# LAYING DOWN THE LINES

# LAYING DOWN THE LINES

## A History of Land Surveying in Alberta

JUDY LARMOUR

BRINDLE
& GLASS

**Library and Archives Canada Cataloguing in Publication**
Larmour, Judy, 1957-
Laying down the lines : a history of land surveying in
Alberta / Judy Larmour.

Includes bibliographical references and index.
ISBN 1-897142-02-1 (bound).--ISBN 1-897142-04-8 (pbk.)

1. Surveying--Alberta--History.  2. Surveyors--Alberta--History.
3. Alberta--Surveys--History.  I. Title.

TA523.A6L37 2005     526.9'097123     C2005-900305-7

**Front Cover photo**
Instrument man working with a transit on John Pierce's survey party subdividing townships north of the 25th Baseline, 1915. Credit: ALSA, Richards Collection, Edgar Mumford Album.
**Back cover photos**
Top: A pre-World War I survey party rafting downstream meets a sternwheeler, northern Alberta [n.d.] Credit: ALSA, Pinder Collection.
Bottom: A survey crew positions their instrument in a challenging spot in northern Alberta before World War I. [n.d.] Credit: ALSA, Pinder Collection.

Author photo: Scotty Aitkin

 Canada Council     Conseil des Arts
for the Arts       du Canada

 Alberta
Land Surveyors'
Association

Brindle & Glass is pleased to thank the Canada Council for the Arts and the Alberta Foundation for the Arts for their support of our publishing program.
We are also grateful to the Alberta Land Surveyors' Association for their contribution.

The Alberta Land Surveyors' Association would like to acknowledge the support of the Alberta Historical Resources Foundation.

Brindle & Glass Publishing
www.brindleandglass.com

1   2   3   4   5   08  07  06  05

PRINTED AND BOUND IN CANADA

For all the hard-working men and women who have ever been land surveyors or worked on survey parties, and for everyone who has contributed to the development of the land surveying profession in Alberta.

# Table of Contents

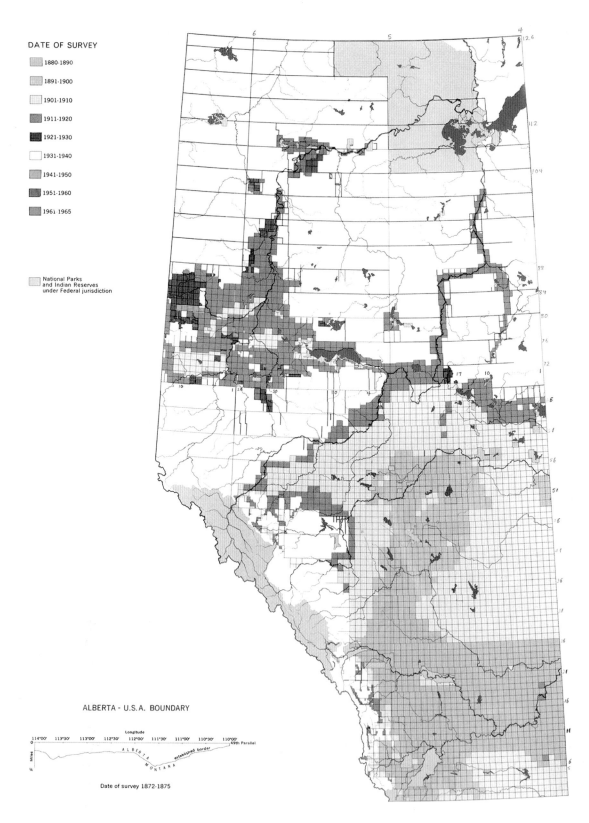

## DATE OF SURVEY

1880-1890

1891-1900

1901-1910

1911-1920

1921-1930

1931-1940

1941-1950

1951-1960

1961-1965

National Parks
and Indian Reserves
under Federal jurisdiction

ALBERTA - U.S.A. BOUNDARY

Longitude
114°00'  113°30'  113°00'  112°30'  112°00'  111°30'  111°00'  110°30'  110°00'
49th Parallel

ALBERTA
established border
MONTANA

Date of survey 1872-1875

*The progress of township subdivision in Alberta from 1880 to 1965.*

University of Alberta / Government of Alberta, courtesy of the Director of Surveys Office

*"Both Canadians and Indians often inquired of me why I observed the Sun, and sometimes the Moon, in the day time, and passed whole nights with my instruments looking at the Moon and Stars. I told them it was to determine the distance and direction from the place I observed to other places; neither the Canadians nor the Indians believed me; for both argued that if what I said was the truth, I ought to look to the ground, and over it, and not to the Stars."*

David Thompson[1]

Under the clear northern sky lies the history of land surveying in Alberta. From a telescope looking to the sky to a satellite looking to the earth—surveying has come full circle. The shape of the planet earth and its complete rotation in one day is fundamental to the science of surveying. Understanding the implications of the curvature of the earth and the measurement of time is the basis for the mathematical calculations that are the work of surveyors. Surveyors tell us where we are on the globe, establish distances and elevations, and show the shape of features such as lakes and rivers. They establish and mark on the ground points from which they can draw connecting lines to stake out our boundaries. We take our many boundaries—national, provincial, natural, and urban parks, private residential properties, airports, roads, oil well sites, and irrigation ditches to name but a few— almost for granted. The notes, sketches, and calculations of surveyors give us maps and plans to order our world.

Modern surveying and mapping in Alberta has a short but astonishingly full history. Surveyors were amongst those who saw Alberta's original natural landscape. Before Euro-Canadian settlement began, they encountered Aboriginal peoples while surveying for the fur trade. Later surveyors were the first harbingers of change that preceded settlement in the late nineteenth century. The wider context of Alberta's history and her resources has shaped the history of surveying in the province, from the surveys needed for maps for the fur trade, to the location of well sites for the oil and gas industry into the twenty-first century.

Beginning in 1872, the Dominion Land Survey laid out the baselines of latitude and meridians of longitude for the township grid system that governs our land holdings and continues to shape our rural landscape today. Surveyors faced the challenge of surveying in the mountains, where they became involved with the development of mountain parks for tourism. They broadened the scope of their practice as they surveyed for irrigation projects and determined the boundaries of coal leases and timber berths. Dominion Land Surveyors meanwhile extended their grid into the huge unsurveyed territory of northern Alberta.

Alberta became a province in 1905. The Alberta Surveys Act of 1910, followed by the establishment of the Alberta Land Surveyors' Association in 1911, signified the importance of the profession. As Alberta swung into a full-scale economic boom, Alberta Land Surveyors were there to meet the hot demand for urban subdivisions. World War I, 1914–18, interrupted the pace of surveying, but surveys were once again in demand as federal topographical mapping continued and the provincial government tackled the development of Alberta's highway system in the mid-1920s. The 1930s brought hard times for surveyors. Land surveyors played a role in the defence of Canada through World War II and the Cold War. The Leduc oil discovery in 1947 marked the beginning of a new resource-based demand for surveying, as the oil and gas industry kept surveyors busy. During the 1950s and 1960s Alberta became increasingly urban and many surveys were needed for the required infrastructure of a modern society. As the twentieth century drew to an end, surveyors adopted new technology and embraced a digital world.

This book traces the story of surveying in Alberta and the men who quite literally shaped the province, beginning with the legendary David Thompson. It shows an evolving profession and a practical science as it developed in Alberta to the present. The first part of the story is based on extensive archival records. The years since World War II are, fortunately, also documented by first-hand accounts recorded as oral history interviews, conducted by the Alberta Land Surveyors' Association. Surveyors have always been a hardy bunch, good walkers, and good talkers. They are ready for almost any job and able to put up with almost anything in the field. They work hard for long periods away from the comforts of home. Surveyors love to share stories of camp life and food—good or bad. Many years later, they can recollect the dramas of transportation across rugged terrain, paddling a canoe or driving a truck in fifty-below weather. Surveyors have tales of battling extreme heat, wind, storms and bitter cold. Nothing, however, quite compares to the horror of mosquitoes and blackflies. All this has produced the surveyor's indefatigable sense of humour.

The intense experience of being outdoors in challenging working conditions, combined with a mentor or apprenticeship tradition, has resulted in the forging of close bonds and extraordinary teamwork among the men, and now women too, who have chosen this demanding occupation. Alberta's land surveyors, beginning with men such as Allan Patrick, William Pearce, Arthur Wheeler, Lionel Charlesworth, Richard Cautley, James Wallace, Fred Seibert, and Jean Côté, have had a major impact on the province through their commitment to the profession and the role it plays in our society. While surveyors in Alberta have shared many aspects of work with those in other provinces and in other countries, their surveying experience has been quintessentially Albertan. Surveying is, after all, about place—about finding and marking place.

## CHAPTER ONE

# Exploratory Surveys

*Connections and Context for Land Surveying in Alberta*

## ESTABLISHING COORDINATES: THE FIRST PREMISE OF SURVEYING

In our minds' eyes, we see Canada stretched out on top of one side of the globe, set apart from Europe by the great blue-green Atlantic. But this clear sense of where we are on the globe was once not so. The seventeenth-century navigators, setting out from Europe, knew where they were in relation to the equator, as they could establish latitude with relative ease by measuring the angle of the Pole star (Polaris) above the horizon, or the position of the sun at noon. How far they had sailed in an easterly or westerly direction was more problematic. Longitude was generally calculated by dead reckoning, often with disastrous results and loss of life.

Longitude, the angular distance east and west measured from the meridian that runs through the Royal Observatory established at Greenwich in England in 1675, can be easily determined from the difference between Greenwich time and local time. Longitude is expressed in degrees or minutes, the complete angular distance around the world being 360 degrees. Each 15° is equivalent to one hour's local time difference. Therefore, if local time can be established in relation to Greenwich time, it is possible to figure out one's position in degrees of longitude. By correlating it with degrees of latitude, a global location can be established. From 1675 British cartographers based their work on Greenwich time. In 1880 Greenwich Mean Time was established, and in 1884 the meridian passing through Greenwich was adopted as the world's prime meridian at 0° longitude, from which all nations orient their maps.

An early method of finding Greenwich time was to make astronomical observations of eclipses of the moons of Jupiter. These difficult and lengthy procedures required perfect conditions for any accuracy, and were almost impossible at sea. In 1714 the British Parliament offered a huge reward to the man who could devise a simple method of measuring longitude. The solution rested on a simple but elusive device—a clock to keep accurate Greenwich time that could be carried far from the shores of England. The clocks invented by John Harrison of Britain between 1730 and 1770 ultimately resulted in the use of large, expensive chronometers on board ships.[1]

In the Canadian North-West, however, astronomical observations remained the only way to establish coordinates for surveying. Initially, in the late eighteenth century, they were approximations, but instrumentation improved as the nineteenth century progressed and levels of accuracy increased. Although pocket chronometers were available by the mid-nineteenth century, they remained fragile and unreliable instruments. Rough travel over land caused inaccuracies, forcing surveyors to take astronomical observations to verify Greenwich time. Finally, the new technology of the telegraph meant that simultaneous Greenwich time could be checked through linked observatories, and communicated to wherever the telegraph system extended.

## SURVEYS IN THE INTERESTS OF GREAT NATIONAL AND ECONOMIC RIVALRIES

While the scientific problem of longitude was preoccupying European mariners, a power struggle on land in the New World led to the first exploratory surveys. As soon as the Hudson's Bay Company (HBC) began to trade for furs with the Aboriginal peoples of Canada from the shores of Hudson Bay, from 1670, Britain and France vied for control of the vast territories of the North-West. The French fur traders of New France who controlled the St. Lawrence River moved westward, establishing trading posts to exchange European goods for furs with Native peoples. By 1754 the HBC, alarmed by their competitors' western inroads and success, sent out Anthony Henday to win back some ground with the help of Native guides whose survival skills on the land ensured his safe travel. Henday over-wintered in the foothills of central Alberta before making it all the way to the Rocky Mountains, where the French had not yet gone. In the same year, 1754, Britain and France went to war in North America, and two years later the hostilities expanded to a worldwide conflict, generally referred to as the Seven Years' War, involving the colonial powers of Europe. In North America, the tide turned in favour of the British, and New France fell in 1760. Britain claimed control of Canada through the Treaty of Paris in 1763, and French traders lost control of the St. Lawrence. Little changed in the fur trade, however, as it did not take long for English-speaking independent traders operating from Montreal to take up the slack.

Among those independent Montreal traders pushing westwards in competition with the HBC was Peter Pond. In 1778 he discovered a significant portage—Methy Portage—connecting the Churchill River system with a stream flowing westwards into the Athabasca River. Pond's report on the rich fur resources of Lake Athabasca, along with a number of his maps—the first of the western interior of Canada—soon had the attention of the HBC. Pond, however, used a compass and guestimates to establish longitude. His estimates placed Lake Athabasca less than a hundred miles from the Pacific! When the HBC compared Pond's claims with results determined from longitude established on the charts of Captain James Cook, who had mapped the Pacific coast of Canada, with a chronometer on board, the dilemma was clear. Was Pond incorrect or had he found a short route to the west coast that would give Britain access to Asia?

The dilemma awakened the Hudson's Bay Company to the value of accurate maps of the North-West based on astronomical observations. The company hired British practical astronomer Philip Turnor, compiler of the *Nautical Almanac* issued by the Royal Observatory, Greenwich, as its surveyor. His job included the training of others within the company to make astronomical observations, before he finally travelled to Lake Athabasca to establish its coordinates in 1790.[2] Peter Fidler, one of his two most famous students, went with him. However, David Thompson, Turnor's second student, ultimately proved to have a greater impact on the history of surveying in Alberta.

## DAVID THOMPSON: ALBERTA'S LEGENDARY EXPLORATORY SURVEYOR

"In the month of May 1784 at the Port of London, I embarked in the ship Prince Rupert belonging to the Hudson's Bay Company, as apprentice and clerk to the said company, bound for Churchill Factory, on the west side of the bay." [3] So began the adventure that would last a lifetime for fourteen-year-old David Thompson, who had shone at mathematics at London's charity Grey Coat School near Westminster Abbey. By September he found himself at Churchill Factory in a world of approaching winter. In fall 1785 Thompson was summoned to York Factory, some 150 miles south, to depart on exploratory travels to expand the fur trade into the country that would later be part of Alberta. The HBC had renewed concerns about competition when the independent Montreal traders amalgamated their interests to form the North West Company in 1784. By 1787 Thompson had paddled upstream along the North Saskatchewan River, travelling overland south-west to the Bow River in 1788.

A leg injury caused David Thompson to spend the winter of 1789–90 at Cumberland House on the North Saskatchewan River, in present-day eastern Saskatchewan. At the beginning of October 1789, Philip Turnor, the Hudson's Bay Company's surveyor, arrived by canoe. "This was a fortunate arrival for me," Thompson recalled. "Under him I regained my mathematical education, and during the winter became his only assistant." Thompson eagerly devoted himself to making astronomical observations to establish the exact location of Cumberland House. He had caught the surveying bug, but he was unable to accompany Turnor on his travels to Lake Athabasca in spring 1790 due to a severe inflammation of his right eye, which he blamed on "too much attention to calculations in the night." [4] Peter Fidler, who had also been training at Cumberland House under Philip Turnor, took Thompson's place. By the next year, Thompson had recovered his health, and his apprenticeship in the trade was complete.

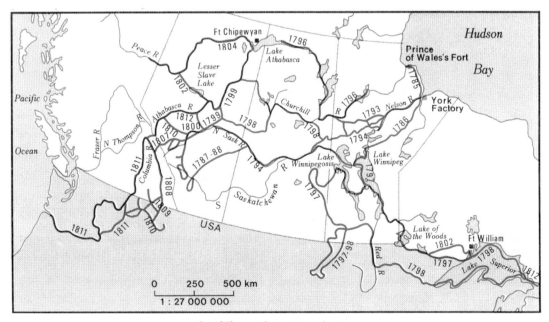

*David Thompson's extensive explorations.*
THE CANADIAN ENCYCLOPEDIA AND HISTORICA FOUNDATION

Thompson was sent west to establish trade relations with Native trappers. The HBC informed Thompson that any information that "can tend to form a good Survey and Map of the Country Inland [*sic*] will always be particularly acceptable to us."[5] The company presented him with a compass, a thermometer, and a case of instruments, and by 1794 gave him a raise—at his own request—of 400 percent! He was charged with the task of finding an efficient route from Hudson Bay to Lake Athabasca. Nevertheless, in 1797 Peter Fidler was appointed chief surveyor and mapmaker to the HBC. Thompson left the HBC abruptly, despite an excellent salary and approval of his performance as trader and surveyor, to join the rival North West Company. Thompson and Fidler bore a lifelong hostility as they pursued their jobs as surveyors to rival companies that would not merge until 1821. Personality issues and money aside, Thompson must have thought the North West Company offered more freedom to survey new routes.

The North West Company was happy to have a surveyor and generously supplied Thompson with canoes, horses, men, and supplies. In 1799 Thompson's explorations again took him through territory now within Alberta, this time with trading as well as surveying objectives—a measure of his rising importance within the company. He set out with a small group of Métis employees to locate, survey, and map the routes between North West Company posts. Along the way, Thompson met Charlotte Small, a Métis woman who became his wife and paddled his canoe alongside him. By 1807 Thompson had covered thousands of miles, through Alberta and over the great divide of the Rocky Mountains into British Columbia, where he established trade with the Kootenay Indians.

David Thompson's method of surveying was based on what he learned from Philip Turnor: the determination of longitude through lunar observation. With three hours and a telescope in hand, he could establish Greenwich time by observing the moment of eclipse of one of the moons of Jupiter. Alternately, calculations could also be made in relation to the moon's movement around the planet earth, which moves approximately 13° each day in relation to the fixed stars. By observing the angle between the moon and two fixed stars, Greenwich time—and hence longitude—could be calculated with reference to the astronomical tables in the *Nautical Almanac*.[6]

Thompson made a track survey of his route using a magnetic compass for bearings and estimated distances between points. He took astronomical observations for latitude and longitude as a check, averaging out errors in the compass survey between the fixed points. "My instruments for practical astronomy, were a brass Sextant of ten inches radius, an achromatic telescope of high power for observing the satellites of Jupiter and other phenomena, one of the same construction for common use, Parallel glasses and quicksilver horizon for double altitudes [artificial horizons for using the sextant]; Compass; Thermometer, and other requisite instruments, which I was in the constant practice of using in clear weather for observations on the Sun, Moon, Planets and Stars; to determine the positions of Rivers, Lakes, Mountains and other parts of the country I surveyed from Hudson Bay to the Pacific Ocean."[7] Thompson noted that John Dolland of London made his instruments. Dolland developed the achromatic lens after 1757, which was an improvement on the refracting lens in telescopes available to that time. Achromatic lenses produced better telescopic images than were previously possible, and revealed fainter objects, producing more accurate results.[8]

Surveyors and historians alike have taken a good deal of interest in the level of accuracy that Thompson was able to achieve. By all accounts, the location of Thompson's astronomical observation was usually within a mile or so of the true location. Historian William Stewart concluded that Thompson's location of latitude was within a mile of correct, his longitude within two miles. Stewart noted that Thompson's magnetic bearings contained "inconsistent and irregular errors" and that he recorded distances only to the nearest quarter mile. Thompson was unaware of problems associated with the earth's magnetic field that would challenge surveyors who came after him. "It is a fact then," Stewart warned, ". . . that the latitudes and longitudes given in Thompson's notes cannot, in general, be accepted as defining the position of old trading posts or other points of interest."[9]

Thompson kept meteorological observations as well as field notes in his journals, recording the temperatures he encountered over a number of years. He was quite determined to know how cold it could be in the North-West. Thompson became suspicious of the accuracy of his first thermometers: "one of Spirits, and one Quicksilver; each divided to forty-two degrees below Zero, being seventy four degrees below freezing point." The mercury froze, and it appeared to Thompson that, as the spirit approached the bulb, it seemed to take two or three degrees of cold to correspond with a drop of one degree registering on the thermometer. He wrote to Mr. Dolland in London requesting a thermometer divided "to upwards of one hundred degrees below zero." By the winter of 1795, from halfway round the world, came "a thermometer of red coloured spirits of wine, divided to 110 degrees below zero, or 142 degrees below the freezing point."[10] Thompson tested it out at Bedford House on Reindeer Lake. On December 18, he confirmed his suspicions. The new thermometer read fifty-six degrees below zero while the older small spirit one would not descend beyond forty-one degrees below zero.[11] Thompson experienced a good deal of difficulty establishing altitudes and requested a "mountain barometer" for his work in the Rocky Mountains. Twice a barometer arrived broken, so he gave up and resorted to the boiling water method—the lower the temperature of the boiling point, the greater the altitude—and making the necessary calculations, which proved to be quite inaccurate.[12]

Thompson's surveying career in western Canada concluded with travels through southeastern British Columbia. In 1811 he set out with a canoe party to find where the Columbia River led, and arrived at Astoria on the Pacific coast just weeks after the American Pacific Fur Company established a fort there. By 1812 Thompson was ready to retire from the North West Company, and he settled in Quebec. He then began work on a series of remarkable maps of the Canadian North-West based on his many surveys. In 1813, in completion of his contract with the North West Company, he delivered his *Map of the North-West Territory of the Province of Canada from actual survey during the years 1792 to 1812*. The map passed to the HBC on the merger of the two companies in 1821 and the rights to the map were sold to the Arrowsmith mapping firm in Britain.[13] Arrrowsmith continued to incorporate Thompson's work in the ongoing editions of its map of North America, which would not be supplanted until the Dominion Land Survey produced maps based on its surveys begun in the 1870s.

In 1816 David Thompson began a new phase of his career. He was appointed astronomer and surveyor by the British Foreign Office for the international boundary between Canada and the United States of America, established through the Treaty of Ghent at the end of the War of 1812. He worked on the section west from St. Regis on the St. Lawrence River. In 1824 his survey party reached the northwest shore of the Lake of the Woods, where Thompson left a monument to mark the location of the western termination point of the international boundary. Thompson then continued to perfect his maps. He provided a set for the British government in 1826 and then a final set in 1843. [14]

In the early 1840s, Thompson used his maps to urge Britain to make a claim to the Oregon country where the North West Company bought out American interests at Fort Astoria, and which had become a bone of contention between Britain and America. The territorial dispute was eventually resolved in favour of the claims of the United States of America. A huge potential Canadian territory of three hundred thousand square miles was lost through the Oregon Treaty of 1846, when the forty-ninth parallel west from the Rocky Mountains to the Pacific was declared as the international boundary. This was a continuation of the forty-ninth parallel as the international boundary west from the Lake of the Woods to the Rocky Mountains, previously agreed on in 1818. [15]

Although Thompson was well versed and involved in the political questions of territorial expansion of nineteenth-century Canada, he was not well known to his contemporaries. In 1843 a now impoverished David Thompson returned to his detailed survey journals of earlier days and sat down to write up an account of his travels and work. He died in 1857 and the manuscript languished unpublished for over half a century. David Thompson was virtually forgotten. Finally, in 1916, *David Thompson's Narrative of his Explorations in North America* was published on the instigation of geologist Joseph Burr Tyrrell. Tyrrell, impressed by the accuracy of the map of the North-West still used by the Dominion Government of Canada in the 1880s, was curious to know more about Thompson. [16] Hailed as a masterpiece of geographical writing, Thompson's *Narrative* grabbed the imagination of men involved in the contemporary surveying of western Canada.


CANADA ENVISIONS HER WESTERN HORIZONS

By the 1850s America began to develop farmlands on the frontier of the Midwest. In Canada, too, suitable land for settlement in the east was running out. As a land crisis loomed, politicians in the Province of Canada (now parts of Ontario and Quebec) turned their eyes westwards to Rupert's Land—the land of the Red River Settlement and beyond. The Hudson's Bay Company, through a Royal Charter, held Rupert's Land. Although knowledge of that land was limited outside of Aboriginal communities and fur trade circles, Canada opposed the upcoming renewal of the HBC's privileges, and made it clear to Britain that the intent was to claim title for Canada. A rationale for doing so became paramount, spurring an assessment of western soil, climate, natural resources, flora and fauna, and potential for agricultural development. The North-West was hailed as Canada's Promised Land, where her future lay as a nation rather than as a colony. [17] As Fort Garry and Red River Settlement were effectively cut off from the Province of Canada by the vast region of the Canadian Shield, it was necessary to travel through Minnesota to get there. A long-established transportation and trade route used the Red River to link Fort Garry with the US railhead at St. Cloud. The Canadian government sent out expeditions under Simon J. Dawson and Henry Y. Hind to survey an all-Canadian water and land transportation route from Fort William at the west end of Lake Superior to Fort Garry in 1857 and 1858, and to go further west to report on the vast lands beyond the Red River Settlement.

During those same years, the British North American Exploring Expedition also investigated the prairies. When adventurer John Palliser approached the Royal Geographical Society for funding to examine the country along the forty-ninth parallel between the Red River and the Rocky Mountains, and to explore passes through the mountains, he got more than he hoped for. The British government, keen to have more information about Rupert's Land, found five thousand pounds to send a scientific expedition. Palliser, a member of the lesser Irish aristocracy, could hardly believe his luck. He was a competent astronomer, fluent in French, and an avid sportsman, who had been on hunting expeditions in the Far East and the American Midwest. Eminent Scottish geologist and naturalist James Hector and French botanist Eugene Bourgeau joined Palliser's expedition party. Thomas Blakiston, an officer in the Royal Artillery, took magnetic observations. His observations were to form part of the British government's wider study of the earth's magnetic force and the problem of magnetic declination. (By this time, it had been discovered that the magnetic needle of a compass deviates in varying amounts from the true poles, as defined by the earth's rotational axis, in different geographical locations). John W. Sullivan, an Irish

*A portrait of John Palliser and James Hector taken in England before embarking for Canada.*
GLENBOW ARCHIVES, NA-588-1

mathematician who taught at the naval college at Greenwich, took charge of astronomical observations and secretarial duties. Native and Métis guides made up the rest of the party that set out laden with supplies in the summer of 1858.

Palliser is best known for his condemnation of the lands in present-day southwest Saskatchewan and southeast Alberta as arid and unsuitable for agriculture—the so-called "Palliser's triangle." Palliser also sought to find suitable passes for transportation through the Rocky Mountains, and details of his explorations of Kicking Horse Pass and the Kananaskis Valley were studied by surveyors for the Canadian Pacific Railway (CPR) in the early 1880s. The expedition sought a pass in close proximity to the forty-ninth parallel, as the North American Boundary Commission was concurrently working east from the Pacific to the Rocky Mountains. Blakiston, who by this time had left the expedition, having fallen out with everyone, crossed the mountains by the North Kootenay Pass in August 1858. On his return from the Tobacco Plains of British Columbia a month later, he took a more southerly pass, which appeared on Palliser's map as Boundary Pass, now named South Kootenay Pass. Blakiston, keen to have his coordinates correct, appointed a different man each day whose sole duty was to carry the chronometer carefully!

Palliser and Sullivan crossed the Rockies through the North Kootenay Pass in August 1859, without the benefit of Blakiston's latest maps, which he refused to give up. They travelled south to the HBC post at Fort Shepard on the Columbia River, and determined the latitude coordinate of this fort to be 49° 1'—this was three-quarters of a mile inside Canadian territory. This had been a matter of some concern to the HBC as the North American Boundary Commission advanced from the coast. Palliser continued west, reaching an astronomical site for the commission on the Kettle River, its eastern outpost. [18] When he wrapped up his expedition in 1860, Palliser had fulfilled the original hope of the British government that his explorations through the mountains should be of use to the commission. [19] Two years later, in 1862, surveyors determined the position of the final boundary monument in Akamina Pass, just to the south of South Kootenay Pass, on the forty-ninth parallel. Palliser's expedition had stretched over three summers and he submitted three major reports—an interim report in 1859, more complete accounts in 1860 and 1863, along with a map in 1865.

The fever of excitement about the future of Canada's North-West abated somewhat in the 1860s. The world was an unsettled place as Americans embarked on a horrendous civil war, ostensibly over the issue of slavery that divided the abolitionist North from the plantation society of the South. Britain's sympathetic hand to the South, providing armaments and even naval ships, led to an international dispute about the freedom of the seas. When the North won in 1865, Britain acquiesced to the new power reality, reduced her expenditures, and gradually withdrew from North America. The provinces of British North America realized they would be left to look out for themselves. Within Canada the movement to unite the provinces within a confederation focused on a common destiny within British North America.

The passage of the British North America Act led to the proclamation of "one Dominion under the name of Canada" on July 1, 1867. The United States chose the same day to purchase Alaska from Russia, begging the question as to their intent towards Rupert's Land. Canada's elevation to nationhood had not come easily, nor was it a sure route into the future. It was time to check American attempts to annex or acquire the interests of the Hudson's Bay Company in Rupert's Land. In the eyes of the new national government under John A. Macdonald, the assertion of Canada's sovereignty in the great North-West was clearly a race against time and the urge for territorial expansion in Washington that was mirrored in American populist feeling.

The first step to block American expansionism was to acquire Rupert's Land from Britain, followed by the building of a railway across the plains and through the Rocky Mountains to link Canada with British Columbia. The railway would likely entice British Columbia into Confederation, and carry thousands of settlers west to farm. Grain and other resources would be shipped east while the manufactured products of the east would be shipped west. And finally, Macdonald's national policy envisioned a tariff imposed on goods imported from the United States. The Dominion of Canada would have its own empire north of the forty-ninth parallel from sea to sea, based on British values and traditions. The international boundary from the Lake of the Woods to the Rocky Mountains had, however, never been surveyed.


SURVEYORS CLOSE THE FORTY-NINTH PARALLEL

In 1872 the second phase of the survey of the international boundary in western Canada, long put on hold due to the American Civil War, began. The North American Boundary Commission, comprising joint British and American commissions, surveyed the forty-ninth parallel west across the prairies to the Rocky Mountains. Survey parties with the British and the American commission co-operated, each working from their own side of the forty-ninth parallel. The Dominion Government of Canada shared in the organization and cost of the British commission, which included Canadian surveyors. Canada immediately proposed the appointment of Donald Roderick Cameron, a British army officer in the Royal artillery, as British commissioner. He was the son-in-law of Charles Tupper, a member of the Canadian cabinet. An abrasive and obstinate man by all accounts, Cameron did not get on well with the rest of his commission team nor the American Commissioner Archibald Campbell, and eventually the Canadian government regretted his appointment. Chief Astronomer Captain Samuel Anderson and his two assistant astronomers were also British army officers. Among the rest of the fourteen men on the commission were two Canadian surveyors and their assistants, along with four sub-assistant astronomers. Canadian support staff and daily labourers made up the rest of the scores of men who set out to survey the boundary.

The border survey began at the Lake of the Woods. Immediately it was apparent that there were issues to be resolved. At the outset, the North American Boundary Commission's hope to settle the location of the border by completely scientific methods was dashed, as it attempted to sort out the legal and political ramifications of a number of international treaties. It was agreed by the Webster-Ashburton Treaty in 1842 that the boundary was to run due south from the northwest corner of the Lake of the Woods to the forty-ninth parallel and then west to the Pacific. David Thompson's inter-

*North American Boundary Commission staff. This photograph includes most of the men with the British commission who were employed in the 1874 season to the Rocky Mountains. Back row: George F. Burpee, sub-assistant astronomer; William F. King, sub-assistant astronomer; George C. Coster, sub-assistant astronomer; Lawrence Herchmer, commissary; Captain Samuel Anderson, chief astronomer; Professor George Dawson, geologist; William Ashe, sub-assistant astronomer; Lindsay A. Russell, Deputy Surveyor General of Canada. Front row: Lieutenant William J. Galwey, assistant astronomer; Lieutenant Arthur Clitheroe Ward, Secretary, British Commission; Captain D. R. Cameron, British Commissioner; Captain Albany Featherstonhaugh, assistant astronomer; Doctor William George Boswell, veterinarian; Doctor T. J.W. Burgess, surgeon.*
GLENBOW ARCHIVES, NA-249-1

*George M. Dawson, botanist, at the site of David Thompson's witness monument at the Lake of the Woods. The survey party verified the authenticity of the monument and then rebuilt it with new materials.*

national boundary survey identified the northwest corner of the Lake of the Woods as 49° 23' 55" north latitude and 95° 14' 38" west longitude—a position that was in the lake. Surveyors would have to survey a line south from this position before the survey west along the forty-ninth parallel could even begin. Survey parties eventually found David Thompson's witness monument of 1824 in a marsh of shallow water. (A witness monument is a monument placed a known distance from the true position, where that position is inaccessible). Donald Cameron described the witness monument in his diary as having originally comprised a double tier of logs. That it was built of oak was a factor in confirming it was indeed Thompson's monument.[20] A sight line was then surveyed from Thompson's position of the northwest corner to the forty-ninth parallel. From Canada's perspective, there was a logical problem to this solution—the line would cut off a triangle of land on the northwest shore of the Lake of the Woods that connected Dawson's Road to Red River, putting Dawson's Landing within American territory. This issue, although not resolved to Canada's satisfaction, lost much of its strategic importance when the Canadian Pacific Railway replaced the water route and Dawson's Road.[21]

The British commission defended Canada's territorial interests as a second issue arose. The forty-ninth parallel is not a straight line on the earth's surface, but actually a curved line, angling northward as the viewer looks west. The North American Boundary Commission intended to locate the forty-ninth parallel by astronomical observations twenty miles apart. Agreement on how to survey the boundary became a major hurdle. The Americans proposed a straight line between each monument, but Cameron and the British commission quickly pointed out that Canada would have lost about two hundred acres every twenty miles! Canada successfully proposed a curved-line border following the parallel of natural latitude between each monument. Once the first monument was erected on the forty-ninth parallel, the British commission was on its way west. The British and American commissions worked in a spirit of cooperation, establishing alternate astronomical stations and boundary markers.

Captain Samuel Anderson worked with a reconnaissance party of about thirty Métis from Red River who knew the country. They moved about a hundred miles or more ahead of the survey parties, to get a grasp of the lay of the land. Anderson used a sextant and pocket chronometers to determine his position and prepared sketch maps of the country that, upon his return to base, were given to the officers in charge of working parties. Anderson thus determined a suitable route for the heavy supply trains, selected sites for sub-depots to provision the camps, and marked the

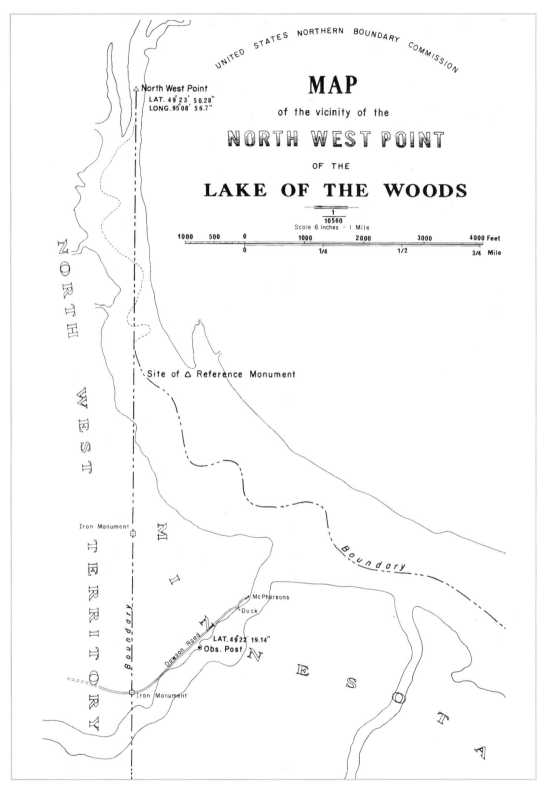

*Map of the vicinity of the northwest point of the Lake of the Woods by the United States Northern Boundary Commission (1878) as depicted in Don W. Thompson,* Men and Meridians, *volume 2, Ottawa: Department of Energy, Mines and Resources, 1967.*

REPRODUCED WITH THE PERMISSION OF THE CANADIAN REPRESENTATIVE,
INTERNATIONAL BOUNDARY COMMISSION & SURVEYOR GENERAL OF CANADA LAND

*The boundary monuments, located every three miles, were substantial earthen mounds, seven feet high by fourteen feet in diameter, surrounded by a circular ditch. When boulder stones were available locally, they were arranged to form a conical cairn, also surrounded by a ditch.*

GLENBOW ARCHIVES, NA-218-1

*Surveyors set up observer tents at astronomical stations, from which they were able to take precise readings. The tents were usually on an elevated spot from which an uninterrupted sight line could be obtained for a distance of approximately three-quarters of a mile. Not even the smallest vibration in the ground could be tolerated, so animals were tethered some distance off, and the sleeping and cook tents were pitched some distance away to avoid any disturbance. The large Zenith telescope can be seen in the doorway.*

GLENBOW ARCHIVES, NA-249-22

position of the astronomical stations within about one hundred yards of the boundary line. All this planning ensured the astronomical observations could be made efficiently and campsites set up without delays.[22]

The British commission had the most technically advanced surveying equipment of the day. The astronomical parties each carried several types of transits, levels, chronometers, and tapes and chains for measuring distances.[23] Astronomical stations, alternately British and American, were positioned at distinguishable natural features approximately twenty miles apart. As assistant astronomer Captain Albany Featherstonhaugh later explained to the Royal Geographical Society, "the connection of two astronomical stations was effected by the laying of a line from one of the stations at right angles to the meridian, and prolonging this line until it struck the meridian of the second station, the whole distance being chained, and pickets left in the ground. The proper offsets to the Parallel were then measured wherever permanent marks were intended to be erected."[24]

The surveyors for each commission surveyed six miles on either side of the forty-ninth parallel and mapped rivers and other features. The surveyors on the Canadian side traversed the watercourses and ridges from their intersection with the boundary to the six-mile limit. Topographers used the chain lines as a base from which to sketch the natural features in the areas between the check lines, plotted on a sheet on a scale of four inches to one mile. The sheets were ultimately fitted together, and scaled down to a scale of one inch to a mile.[25] A set of twenty-four topographical maps on a scale of two miles to an inch was finally produced, as well as a map of the entire boundary from Lake Superior to the Rocky Mountains on a scale of sixty miles to one inch.

It took two years for the North American Boundary Commission to reach the meridian of 110° longitude. The 1874 season began from the end of the line of the previous season at Wood Mountain, west of present-day Moose Jaw, Saskatchewan. The parties

*Long trains of oxen and horses hauled covered wagons packed with instruments, supplies, and food west to the new depot at Wood Mountain in 1874.*

with the British commission marched west from their winter quarters at Dufferin in Manitoba. Along with officers and surveyors, the British commission included teamsters, cooks, axemen, and other labourers—250 men in all. Speed was of the essence if the commission was to complete its work by autumn. The work was streamlined in various ways, and the three survey parties were reduced to one under Lieutenant Rowe of the Royal Engineers. Rowe took a bad fall on June 11 and fractured his skull even before he got to the starting point for the survey. He was left critically ill in the care of the commission's physician, while the other surveyors carried on the work without him. During July they finally reached 110° longitude on the forty-ninth parallel, which would later mark the Alberta–Saskatchewan boundary.

Once west of Wood Mountain, the British commission reduced the survey and mapping of the topography north of the forty-ninth parallel from six to three miles. The distance between the astronomical observation stations was averaged at twenty-one rather than twenty miles for the remaining distance to the mountains. The open plains made it easy for the parties with the British commission to stick close to the forty-ninth parallel, which Anderson's reconnaissance party of Métis scouts followed as far as the Milk River. Here they were stopped in their tracks by a deep ravine. Anderson travelled along the cliff edge, scouting for a crossing. Turning south, he eventually found a suitable spot, almost ten miles into the United States. The commission continued on its way just south of the forty-ninth parallel, where the route was easier and provided more water, travelling north to the line at intervals to establish astronomical stations and erect monuments.

The British commission blazed trail ahead of its American counterpart through what is now northern Montana. Anderson monitored the American rate of progress during the summer of 1874: "The Americans are coming on as fast as they can, and I hope they will not delay us at the last," he declared from a point eighty miles east of the Rocky Mountains on the Canadian side of the forty-ninth parallel. "We have of course saved them great trouble and expense, as all they have to do is follow our track and take up the work at points that we leave for them, so that they lose no time in going straight to the scenes of operation and commencing work at once."[26]

Anderson also monitored the American commission's dealings with the Native peoples of the plains. "Fortunately we are so far ahead of the Americans, about 100 miles, that the British parties have been the first to come in contact with the Indians, and so far there has been much shaking of hands, smoking of pipes, and other amicable exchanges," Anderson assured his mother in a letter dated July 21, 1874.[27] Once on the Canadian prairie, home to the Blackfoot, Anderson was again concerned about the approaching American military escort and the message it would give on the Canadian side of the forty-ninth parallel. "At present I think the Indians are keeping out of our way on purpose, as it can not possibly be with their wonderful system of scouting, that they do not know where we are working . . . I should prefer to meet the Indians and come to some under-standing with the chiefs, and the only reason that I can see for their keeping out of the way is the knowledge that the Americans and ourselves are working together, and that they are afraid to meet the American troops."[28]

At the end of July the American and the British commissions camped together south of the forty-ninth parallel at the edge of the Sweet Grass Hills. Here the Rocky Mountains, with snow on the summits glinting in the sun of early morning, first came into view on the western horizon. The British commission then headed northwest, the reconnaissance party pushing on to the St. Mary River, where a suitable site was found for the final depot. Three astronomical stations were estab-lished between West Butte and the St. Mary River. The survey party completed a traverse of the St. Mary River, and continued west.

The British commission finally arrived at the scenic shores of Waterton Lake, named by Blakiston in 1859. Anderson described the dramatic vista: "The horizontal strata of the plains are suddenly broken by the crumpled rocks of the mountains, elevated by a great convulsion of nature."[29] They set up camp and explored the area around the still waters of the lake. The photog-raphers were soon at work, carefully removing their glass plates from the wooden boxes and set-ting up tripods to take views of the stunning scenery and geology of the mountains.

On a warm August morning, Anderson, sporting a straw hat, set out with his scouting party and four axemen, following a trail up the South Kootenay Pass. George Dawson, a Canadian botanist and naturalist who had accompanied the commission from the outset, eagerly joined them. He recorded the appearance of the exposed reddish sandstone as he climbed, and noted the remains of buffalo "as far as the last patch of meadow land, on the east side of the watershed."[30] It was a hard slog, and the axemen were kept busy, as fallen timber strewn on the track was too high for the horses to step over. By this time, low branches had shredded Anderson's hat. Finally, to their relief, the track intersected with the trail cut by a party with the North American Boundary Commission working from the Pacific to the Mountains thirteen years previously. It was a better trail, but at one point beavers had been busy damning up the valley. The horses waded through three or four feet of water—not without mishap. "In riding thro' the beaver swamp, we came to an awkward ditch into which all the animals had to plunge headforemost for 2 or 3 steps, and some of them rolled over instead of coming out straight on the other side, and some of the baggage suffered, but none of the instruments fortunately."[31] They pressed on towards the summit. Anderson was impressed by the clarity of the axe marks left on the trees in 1861. He noted that the thirteen rings of growth on the trees "were wonderfully distinct." As time was of the essence, Dawson was "only able to devote a few spare hours to the collection of plants," all of which he listed in his report published in 1875.[32]

On August 18, they embarked on the final stretch south to the Akamina Pass. It was a hard day's climb to Camp Akamina at the head of the valley. This was where the North American Boundary Commission had camped at the end of the first phase in 1862, at an elevation of about six thousand feet above sea level. Dawson noted it was a "sheltered hollow characterised by thick spruce woods of thick growth." About a mile from the camp, out on a saddleback with precipitous sides, they located the boundary monument. Anderson was clearly thrilled to be the link between the previous survey east to the Rockies and the second survey west to the same monument: "altho' only a rough cairn of stones, [it was] in perfect preservation and not a stone had rolled out of place."[33]

The demarcation of the longest stretch of surveyed border in the world had finally been completed right in the heart of the Rocky Mountains, and its significance was both practical and political. The North American Boundary Commission had established the first monuments along the forty-ninth parallel, which later surveys, including provincial boundary surveys, would tie into. There was also a clear political connection between the timing and pressure to complete the international boundary along the forty-ninth parallel and the national vision for the Canadian Pacific Railway to run to the Pacific Ocean. It was no accident that the map accompanying the published account of the North American Boundary Commission of 1872–74, presented by Samuel Anderson to the Royal Geographical Society in Britain in 1876, included the proposed route of the CPR through the Yellowhead Pass to the Pacific.

## EXPLORATORY SURVEYS FOR A CANADIAN TRANSCONTINENTAL RAILWAY

The interests of the Dominion of Canada and the British Empire were one and the same as Ottawa worked hand in hand with British investors to build a transcontinental line across Canada through the Rocky Mountains to the Pacific Ocean. Sandford Fleming, an engineer and surveyor trained in Scotland, was chief engineer for the Canadian Pacific Railway. In 1871, he was placed in charge of numerous preliminary exploratory surveys of alternative routes across the prairies and through the mountains to the Pacific Coast. Fleming sought John Palliser's advice and always had a copy of his report tucked into his bag while out in the field.[34] The report came in handy: all the map work was

*Charles Horetzky's photograph of a CPR reconnaissance survey party*
*at the entrance to the Yellowhead Pass [1871–72].*
GLENBOW ARCHIVES, PB-885-25

based on astronomical coordinates for latitude and longitude. Keeping Palliser's negative assess-ment of southern Alberta in mind, Fleming himself kept north, surveying the valley of the North Saskatchewan River.

The results of all the surveys, from both the British Columbia side and the eastern side of the mountains, convinced him that the best way to cross the mountains to the coast was through the Yellowhead Pass. Survey photographer Charles Horetzky was convinced that the Peace River or Pine River Pass presented a more favourable route to the coast. When Fleming dismissed Horetzky's recommendation in his *Report of the Surveys and Preliminary Operations of the Canadian Pacific Railway, up to January 1877*, Horetzky made a public furor in a pamphlet published in 1880.[35] Nevertheless, Fleming's exploratory route through the North Saskatchewan Valley and the Yellowhead was accepted by the CPR. Ultimately, however, the CPR line was built across the southern plains and through the Kicking Horse Pass. Nevertheless, the comprehensive exploratory surveys undertaken under Fleming's direction were invaluable. They provided the first land surveyors working for the Canadian government with information about the topography and series of coordinate positions against which to check their own observations. Meantime, the telegraph line that Fleming had ordered to be built south of the North Saskatchewan River in advance of the rail line, brought a time signal by 1876 as far as Hay Lakes, south of Fort Edmonton.

Astronomical observations were the core surveying activity to establish initial coordinates and positions during all early exploratory surveys as well as the international boundary traverse survey of the forty-ninth parallel. At the end of the eighteenth century, David Thompson attempted to achieve accuracy within a mile; by 1872 the surveyors on the North American Boundary Commission were able to aim for positions along the forty-ninth parallel within yards of the true position.

Exploratory surveyors—beginning with Philip Turnor, Peter Fidler, and David Thompson—went to work with a purpose to solve the questions and meet the demands thrown up in the political and economic context of their era. They built on each other's work. Thompson provided many of the first records of latitude and longitude coordinates for locations in what would become Alberta. Palliser's party carried Thompson's maps, and provided additional knowledge of southern Alberta as well as the mountain passes of British Columbia that would assist the North American Boundary Commission in its work marking the forty-ninth parallel. Sandford Fleming carried Palliser's report as he surveyed potential routes for the CPR.

Their work would soon play an important role in the first land surveys carried out by the Dominion Government of Canada in the valley of the North Saskatchewan River, creating property boundaries where no such concept had previously existed.

## CHAPTER TWO

# Laying the Grid

*The Dominion Land Survey Goes to Work*

## "ONE GREAT COUNTRY BEFORE US"

On the passing of the Dominion Lands Act of 1872 the Dominion of Canada officially embarked on the enormous task of surveying thousands of square miles west of the burgeoning settlement at Winnipeg on the Red River. "We had," Sir John A. Macdonald remarked a decade later in the House of Commons, "the advantage of having one great country before us to do as we liked and one vast system of survey, uniform over the whole of it."[1] It was not, however, quite that simple. Initially, it took time, trial, and error to work out a township system that included free homesteads, school land, railway land, and sections for the Hudson's Bay Company. Although the goal was to establish a grid of meridians and baselines before extensive township subdivision, the rapid construction of the Canadian Pacific Railway forced the Dominion Land Survey to begin township subdivision on the lands granted to the railway, before the outline grid was complete further north. As the CPR line advanced westwards into southern Alberta by 1883, it provided a catalyst for the speedy survey of a vast network of townships over the southern plains.

Despite Macdonald's optimism, the first surveys got off to a rocky start. The survey of the North-West actually began in August 1869, before Rupert's Land was turned over to Canada and before the Dominion Land Survey was set up. Surveyor Lieutenant-Colonel John Stoughton Dennis arrived at the Red River Settlement, with instructions from William McDougall, Minister of Public Works in Ottawa, to begin surveying land holdings for future settlers. He was not to disturb the holdings already established by Métis settlers, according to the river lot system that had been transferred from the old land holding system of Quebec. He found tensions running high in the settlement, which was technically still under the jurisdiction of the Hudson's Bay Company. The Métis, already nervous about the transfer of Rupert's Land, had been enraged by the boorish behaviour of a road survey and building crew under John Snow. Snow's party was to establish a road east from the Red River Settlement but, as the story goes, Snow and the paymaster Charles Mair, along with others on the survey crew, staked out speculative land for themselves near the Métis settlement and allegedly refused to pay the Métis they employed the wages due to them. Dennis, nevertheless, began work, establishing a meridian ten miles west of Pembina on the forty-ninth parallel to provide a governing line for his survey. Joined by two other surveyors, Milner Hart and A. C. Webb,

Dennis began the subdivision of land north of the Assinniboine River, east of the Red River Settlement. Armed Métis stopped one of the survey parties on October 11, 1869, and forbade them to survey Métis land.

The survey had become a political issue and all surveying stopped by December 1, the date on which the transfer of Rupert's Land was to take place. Dennis, a former British military officer, armed a small number of his survey parties and retreated to Fort Garry, ready to face a Métis militia led by Louis Riel. The Red River Settlement plunged into crisis, its inhabitants divided by race, language, religion, and political aspiration. Riel clearly had the upper hand and soon claimed initial victory without bloodshed. The Métis declared a provisional government, led by Louis Riel, and demanded that Canada negotiate the terms on which the settlement around Red River would be administered as part of the Dominion. Surveyor John Stoughton Dennis promptly returned east. Some of the men on the survey crews ended up imprisoned, along with many of the leaders of the Canadian English-speaking Red River settlers, in Fort Garry, by then under Métis control. The crisis almost escalated into a local civil war, and spawned national sympathies and outrage on the part of both English and French Canada following the execution of survey party member Thomas Scott. Further violence was averted through the creation of the Province of Manitoba in May 1870. The lands further west were named the North-West Territories, presided over by a Lieutenant-Governor. [2]

Finally, in 1871, plans for the survey of the North-West resumed with the creation of the Dominion Land Survey. John Stoughton Dennis, no doubt the wiser for his experiences in 1869, returned to Red River as the first surveyor general of Canada. He worked with Adam George Archibald, first Lieutenant-Governor of Manitoba, to develop a system that was similar to the rectangular township system used in the American Midwest, except it provided for public road allowances and allowed for river lot

### Execution of Survey Labourer Thomas Scott

Thomas Scott, a veteran Ontario militiaman, joined John Snow's survey party as a labourer at Red River in 1869. An unpredictable troublemaker, Scott, as the story goes, soon offended the Métis with his racist and anti-French views. He then assaulted Snow, who fired him. Scott joined a group in the Red River Settlement that was determined to oppose Riel. On December 7, he was imprisoned at Fort Garry when Riel assumed control. A month later, Scott and 120 others broke out and escaped to Portage La Prairie. Here Scott joined a militia group led by A. C. Boulton, one of John Stoughton Dennis's surveyors. By February 18, 1870, Riel had Scott back behind bars. Scott taunted his captors, who placed him before a tribunal for insubordination and found him guilty. Riel, as Métis leader, chose not to spare his life, and Scott was executed by a firing squad on March 4, 1870. [3]

land holdings as required. The first *Manual of Instructions for the Survey of Dominion Lands* was published in 1871 and set out how the system would proceed. On April 25, 1871, the House of Commons voted to adopt the Dominion Land Survey system that became law under the Dominion Lands Act of 1872.

The survey grid was to be laid out "square" on north-south meridian lines of longitude and east-west baselines of latitude established through astronomical observation. From the Principal Meridian successive initial meridians, approximately 4° longitude apart, were established to run north from the forty-ninth parallel, which formed the 1st Baseline. Successive east–west baselines to be established every twenty four miles along the meridians would then form a grid. However, as the meridians of longitude follow the curvature of the earth, they converge as they go further north; therefore, the distance along the baselines between the meridians decreases. In order to lay out uniform blocks of sixteen townships—to be subdivided later—within this controlling grid, surveyors had to make adjustments by establishing correction lines between the baselines. The "jogs" at the correction lines increase as they go west, resulting in a fractional range adjacent to the next initial meridian. Townships six miles square, comprised of thirty-six sections, each section being 640 acres, more or less, were to be numbered beginning at the forty-ninth parallel, from 1 to 126 northward, and according to ranges numbered westward from each Initial Meridian.

In 1872 the work of the Dominion Land Survey formally began as Canadian surveyors, in conjunction with their colleagues working on the North American Boundary Commission, established a historic link from the observatory in Selkirk over hundreds of miles of telegraph line with the Chicago observatory. On a series of crisp winter nights, repeated time checks with Chicago produced the coordinates for the Principal or First Meridian for the prairies. It was established at 97° 27' 28.41" West Longitude. From the Principal Meridian, a basic survey grid could be laid out westwards beginning with a series of partial baselines and meridians to establish governing lines of survey.

The work went slowly in the first years of the survey in the settlement area west of the Principal Meridian in the Province of Manitoba. During 1872, eight surveyors ran block outlines, twenty-two others marked out river lots, while five surveyors made advance exploratory surveys.[4] The survey of land reserved for the Hudson's Bay post at Fort Edmonton in 1873 by William S. Gore, DLS, was the only work undertaken during the first years of the Dominion Land Survey in territory that became Alberta.

In an attempt to speed things up west of Manitoba, the "Special Survey" was set up by order-in-council in 1874 as the advance "shock troops" of the Topographical Surveys Branch. Under the supervision of Lindsay Russell, DLS, Assistant Surveyor General, the Special Survey embarked on laying out the grid of meridians and baselines throughout the North-West. The surveyor general emphasized how surveyors would "contribute towards the construction of the railway by facilitating the location of the land grant along the line."[5] The Special Survey was also charged with gathering information about the soil, timber, minerals, flora, and fauna of the vast country of the North-West.

Canada, however, plunged into a major economic depression during the 1870s, with limited government funds available for surveys. It was a difficult start for a new country whose development seemed forever on hold. The western section of the Canadian Pacific Railway had only progressed from the Lakehead on Lake Superior as far as Winnipeg by 1876. Meanwhile, local government in the North-West was established

## The Administration of Land

As the Dominion Land Survey began its work, Canada was also developing a system for administering land in its new territories. In 1873 the Dominion government set up the Department of the Interior, which, through its various branches, would shape the development of the vast lands under its jurisdiction. The Dominion Lands Branch, established in 1871 under the Department of the Secretary of State and transferred to the Department of the Interior in 1873, played a central role. The subsequent regulation of land acquisition and its use through homestead entry, grants, and leases, was tightly controlled from Ottawa through a web of local Dominion Land agencies and timber agencies. The survey of land for settlement and crown leases remained in the hands of the Topographical Surveys Branch, despite changes in the administrative structure of the old North-West.[6]

through the North-West Territories Act of 1875.[7] Although the Lieutenant-Governor and a five-man council along with elected representatives had little autonomy, they consistently agitated for the rapid survey of the North-West Territories. In 1876 the Special Survey finally set foot on land within the boundaries of the future Province of Alberta. By that time, the Special Survey had been divided into two divisions, east and west. William F. King, DLS, led the west division. He followed Sandford Fleming's proposed route for the CPR west from Battleford, anticipating a demand for land from settlers along the North Saskatchewan River. King's work in 1876 took him as far as Fort Edmonton. His most important task was to establish the Fifth Meridian at 114° longitude, just west of Edmonton.

## THE LONG ROAD TO THE FIFTH MERIDIAN

The difficulties in the running of the Fifth Meridian faced by both King and Montague Aldous, DLS, who was sent to assist him, reveal a good deal about the process of putting together the vast geographic grid during the 1870s. Meridians of longitude were still difficult to establish. A pocket chronometer, the stars, and possibly the telegraph, along with a theodolite, compass, and chains for measuring out distance, remained the tools available to surveyors. In late 1877 William King set up an astronomical station just west of Fort Edmonton and established the 14th Baseline, along which he hoped to run a line westwards to establish the Fifth Meridian at 114° longitude.[8] King attempted to establish longitude at Edmonton using a time signal over the "not very reliable" telegraph system that had been laid by the Canadian Pacific Railway as far as Hay Lakes. Upon establishing his position, he planned to run a survey line west to establish a tentative meridian line.

In spring 1878, King waited over a month at Hay Lakes for a signal, delayed on account of an extensive prairie fire in late March that destroyed much of the telegraph line between Battleford and Hay Lakes. While waiting, he assessed what information he did have: "I am much obliged to you for Palliser's longitude of Edmonton which differs very much from the CPR longitude, the latter being 113° 40' 54", the difference from Palliser's being about 18 miles," he wrote to newly appointed Surveyor General Lindsay Russell. He noted that he hoped to have "startling results when I am able to get some moon culminations."[9] Ultimately, however, he failed to establish an exact longitude. Meanwhile, the eastern section of the Special Survey had discovered that the longitude for Battleford established by the CPR exploratory survey parties was out by about eleven miles. This underlined the necessity for the Dominion Land Survey to run the 14th Baseline all the way west from the Fourth Meridian at 110° longitude to establish the Fifth Meridian.[10]

### Every Surveyor Had a Theodolite

A theodolite is a surveying instrument designed to measure horizontal and vertical angles or to establish straight lines. It has a telescope mounted between a pair of vertical standards attached to a revolving circular plate. The instrument has graduated circles for measuring angles in both the horizontal and vertical planes. It is secured to a tripod to provide a stable and level platform for field work. Theodolite was a British/Canadian term and in the United States the similar instrument was called a transit. In Canada, the term transit was also used, increasingly so as the twentieth century progressed.

Montague Aldous was appointed to undertake this rather daunting task as part of the ongoing work of the western branch of the Special Survey. He set out from Winnipeg in spring 1879 with assistant Charles Magrath, DLS, and his party of four chainmen, three axemen, one mounder, and a cook. After a month rattling over the prairie in buckboards and carts, they arrived at the Fourth Meridian, which surveyors had marked on the 11th Baseline with an iron bar during the previous summer. Aldous confirmed its location by astronomical observation and ran a line north to the 14th Baseline. Here, joined by King, he discovered a problem. The distance his party had chained out between the 11th and the 14th Baseline differed from King's results by eleven chains, or approximately 725 feet. Astronomical observations then placed the 14th Baseline ninety-three feet too far north. Aldous and King compromised and established the baseline seventy feet to the south! With this piece of the geographic grid filled in, they could strike out west from the Fourth Meridian into what is now the Province of Alberta.

By the end of October, Aldous reached the Edmonton area, tying in with King's astronomical station to make further observations, before reaching 114° longitude or the Fifth Meridian on November 5, 1879. The problem of confirming its accuracy remained as Aldous still did not know the time accurately. "I have broken the chain of my mean time watch and take the liberty of sending it down to you for repair, try and get it repaired and mailed to me as soon as you can," he wrote Lindsay Russell from Edmonton in December. "I wish we could manage to get the longitude for this place . . . the telegraph station is now in here and it would be so much better to get the 114th meridian in its right position before producing it north or south."[11] He finally did so,

*An undated portrait photograph of Montague Aldous.*

working with John Walter's telegraphic office at the ferry crossing, as it would be months before his watch might return from distant Ottawa. It was now possible to continue expanding the grid by extending the Fifth Meridian, initially as far as Pigeon Lake, and then hundreds of miles south to the international boundary—a daunting task.

Spring came late in 1880, and it was April 14 before Aldous was able to set out from Edmonton for a point north of Pigeon Lake, back to the position from where he had produced the Fifth Meridian south from the 14th Baseline during the winter season. On the first day of May, they carried the line across the ice on Pigeon Lake. Aldous left his party in the charge of Charles Magrath from May 16 to June 4, and returned to Edmonton in an attempt to get a telegraphic communication with William King to confirm the longitude. Magrath faced major hurdles in running the line south across Gull Lake: "The distance is about eight miles and production of the line and angular observations had to be effected at night with the aid of fire signals."[12] Aldous and his party continued south through the summer, heading into rough and hilly country in the Porcupine Hills at the 5th Baseline. When he reached the 4th Baseline he could continue no further, because the country was so mountainous. He then ran a line east for some distance before once more turning south, passing about five miles east of Fort Macleod. "When in about the same Latitude as the Fort I ran west on a convenient section line and connected our survey with the flag staff in the N.W. Mounted Police barrack yard," Aldous reported.[13]

Then, taking their lives in their hands, the survey party crossed the Belly River eleven times before they were able to continue surveying a line directly south to the St. Mary River about twenty miles from the international boundary. As it was unsafe to cross the river, they ran west a distance along the 2nd Baseline and then swung 90° south, tying into the international boundary on July 30, 1880.[14] The completion of the survey of the Fifth Meridian south to the forty-ninth parallel was no small achievement. Aldous was working with equipment that was not much more sophisticated than that used by David Thompson, and the technology for establishing longitude had advanced only as far as the additional check of a time signal by telegraph. Aldous's survey of the Fifth Meridian, in conjunction with the establishment of the Sixth Meridian in the Peace River area in 1883, formed a basic framework that was connected at sufficient points to govern the future survey of townships in Alberta.

## The Unexpected Challenge from the Canadian Pacific Railway

The financial dramas and scandals attendant on the financing and construction of the Canadian Pacific Railway filled the newspapers in Toronto, Montreal, and Halifax. The twists and turns of events must have seemed divorced from the realities of daily work for the few surveyors out along the North Saskatchewan River. In 1879, Aldous, for one, was more concerned that the survey would never be able to keep up with settlement already beginning along the North Saskatchewan in anticipation of the Canadian Pacific line through the Yellowhead Pass to the coast. While carrying out exploratory surveys of the Edmonton and St. Albert Settlements, Aldous became convinced that there was an urgent necessity for township subdivision surveys of adjacent land, warning "that every year's delay will result in an endless amount of difficulty amongst those who are now taking up land in the country."[15] Within six months, however, the boom on the North Saskatchewan River came to an abrupt end.

On October 21, 1880, everything changed. The Dominion government struck a new deal that would ensure the CPR's completion. It signed an agreement with a syndicate of businessmen—Donald Smith, George Stephen, and James Jerome Hill. It paid the syndicate 25 million dollars in cash, and turned over

### Chains and Chaining

Surveyors measured the distances they covered on the ground using the imperial Gunter's Chain made up of 100 steel links, each link being .66 foot or 7.92 inches long. The exact width of a road allowance in rural Alberta is one chain, sixty-six feet. Eighty chains equal a mile, the width of a section of land. Ten square chains equal an acre. Each survey party employed a number of chainmen for this work. Chainmen had to take an oath to fulfill their duties with honesty and accuracy. The possibilities for error were many, and distances were check-chained with a chain graduated in feet. It was necessary to correct and adjust for slope of the land, sag and tension in the chain. The chain length was also affected by temperature. If the error in chaining exceeded two feet in a mile, it had to be re-chained. By 1900 the Gunter's Chain had been replaced by steel bands marked in feet, which, although easier to use, also required careful use and correction.

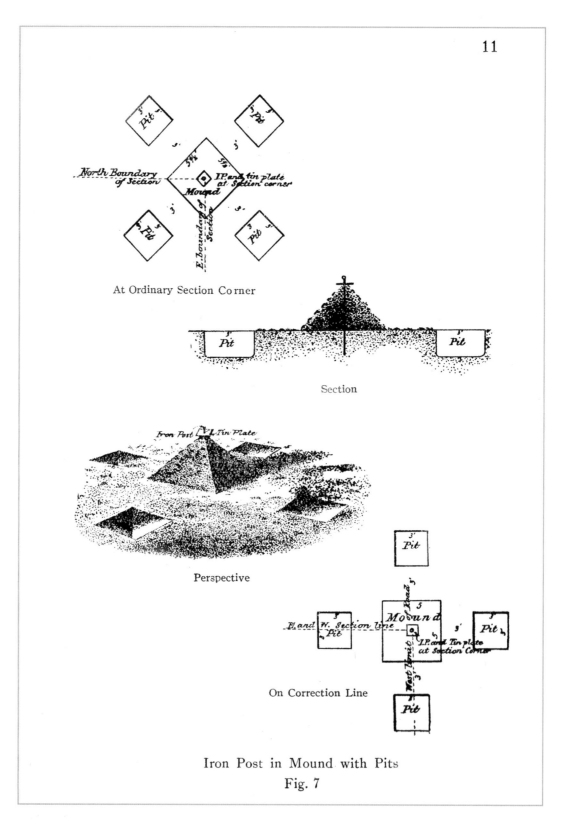

At Ordinary Section Corner

Section

Perspective

On Correction Line

Iron Post in Mound with Pits
Fig. 7

*A page from* Description of the Boundary Monuments Erected on Surveys of Dominion Lands, 1871–1917
*showing iron post in mound with pits as used on prairie landscape between 1882 and 1886.*
Published in 1917, Canada, Department of the Interior

the completed sections of line as well as all surveys pertaining to its route through the Rocky Mountains. In addition, the Dominion of Canada gave the syndicate twenty-five million acres as a land grant subsidy and agreed to pay for them to be surveyed (later assessed at 37 million dollars). This was all part of the price for bailing out the nation's sinking dream of a rail line from sea to sea.[16] The agreement was ratified as the Canadian Pacific Railway Act of 1881.[17]

The unexpected then happened. The new owners decided Fleming's Yellowhead route was too expensive, and simply announced they wished to change the route to a southern one. Parliament acquiesced. The final realignment of the CPR in 1882 ensured its passage west from Regina into southern Alberta through Medicine Hat, Calgary, Banff, across the Kicking Horse Pass, and on to Kamloops in British Columbia, where it joined the route suggested by Sandford Fleming to the coast.[18] Public attention shifted from the valley of the North Saskatchewan to the potential of southern farm and ranch land as speculators switched tracks. But reaction had already been swift in the Ottawa office of Surveyor General Lindsay Russell. The new Canadian Pacific Railway argued that it should survey the millions of acres of land included in their land grant, but the Dominion Land Survey quickly sprung into action to prevent this, and persuaded the Minister of the Interior that the Topographical Surveys Branch could rise to the challenge of surveying the 25 million acres across the southern prairies.[19]

Forced to reassess the situation, the surveyor general had to figure out in a hurry how he could possibly meet the increased demands on his resources to subdivide so many townships along the CPR rail line. Russell took action to ensure that there would be enough surveyors ready and willing to do the work for the right remuneration.[20] In a lengthy letter to John Stoughton Dennis, Deputy Minister of the Interior, Russell proposed changes for greater efficiency in carrying out the survey arrangements being made with the syndicate for the construction of the CPR, and asserted his opinion that the contract method of employment used by the survey was not the best. Russell further spelled out what every surveyor knew to be true: "The special difficulty or obstacle to the demarcation and measurement of a survey line in any particular place cannot be known until the survey is being made, and it is but the merest leap in the dark for a surveyor to undertake to effect properly for a certain sum any surveying operation on a piece of ground that he has not previously thoroughly inspected."[21] Russell noted that paying by the mile encouraged a man to rush his work through where conditions were favourable. He drove home his case by noting that a recent American commission had concluded that salaried surveyors did a better job.

### Dominion Land Survey Monuments

The type of monumentation or markers initially varied according to whether the landscape was prairie or bush. Monumentation posed numerous problems that resulted in a series of changes from 1871. Between 1871 and 1880, at township corners in bush country a surveyor could employ a bearing tree, a wooden post in conjunction with a bearing tree or trees, or a stone with a small pyramid of stones around it, while on the prairie he was required to mark with a post, mound, trench, and pits. Section corners were marked with a wooden post in the same way, as were quarter sections where a wooden post could be made from available timber. Otherwise, a mound trench and pits would suffice.

Iron posts were first placed at the corners of township blocks only, and then from 1882 they were also used at prairie section quarters. The posts were driven about one foot deep through the centre of the mounds, leaving about two inches projecting above the ground. A cold chisel was used to mark the section number on the southwest face of the iron post, and a square tin plate marked with a cold chisel with N, S, E, and W, was slipped over the post.[22] The Topographical Surveys Branch soon replaced the solid iron bars with iron tubing or pipes, but continued to use the tin plates until 1890.

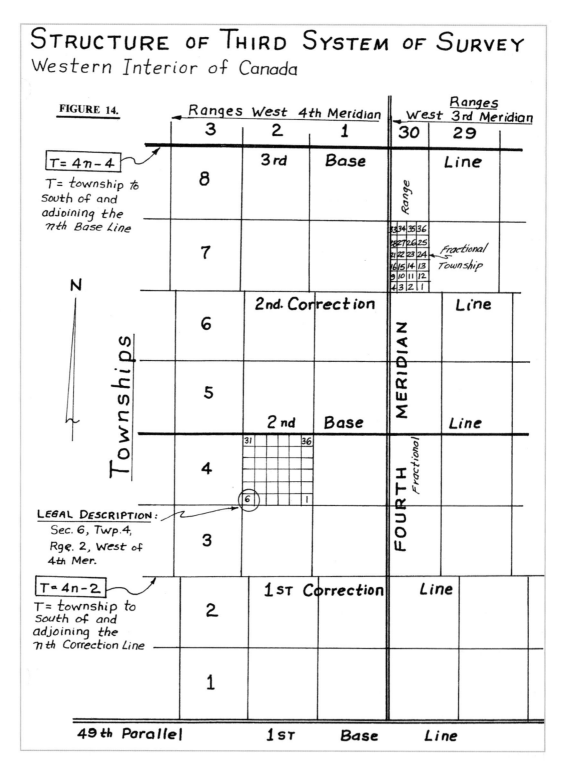

*The Third System of Survey in Alberta.*

DOUGLAS BARNETT, "EARLY SURVEYS AND SETTLEMENTS IN CENTRAL ALBERTA," UNPUBLISHED MANUSCRIPT, 2000

Russell wanted to be sure there would be a sufficient number of competent surveyors willing to do the work in the North-West Territories. The dreadful weather there during the season of 1880 had not been good for surveyors' pocket books, and little profit, or even loss, was no incentive to take on further work. Russell's pleas for improving working conditions for surveyors and instigating daily or yearly pay fell on deaf ears. In February, the Minister decided to continue the process of awarding township subdivision contracts after competition by tender, allowing that the block township outlines, the Special Survey, and inspection should be done by surveyors known to the surveyor general as especially able and reliable and, of course, who would also be approved by the Minister.[23] Letters of contract subsequently laid out more detailed instructions for the scope of work to be undertaken by surveyors in the field, which by December 1881 had resulted in the survey of a total over nine million acres—but only a very small portion of them were in Alberta.

By 1881 the efficiency of the system of survey itself was under scrutiny, and it was decided to make road allowances a little narrower. The decision to decrease the road allowance from 1.5 chains to 1.0 chains, or sixty-six feet, for all subsequent surveys not only put thousands more acres into farmland, but also reduced the cost of survey by about 2.5 million dollars.[24] Surveyors, however, had trouble aligning their work between the old First System of Survey, applied to townships in Manitoba and the Prince Albert area of Saskatchewan, and the new Third System of Survey.[25] Although all townships within Alberta were subdivided on the Third System of Survey, the change affected the preliminary grid outline work done before 1881, which required correction.[26]

An updated *Manual of Instructions for the Survey of Dominion Lands*, published in 1881, provided detailed instructions for the Third System of Survey and included tables of logs and trigonometric functions, for the convenience of surveyors, as well as astronomical and geodetic tables.[27] Montague Aldous, by now undoubtedly the surveyor who had walked the furthest in Alberta, set out in spring 1881 with a copy in his bag, ready to survey nineteen block township outlines west of the Fifth Meridian between the 5th and 7th Baselines west of Fort Calgary. At the same time, Lachlan Kennedy, DLS, subdivided the townships that Aldous laid out.[28] They soon ran into difficulties working according to the new Third System of Survey. As smaller townships of the Third System brought the baselines closer together, Aldous had to send out correction survey parties to relocate posts and mounds. Additionally, the degree of accuracy for meridians became more significant as township subdivision progressed.

As problems encountered with the Fifth Meridian continued, they revealed the difficulty of filling in the township grid when it was laid out over thousands of square miles. It turned out that Aldous had made errors chaining the Fifth Meridian. Furthermore, chain measurements had led to inaccuracy in the distance between the Fourth and Fifth Meridian. The Inspector of Surveys, William King, explained to Edouard Deville, who became surveyor general in 1885, that although Aldous had corrected the posts on the meridian from the 14th to the 11th Baseline in accordance with the Third System of Survey, as well as proportionally correcting the error of 9.77 chains—approximately one-eighth of a mile—throughout his whole line, an error margin still remained.[29] The result, of course, was that township subdivision plans later tied into Aldous's survey would not fit the grid exactly. Montague Aldous, it appears, was better at astronomical observation than supervising chaining.

## The Dominion Land Survey: A Machine in Motion

From the early 1870s to the mid-1880s, the Dominion Land Survey developed a system for transporting and supplying surveyors for fieldwork. Just getting to Winnipeg from eastern Canada was challenge enough. Once there, the trip further west, to the North Saskatchewan River district in Alberta, for example, was another logistical problem. It required hauling survey equipment in Red River carts over the Carlton Trail each summer. For surveyors working in southern Alberta, the quickest way west was generally to take the US railway route, then travel overland from Fort Benton in Montana to Fort Macleod. The alternative was a long trek across the plains.

In the spring of 1881, Montague Aldous had been given instructions to go by rail from Winnipeg to Bismarck, North Dakota, take the river steamer west to Fort Benton, and then proceed north over land to Fort Macleod. When he heard about high waters on the Missouri, Aldous decided it would be better to go over land from Winnipeg. "My men and horses are in good condition, a walk of 850 miles has put them all in good training," he wrote from Fort Macleod on June 23, 1881.[30] As the end of steel crept west of Winnipeg, the trek became easier and cheaper. During 1883 the Survey secured reduced rates on the CPR and the Grand Trunk Railway for surveyors. In 1884 Calgary became the starting point for surveys in Alberta, and the Survey established a government depot for storing outfits over winter from one year to the next, as it did in Edmonton.

Surveyors did not have an easy time of it organizing supplies and, most importantly to them, getting paid for their expenses. The issue of their personal financial outlay at the beginning of the season was contentious as they were only allowed to claim according to a fixed rate. In 1879 William King, considering the logistics of outfitting his survey party at Fort Edmonton, reported that flour in Edmonton cost twenty dollars for one hundred pounds! Goods freighted for two months from Winnipeg, arrived late in the season and were frighteningly expensive. Supplies for southern Alberta in 1880 came by bull train from Fort Benton to Fort Macleod, where they cost considerably more than at Winnipeg, but certainly less than at Edmonton. Flour, for example, that cost $2.75 for forty pounds in Winnipeg, cost $7.50 at Fort Macleod. Montague Aldous noted that rations for one month for his party cost $12.48 in Winnipeg, as opposed to a total of $19.19 in Fort Macleod. When the railway reached Medicine Hat, and then Calgary, the situation changed, but it was still a major expense to have goods freighted from the end of steel. In 1884 it cost $271 to transport goods overland from Calgary to Victoria settlement on the North Saskatchewan River for township outline surveys.[31]

Along with food, blankets, and clothing, surveyors had to transport tents, cooking stoves, plates and utensils, survey equipment that included a fragile transit carefully packed in an instrument box, wire, rope, axes, inscribing irons, chains, and heavy iron monument posts. The posts were shipped from Winnipeg, where they were made—thirty-five thousand of them in 1884. By 1883 surveyors picked up their iron posts at Medicine Hat and heaved them into their carts as they set out for the survey location. In 1882 the Survey contracted John Campbell's carriage factory in London, Ontario to supply one hundred carts. These carts were generally protected with covers made from Canadian Duck cotton. Surveyors walked or rode on horseback, used carts and buckboards, and the few who worked in Alberta in the winter during these early years used snowshoes and sleighs to get about. Crossing rivers was a major problem in a land without bridges, and the Survey ordered twenty-four twelve-foot folding canvas boats from Strathan Folding Canvas Boats at Chagrin Falls, Ohio, in 1881.[32] If no boat was available, surveyors made makeshift rafts.

Horses to transport all this equipment and provisions posed a significant expense and logistical headache for the Survey. Horses were scarce to buy and even harder to take care of and feed properly, especially in districts with no natural hay. From the beginning of the Survey's operations in Alberta, long-standing arrangements were made to overwinter horses. John Lineham of Fish Creek, for instance, kept the horses and stored the outfits of a number of Dominion Land Surveyors, including William King, Lewis Ord, Tom Kains, Thomas Fawcett, and William Ogilvie.[33] Surveyors were required to have a list of all storage items signed by a notary public before forwarding it to Ottawa.

## LAND SURVEYORS ENCOUNTER SOUTHERN ALBERTA

Alberta provoked strong feelings in those surveyors who first encountered her—beautiful and bounteous on one hand, ugly and barren on the other. While her skies were often welcoming, sunny, and bright, they could turn quickly and become ferocious, like the hidden dangers of her features. Surveyors in southern Alberta wrote long descriptions of the country where they worked as part of their official reports to the surveyor general. These were often included with more technical aspects of their work in the annual reports that the Department of the Interior delivered each year to Parliament.

Lachlan Kennedy, who worked on township surveys in the Bow River area, where ranching had already become big business, left a picture of southern Alberta as he saw it. He was impressed with the varied landscape, noting the rolling foothills with spruce, grey willow, white poplar, and cottonwood to provide shelter and ample fuel, and springs and streams that ran with pure water. Kennedy, less than impressed with the "innumerable quantity of flies of which the mosquito is the most formidable factor," was perhaps the first surveyor to include in an official report a discussion of the pest that bedevils those working outdoors! The weather, he warned, while generally pleasant, was unpredictable. On July 21, 1881, surveying on the headwaters of Pine Creek, now within Calgary, Kennedy and his men were struck by hailstones at least the size of walnuts, which left four of them black and blue for two weeks afterwards. The storm was about two miles in width and cut a swath through the vegetation, killing several prairie chickens and an eagle.[34]

In 1882 Otto J. Klotz, DLS, surveying the 5th Baseline between the Fourth and Fifth Meridian, crossed the South Saskatchewan River four miles south of the baseline and continued west across what is now Canadian

### Triangulation: A Tried and True Procedure

Surveyors employ trigonometry where they can not run a straight line to measure distance, such as over the terrain encountered by Thomas Drummond, DLS, running the 6th baseline in 1882. If two angles and one side of a triangle are known, then the remaining angle and sides can be calculated. Drummond measured the angle at which he deviated from the baseline. He chained a distance along this tangent, and then angled a line back towards the baseline at a known angle to his tangent. He calculated the length of the other two sides of the triangle and chained back to the baseline. Back on track, he resumed running the 6th Baseline.

Forces Base Suffield. Klotz had to kill many a rattlesnake along the steep banks of the South Saskatchewan River. "Working with parched lips for want of water, under a tropical sun, was rather hard," he noted.[35] Saline ponds unfit for man or beast provided no respite until they reached the welcome sight of the Bow River with its clear blue waters.

Some distance north of Klotz's party, Thomas Drummond, DLS, was surveying west along the 6th Baseline. He was also unimpressed with the dry land east of the Bow River: "very peculiar, for the most part a sort of yellow alkaline clay . . . this clay seems heavy enough, but, either from some property of the soil or from lack of moisture, grows very poor grass; in many places there were patches with no vegetation at all." Where the Red Deer River ran close to the 6th Baseline— through today's Dinosaur Park—the four-hundred-foot-high banks hampered Drummond. It resembled, he noted, the badlands along the international boundary, and was aptly named Dead Man's Canyon. Ravines ran out from the river, making it impossible to place posts in the ground along the actual baseline, and at one point he had to make a triangulation of about three miles.[36]

## SURVEYORS SEE THE CANADIAN PACIFIC RAILWAY EDGING EVER CLOSER TO THE ROCKIES

As surveyors worked in southern Alberta in 1882, the long gleaming steel of the Canadian Pacific Railway edged its way across the plains. By the time it reached Regina, Dominion Land Surveyors were running the necessary lines for railway surveyors to tie into. In 1882 Charles Magrath surveyed the 4th Baseline between the Fourth and Fifth Meridians, following it down into the valley of the South Saskatchewan River. "The Bull's Head Coulee enters the valley from a south-easterly direction, and it is down this coulee that the proposed route of the Canadian Pacific Railway approaches the river," he reported at the end of the year.[37] In early summer 1883, a short step ahead of construction, railway surveyors working for the CPR arrived at Medicine Hat. The clank of hammer on metal echoed as Medicine Hat quickly became the centre of a great deal of activity. A tent city, occasionally graced with more substantial buildings such as the American Hotel, sprang up. Eventually, the first plume of black smoke was seen on the horizon on June 10, and a locomotive pulled up to the end of steel. The cars disgorged supplies to be freighted west and north to the North Saskatchewan River valley. Among the passengers were Dominion Land Surveyors. They reported to William King, Inspector of Surveys, and picked up iron posts before heading in to the field.

King moved his office from Regina to Medicine Hat to coincide with the arrival of the CPR in 1883. He had a house built in the new settlement and found that his work went better under a solid roof than from a tent. Charles Biggar, DLS, assisted him, and by August, they had allotted 375 townships to be surveyed. There were so many parties in the field that year that the Topographical Surveys Branch set up its own mail service, employing eleven men whose job it was to bring instructions to surveyors in the field and return with progress reports and drawings, in an effort to cut down on delays and losses in the field.[38]

The surveyors who spread out north and south of the CPR line as it headed for Fort Calgary in 1883 were under a great deal of pressure to complete the township subdivisions according to their contracts. The pace of construction was relentless, the railway bridge across the South

*Surveyors with the CPR pose with their theodolites at Medicine Hat, Alberta, in 1883.*

Saskatchewan was up in record time, and by July 14 the railway had been extended seventy-five miles northwest of Medicine Hat. By the beginning of August, the end of steel was little more than thirty miles from Calgary.[39]

Despite Lindsay Russell's previous protests against contract work, the Department instituted a bonus system as an incentive for efficiency. Surveyors who completed all of their contract work by January 1, 1884, would receive a bonus of 15 percent on the total amount of their payment.[40] In early fall 1883 a number of surveyors who had finished their fieldwork took on extra townships—confident they could still complete all the work before the deadline. Atrocious weather, which marked the beginning of the season in July, unexpectedly brought the early onset of winter in October. There was no way the work could be finished in conditions that quickly became life-threatening.

George Roy, DLS, reported in detail on October 3, 1883, how he was only able to complete two of the six townships remaining on his contract for additional townships. "Rain came on at noon—a rain mixed with snow," he reported to Edouard Deville in Ottawa. "The bad weather soon became tempestuous and for two days I could not leave my tent." Spells of bad weather prevented him from finishing the survey until October 24. The ground was by then frozen eight to ten inches deep with ten inches of snow on the ground, and the survey party had to use an axe to make the mounds. One of his men had a frostbitten foot and another suffered from a sore throat, barely able to speak. Another had snow blindness and could hardly see. His three remaining horses could hardly stand, as they could not get sufficient feed. "Furthermore," he added, "my men had been told that one of the men belonging to Mr. Francis, a neighbouring surveyor, had become lost in a snow storm and was found some days after frozen to death. Suffering from intense cold, discouraged by the bad weather and the delayed work, seeing the state we were in, this last news did not serve to encourage them." Roy, perhaps fearing a mutiny on the line, decided it was time to quit for the season.[41] Roy was among a number of surveyors who did in the end receive the bonus, deemed to have faced circumstances beyond their control.

**Spending Big Bucks**

The years 1881–1884 were ones of exponential financial outlay on surveys by the Canadian government. Expenditure in the North-West Territories in 1880 was $147,802. In 1881 it jumped to $334,681, and then took another leap in 1882, to $511,882, in response to the challenge presented by the Canadian Pacific Railway land grant. The year 1883 marked a further increase—to $562,221. Expenditure peaked at $728,441 in 1884, as the subdivision of townships in the CPR lands in southern Alberta was completed.[44]

The death of one of his men seems to have weighed heavily on John Francis, DLS. His survey returns remained incomplete over the next two years, while he found solace in alcohol, much to the worry of his family.[42] He eventually recovered his professional edge and continued his career in surveying with the Dominion Land Survey in Alberta and later in a private practice in Manitoba. Another surveyor found the work in 1883 so stressful that he suffered a mental breakdown, seemingly from exhaustion, anxiety, and lack of sleep.[43] The pressure of subdivision in 1883, and the bonus system, which was not repeated, had driven home to both surveyors and the surveyor general that the western frontier of Alberta could be an unpredictable and dangerous place. The safety of survey parties was a very real concern for the future.

### Squatters' Concerns with the Surveys for the CPR

The earliest settlers in southern Alberta, squatting in small communities, were less than pleased to see all the emphasis put on subdividing townships along the CPR. Many wished to apply for homesteads, but could not as their land remained unsurveyed. Settlers in the district around Fort Macleod did not have far to travel for a hotel, or stores where they could buy harness, hardware, groceries, and dry goods. They could make stage connections to Pincher Creek, avail of financial, legal, and real estate services, or entertain themselves at a billiards parlour, but they saw no imminent legal security for their land holdings. The *Macleod Gazette* fiercely championed their interests. "There is no more interesting subject to the squatter than the progress of Dominion Surveys," declared an editorial on April 24, 1883. "He looks for the time when it shall have reached his section of the country for the perfecting of his title to the land he is on . . . no provision is made for him; he must wait patiently for the regular survey, probably dragging itself along at a snail's pace hundreds of miles east of him." Dismayed squatters at Pincher Creek, High River, along the Belly River, Sheep Creek, and Fish Creek, could see waiting a long time, while Dominion Land Surveyors were subdividing country that might not be settled for twenty years. The same problem existed along the Red Deer River, and the *Gazette* proposed—to no avail—an interim subdivision survey that could be verified at a later point to cover a strip of land a hundred miles east of the Rockies as far north as the Red Deer River.

In the meantime, the *Macleod Gazette* demanded a survey for an official townsite at Fort Macleod. A settlement had grown up in the 1870s around the North-West Mounted Police (NWMP) post, strategically built on an island in the Oldman River. Not only did everything have to be ferried across to the island, but the erection of more buildings close to the post had been prohibited, stalling further investment in business at Fort Macleod.[45] Finally, in March 1883, the citizens began to move their buildings from the island to the north bank of the river in the hope of influencing the government as to an appropriate spot for a townsite.[46] On July 24, the *Macleod Gazette* declared: "We can find little excuse for the absurd delay in laying out and selling the lots in our new town." The very next month, Archibald McVittie, DLS, arrived to lay out the townsite, which included a new NWMP reserve. At the insistence of Major Crozier of the NWMP, McVittie included an esplanade along the river as a pleasant carriage drive or promenade for the future townspeople.[47] By 1884 many of the new townsite lots had been sold off by auction, and the government retained the title to the remainder.

Further north, as the CPR line approached, squatters waited with apprehension at Calgary. A fledgling settlement had also grown up there during the 1870s around the North-West Mounted Police fort at the confluence of the Bow and the Elbow Rivers, as well as on the east bank of the Elbow. By 1883 the Dominion government had forbidden building west of the Elbow River, and stayed all requests to lay out a townsite before the railway arrived. Merchants consequently put up their goods in tents. This situation, according to the *Macleod Gazette* of July 24, 1883, was retarding the development of a flourishing good-sized town. When the CPR chose the location of its townsite, it did exactly as it had done elsewhere across the prairie—it ignored the existing settlement and the wishes of settlers.[48] It selected Section 15, Township 24, Range 1, West of the Fifth Meridian,

*Archibald McVittie, DLS, n.d.*
GLENBOW ARCHIVES, NA-1046-7

which lay west of the Elbow—where there were in fact already some squatters by the summer of 1883.[49] The Bow River runs through the north part of Section 15, which today comprises the area between Fourth Street SE and Fourth Street SW running as far south as Sevententh Avenue. The CPR chose the west side of the section for the location of the station grounds, on today's Ninth Avenue.

The Dominion government then established a rival townsite, to the west on Section 16, cashing in on valuable proximity to the CPR railway station. Today, this land lies west from Fourth Street SW to Fourteenth Street SW. In April 1884, Archibald McVittie began surveying town lots. He surveyed avenues running parallel to the railway line and streets running perpendicular to the avenues, both of which were sixty-six feet wide. Regular blocks were to be laid out 500 feet long along the avenues by 280 feet along the street. McVittie was told to lay out the irregular blocks adjoining section lines as he saw fit. When asked by Surveyor General Edouard Deville to explain missing posts on his survey in fall 1884, McVittie drew a picture that would have made many a surveyor's heart sink: "In the summer a race course was laid out and all the posts in the way removed."[50]

## THE SHAPING OF A PROFESSION

When the Dominion Lands Act of 1872 set the survey and settlement of the West in motion, not only did it set out the system of survey to be used, it also regulated the profession of surveyor, setting up a board of examiners and, by 1875, establishing the professional commission of Dominion Land Surveyor. From 1875, all surveyors were obliged to sit the DLS examination, which tested their knowledge of a syllabus established under the 1872 Dominion Lands Act. Surveyors who headed out west had to prove their knowledge of a rather intimidating subject list—Euclid, Plane

Trigonometry, Mensuration of Superficies (measuring distance on the ground), Plotting and Map Drawing, Spherical Trigonometry, Astronomy, and Geology—as well as show their aptitude for practical surveying operations and use of instruments. A more exacting range of knowledge could earn a Dominion Land Surveyor the higher commission of Dominion Topographical Surveyor, or DTS, introduced in 1876, and for which eighteen surveyors had qualified by 1887—eleven of whom surveyed within the future province of Alberta.[51]

Dominion Land Surveyors were bound by procedural rules for every step of their job. They had to keep field notes and a daily diary, fill out forms for supplies, and keep inventories of equipment on hand. In Ottawa things were done by the book. Surveyors out in the field, however, faced dire weather and were often frustrated by complaints from Ottawa about lack of communication or delays, as they struggled to do their job. Sometimes the conditions were such that the monumentation could not be done exactly as prescribed, or instructions for the survey carried out exactly as set out by the surveyor general for each specific contract. There was, however, little room for deviation, as every surveyor knew his work would ultimately be thoroughly scrutinized.

The Dominion Land Survey ensured a system of checks and balances for surveys by having an inspection of surveys done in the field. By 1884 there were four examiners assessing the work done. Although the amount of time they could spend checking chaining and inspecting monumentation was limited given the number of contracts they had to check, the inspectors expected the

*Group of Dominion Land Surveyors at Winnipeg, Manitoba, May 1882.*
*Back row: James K. McLean; T. R. Hewson; Lewis R. Ord; J. F. Harden; H. C. Denny; Charles E. Wolfe.*
*Middle row: Charles F. Miles; F. W. Armstrong; Thomas Kains; Charles A. Magrath; H. B. Proudfoot.*
*Front row: A. F. Cotton; T. Drummond; H. F. Bray.*

surveyors to uphold standards. "This survey has been performed in a rough and careless manner," concluded examiner Milner Hart, about a subdivision in southern Alberta in 1883. He complained about the chaining and noted: "The quarter section mounds which were too small were not in line with the section mounds, and the pits were poor and not well shaped." [52]

Before a surveyor's final return of survey—to include field notes, sketches, daily diary, and all calculations—would be accepted for payment, he might have to address detailed lists of corrections or questions raised by the survey inspection. When the surveyor general was less than pleased with the initial returns of his contractors, they were soon faced with a point-by-point detailing of omissions and contradictions in figures—and a barrage of questions as to how exactly distances were calculated! All this usually indicated the surveyor had a good deal more work to do before his contract would be paid out. The extensive correspondence on many survey contracts show that the surveyor often contested the findings of the examiner, generally on specific points or contrary evidence. Most vociferous were surveyors who had their expense claims questioned or final payments withheld.

In April 1882 surveyors formed the Association of Dominion Land Surveyors. Among the founders were at least ten men who worked in Alberta, including Otto Klotz, Dominion Astronomer, who was elected president, along with William King, Lewis Ord, William Ogilvie, and Charles Magrath. One of their first moves was to draw up a resolution asking the government for more pay. Surveyor General Edouard Deville was a little wary of the purpose and intent of the Association. "With a very few exceptions, the work of Dominion Land Surveyors is limited to surveys under instructions from the Minister of the Interior and there is no prospect of a change as new provinces will be formed and Provincial Land Surveyors appointed before private surveys are required. The Minister of the Interior being responsible for the work performed by surveyors, it seems equitable that he should have control of the profession. From a general point of view, I fail to see what advantage would be secured or improvement made by the proposed incorporation." [53] The surveyor general retained the right of examination and granting of commissions, and the Association of Dominion Land Surveyors remained unincorporated, acting as a lobby group and for professional exchange. [54]

The rapid expansion of the Dominion Land Survey into southern Alberta was directly linked to the construction of the Canadian Pacific Railway. By 1883 the survey parties of nine Dominion Land Surveyors had laid out a basic framework of meridians and baselines for extending the township grid in Alberta. [55] They worked in harsh and trying conditions and their achievements can only be described as extraordinary. They set a tradition of rugged determination against the odds of terrain and climate that was embraced by land surveyors following in their wake. By 1884 the first wave of township outline and subdivision surveys as far west as the Rocky Mountains was completed. Almost all the townships surveyed were in southern Alberta. Not until the late 1890s did John A. Macdonald's next step for the national policy fall into place. As his vision of a huge immigrant influx to the prairies was finally realized, Dominion Land Surveyors were again busy surveying trails and subdividing townships along the North Saskatchewan River and in central Alberta. In the meantime, surveyors tackled other challenges; the most immediate was to mark out boundaries for the first Indian reserves in Alberta.

## CHAPTER THREE

# People Facing Change

*Land Surveyors, Aboriginal People, and the Grievances of the North-West Territories*

## SURVEYORS MEET ABORIGINAL PEOPLES FACING CHANGE

As Canada prepared to introduce the township system, the question of how to accommodate the Aboriginal residents of the North-West, who claimed the land as theirs from time immemorial, became an urgent issue. During the 1870s, their way of life as plant gatherers and migratory hunters changed dramatically for Aboriginal peoples. The quantities of game decreased through indiscriminate use of firearms and even poison. As the buffalo were hunted down to near extinction, a smallpox epidemic in 1870 brought death and demoralization. The unscrupulous activities of American whiskey traders from Montana, who exchanged cheap and addictive spirits for horses and pelts, resulted in poverty and violence. In 1873, American trappers looking for stolen horses crossed the forty-ninth parallel and attacked an Assiniboine camp in the Cypress Hills. The massacre of up to thirty Assiniboines alarmed the Dominion government and instigated the famous North-West Mounted Police march west. On the southern plains, the whiskey traders subsequently vanished, but starvation became the new reality, heightened by the influx of four thousand Sioux refugees into the Cypress Hills following the massacre of the American General Custer's troops south of the border in 1876.

Canada wished to avoid the horrifying bloodshed that had accompanied the occupation of Aboriginal lands in the American west. The Dominion government's aim was to placate Native peoples and ensure their acceptance of the new order of things. The Natives of the plains were alarmed by the encroachment of white settlers, but the chiefs, mindful of the military force used in the United States of America, felt they had little recourse other than to seek peace—first with each other through the Blackfoot Confederacy, and then with the Dominion government through treaties. Gradually, as part of the provisions under Treaty Six signed at Fort Carlton and Fort Pitt in 1876, Treaty Seven at Blackfoot Crossing in 1877, and Treaty Eight signed at Lesser Slave Lake in 1899, Native leaders acquiesced to the idea of reserve lands for their peoples.

The Indian Act of 1876 defined the system of reserves to be set aside for the members of bands who adhered to a treaty. A cash annuity was to be paid to band members, which was later generally referred to as treaty money. A reserve, within the meaning of the Act, was a tract of land set aside for the use and benefit of the band, but the title remained vested in the crown.[1] The location of reserves was to be decided according to the treaties and the wishes of the chiefs. Dominion Land

*A Blackfoot camp on the southern plains, 1870s.*
GLENBOW ARCHIVES, NA-249-78

Surveyors would then negotiate agreements on the final boundaries of reserves when they arrived to locate and survey them.

Surveyors were keenly aware that, for Native peoples, their arrival meant that white settlers were not far behind. The surveyors knew that the Native peoples on the southern plains of Alberta held a deep mistrust of the government. The Blackfoot Confederacy, along with the Plains Cree, had less contact with white society and the Dominion government than the Woodland Cree of the north, who had been partners in the fur trade for generations. Dominion Land Surveyors faced a weighty job. The evidence suggests that they developed a careful relationship with Aboriginal peoples, one that was shaped by individual personalities and changing political circumstances. The land surveyor assumed the enormous responsibility of balancing the interests and demands of Aboriginal peoples with the policy of the government.

## DOMINION LAND SURVEYORS BEGIN THE SURVEY OF RESERVES UNDER TREATY SEVEN

The first major reserve surveys in Alberta were done for the signatories of Treaty Seven. In September 1877, the chiefs of the five First Nations of Treaty Seven—the Blackfoot (Siksika), Blood (Kainah), Sarcee (Tsuu T'ina), Peigan (Pickani), and the Stoney (Nakoda)—gathered on the flats at Blackfoot Crossing on the Bow River to meet with the treaty commissioner who secured their signatures to Treaty Seven. The reserve for the Blackfoot Confederacy—the Blackfoot, Blood, and Peigan of southern Alberta—according to Treaty Seven, was to be a long strip of land four miles wide stretching 120 miles along the Bow to the forks of the Red Deer and South Saskatchewan Rivers. The Department of the Interior sent two surveyors, Allan Patrick, DLS, DTS, and William Ogilvie, DLS, to begin a preliminary survey of the reserve. The determination of the boundaries of the reserve and its size was a huge job for the surveyors, who were expected to translate the generalities of the treaty into a parcel of staked land.

Allan Patrick began survey work for the Blackfoot Confederacy reserve at its eastern edge, which lay within present-day Saskatchewan. He had completed almost six weeks of work when, on a late September day in 1878, Chief Big Bear rode into the camp accompanied by almost one hundred of his men. According to Patrick's account of events, Big Bear declared that the country the surveyors were in was Cree territory, and that he wished no kind of work to be done "by the surveyors or any other white men."[2] Big Bear, half-Cree and half-Obijwa, was the impressive leader of up to two thousand plains Cree. He had refused to sign Treaty Six and headed a campaign for Indian peoples to unite in the face of white settlement through the selection of contiguous reserves.[3] Patrick did not argue but rode west to report the incident to the North-West Mounted Police at Fort Walsh. Colonel Macleod arrived from Calgary and rode out to Big Bear's camp. What transpired is uncertain other than that Big Bear "offered no more resistance," according to Patrick.

Meanwhile, during the same summer of 1878, William Ogilvie was surveying further west around Blackfoot Crossing. When he arrived at the Crossing, he found that the Blackfoot, who had gathered for a treaty annuity payment, were incensed. Someone had "either ignorantly or maliciously told them I was coming to mark out a small piece of land around the crossing on which they were to be shut up and compelled to devote themselves to agriculture," Ogilvie later recalled. "I immediately sought an audience with Crowfoot . . . and explained fully and clearly to him the object of the survey. This put him and his people into good humour and from the time I commenced the survey until I finished it I was not interfered with in any way."[4]

The partial surveys undertaken by Patrick and Ogilvie, however, were not destined to define the boundaries of the reserve for long. Big Bear's intervention was a reminder of the potential for hostility from Native peoples, and of the need to recognize their traditional lands. The area to be encompassed by the reserve for the Blackfoot Confederacy not only encroached on the lands claimed by the Cree, but did not include the traditional lands of the Blood or the Sarcee, neither of whom were satisfied with the arrangement of one large reserve. In 1879 the Blood sought to withdraw and take up their allotted share of land elsewhere and the Sarcee followed suit, willing to surrender their interest in the Blackfoot Confederacy Reserve. Moreover, in 1881 the Canadian Pacific Railway announced its southern route. It was clear that the line to Calgary would run through the reserve. This provided the final impetus for changing the boundaries of the Blackfoot Confederacy Reserve.

In 1882 John Nelson, DLS, surveyed land bound by the Belly, Oldman, and St. Mary Rivers, for the Blood Reserve. Nelson then discussed the boundaries of a reserve with the Sarcee, before moving northeast to Blackfoot Crossing in the fall of 1882, where he reassesed the boundaries of the original Blackfoot Reserve. Nelson began work on October 22, 1882, on a survey of the Bow River as a preliminary step to redefining the Blackfoot Reserve. Chief Crowfoot of the Blackfoot agreed to an amendment to Treaty Seven signed on June 20, 1883, that released the reserve described in Treaty Seven to Her Majesty the Queen. Shortly afterwards Bull's Head, the Sarcee Chief, signed an amendment document on June 27 and Chief Red Crow of the Blood followed suit on July 2, 1883, surrendering their share of the Blackfoot Reserve.[5]

The survey of the right-of-way for the CPR line went ahead. The Indian Department hailed this as a diplomatic success: "The construction of the Canadian Pacific Railway rendered it advisable to obtain from the Indians a surrender of the tract . . . and it is a most important addition to the property of the Dominion, as there is very valuable land within it, and it possesses also desirable mineral resources."[6] John Nelson consequently spent June and July of 1883 surveying the boundaries of a new Blackfoot reserve. It contained 470 square miles on the Bow River, which lay directly south of the Canadian Pacific Railway.[7] The Blackfoot accepted the reserve as described in a further amendment to Treaty Seven dated February 7, 1884.[8]

In the meantime, Allan Patrick surveyed other reserves in southern Alberta. Late in summer 1879, Patrick made a survey of the Oldman River in conjunction with a reserve for the Peigan. He worked closely with the Indian Affairs Branch, riding around with Edgar Dewdney, Indian Commissioner, who selected the boundaries of the Peigan Reserve and the location of the associated Indian farm and timber limit. Once these were decided upon, Patrick left his assistant, John Nelson, to survey the Peigan reserve for Chief Eagle Tail on the edge of the Porcupine Hills. Allan Patrick, along with Dewdney and Colonel Macleod of the North-West Mounted Police, then determined the location of a reserve for the Stoney Indians in the foothills of the Rockies.

At Morleyville, Patrick met with John McDougall, Methodist missionary, to discuss the boundaries of the proposed reserve. Controversy surrounds McDougall's role in the negotiations for Treaty Seven and implementation of its provisions for reserves. Stoney oral tradition holds that McDougall was in conflict of interest. It is believed that, at the very least, McDougall did not indicate the range of the Stoneys' traditional territory, but rather put his own convenience and perspective as a missionary before the needs of the three groups among the Stoneys. Archival records show that the Department of Indian Affairs thought McDougall was in conflict of interest when he later applied for a personal grazing lease on the reserve in 1891. Hayter Reed, then Indian Commissioner, informed McDougall that the Minister of the Interior thought this would be an unwise precedent.[9] One can only guess at the influence McDougall brought to bear on Allan Patrick surveying the reserve in 1879 in the absence of most of the Native leaders. Only Chief Chiniki was present when he arrived. Patrick, according to his field notes, began the survey on August 5, 1879, with an astronomical observation to establish an initial location from which to run his lines. His judgment of the reserve's potential as suitable for both cattle and farming was later undermined by an official report of the Department of Indian Affairs in 1883. It noted the reserve was unsuitable for agriculture, being so near to the Rocky Mountains and subject to severe summer frosts.[10]

Whatever shortcomings Allan Patrick may have displayed in failing to address the conflicting currents of interest among the Indian Affairs Branch, the Methodist missionary, and the Stoney bands under chiefs Chiniki, Bear's Paw, and Jacob, he was not a man without compassion. Alarmed by the disappearance of the buffalo as a food source, Patrick supplied large quantities of food to starving people. Nonetheless, in January 1880 he concluded his official report from Fort Walsh on a

*Allan Poyntz Patrick, DLS, DTS.*
GLENBOW ARCHIVES, NA-176-1

rather self-congratulatory note. "After an intercourse of some two years with the original occupants of the soil, I cannot refrain from mentioning what I think a matter of utmost congratulation, namely: that all our relations with them have been, with exception of the slight misunderstanding with Big Bear, friendly. Had this been otherwise, our work might, on several occasions, have been seriously interfered with, if not stopped, for a considerable length of time."[11]

## THE DEPARTMENT OF INDIAN AFFAIRS SETS UP ITS OWN SURVEY BRANCH

On May 7, 1880, the Indian Affairs Branch of the Department of the Interior became a department in its own right. The new Department of Indian Affairs assumed responsibility for Aboriginal peoples through the provisions of treaties signed from the 1870s and the administration of the Indian Act of 1876. The Department of Indian Affairs immediately set up its own Survey Branch and employed Dominion Land Surveyors to carry out surveys on Indian reserves, with John Nelson, DLS, in charge. The survey of reserves under the Department of Indian Affairs progressed slowly in Alberta; in some areas there was little pressure to survey them before township subdivision surveys or settlement was imminent. The selection and marking out of Indian reserves by land surveyors was, nevertheless, an increasingly challenging job.

Surveyors within the Department of the Interior did not approve of the transfer of the responsibility for surveying reserves to the Department of Indian Affairs in 1880. The division of survey work between two government departments certainly caused problems in the field. The Department of Indian Affairs was often slow to survey reserves, as negotiating specific boundaries took time. Surveyors working for the Topographical Surveys Branch learned to exercise diplomacy while surveying land in close proximity to Indian reserves. They adopted a policy of not placing posts and mounds when running meridians, baselines, or other controlling lines for townships across Indian reserves, to cut down on possible disputes.

In 1884, Otto Klotz, DLS, DTS, working for the Topographical Survey, on land adjacent to the Blood Reserve noted: "the several mounds were not planted out of discretion to prevent collision

### Charles Magrath, DLS, DTS, on the Need to Build Trust

Early in 1884, Charles Magrath was running township outlines for the Topographical Survey in the Saddle Lake area near the North Saskatchewan River, where the Cree Chief Pakan wished to locate a reserve for his people. An Indian delegation arrived in his camp to express its concern at surveys being run while Chief Pakan was away in Regina meeting with the lieutenant governor of the North-West Territories. The men all sat together, and a three-hour discussion through an interpreter began. "If I could have talked to the Indians in their own language, I could have removed their fears in a very short time," Magrath later recalled. He finally persuaded the delegation that he would not impose on the area for the reserve.

The meeting ended and Magrath continued with his survey without complaints. Later, Arthur Cotton, DLS, began surveying from lines established by Magrath, but Pakan asked him to stop because the location of the reserve was still not settled. Cotton, however, according to Magrath, "was not diplomatic with the chief and said he intended on going ahead with his work." The following day Cotton's assistant put his instrument on one of the lines that were to be projected into the district. Magrath related how Chief Pakan, "a tall spare [sic] individual stepped forward and picked the theodolite up, and carrying it off the line, pointed toward Mr. Cotton's camp and made it clear that the surveying party had better return there."[13]

with Indians . . . for invading their ground, such discretion was supported by the missionary Mr. Trecotte."[12] Conflict was occasionally inevitable. Nathan R. Freeman, DLS, working on surveys for the Topograpical Survey near the Battle River in 1884, reported that the Indians "were inclined to be troublesome but . . . the influence of Mr. Lucas [Indian agent] and a number of presents of tea and tobacco etc. made everything satisfactory." Chief Bobtail, however, did not easily accept the presence of Freeman as he began the subdivision of Township 44, Range 24, West of the Fourth Meridian, where the Indian Chief hoped to claim a reserve for his people. Bobtail asked Freeman to stop his survey south of the Battle River. When he refused, Chief Bobtail, Freeman reported, "came around firing guns to intimidate us." [14] A lack of communication between the two departments cannot have helped to earn the trust of Indian leaders.

By 1887 the Department of the Interior became increasingly critical of the paucity of information they received from their surveyor colleagues in the Department of Indian Affairs. "In many cases, where corrections to existing surveys, or new surveys, are to be performed in townships adjoining or in the vicinity of Indian reserves, trouble is experienced, owing to the meager information which we at present have regarding the location and boundaries of many of these reserves," complained Inspector of Surveys John Stoughton Dennis Jr., DLS, DTS. Dennis—son of Lieutenant-Colonel John Stoughton Dennis, Surveyor General from 1871 to 1878—argued that the Department of Indian Affairs should issue a small pamphlet with descriptions of each reserve in metes and bounds, which would give surveyors on township subdivisions more to work with than just the monumentation on the ground. [15]

The pace of surveys undertaken by the Department of Indian Affairs also became subject to criticism. William Pearce, DLS, a senior bureaucrat with the Department of the Interior, was especially critical, considering the work to be very inefficient, costly, and slow. "At the rate the Indian Department is conducting its surveys the century will be closed before they are completed," he wrote in 1887 to Thomas White, newly appointed Superintendent of Indian Affairs. Pearce was convinced that all surveys should be under the direction of the surveyor general, and that Dominion Land Surveyors could do many of Indian Affairs' surveys, while working near the reserves. Correspondence in William Pearce's papers shows that, although White agreed with Pearce, behind the scenes at the highest political level there was a departmental struggle over the question of control of the survey of reserves. The Department of Indian Affairs won out as nothing changed for decades to come. [16]

The Survey of Reserves in Central Alberta Under Treaty Six

In central Alberta, surveyors laid out more than a dozen reserves in the area around Edmonton under the provisions of Treaty Six signed in 1876. The first, the Papachase Reserve No. 136, surveyed by George Simpson, DLS, south of the North Saskatchewan River, covered land that now includes Edmonton's Southgate Mall and Mount Pleasant Cemetery. Surveyors then moved south to the Battle River, as well as along the North Saskatchewan, where they surveyed a series of reserves during the 1880s. Often extensive negotiations were required, such as those between John Nelson and Chief Bobtail before the survey of the Montana Reserve. Nelson recorded some of the details in his diary in August 1885: "Bobtail has reduced his demand to a mile square for every three persons." Two days later Nelson wrote, "Bobtail & Coyote his son put in most of the day at my camp." Through an interpreter, Nelson ascertained that Bobtail claimed that he had a large band

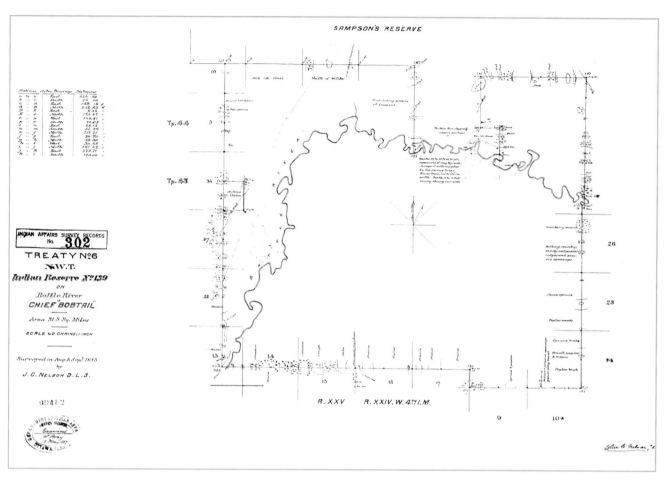

*Plan of Indian Reserve No. 139, Battle River, for Chief Bobtail, later known as the Montana Reserve,
surveyed by John Nelson, DLS, August and September, 1885.*

CANADA LANDS SURVEY RECORDS, 302 CLSR AB

when he first took treaty, and maintained his reserve "should be laid out on the basis of the no. [of
people] then paid." On August 22, Nelson tied the boundary of the reserve into the township system: "Commenced chaining and mounding from the SW corner of Bobtail's reserve going east . . .
the SW corner is on a hill near Battle River. The mound has the appearance of a stone cairn. One
side of the post is marked 'S. 10 Cor. IR Bobtail Res.' & the other side 'Aug. 1885 J. C. Nelson
DLS.' " [17] Bobtail apparently believed in the importance of the surveyor's post, as this specific marking of the post was at Bobtail's request. Nelson's diary reveals his concern with Bobtail's wishes,
which included the inclusion of a tract of timber and a lake within the boundaries of the reserve.

In 1886 Nelson began the work of surveying reserves along the North Saskatchewan River at
Saddle Lake, then Whitefish Lake, Heart Lake, and Beaver Lake. The size of a reserve was dictated by the number of people it would support, generally based on 160 acres for a family of five in
the Treaty Six area. Surveyors found it difficult to establish population figures when they arrived
to do a survey. When John Nelson went to Saddle Lake in 1886 to survey a reserve for the bands
of Chiefs Pakan, Little Hunter, and Blue Quill, he spent some considerable time negotiating with
the parties concerned and the Indian Agent, Mr. Mitchell. On arrival, he was dismayed to find

## Survey of Methodist Church Missions—An Exercise in Cooperation

By the late 1880s the Methodist Church Missionary Society thought it wise to have the mission lands they occupied on Whitefish Lake, Bear Hills, Saddle Lake, Victoria, and Morleyville reserves surveyed to avoid any complications with the claims of Aboriginal peoples. The Departments of the Interior and of Indian Affairs jointly undertook the survey of these Methodist reserves. In 1887, Fred Wilkins, DLS, DTS, met in Calgary with John Nelson, surveyor for the Department of Indian Affairs, and with Reverend John McDougall. McDougall advised waiting to undertake the survey of the Morley mission, wholly inside the reserve, until the Indian leaders returned from the fall hunt. Wilkins accordingly set out instead for Saddle Lake where he surveyed a half-section selected for a mission site—a claim he described as "a most desirable piece of property." At Victoria, the mission had already claimed sixty acres, so he laid out a further 260 acres. Finally, back at Morleyville, Fred Wilkins, John McDougall, and John Nelson decided it would be impossible to reserve 320 acres on the south bank of the Bow without interfering with buildings and other improvements on the reserve, so the mission land was split in two. The surveying of Methodist missions continued well into the twentieth century; the mission at Wabamun Reserve, for instance, was surveyed in 1909.

Chief Pakan was in Edmonton en route to the east. Nelson quickly departed, reaching Edmonton on July 28, and was lucky enough to catch Pakan before his train left. "When I told Pekan [sic] the number of Indians," Nelson wrote, "upon which the computation of the area of his reserve would be based, he replied that he was of the opinion that a greater number had been paid [Treaty money]."[18] Nelson promised that the Indian agent would examine the pay sheets. Pakan assured Nelson that his absence would not halt the survey work, as he had designated a representative to select the reserve.

Nelson, after his meeting with Pakan, first ran the boundaries of a reserve for Little Hunter's band at Whitefish Lake. At a council, the Indian leaders pointed out the lands they wished to be included. The reserve comprised seventeen and a half square miles on the east side of Good Fish and Whitefish Lakes on the trail to Lac La Biche. Nelson arrived on October 5 at Saddle Lake, having surveyed the Washatanow Reserve en route. The reserves for Pakan, Little Hunter, and Blue Quill's band, who were settled to the south at Egg Lake (later known as Whitford Lake), it was agreed, would be laid out in one block. Nelson began work, but waited until Pakan was back from Ontario so he could have the final word. Saddle Lake Reserve No. 128a measured 115 square miles. Nelson concluded positively on his summer's work to his political bosses: "Pekan [sic] said he had confidence in us and that his headmen had reported all that had been done at Whitefish Lake and Saddle Lake, and that he and his whole band were perfectly satisfied."[19]

John Nelson travelled wide distances each year. He had the responsibility of ensuring that the reserves created were acceptable to the Aboriginal leaders. "It has been the custom in this department," he stated in 1888, "where reserves have not been fixed by treaty, to ascertain the views of the chiefs and headmen, and make definite arrangements, as nearly in accordance therewith, as circumstances would permit before proceeding with survey, and consequently, but few alterations have found to be necessary."[20]

## Meeting the Requests of Native Leaders for Ongoing Surveys

In some cases, following the initial survey of a reserve, the Native chiefs requested the services of surveyors with Indian Affairs. In 1887 at Bear Hills, as part of an extension of reserve lands across the Battle River, John Nelson surveyed a line that would divide the timber, good lands, and hay lands equally between Chief Ermineskin's reserve and the reserve of Chief Samson. Nelson employed Pierre, son of Ermineskin, and two members of Samson's band, on his survey party. The chiefs kept a close eye on the proceedings and made some requests for changes as the survey progressed.[21]

In 1888 John Nelson went to southern Alberta to meet with Red Crow, the Blood Chief, who was not satisfied with the size of his reserve. It had been surveyed in 1883, while he was away south of the border to recover stolen horses. Together with Red Crow and two other Blood chiefs, John Nelson and the Indian agent examined the boundary of the reserve, searching out the old mounds that grass had already covered over, and renewed any posts missing. Finally, the party examined the timber limit to be set aside for the Blood. Years later in 1935 the Indian Department proposed swapping this timber reserve, which by then was included within the boundary of Waterton Park, for a tract elsewhere. The Blood objected. As part of a legal deposition a Blood representative stated: "It is true that the limit is ours, the Queen put the stakes in for us, it is not right for us to pull those stakes, we cannot make a trade."[22] The timber limit remains part of the reserve today. In 1893 he was back to the Blood reserve; this time Nelson's survey party, which included residents of the reserve, subdivided part of the reserve along the Belly River into eighty-acre lots where individual band members had built houses and fences.[23] This policy, originally based on the survey of forty-acre lots, had been determined by the Department of Indian Affairs to encourage individual farming operations to be developed by reserve residents.[24]

## Surveyors and the "Surrender" of Reserves in Southern and Central Alberta

Almost as soon as surveyors began the survey of reserves, the boundaries were in many instances redrawn for a number of reasons, including pressure from settlers, expropriation for rail and road rights-of-way, as well as a change in demographics on the reserves. The surrendered portions of Indian reserves were available for sale for settlement, road and rail rights-of-way, or resource exploitation. In any such case, a surveyor was required to subdivide the surrendered lands and re-survey the boundary of the reserve in question.

In 1884 John Nelson re-surveyed the boundaries of the Papachase Reserve, following complaints from white settlers that reserve land took in their hay fields and woodlands. Then in 1888, the entire reserve was surrendered, any remaining residents transferred to the Enoch Reserve, and the lands offered for sale by auction in 1891.[25] In 1897 the Sharphead Reserve, south of the Battle River west of Ponoka, was surrendered, and the following year Archibald Ponton, DLS, subdivided the four townships that comprised its former acreage. In January 1902, the Enoch band surrendered the northern section of their reserve No. 135 at Stony Plain, and in July Ponton arrived to do the necessary survey to subdivide the area into quarter sections "to be sold for the benefit of the Indians."[26]

# ALBERTA

# Plan of Township 1 Range 28 West of the Fourth Meridian

FOURTH EDITION (CORRECTED)                                                          SCALE 40 CHAINS TO AN INCH

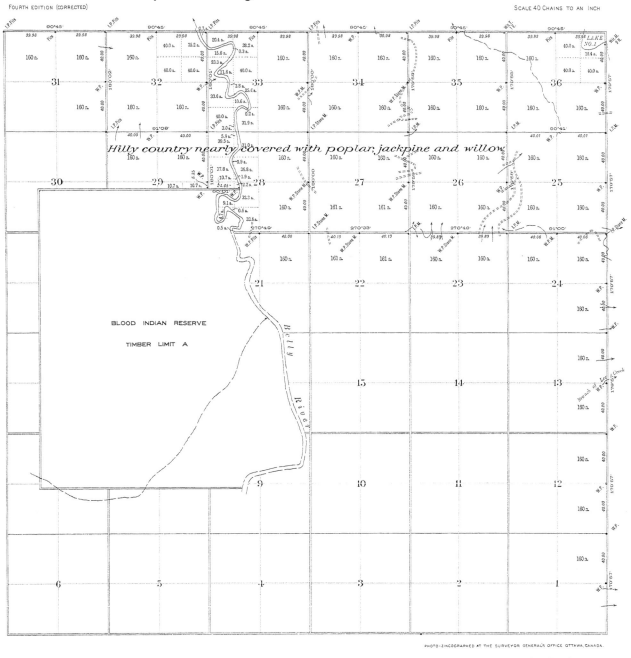

*Hilly country nearly covered with poplar, jackpine and willow*

BLOOD INDIAN RESERVE

TIMBER LIMIT A

Belly River

PHOTO-ZINCOGRAPHED AT THE SURVEYOR GENERAL'S OFFICE OTTAWA, CANADA.

Compiled from official surveys by

| | | | |
|---|---|---|---|
| A. Driscoll | D.L.S. | 30th July, | 1888 |
| C. A. Magrath | D.T.S. | 21st April, | 1893 |
| F. W. Wilkins | D.T.S. | 5th October, | 1896 |
| J. E. Woods | D.L.S. | 4th August, | 1900 |
| G. J. Lonergan | D.L.S. | 17th July, | 1901 |
| C. F. Miles | D.L.S. | 10th October, | 1905 |

Areas in acres are marked on all lands surveyed.

Distances are in chains.

Bearings are reckoned from the astronomical meridian

through the centre of the township.

Areas are taken to the banks of Belly river.

Department of the Interior, Ottawa, 4th December, 1906

Approved and Confirmed,

*E.Deville*

Surveyor General

*Plan of Township 1, Range 28, West of the Fourth Meridian, showing boundary of the Blood Indian Reserve Timber Limit A.*

DIRECTOR OF SURVEYS OFFICE, FOURTH EDITION CORRECTED, APPROVED AND CONFIRMED, 1906

Some cases involved the surrender of small portions of reserves to facilitate the development of rail lines. In April 1891, Archibald Ponton was involved in securing the surrender of forty acres to be surveyed as a right-of-way for the Calgary and Edmonton Railway through the Samson Reserve at Bear Hills. At Hobbema, however, Ponton could not persuade Chief Ermineskin to surrender part of his people's reserve for a townsite at the siding on the Calgary and Edmonton Railway built in 1891. A townsite eventually developed off the reserve just southwest of the siding, on the west side of today's Highway 2a.[27] In southern Alberta, where the new Canadian Pacific Crows Nest Pass Railway line was to be built west from Lethbridge, Richard Jephson, DLS, surveyed a railway right-of-way and station grounds on the Blood Reserve and then through the Peigan Reserve in 1897.

In 1893 Archibald Ponton stepped from a Canadian Pacific train onto the wooden platform at Gleichen to visit the Blackfoot Reserve. Although portions of the reserve had been surrendered in 1886 and 1889,[28] the Blackfoot Reserve, as the Government had determined, was still in excess of the present or future requirements of the band. Ponton's job was to assess the lands that were to be sold. The money raised was to be invested in a cattle herd for the reserve.[29] Whatever Ponton's assessment was, nothing happened. Then, in 1901, the appointment of J. A. Markle as Indian Agent marked what historian Hugh Dempsey has described as "a campaign to acquire the Blackfoot lands." In 1908 Markle was appointed Inspector of Indian Agencies with responsibility for implementing land surrenders. He cut back rations on the Blackfoot Reserve and then focused his energies on persuading the Blackfoot that the surrender of land was in their best interests, so that they would have plenty of money for food and for farming.[30] James McLean, DLS, finally completed the survey of the surrendered portion—125,000 acres—in 1911.[31] About sixty thousand acres sold by auction in summer 1911, and a further fifty-five thousand acres sold in 1917. Much of the surrendered land became part of the CPR irrigation block.

Surrender of reserves also took place because Métis members of bands frequently withdrew from reserves to take up scrip—160 freehold acres or a promissory note of equal value—to which they were entitled as peoples of mixed blood. The population of reserves consequently dropped. As result, the survey of surrendered reserve lands continued apace from 1905.

## THE GRIEVANCES OF THE NORTH-WEST: DEMANDS FOR THE SURVEY OF RIVER LOTS

The Métis also pressed their land claims with the new dominion. Canada accepted the principle of granting river lots rather than quarter sections following the Métis resistance at Red River in 1869. The Métis were not alone in demanding special surveys. The Hudson's Bay Company received reserved river front lands around trading posts, as well as a land grant included within the township survey, in compensation for the surrender of Rupert's Land. White settlers, who had formed commercial and farming centres around the HBC posts such as at Fort Edmonton, demanded river lot surveys. All who had established themselves before 1870 were entitled to a special survey to maintain their original boundaries. Those who settled after 1870, but before the arrival of the Dominion Land Survey in their area, were to have their claims addressed at the discretion of surveyors on the ground.[32] Other surveys were required to create reserves for the North-West Mounted Police posts and for Methodist and Oblate missions. All of these surveys were carried out simultaneously with establishing the township grid system.

Settlements established before the regular township survey were usually laid out in river lots. River lot surveys posed challenges for surveyors working for the Department of the Interior, which were similar to those faced by surveyors working for the Department of Indian Affairs on Indian reserves. The principle of river lot properties, carried from Quebec to Manitoba where they were guaranteed through the Manitoba Act in 1870, was applied throughout the rest of the North-West Territories. In a world of river and lake transportation, land with access to river frontage was considered a prime location, especially for those involved in commerce. Most settlers chose long narrow ribbon lots facing onto the water. John Walter, lumberman and ferry operator, and John McDougall, merchant, were as eager to have their river lots near Fort Edmonton surveyed as their Métis neighbours.

The Manitoba Act of 1870 confirmed the principle of land grants for the Métis, but its implementation was another matter. In Manitoba, the Métis were granted the right to a land grant of 160 acres or paper scrip of equal value to be used to acquire land in the future. Settlers across the North-West Territorites were not long in demanding similar consideration. In 1878 Métis from St. Albert, St. Laurent, Cypress Hills, and Prince Albert petitioned the Dominion government for the extension of such land grants to Métis outside Manitoba. Finally, in 1879, the Dominion Lands Act of 1872 was amended and Métis land claims were addressed "by granting land to such persons to such extent and on such terms and conditions as may be deemed expedient."[33] Although the surveyor general in effect had carte blanche to survey river lots as he saw fit, the political perspective and interests of the Minister of the Interior was an important factor in shaping the course of such surveys over the next decades. The survey of river lots progressed slowly during the 1870s, which were bleak economic years for Canada. The cost of surveying numerous river lots was much more expensive than adhering to the township system. In the early 1880s, as the Dominion Land Survey concentrated its efforts on ensuring that the subdivision of townships was keeping pace with the construction of the CPR across the prairies, laying out river lots remained a lesser priority.

These policies caused problems in the Edmonton district, where the first surveyor in the area, William Gore, DLS, had surveyed the HBC reserve at Fort Edmonton in 1873. Then in 1878, William King, DLS, DTS, made a preliminary survey to locate the improvements of the settlers—their houses, stables, pastures, and fences—most of which were on the north side of the river. The settlers themselves had placed fences to delineate the property boundaries they wanted and, in some cases, King solved disputes. By 1880 settlers on the North Saskatchewan near Fort Edmonton had grown increasingly impatient for an official survey to be made in anticipation of the proposed Canadian Pacific Railway route to the coast through the North Saskatchewan River valley. Together with settlers at Fort Saskatchewan and St. Albert, they sent a petition to the Department of the Interior in Ottawa in 1880, in which they stated they were suffering great inconvenience and loss because the country remained unsurveyed. In February 1881, the surveyor general promised that, along with general township subdivision, surveyors would lay out river lots with a frontage of ten chains on the river, extending back to a section line at the rear. Nothing happened.

In January 1882, William Newton, Church of England clergyman in Edmonton, warned, "the

Plan of Edmonton Settlement, surveyed by Michael Deane, DLS, in 1882.
DIRECTOR OF SURVEYS OFFICE, OFFICIAL PLAN OF EDMONTON SETTLEMENT, APPROVED AND CONFIRMED, 1883

absence of surveys is made an excuse for a great deal of lawlessness, and this lawlessness is on the increase." [34] He was right. When a "land jumper" built a house on land claimed by a syndicate of Edmonton's businessmen, the affair grew into a vigilante drama. It ended when a small mob pushed the house off the riverbank, to smash on the ice below. [35] This incident highlighted the need for the survey at Edmonton, which finally went ahead in summer 1882. The *Edmonton Bulletin* hailed the arrival of Michael Deane, DLS, in Edmonton on July 27, 1882, with considerable coverage. King's preliminary plan of 1878, which showed creeks, wooded areas, and trails, was the basis for the official settlement survey undertaken by Deane. Deane declared he would lay out river lots within the area surveyed by King in 1878, and hear any disputed claims. By August he was ready to begin the survey of river lots on the south side. Lot No. 7, comprising 269 acres, was claimed by Lawrence Garneau, whose name was later given to the residential subdivision around the University of Alberta.

In the fall of 1882, Michael Deane went to St. Albert, where the Oblate Fathers of Mary Immaculate had established a mission in the 1860s, and began laying out river lots as the settlers demanded. Then, inexplicably, an order to stop his survey came from Ottawa following a decision that surveys in the area were to be done on the township system. The *Edmonton Bulletin* of December 26, 1882, reported: "The colony of St. Albert is considerably excited just now and very much dissatisfied with the unjust manner in which it seems the people are to be treated." There were, as the *Bulletin* noted, two hundred families established on both sides of the Sturgeon River. "And now it would appear our very existence is to be ignored . . . our right to a river claim survey is not to be recognized. We are told we must be content with a township survey. Such arrangement is both unjust and absurd for it ruins the whole settlement." The *Bulletin* concluded with the statement of the people of St. Albert that if they did not get river lots "they will protest and give in to nothing short [of] open force." Oblate priest Father Leduc evidently led a convincing delegation to Ottawa in March 1883, as the next month land surveyor Michael Deane returned at St. Albert to lay out river lots.

Later in 1883 Deane moved to Fort Saskatchewan, but found that William King's preliminary survey of 1878 needed considerable readjustment to satisfy the claims of the settlers. Difficulties also emerged at Victoria Settlement on the North Saskatchewan River, east of Edmonton, when Tom Kains, DLS, arrived in fall 1884 to mark out river lots. His instructions were to survey "lots about two miles deep to embrace all the lands taken up before the transfer of the North West to the Dominion" and to include such other lands he judged fit to include. When he arrived at Victoria, he discovered settlers on the north side of the river west of the HBC reserve, but noted that they had taken up their claims so recently that they were not entitled to a special survey. Kains was unable to take statutory declarations "as the majority of the settlers were absent on a duck hunt." [36] Eventually, he laid out nine lots beside the HBC reserve.

The same year, 1884, Charles Magrath, arrived at Lac La Biche to survey river lots. An Indian reserve was to be established close to the settlement around the HBC post. Magrath was hesitant to rush in without due consideration of the difficult situation he faced. Magrath questioned whether the settlement at Lac La Biche ought to be surveyed before the reserve. "It appears that the Lac La Biche settlement extends along the east, south and west sides of the Lake, a distance of about 30 miles, and that there are about 30 settlers, a number of whom are Indians and take treaty money. These Indians . . . desire to be placed on their reserve, which they wish to have located along the eastern side of the lake." As Magrath pointed out, when asking Surveyor General Edouard Deville what he should do, the reserve area "would take in part of the settlement and also a number of the settlers would move onto the reserve."[37] The result was postponement. In 1887 the reserve was finally surveyed, but the settlers had to wait another two years for their survey.

## The Role of Surveyors in the 1885 Rebellion

By 1884 agitation for river lot surveys had escalated among the Métis at Prince Albert and Battleford in Saskatchewan. William Pearce, DLS, in his capacity as head of the Dominion Land Board, investigated Métis land claims along the South Saskatchewan River. Unfortunately, by early 1885, as the wheels of bureaucracy barely moved, many Métis came to believe that the government did not intend to grant them title to their river lots. In spring 1885 they took action and Louis Riel led a coalition of Métis, Native, and white settlers in armed rebellion against the Dominion. The Canadian Pacific Railway sped a military force west under Major-General Middleton. The ordinary business of commerce, farming, and indeed surveying, came to a halt in the North-West Territories. As troops moved in on Batoche, Major Samuel Steele, of the North-West Mounted Police stationed at Fort Saskatchewan, led a troop east from Alberta. The military might of the Dominion government soon defeated the Indian and Métis insurgents. Relations between white and Aboriginal peoples in the North-West hardened in the face of the hanging of eight Native leaders and Louis Riel on charges of treason.

The issue of surveys and their role in sparking the rebellion immediately attracted political attention. In his 1885 report to Parliament, the Deputy Minister of the Interior affirmed the willingness of the department to grant river lots: "In no case where settlers have been found on a river front in advance of the survey, and desired their holdings should be laid out with river frontages, has the privilege been refused." The Deputy Minister denied that surveys were at the root of Métis grievances. He asserted: "The only complaint which has reached the Department about surveys has come from the South branch of the Saskatchewan and from French [Métis] who went into possession of their holdings long after the lands had been surveyed on the rectangular principle and in respect of these the department has always been ready to practically meet their wishes by allotting to them their holdings in legal subdivisions, which would give them their lands with narrow frontages upon the river and extend then back one or two miles . . . as if they had been laid out on the river lot system from the beginning."[38]

The evidence, however, suggests this was not the whole truth. Settlers at St. Albert, for example, had quite a struggle to persuade the Department of the Interior to survey river lots. Yet, nowhere in the Métis Bill of Rights of 1885 was the survey of river lots *per se* specifically mentioned. Métis demands included a census to enumerate those with land claims, a call for early granting of patents to land, assistance with purchasing farm implements and seed, extended hunting rights, and the establishment of the provinces of Saskatchewan and Alberta.

Surveyors have emphasized that the river lot surveys carried out by Dominion Land Surveyors

## The Dominion Land Survey Intelligence Corps, 1885

In late March 1885, when news of violence at Duck Lake reached Ottawa, a group of Dominion Land Surveyors meeting at the city's Russell Hotel organized a militia unit. They believed their knowledge of the country—its conditions, transportation, and camping locations—would be useful in support of the troops. Twenty-five-year-old Arthur Wheeler, initially offered its command, declined. John Stoughton Dennis Jr. assumed the honour—earning the corps the nickname of "Dennis's Scouts." The Dominion Land Survey Intelligence Corps of fifty-five men—twenty-two surveyors and their assistants—went west. Among them were surveyors who made their mark on surveys in Alberta, including John Stoughton Dennis Jr., Arthur Wheeler, brothers Thomas and Adam Fawcett, Alfred Driscoll, Lewis Ord, Bryce Saunders, and James McLean. The surveyors, decked out in black leather jackets with white canvas bandoliers, felt hats with a red flannel band, cord breeches, and long riding boots complete with spurs, first patrolled the area between Swift Current and Long Lake. Joining Middleton's force at Batoche on May 10, they came under fire from the Métis dug in along the riverbank. A bullet hit Wheeler as he was strolling out to inspect a rifle pit; it ripped through his shoulder, while narrowly missing Lewis Ord. The action had begun.

On May 12, Middleton's forces secured the capture of Batoche—but not without a casualty among the surveyors. Amidst the glint of bayonets, the boom of field guns, the chaos of whizzing bullets, and the crack of repeating rifles, "someone called out 'Kippen's gone.'" Alexander Kippen had been shot in the head and killed instantly, and his death, Wheeler admitted, "brought home the reality of the game we were playing." Thomas Fawcett took a burst of buckshot in the chest, and Jim Garden suffered wounds.

The skills of the surveyors came into their own in the unsuccessful attempt to pursue Chief Big Bear through bush country in early June. The surveyors proved their worth as they speedily cleared roads, throwing down brush on soft places for wagons and artillery to pass over, and cut down poplar trees to build bridges. Although the surveyors navigated the land well, Big Bear knew it better and outwitted Dennis's scouts. On July 12, 1885, the DLS Intelligence Corps disbanded. In April 1934 Wheeler wrote about the Corps in *The Canadian Surveyor*: "The majority of our corps were young fellows and we had the fun of the excitement." In retrospect, he reflected, "the whole episode seems inglorious."

*"Dennis's Scouts," 1885.*
ALSA, Weir Album

were not linked to the events of 1885. "Why Blame the Surveyors?" asked an editorial in *The Canadian Surveyor* in January 1926. It was arguably not the actual surveys, for river lot or section, but the tortoise approach to carrying them out, and in granting patents to the land, that rankled the Métis. As Frank Oliver publisher of the *Edmonton Bulletin*, noted in an editorial on May 15, 1886, it was not any one grievance or even the sum of the grievances that had caused the rebellion. Rather, he wrote, "it was the sense of wrong to which they gave rise. The feeling that the doors of justice were shut. That these were only the beginnings of wrongs for which there was to be no redress." In Alberta, where surveys had in fact been completed by 1885 for most of the main Métis settlements along the North Saskatchewan River, no Métis took up arms. The seemingly obstinate tardiness of the government in Ottawa dealing with land claims irritated residents of the North-West, white and Métis alike. Dominion Land Surveyors engaged in the actual surveying of land had little to do with the causes of the rebellion. Most, however, had little sympathy for the rebels, and some even took up arms against them.

### River Lot Surveys: An Unresolved Issue

After 1885 a series of ongoing commissions finally addressed the Métis land claims, whether river lots or quarter sections. Many Métis migrated from Saskatchewan into Alberta, heading to areas where their people had already established communities. Phidime Belanger, DLS, laid out the two lakeside settlements at Lac Ste. Anne and Lac La Biche in 1889. Dense smoke from bush fires hung heavily in the air when Belanger arrived to survey the waterfront lots for settlement at Lac Ste. Anne, which extended about six miles along the south shore. Those who lived at the lake included Natives and Métis, an HBC official, and Oblate missionaries. Belanger reported on the hard work required to open up the lines that ran through timbered stands for surveying the lots into 160-acre parcels. One lot was taken up by the Oblate fathers, in compensation for land on which they had, according to Belanger, a claim of some forty years standing, but which had been possessed by squatters.

Belanger surveyed seventy-three lots before moving his survey party to Lac La Biche. There, the task was more difficult, as the settlement extended about forty miles along the winding shore of the lake. It took Belanger a full three months to confer with residents and to survey the settlement and the trail that crossed it. He undertook a traverse survey along the shore, planted posts to mark the frontage of each lot, and a rear line, with posts to mark the varying width and depth of the eighty lots.[39]

The survey of river lots was a constant source of difficulty and controversy, as well as friction between Surveyor General Deville and the Minister of the Interior. Deville, always holding to the principle of providing river lots, attempted to come up with a solution that would satisfy all parties and make the survey of river lots easier and cheaper. The idea was to form river lots from subdivisions of quarter sections—a quarter section could be divided north–south or east–west (depending on the direction of the river) into two 80-acre parcels. In 1883 the *Manual of Instructions for the Survey of Dominion Lands* made provision for the laying out of such a system of river lots on the Saskatchewan, Red Deer, Bow, and Belly rivers. The river lot system devised by Deville meant

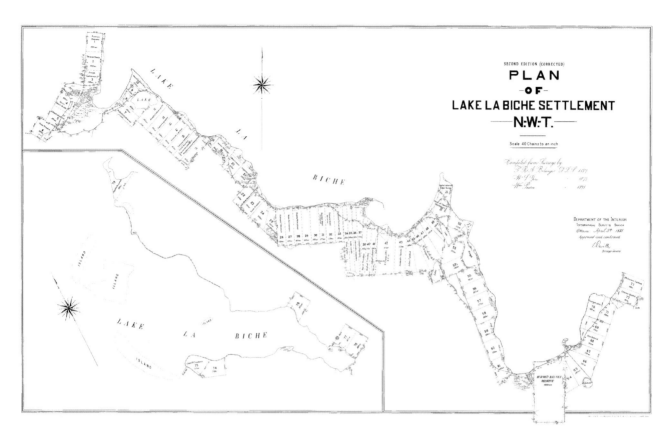

*Lac La Biche Settlement.*
DIRECTOR OF SURVEYS OFFICE, LAC LA BICHE SETTLEMENT, SECOND EDITION CORRECTED, 1895

that more settlers along a river would have waterfront access and the value of each lot—one-quarter mile wide and about one mile deep—was the same. The boundary of each river lot would be formed by the river on one side, and section lines, quarter section lines, or the boundary of a smaller parcel—a legal subdivision (LSD)—on the remaining sides. Opposition to these proposed river lots from settlers and speculators was almost immediate. Deville admitted it was not difficult to see why: "If a quarter section crossed by a large river is more valuable than a river lot, it is not because it affords increased facilities for farming: the settlers can only farm on one side of the river. But he can sell the other part of his quarter section to the owner of land on the opposite side, who must have water frontage."[40]

By December 1886, the Department of the Interior had come up with a list of river lot settlements to remain in place and for locations where a river lot survey was to proceed. These were lots where an occupant had settled prior to the time of survey. All other river lot surveys, it was decided, should be cancelled, the monuments removed, and quarter section lines and corners marked accordingly. Dominion Land Surveyors led correction survey parties in 1887 and 1888 to remove the posts marking river lots in central as well as in southern Alberta. In townships adjoining the South Saskatchewan, Bow, and Belly Rivers, there were many surveyed river lots that settlers had not taken up.

Duhamel on the Battle River in Township 46, West of the Fourth Meridian, was one settlement where the Métis were guaranteed title to their land. The appearance of a survey party under John McAree, DLS, DTS on the Battle River in 1887 alarmed not only the Métis, but also the Roman Catholic Church, which sought to strengthen Catholic settlements in the west. Bishop Grandin of St. Albert, writing to the Minister of the Interior, declared that the Métis were "very much excited" due to the actions of surveyors in the vicinity. "His Grace's letter probably refers to some adjoining townships in which river lot posts were removed," Surveyor General Deville explained, "but he must have been misinformed when speaking of the excitement of the people, as in no case was a post removed without the consent of the settlers."[41] The local agent of Dominion Lands investigated the matter on the Battle River, and concluded that no settler who had been on the land before the area was surveyed had their property boundary interfered with by the surveyor.

From 1890 the Department of the Interior determined that it should not carry out any more river lot surveys.[42] Yet, whatever the views of the Minister, Dominion Land Surveyors continued to survey river lots when expedient. In May 1896, when Joseph Woods arrived to subdivide a township near Victoria settlement, the status of as yet unsurveyed river lot claims by the Métis were thrown into question. Métis settlers had long expected that the land they claimed along the river would be surveyed into river lots. In 1884, when surveying the HBC reserve, Tom Kains, DLS, had respected the claims of at least some of the settlers and surveyed out nine lots west of the HBC reserve. Now more than ten years later, this expectation on the part of later settlers, and the offspring of those who had originally migrated from Red River, seemed about to be dashed. The Métis acted fast, calling on Frank Oliver, recently elected Liberal Member of Parliament for Edmonton, to lobby Ottawa on their behalf. Woods was told to halt his township subdivision survey, and later in the fall, he returned to lay out eleven river lots at Victoria, and eighteen at Lobstick some distance further west. At Lobstick, the lots averaged about twenty-two chains by seventy chains in depth, and Woods carefully laid his lines to accommodate the location of houses, stables, fences, and trail alignments established by the settlers.

Individual surveyors had a good deal of leeway in dealing with the land claims of the settlers they encountered at Edmonton, St. Albert, Lac Ste. Anne, and Lac La Biche among other settlements. The surveyor general's attempt to adapt the township system to allow for an alternative system of river lots as legal subdivisions of township sections, rather than irregular shaped lots of varying acreages, did not meet with political favour. Correction surveys were made in 1887 and 1888 to remove the posts and mounds defining unclaimed river lots. Despite a decision to survey no more river lots in 1890, a reversal of policy followed the election of a Liberal government in 1896. Dominion Land Surveyors continued to survey river lots for settlements where there was demand well into the twentieth century.

The dealings of the Dominion government with Aboriginal peoples and the grievances of the North-West had pushed land surveyors to the forefront, often in a position that required considerable skills in negotiation and public relations. The land surveyor had little to do with the actual policy and politics of surrender of Indian reserve lands; his job on the ground was to advise, evaluate, and survey boundaries and also to subdivide surrendered lands. The survey of new reserves and the adjustment of reserve boundaries continued in the twentieth century. Surveyors laid out reserves under Treaty Eight, as the Dominion Land Survey System extended into Alberta's vast North—a region apart from all others.

Meanwhile, land surveyors had many surveys to undertake as settlement spread across the southern plains. One of the first issues to arise, however, was the need for a consistent water supply and for irrigation. Irrigation would require a range of surveys and a new perspective on the management of water and river lands.

CHAPTER FOUR

# Mastering a Dry Land

*Land Surveyors and Irrigation*

## IRRIGATION: A VISION FOR SOUTHERN ALBERTA

Dominion Land Surveyor William Pearce watched the landscape slipping by as his train rattled its way west in September 1883 on the brand new Canadian Pacific line from Medicine Hat to Calgary. Struck by his first impression—land flat and dry as far as the eye could see—Pearce asked a fellow traveller what he thought of it. The traveller, an agriculturalist from Colorado, pointed out the possibilities of using the Bow River for irrigation. He and Pearce were soon engaged in a lengthy discussion. Pearce had seen the benefits of irrigation while on a visit to Colorado and Utah in 1881. The two men parted company in Calgary, but Pearce stored away the kernel of the conversation.

Pearce, who found a ready ally in John Stoughton Dennis, Jr., DLS, Chief Inspector of Surveys, became the most influential government promoter of irrigation as the salvation of agriculture on the semi-arid plains of southern Alberta. He noted the successes of individual farmers in southern Alberta, including John Glen and John Ware, in diverting streams and flooding their land. Clearly, excellent crops of grain and vegetables could be raised. Several things struck Pearce from these projects. First, it would take a systematic plan to implement large-scale projects for widespread results; second, a survey should be carried out to get the required accurate information; and third, legislation was required to put licensing regulations and procedures in place for diverting water in the public interest. In addition, Pearce realized that public pressure would be necessary to push the government into action. His article on "Settlement and Irrigation" in the *Lethbridge News* in November 1889 started a long editorial campaign in the fledgling southern Alberta press.

Pearce's vision of large-scale irrigation works on consolidated tracts of land required systematic research, and he sought technical information on all aspects of irrigation projects wherever he could obtain it. As he explained to one California expert, he was starting from scratch in an area where even climatic conditions were an unknown.[1] Pearce also sought to interest his fellow surveyors in irrigation, addressing the Association of Dominion Land Surveyors in 1889. He pointed out the significant role the surveyor could play in the successful implementation of irrigation schemes in southern Alberta, "for not only does it involve . . . extensive topographical surveys, but it also affords scope for ingenuity in the gauging of streams, in devising an economical flume for

### Pearce's Controversial Calgary Irrigation Company

In 1892 William Pearce set out to prove that irrigation worked by establishing an irrigation company to irrigate land west of Calgary, with his own farm serving as a demonstration project. In partnership with engineer John Turner Bone, lawyer John Pascoe, and surveyor Richard J. Jephson, he founded the Calgary Irrigation Company. The next year the company embarked on Alberta's first corporate large-scale irrigation project with the construction of head-gates on the Little Bow River and canals adequate to irrigate forty-five thousand acres. Despite damage from a flood in June 1893, an unsuccessful legal challenge for water rights on the Bow from the Springbank Irrigation Company led by Senator James Lougheed (grandfather of Alberta's future Premier, Peter Lougheed), and numerous charges of conflict of interest against him, Pearce pressed forward. By 1899 the Calgary Irrigation Company had completed the construction of sixty miles of canals. Pearce touted his own farm in Inglewood as a model for irrigated farming. *The Calgary Tribune* delivered a biting criticism of Pearce's tillage lands, questioning the viability of his canal system. "Anybody who had a practical knowledge in irrigation would first take the water to the highest point possible of the field and from thence draw his laterals, and with ease distribute the water to all other points of the field." [2] The Calgary Irrigation Company was never able to attract settlers to purchase its lands. Less than four hundred acres were ever irrigated. The Department of the Interior was less than impressed. Pearce, in conflict of interest, was warned to withdraw from the company, which was finally liquidated in 1905 and its water rights were withdrawn in 1907.

*William Pearce, DLS [ca.1880s].*
GLENBOW ARCHIVES, NA-339-1

the measurement of water supplied to ditches, and in ascertaining what is the 'duty of water' [how much water needs to be allocated] in the irrigable tract, which duty will vary according to location and soil." [3]

In early 1891, Pearce presented a lengthy report on irrigation. Its conclusions alarmed the government, which feared that immigrants would avoid southern Alberta if they believed it to be arid. Anthony Burgess, Deputy Minister of the Interior, reminding William Pearce that he was a civil servant, refused him permission to deliver a paper on irrigation to the International Irrigation Congress in 1891. [4] Pearce and others, however, were not to be silenced, and the government was soon forced to admit the futility of farming in arid conditions. In a 360° turnaround, the government introduced an irrigation bill—which Pearce played a major hand in drafting—in the House of Commons in February 1893.

Settlers would no longer have the right to divert the water flowing through their land without a license. [5] It introduced regulations governing application for a license, right-of-way surveys, and construction of irrigation works. The government promised a general survey to determine suitable locations for irrigation. Pearce, who had little confidence in the political will in Ottawa to address irrigation, used every strategy in the book to get public opinion behind the irrigation bill prior to its second reading. He galvanized support from the press, notably the *Lethbridge News*. The call for irrigation gained popular momentum, through local irrigation leagues and meetings. "The feeling in the country is for irrigation or leaving the country altogether," as one supporter put it.[6]

The North-West Irrigation Act became law in July 1894. Pearce was relieved that the sweltering heat in Ottawa that day had discouraged much debate in parliament. Pearce, along with John Stoughton Dennis Jr., travelled to the Fourth International Irrigation Conference, held in September in Albuquerque, New Mexico. In front of an American audience, Pearce extolled the highlights of the 1894 Act, and triumphantly sent newspaper cuttings covering his speech to Anthony Burgess. Deputy Minister Burgess responded that he was amused at Pearce's statement that the Act was the pride and admiration of his country. "I hope that the experience we have in the next few years will prove you were correct in your statement."[7]

## THE CANADIAN IRRIGATION SURVEY BEGINS ITS WORK

In 1894 the Topographical Surveys Branch launched the Canadian Irrigation Survey, distinct from the Dominion Land Survey, under the leadership of John Stoughton Dennis Jr., who reported to the surveyor general. Its Herculean task was to work out when and where irrigation systems could be built in the districts of southern Alberta and western Assiniboia. The irrigation survey quickly focused on southern Alberta, as it soon became clear that it was here, rather than on the plains of Saskatchewan, that irrigation had the most potential. The Canadian Irrigation Survey assessed the conditions in southern Alberta—an area of semi-arid lands that do not consistently have sufficient rainfall or residual soil moisture for the successful production of crops. The definition of semi-arid, as understood in the 1890s, was less than fifteen inches of rain per year. The levels of precipitation in southern Alberta, both locally variable and cyclical, were not well documented and surveyors working on the Canadian Irrigation Survey had no records on which to base their work. The survey, working without detailed climatic data, focused on a projected irrigation area drained by four major rivers: the St. Mary, the Milk, the Belly, and the Bow, along with their main tributaries. Irrigation projects required an understanding of the hydrology of each.

The basic objective of the first irrigation schemes in western Canada was to capture the spring runoff for use over summer and fall. This required damming and diversion of a river or stream and channelling the resulting water supply through a ditch or flume to the area where water was needed to irrigate the soil. The surveyor's job was to find the best location for the diversions and direction of the ditches, which spread out in an ever-smaller web culminating in "turn outs" or dammed diversions to spread water over a farmer's field. The surveyor needed to know the slope of the land and amount of water available in order to plan for the canals and diversions. The rate of water flow upstream in the foothills determined the engineering requirements of the ditches or channels far below on the plains. What would happen to the flow when floodwaters

*John Stoughton Dennis, Jr., DLS, DTS [ca. 1914].*
GLENBOW ARCHIVES, NA-2430-1

*A topographer sketches contour lines on a map sheet in the field in southern Alberta as part of levelling work for irrigation.*
PROVINCIAL ARCHIVES OF ALBERTA, A.5019

raced down? Would it overflow and destroy the ditches in a period of heavy rainfall? Or, during very low precipitation, would the slope and flow be adequate to keep whatever water was available moving through the ditches and channels? How much evaporation would take place in the ditches and channels? How much land could be irrigated? How much water would this require?

Surveyors with the Canadian Irrigation Survey sought answers to these questions to aid the developers and engineering specialists constructing large irrigation blocks that would later benefit thousands of settlers. "I have discussed the proposed scheme of making the irrigation survey with all the surveyors and engineers in this district who are engaged in locating or constructing irrigation ditches," Dennis informed Surveyor General Deville, "and am pleased to be able to report that they all approve of the scheme and say that it will furnish the general information of which they are so much in need."[8]

Planning irrigation projects required detailed topographical maps, but in 1894 there were none of southern Alberta. Dennis defined this new type of survey as "one which gives not only the geographical positions of points and objects on the surface of the ground but also furnishes the data from which the character of the surface may be delineated with respect to the relative elevations or depressions."[9] Topographical surveying for irrigation demanded accurate levelling to determine the gradient of the landscape. Levelling is a process of measuring vertical distances, using a variety of different instruments, to establish elevations. Upon determining differences in elevation between two points, the degree of slope can be calculated. The Irrigation Survey used the existing grid system of township outlines to locate permanent topographical features. The survey parties shot levels at intervals of 330 feet or less along established baselines and township outlines of rectangular blocks of land ranging from 144 square miles to 576 square miles.

Once the elevations of permanent features on the township outlines were established, the topography was filled in on the map as fifty-foot contours. The topographer sketched in the field, working on cross-section sheets, and checking his elevations by closing in on surveyed elevations. He paced out distances or used a micrometer—an instrument used with a telescope to measures distances—or an odometer, checking for accuracy each mile at the intersection of each section boundary.[10] Readings taken with the British barometers made by the trusted Dolland and Company of London, despite atmospheric variations, proved sufficiently accurate for those elevations located between the main line levels. This, as Dennis stressed, was a fast and economical way to produce sufficient data for cartographers to determine fifty-foot contours for the issue of "a very fair topographical map."

Levelling, traverse surveys of rivers and streams—a type of surveying in which distance and direction of lines between points were obtained by or from field measurements along their course—and the new technology of photo-topographic surveying in the foothills, all provided data to produce the first topographical maps. These maps, in conjunction with an understanding of the hydrology or gauging of water flow, were to form the basis for irrigation project planning and construction, including the St. Mary's project and the massive irrigation works eventually undertaken by the CPR.

The work of the Canadian Irrigation Survey began early on the morning of June 13, 1894. It comprised two divisions, A and B, each with levelling parties. John Stoughton Dennis Jr. supervised two parties in Division A, while Arthur Wheeler, DLS, took charge of Division B. The levelling parties, led by Thomas Green, DLS, and Mr. Davy, a certified engineer, set out from the joint camp on the Bow two miles upstream from Calgary to establish an elevation benchmark from which the two divisions would work. The established elevation above sea level of the Canadian Pacific Railway bridge over the Elbow was used to determine the elevation of the northeast corner of Township 24, Range 2, West of the Fifth Meridian. Today, this location is within the city of Calgary, just off Crowchild Trail at the corner of Northmount Drive and Northland Drive, NW. This established a benchmark against which all subsequent elevations for the irrigation survey would be determined. The survey parties of each division then went their separate ways.

The levelling party of Division A progressed west and south from Calgary along the township lines already established by the land survey system. Benchmarks were established at township and section corners along the main levelling routes at irregular intervals and at the nearest prominent points to the cross-section locations of rivers. By the end of the first season, forty-three elevation benchmarks had been established. They were identified by iron bars, marked by steel dies, with a crow's foot, the letters "B.M.," and odd numbers.[11] Division B under Arthur Wheeler set out to investigate the waterways on the plains of southwest Alberta, taking current meter readings and levels to determine the flow of water as well as the estimated discharge at high water. It located twelve possible reservoir sites and four catchment areas.[12]

The next summer, 1895, Dennis was placed in charge of the Irrigation Survey. He opened an office in Calgary, and he was soon buried in a mountain of paperwork connected with regulations and applications for water rights under the Irrigation Act. It was some time before he could join Division A, which, under the leadership of Thomas Green, was continuing levelling work on the plains. In July Dennis investigated locations on the St. Mary River for an irrigation canal. His survey parties identified the best location for the canal intake at Kimball, approximately six miles north of the international boundary. Two years later, an order-in-council reserved the waters of the St. Mary River for future irrigation development. The federal government did not intend to construct a system, but wished to ensure the water would not be frittered away by small projects and remain available for one large undertaking.[13]

## SURVEYING IN ALBERTA'S FOOTHILLS

Meanwhile, beginning in 1895, Wheeler's smaller party gathered information on the hydrology and topography of the foothills and eastern slopes of the Rockies, in today's Kananaskis country, beginning west of where the Dominion Land Survey had completed its work. Beginning at an established section corner, Wheeler surveyed up a number of valleys beginning with Jumping Pound Creek, the Elbow River, Fish Creek, Sheep River, and Highwood River, and then worked south to the Waterton River.[14] The gauging of streams was central to Wheeler's investigations in the mountains. His party made measurements of the flow of all major rivers and streams south of the Bow, as well as estimations from the high water line evident along the banks.

Working on fast-flowing streams was a tricky business and care was needed to avoid potentially fatal accidents. On paper, the notation "took a cross-section of stream" sounds innocuous. But in reality this task was exacting. A steel wire marked with brass tags at ten-foot intervals stretched taut at right angles across a stream provided the base reference for cross-section measurements and rates of velocity. First, the surveyor had to run a light cod line across the stream—risking his life in one of the notorious portable "Acme" folding canvas boats provided by the department—to haul the heavier steel wire across to the far bank. Once the wire was in place, a rope or cable, on which a pulley ran, was strung across thirty feet upstream. The boat was fastened to the pulley and held in place by a tackle system that allowed the boat to be positioned exactly over the cross-section to take depth readings at regular intervals using a specially constructed sounding rod.

The surveyor next determined the area of high water and flood lines with reference to the cross-section line by taking measurements using a level and gauge rod. Finally, he determined the velocity of the stream using a current meter at intervals along the cross-section wire before returning to shore. The gathered data allowed the calculation of the actual flow of the stream as well as the potential flow at high and flood water levels. Current meters had to be rated to ensure their accuracy. By the end of the initial season of 1894, a rating station had been set up in a pond where the Bow River was dammed by the Calgary Water Power Company. The use of battery-operated electric current meters by 1898 allowed for measurement of the rise and fall of streams over a considerable period of time to give much more accurate estimations of velocity.[15] As

Wheeler pointed out, "this branch of the irrigation surveys work is of great importance in the administration of water rights and avoidance of legal difficulties."[16]

Wheeler recorded information on potential reservoir sites, drainage systems, and the heights of main summits and heights of land between the water systems, as well as timbered areas, and other topographical features in his notes. In the foothills, however, it was considerably more difficult to pace out distances, take levels, make notes, and do sketches of the terrain than on the plains. As a result, Wheeler switched to a technology new to his profession—photographic surveying or photo-topographic surveying, as it became known.

### Photo-topographic Surveying for Mapping

Arthur Wheeler had been introduced to photo-topographic surveying in 1885 when he was working in Ottawa. Edouard Deville, Surveyor General, was preparing to apply photography to survey work along the railway belt through the Rocky Mountains. Deville applied technology developed in 1849 by a French scientist, Colonel Laussedat, for taking photographs from which perspectives could be drawn. The application of Laussedat's principle to surveying challenged surveyors across Europe, but it was in Canada that it received the most extensive attention. Deville engaged in extensive research, carrying on correspondence with European surveyors and instrument manufacturers, before coming up with a Ross camera for the Dominion Land Survey. James J. McArthur, DLS, used it for a pioneering survey of about two thousand miles in the Rocky Mountains in 1891–92, and cameras were also used on the Canada–Alaska Boundary survey in 1893. Deville's enthusiasm for surveying with a camera was boundless: "Can anything more convenient be conceived than a method which enables a topographer to gather rapidly on the ground the material for his maps and to construct them in his office?"[17] Arthur Wheeler was soon to find out, as, armed with a copy of Deville's *Photographic Surveying*, published in 1895, he spent the next five years perfecting the application of photography to detailed topographical mapping in the foothills of Alberta.

In 1895, while waiting for his camera to arrive, Wheeler set up a framework for the triangulation work needed to orient the camera stations on mountaintops, marked by a cairn with a flag that would be visible for a considerable distance. On June 20, he located two "trigonometrical" stations. Station No. 1 was on "cox comb peak" at two thousand feet above Jumping Pound Creek.[18] Wheeler then surveyed up the Elbow River and climbed to establish eight more trigonometerical stations, thus beginning a network of triangles. The relative positions of the stations, which were tied into traverse lines, were checked by magnetic bearings at each station. Finally, a messenger arrived in camp with a letter for Wheeler—the camera had arrived in Calgary. Wheeler immediately set off to get it, leaving his

*This was the Ross camera used by Arthur Wheeler—a basic metal survey camera mounted on a tripod and equipped with a Zeiss anastigmat, a distortion-free lens, with 141 millimetres focus.*

assistant to locate a course for the diversion of the Elbow River to the north branch of Fish Creek.

Wheeler was soon back with the camera and equipment and eager to get to work. He could now take photographic views, from various perspectives capturing identifiable features for mapping, and measure the angles between the selected stations. He used a three-inch theodolite, especially built for the work, to obtain the azimuth (to level the camera in both directions) and elevation of stations in the photographic views, and to establish the relative positions of the stations to one another. This was a more accurate method than the former method of using magnetic bearings.[19]

Wheeler experimented with different types of glass plates and lengths of exposure. Shooting through an orange- or lemon-coloured screen equalized the relative sensitivity of the various rays of the spectrum. The intensity of the light was the trickiest thing to determine correctly, and he discovered it was better to err on the side of overexposure, as a lengthy exposure captured details in the far distance. The sequence of camera stations in a day's work followed the course of the sun. Only so many views could be taken in a day because it was necessary to wait until dark to transfer the glass plates from the camera to their box. As Wheeler learned the hard way, daylight would permeate the dark tent he used when handling the plates and leave them fogged.[20]

It was, as Deville warned, tricky work. Wheeler was eager to develop some of the plates in the field, to see how the prints would work out. Deville was less than enthused about the results that he received in September and ordered Wheeler to forward the plates to Ottawa for development and printing.[21] From his tent on Sheep Creek, Wheeler penned a promise to obey orders, but defended his decision to develop some plates in the field to check whether the points he had used on the rounded contours of timbered slopes to obtain azimuth readings were in fact recognizable in the photographs.[22] By the end of the season, Wheeler's party completed its explorations between the Bow and the Sheep rivers.

Operations for 1896 began in the Bow Valley, from a base established for triangulation in connection with the railway belt photo-topographic survey in the Rockies. Wheeler used this base to carry the system of triangles south and ultimately to the international boundary. But luck was not to be on Wheeler's side, as forest fires broke out on the west side of the Rockies and in the Selkirk mountains. The smoke poured east, obscuring the views Wheeler wished to photograph. He had to give up and spent the rest of the summer setting up further stations required to continue the triangulation south. Then, having waited out a snowstorm in early September, a frustrated Wheeler had to close his season in October.

The season of 1897 also got off to an unpromising start, smoke from forest fires once again obliterating photographic views. Then it rained heavily from June 15 to June 18, 1897, causing flash floods. Arthur Wheeler was impressed by the power of nature: "Streams, previously of small dimension . . . became raging torrents, utterly impassable, carrying down huge trees as though they were twigs; spreading far and wide over the country, sweeping away bridges, dams, headgates and ditches; obliterating fords of many years . . . and in some cases carving out entirely new channels. The full force of the immense power let loose was felt more particularly along the courses of the larger streams as the floods, swelled by numberless tributary torrents, rushed irresistibly towards the open plain . . . towns and villages were inundated in their lower levels, houses overturned; trains blocked, large tracts of fertile agricultural land left beds of gravel; and farmers and

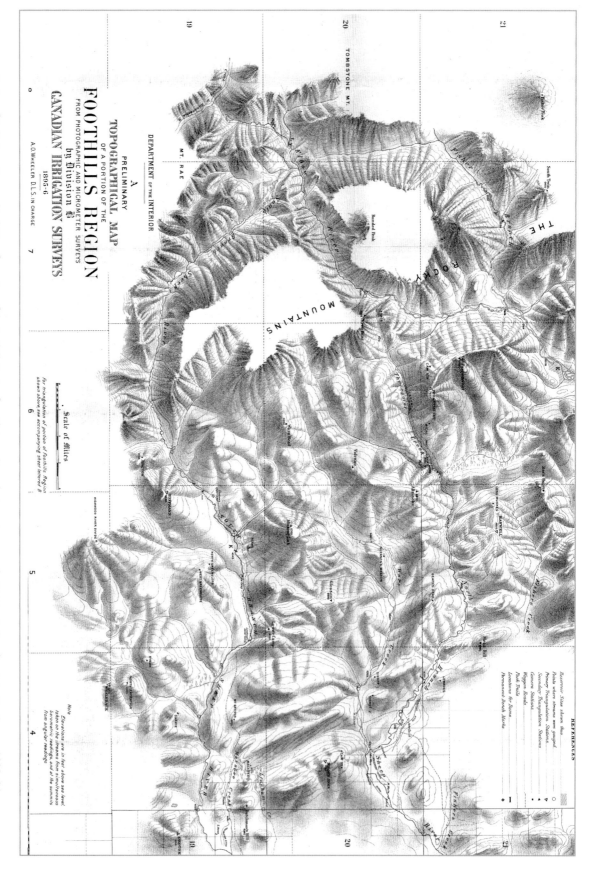

Portion of Preliminary Topographical Map of a portion of the Foothills Region from Photographic and micrometer surveys by Division B, Canadian Irrigation Surveys, 1895–96 (Sheet A), as published in the Annual Report of the Department of the Interior, 1897.

COURTESY OF THE SURVEYOR GENERAL OF CANADA LANDS

ranchers compelled to leave their homes in the bottoms and seek refuge on the higher ground."[23] Wheeler, who repeated this passage in at least three official reports, emphasized the destructive effect of such flash flooding on early irrigation works and raised fears as to its implications for proposed larger irrigation schemes.

From a surveyor's point of view, the deluge provided an opportunity to study flood levels. On Jumping Pound Creek where his party was camped, the depth of flood water was twelve feet in comparison to an average of five. Wheeler knew then that the astoundingly high level of flood water they had estimated in 1894, from wash lines on cut banks and barked trees while gauging streams, was correct. The rain finally extinguished the forest fires, and by the end of the 1897 season he was able to take 530 photographic views.[24]

Wheeler's data from photographic and micrometer surveys was used to produce the first topographical maps of southern Alberta's foothills, published in conjunction with the department's report for 1897. The report provided a general plan of areas that could be irrigated along with topographical maps of the areas covered by Division B, and a diagram of the rise and fall of the Bow River. Sheet A was a topographical map covering the foothills. Anyone seeing this map for the first time must surely marvel at Wheeler's accomplishment. The number of triangulation and camera stations certainly indicates the staggering amount

*Perspectograph designed for topographical work by the Dominion Land Survey, used to illustrate Edouard Deville's* Photographic Surveying *(1895). The plotter was supposed to trace the photograph with one arm of the machine. The other arm, via a complex linkage, was designed to transfer the points onto a flat map held on a drawing board.*
LIBRARY AND ARCHIVES CANADA, C007806

of climbing done in a short period of time. Elevations in feet above sea level were marked along streams, taken from simultaneous barometer readings, while those on the peaks were taken from angular readings. Among the softly shaded contour lines of the peaks are open white spaces where no triangulation work had been possible. Reservoir sites, gauging points, and benchmarks were included on the map.[25]

Wheeler spent the winter of 1897–98 in Ottawa and, assisted by his brother Hector, developed over five hundred negatives, and then plotted contour lines by hand from print enlargements.[26] In summer 1898, he extended the photo-topographic survey into the headwaters of the Oldman and Livingston Rivers, and the following winter he continued his mapping work in Calgary. It was, Wheeler lamented, a painfully slow task drawing contours at intervals of fifty feet.[27] He wrote to Deville for elaboration on several points in *Photographic Surveying*, and inquired about using the perspectograph instrument that Deville had described. To Wheeler's disappointment, Deville responded that the instrument did not work well and was not accurate in its rendering of contours. He advised Wheeler to go on plotting by hand! Wheeler, nevertheless, pursued the issue, and in May

Deville promised to send a couple of perspectographs made to fit the exact focal length of the enlarged photographs from which Wheeler was working.[28]

In late December 1899, Wheeler forwarded a box of his negatives to Ottawa, noting his disappointment: "while they will produce a good set of working prints, they required a good deal of spotting. I think this is largely due to the age of the plates and the amount of transportation they have received."[29] By late February 1900 another map was ready to be printed by the Toronto Litho Company, with Wheeler's orders that canals and ditches should be in black; springs, streams, lakes, and all watercourses in blue. Wheeler was, however, bitterly disappointed when he got the proofs. "The Toronto Litho Company has made a clumsy copy of a well and accurately drawn map. I had intended that a Photo-lithograph [sic] should be made and requisitioned to that effect. So that the map would be in keeping with our general maps sheets 1 and 2; and also that the original could be preserved for future use for corrections." Wheeler was incensed that the time he had spent was wasted and claimed that that the original map was ruined for further use.[30] Meanwhile, surveyors and engineers waited impatiently for maps indicating suitable irrigation areas and routes for irrigation ditches.

### SURVEYORS GO TO WORK ON PLANS FOR IRRIGATION PROJECTS

The Irrigation Act specified that Dominion Land Surveyors had to be employed for the survey of rights-of-way for irrigation ditches. Clear and explicit rules, John Stoughton Dennis Jr. argued, were required for doing surveys for rights-of-way, and for their registration. Preliminary surveys were to be made of locations staked out for main ditches and laterals, as required by the act of incorporation for irrigation companies, and the Irrigation Act. Then, when the routes of ditches were located and construction had begun, a final survey was required to convey title to the right-of-way.[31] Most importantly, the 1894 Act stipulated that all right-of-way plans had to be signed by a Dominion Land Surveyor. According to the Irrigation Act, individuals and companies planning, or who had constructed, irrigation works were obliged to comply with the licensing regulations of the Act and register surveyed plans.

Dominion Land Surveyors soon began irrigation survey work. These were small projects done for individuals preparing final plans for irrigation ditches already in place, or drawing up preliminary plans for proposed irrigation works. Rancher John Ware hired James A. McMillian, DLS, to prepare a survey plan showing the location of the ditch he had constructed to divert water from the north fork of the Sheep River onto his lands. Other Dominion Land Surveyors, including George F. Austin, L. A. Hamiliton, and Allan Patrick, produced plans for small irrigation works south of Calgary.[32]

The 1897 flood wiped out many small irrigation projects underway in southern Alberta. William Pearce refused to be discouraged: "In spite, however, of the disaster, while it has proved a very great loss to irrigationalists, it has not in the slightest discouraged them, at least they are so thoroughly impressed as ever of the necessity of irrigation."[33] The flood, however, reinforced the understanding that cyclical drought and flash flooding could wreak physical and economic havoc in southern Alberta.

It also seems to have dampened the enthusiasm of the Department of the Interior for the administration of irrigation, and when the government of the North-West Territories requested to take over the survey, the Dominion government agreed. In spring 1898, Dennis was appointed Deputy Commissioner for the Department of Public Works in the North-West Territories, and Arthur Wheeler was placed in charge of the Canadian Irrigation Survey.

Dennis admitted privately in December 1898 that all the government surveys and records "will no doubt be of very considerable value in time, but heretofore it has been of no assistance to the enterprise carried into effect."[34] Irrigation in late 1898 was still in its infancy. While Arthur Wheeler and other surveyors did the background work for the necessary maps and understanding of hydrology to make it possible, the actual construction and operation of irrigation projects was far behind. There were, however, plans afoot for much larger irrigation projects than had been realized to this point. The Irrigation Survey was soon hard-pressed to keep its ongoing survey work ahead of major corporate schemes on the drawing board.

Irrigation projects on a large scale were a massively expensive undertaking, and the stumbling block for quick development of plans lay in the difficulty of securing adequate financing. Three large-scale irrigation projects required a range of surveys, from levelling to rights-of-way. First came the St. Mary River project, then the CPR irrigation block, and then finally the controversial Bow River Project. In each case individual land surveyors were closely aligned with the project and played a key role, both at the political, organizational and practical level. William Pearce and John Stoughton Dennis Jr., moreover, continued to shape the irrigation debate in Alberta up to World War I.

THE ST. MARY RIVER PROJECT

The St. Mary River project had its roots in the unlikely alliance between the Galt family who owned the Alberta Railway and Coal Company and members of the Church of Latter Day Saints, who had founded a settlement in 1887 on Lee Creek, in the vicinity of present-day Cardston. Their leader, Charles Ora Card, was an irrigation farmer from Utah with practical experience with the type of irrigation needed in southern Alberta. Eliot Galt, coal and railway magnate of Lethbridge, and his brother-in-law, Dominion Land Surveyor Charles Magrath, saw an opportunity for expansion. Irrigation and colonization of arid railway grant lands would ultimately go hand in hand—a vision shared by William Pearce. The intricacies of railway financing and land policies delayed the scheme, which required extensive surveys and encountered many hurdles before water would flow.

In 1882 the Galt family formed the North Western Coal and Navigation Company (NWC&N) and opened a coal mine at Lethbridge to feed the hungry CPR locomotives thundering west. While Alexander Tilloch Galt, one of the famed Fathers of Confederation, looked after the investment side of the business, his son Eliot remained in Alberta as mine manager. Difficulties with transporting coal by river steamer to Medicine Hat led the Galts to build a railway from Lethbridge that would connect with the CPR line at Dunmore. The Dominion government subsidized the project with a land grant of 3,840 acres per mile of railway—free except for a Dominion Land Survey charge of ten cents per acre.[35] With this deal in hand by summer 1885, Galt's company constructed a narrow

*Charles A. Magrath, DLS, DTS, [1890s].*
GLENBOW ARCHIVES, NA-659-65

gauge line to the newly surveyed townsite of Lethbridge. The company now had land to sell, and Charles Magrath took the job of land commissioner.

Galt next determined to build a second rail line south from Lethbridge to the US border, from where an American railway would carry coal to smelting plants located in Montana. In 1889, with a further land grant in hand, Galt formed the Alberta Railway and Coal Company (AR&C) and transferred all the assets and liabilities of the NWC&N to the new company. Meanwhile, surveyor Charles Magrath, as mayor of Lethbridge in 1890, and then as MLA for the territorial government in Regina, vigorously promoted irrigation for settlement. Galt claimed his lands had no value if they were not irrigated. Behind the public scene, Magrath brought together Galt and Charles Ora Card, along with his fellow church member John Taylor, to sign an agreement in 1891 whereby the two Mormon settlers agreed to lease over seventy-two thousand acres of land from the AR&C with an option to buy after four years.[36] Although they agreed to work together for the irrigation of these lands, through the Alberta Irrigation Company incorporated in 1893, the agreement collapsed for lack of funds. Card, nevertheless, developed his own small irrigation project on Lee Creek.

In 1896 Elliot Galt, ever the business strategist, reorganized the Alberta Irrigation Company, just before the rights granted to it were to expire. British investors were not forthcoming, so Galt looked to Ottawa for financial assistance. Together with William Pearce, Magrath promoted government-sponsored irrigation through the editorial columns of the *Lethbridge News*. The Alberta Irrigation Company had land, a Dominion Land Surveyor on staff, the support of William Pearce, as well as Card's irrigation expertise. Finally the tide turned for the Galts' stalled irrigation scheme. The Canadian Irrigation Survey's reconnaissance survey of the St. Mary River proved favourable, and a preliminary location for a canal was established. By April 1897, the future of settlement looked bright, as railway surveyors located the route for the CPR branch rail line through the Crowsnest Pass. The Galts argued that the rail line guaranteed a future market on the other side of the Rockies for agricultural produce grown on irrigated lands. In Ottawa, Magrath got a favourable reception from Clifford Sifton, the Minister of the Interior in Wilfred Laurier's new Liberal government, who forgave the debt owed by the Galts on the surveys carried out by the Dominion Land Survey on the AR&C's land grant.

With a better financial picture in hand, Galt and Magrath reopened negotiations with the Church of the Latter Day Saints. On September 6, 1897, Charles Ora Card noted in his diary that Magrath had laid out a detailed proposition for a large-scale irrigation scheme that would entice settlers, declaring "that the Lord was inspiring the man."[37] Magrath made subsequent trips to Utah to formalize an agreement with the Church of Latter Day Saints—church members would dig the canals with half payment in cash and the other half in land with water rights valued at three dollars an acre. The land was to be in two separate tracts, each supporting a hamlet.[38]

Magrath was a surveyor, not an engineer. He looked south of the border to seek one of the best-known men in the business, George Anderson of Denver, to plan and supervise the under-

*The intake canal at Kimball on the St. Mary River, located by the Canadian Irrigation Survey in 1898.*
GLENBOW ARCHIVES, NA-922-9

taking that Magrath would head up on the ground. Anderson revised the projected plan for a series of canals proposed by the Canadian Irrigation Survey. The elevation contours, Anderson reported, would allow a system using natural watercourses for the main ditches that would reduce construction costs.[39] The following summer, on August 26, 1898, Charles Ora Card ploughed the first furrow for a permanent irrigation ditch, near the intake at Kimball. In 1899 Galt's company—newly named the Canadian North-West Irrigation Company—needed detailed contour surveys of the Lethbridge district, east of the St. Mary and south of the Oldman River, and applied to the Department of Interior to release R. McIntyre, DLS, from the Canadian Irrigation Survey. The company promised to pay his wages and then share the results of the topographical survey with the government. McIntyre, however, discovered this was unsurveyed land and he had to run the township outlines before he could begin any levelling work.[40]

By summer 1900 Galt's Canadian North-West Irrigation Company had constructed ninety-five miles of canals northwest from the St. Mary River. They included branch canals passing by the new hamlets of Magrath and Stirling and terminating at Lethbridge. The company then embarked on advertising and selling the surrounding lands. John Stoughton Dennis Jr. reported: "The whole district traversed by the canal is rapidly becoming dotted with farms."[41] The irrigation canal brought a remarkable change to the Lethbridge area.

## DENNIS AND PEARCE PUSH FOR CPR IRRIGATION

As the Canadian Irrigation Surveys progressed, John Stoughton Dennis Jr. and William Pearce worked hand in glove pitching irrigation to the CPR. After 1896, when the Liberals assumed power, both Pearce and Dennis ran somewhat afoul of the administration—Pearce for conflict of interest charges arising out of a controversy surrounding his own irrigation company, and Dennis for poor

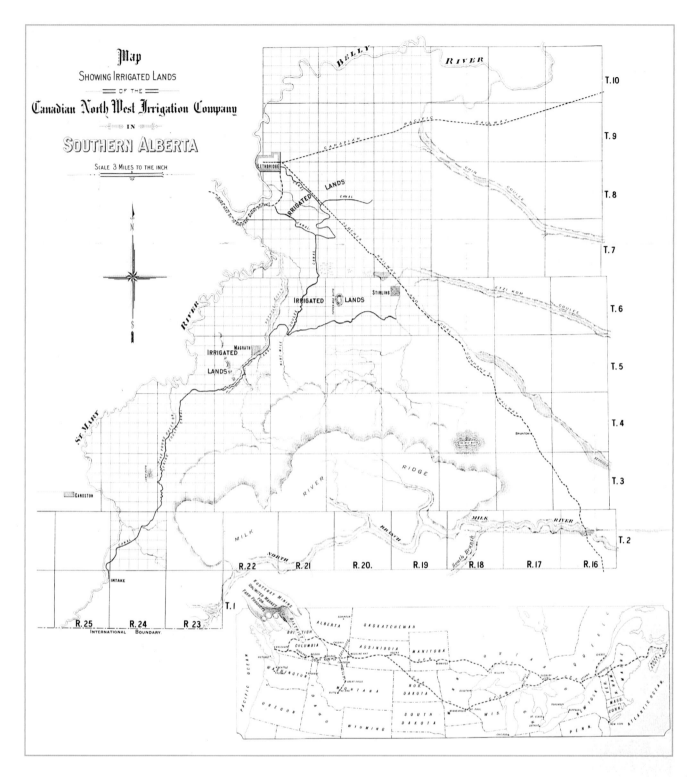

*Irrigation Lands of the Canadian North-West Irrigation Company Lands in southern Alberta, 1900.*
GLENBOW LIBRARY, G3502/2647 J4/1900 MAP

management of funds. When Dennis left the Dominion Survey in 1898, Pearce, despite his rather fractious relationship with the department, was appointed Inspector of Surveys. In their new positions, both men, Pearce in Calgary and Dennis in Regina, basing their arguments on surveys done by the Canadian Irrigation Survey, continued to promote irrigation of CPR lands east of Calgary.

In 1902 the CPR finally decided to go ahead with a massive irrigation scheme divided into three separate blocks, western, centre, and eastern. The company planned to divert water from the Bow River east of Calgary to the east and north, to irrigate CPR land north of the rail line all the way to Medicine Hat. John Stoughton Dennis Jr. promptly left his job with the territorial government in Regina and joined the CPR to oversee the project. As Superintendent of Irrigation, he ran an impressive office in Calgary. Not

*A lateral irrigation ditch running across a farm near Raymond, 1904.*
GLENBOW ARCHIVES, PD-310-96

surprisingly, Pearce followed Dennis to the CPR in 1903, aiding him in drawing up plans for irrigation canals and ditches to be submitted to the Department of the Interior for approval under the Irrigation Act. The CPR western block was soon irrigated, and following the acquisition of a controlling interest in the St. Mary project, the CPR garnered a virtual monopoly on irrigation systems in southern Alberta. It developed a whole scheme of colonization with CPR agriculturalists on

*W. M. Notman Jr., of the famous Montreal photography firm, took this photograph of one of the irrigation canals for Galt's Canadian North-West Irrigation Company in 1904.*
GLENBOW ARCHIVES, PB-863-9

## Hydrographic Surveys in Southern Alberta

In southern Alberta hydrographic surveys became more than a practical necessity for irrigation. Control of water in the rivers that flowed on both sides of the forty-ninth parallel became the issue. The threat of the United States diverting water south of the border had always been an underlying concern of the Canadian Irrigation Survey. Pearce raised this issue in his report of 1891, and the Department of the Interior considered a declared vested interest in the waters of the St. Mary River was the best pre-emptive strike against such a move.[44] Rumours of US proposals to divert water from the St. Mary River spurred on the survey and construction of the St. Mary River Irrigation Canal in 1898. Fear of American plans to divert the Milk River came to a head in 1902, and was a factor in provoking the CPR to finally begin construction of the irrigation scheme that had been sitting on the drawing board for some time.[45]

From 1904 the dispute between the US and Canada drove investigations on the St. Mary and Milk Rivers. Armed with the latest data, William F. King, DLS, the Dominion Astronomer, finalized the negotiations for Canada. They led to the International Boundary Waterways Treaty of 1909, by which Canada and the United States agreed to share available water resources. In Canada, a separate Hydrographic Survey Branch was formed under Penrose M. Sauder, DLS, to undertake work to support the ongoing discussions through an International Joint Commission. Charles Magrath sat as a Canadian representative on the Commission for many years. Finally, in 1921, the Commission signed a further agreement that set out detailed provisions for implementation of the 1909 agreement, which would ensure a supply of water for southern Alberta.[46]

"ready-made farms," supported by an experimental farm at Strathmore, serving the three irrigation blocks that were completed by 1914.

Although the St. Mary Project had required the services of Dominion Land Surveyors, the same was not true for the CPR project—the CPR provided its own surveyors. The Department of the Interior began to receive complaints from farmers who had taken up CPR lands through the settlement scheme, about inadequate water supply from ditches and erroneous classification of land as irrigable. Farmers objected to paying for water in the years when there was adequate rainfall to grow crops, and many fell into arrears on their land contracts and water agreements.[42] The obvious question arose: was the quality of the survey and engineering plans, which the CPR had the privilege of being allowed to undertake itself, not up to par? How closely had the whole project been scrutinized under the provisions of the Irrigation Act?

In 1912 Frederic H. Peters, ALS, Commissioner of Irrigation for the newly formed Irrigation Branch of the Department of the Interior, began to apply pressure on the CPR, requesting plans for a projected reservoir. He indicated that if, in the past, the department had not been strict about submission of plans, it would now require plans to be submitted and approved before any further work was undertaken.[43] Finally in 1913, there was a government investigation of the CPR's western irrigation block. The final report released in 1915 concluded that there was no basis for farmers' concerns about the soil or climatic conditions in the block, but the designated irrigable land was reduced from 367,000 to 225,000 acres, indicating there was a wide margin of error in the CPR surveys. Peters' actions had brought the CPR within the surveying and licensing regulations that applied to other irrigation projects.

## The Controversial Surveys for the Bow River Irrigation Project

For the surveying profession, the third major project in southern Alberta was highly controversial and provoked much criticism. In 1906 James McGregor, President of the Grand Forks Cattle Company located north of Bow Island, acquired a new business associate, Arthur Grenfell, whose father-in-law, Earl Grey, was Governor General of Canada from 1904 to 1911. The partners converted the ranching business into the Robbins Irrigation Company, and acquired 380,373 acres under the Irrigation

Act, forming a triangle south of the Bow River between Medicine Hat and Lethbridge. The pair then hired Dominion Land Surveyor Bryce J. Saunders, formerly with the Canadian Irrigation Survey and Chief Surveyor and Engineer for the Department of Public Works of the North-West Territories. He set out to assess the feasibility of the projected irrigation scheme prior to the capitalization of a new company, the Southern Alberta Land Company, to undertake construction.

Saunders endorsed an earlier report done by engineer John McIntosh, and calculated a 57 percent profit margin for the company! Perhaps it was this that subsequently prompted the Irrigation Branch to allow John McIntosh, rather than a Dominion Land Surveyor, to sign all documents, applications, and plans for the Southern Alberta Land Company. McIntosh immediately submitted a surveyed plan for a main canal with an intake on the east bank of the Bow River some distance west of Arrowwood Creek. The canal stretched southeast through Snake Valley before angling east onto the lands to be irrigated.[47]

William Pearce, despite his belief in the limitless provision of the Bow River, was highly sceptical. He declared the proposed intake location impossible, as it would require a dam and then canals winding through miles of ravines and cutbanks. Charles Magrath was alarmed as to the capacity of the Bow, already diverted for the CPR project, to support another irrigation scheme. He was not reassured by correspondence with Pearce, who wrote on November 19, 1906: "Unless my recollections of the physical conditions along the Bow River are altogether astray, this scheme is financially impracticable. If I am correct, it is a gigantic fraud, and I am astonished at Saunders lending himself to it."[48] Pearce went public with his scathing condemnation of the plan, and as a result the company fired McIntosh and hired Arthur Grace, another American irrigation engineer, to modify the plan before construction began in 1909. Nevertheless, the project continued to go awry.

In 1912 Canada's Governor General HRM Duke of Connaught, and important British investors gathered at Medicine Hat for the official opening of the canal. The collapse of the head gates provided a hiccup to the proceedings. Undaunted, James McGregor drove his VIPs around out on the dusty prairie for eight hours without food or drink, pretending to be lost, so that they would not see the disaster! Dominion Land Surveyor Frederic H. Peters, Commissioner of Irrigation, was less than amused. He launched an investigation, hiring a British engineer, William G. Bligh, for the task. Bligh roundly condemned the engineering as thoroughly incompetent. The Department of the Interior was hesitant to release the report, as it was responsible for ensuring proper construction of irrigation works.[49] The problems with the Southern Alberta Land Company, together with complaints against the CPR, forced the Irrigation Branch to take a tighter rein on irrigation companies. During World War I, moreover, the government of the Province of Alberta passed legislation in 1915 allowing for farmer-run irrigation districts. In the future, only qualified land surveyors would sign all irrigation plans.

Irrigation and the surveys required for it were specific to the situation in southern Alberta, and it widened the scope of surveying work in the province. The early photographic surveys, the levelling work of the Canadian Irrigation Survey, and the actual location surveying for specific irrigation projects, together incorporated several branches of surveying, hydrology, and engineering. The experience surveyors had with irrigation resulted in a complicated relationship between government surveyors, private surveyors, and corporate interests, and illustrated the pitfalls as personalities, public and private interest, became intertwined.

Arthur Wheeler's pioneering work with applied photo-topographic surveying on the Canadian Irrigation Survey was critical to the development of irrigation, and was widely recognized, nationally and internationally in Europe. Pearce, Dennis and Magrath were exceptionally able men who applied their survey training to seek solutions to the problems of western development. In tackling irrigation, they set a trend for leaders within the surveying profession to play a multifaceted role in planning, administrative, and legislative positions. The professional lives and interests of Dominion Land Surveyors working in Alberta became bound up with Alberta's economic development and the society that was evolving in Alberta—a society in which the land surveyor would play an ever more important role.

CHAPTER 5

# Surveyors Meet Settlers
*Trails and Township Subdivision*

## SURVEYORS OPEN UP THE LAND

Once the basic survey grid was in place and the townships along the Canadian Pacific Railway line in southern Alberta had been subdivided, Dominion Land Surveyors worked in cooperation with both immigration and Dominion Land agents to "open up" the land for settlement. Two types of surveys were urgently required, the marking of rights-of-way for trails and the subdividing of townships into sections and quarter sections for settlers. When the CPR constructed the Edmonton and Calgary Railway in 1891, a horde of homesteaders descended on the lush boreal parkland that lay east and west of the rail line through central Alberta. As thousands of people set out along the trails radiating from railway stations to take a chance on virgin black soil, surveyors began further township subdivision surveys. There was a first big push for surveys in 1893, and then again from the turn of the century, culminating in 1903–4. Surveyors, as representatives of the Dominion government, dealt with settlers' concerns, interests, and disputes. This became as much a part of their job as the adjustment of a transit.

## SURVEYING TRAILS

Alberta's surveyors got a first taste of working in the field while settlers were taking up land as they began the survey of the most heavily travelled trails—the precursors of Alberta's highways. Surveyors were expected to do more than merely mark the existing route of a trail and tie it into the existing grid. They sought to mark as direct and level a route as possible, while accommodating the needs of inhabitants, finding the best fording points on rivers, and avoiding lakes and sloughs. Where the vista was limited, trails often meandered; surveying techniques were required to straighten the trail and establish a legal right-of-way.

All roads and trails that predated official surveys were under the control of the Lieutenant-Governor of the North-West Territories in Regina. In 1884 the main overland trail routes were designated "public highways" that would require surveys. This basic principle was reiterated in a revised statute of 1886, which further specified that the decision to survey a trail travelled by the public, which existed prior to regular surveys, rested with the Lieutenant-Governor-in-Council.[1]

The surveyor general in Ottawa did not have control over which trails to survey, nor could he easily respond to the advice of his surveyors in the field. In 1889, for example, he received a petition to open up a new trail from Edmonton to Lac La Biche. As Surveyor General Edouard Deville pointed out, such a survey was not possible because the proposed trail was a new route, a colonization road, and was not provided for under the existing legislation.[2] The issues thrown up by the settlement process over the next decade were reflected in revised legislation that allowed for the survey of colonization roads, generally as a result of petitions for surveys sent to Regina. Legislation also prevented settlers from closing trails, vesting the power to do so in the Lieutenant-Governor-in-council.

## The Evolution of Alberta's Trails

Although river routes remained important in Alberta until well into the twentieth century, Aboriginal peoples also used overland routes following the contours of the land, wearing ruts in the grass and leaving the first trails across the prairie and parkland. Trails linking Métis settlements and hunting grounds, such as those between Tail Creek on the Red Deer River and the Hand Hills and the Neutral Hills in the southeast, became well-established freight trails by the 1870s. Creaking Red River carts inched goods bound for Edmonton from Winnipeg via Battleford, over the Carlton Trail along the North Saskatchewan River. From Edmonton, goods moved south via the Bow Valley Trail. This led south to the Red Deer River Crossing, west of Red Deer, and on to Lone Pine, east of Olds, then continued southwest to the mission at Morley. Other well-worn trails included a route to Rocky Mountain House from Edmonton, a trail from the international boundary linking Fort Benton in the US with Fort Macleod, and trails west into the mountains from Pincher Creek. By the late 1870s, the North-West Mounted Police regularly patrolled the main artery trails on horseback, and the superintendent of each district detailed the condition of trails in his annual report. When the Canadian Pacific Railway line was constructed as far west as the Fourth Meridian (later to form the boundary between Saskatchewan and Alberta), freighters abandoned the Carlton Trail and hauled goods north from the end of steel on the Red Deer Forks Trail. This trail ran north from near present-day Empress, up the east side of Sullivan Lake to Battle River Settlement, and on to Edmonton. Immediately upon the CPR reaching Calgary, freighters forged a trail north to link with the Bow Valley Trail at Lone Pine, and from there followed the old route to Edmonton. The Calgary–Edmonton Trail had been born.

At the same time, any private land affected by a right-of-way for a public trail or road was subject to the homestead rights acquired under the Dominion Lands Act, and administered by the Department of the Interior. Homesteaders were compensated for a roadway across their lands if they had improved their holdings as set out in the Act, proved up and applied for patent, or title, to their land. Settlers, therefore, who did not yet hold title to their land were less than happy when a surveyor began a legal survey of a trail or a road diversion off the road allowance onto their property. The actual survey of trails and of road allowances during the process of township subdivision was in the hands of the Topographical Surveys Branch and surveyors were often caught between a rock and a hard place when making decisions in the field.

## The Survey of the Calgary–Edmonton Trail

The Calgary–Edmonton Trail relieved the sense of isolation Edmonton felt when the CPR decided to build through southern Alberta. On March 17, 1883, the *Edmonton Bulletin* was elated that a trail linked Edmonton with the railway at Calgary and hopeful for an increase in population and the amount of business and mail that would come their way. A stagecoach hauled mail and passengers north on a weekly basis from July 1883. For a whopping twenty-five dollar fare, a traveller was jarred to the bone, and spent five nights sleeping in designated "stopping places,"—Alberta's first rough and ready bed and breakfast establishments. Here travellers could find feed for horses, sustenance and rest, and mail could be picked up. The enthusiastic approach to commerce and communications was, however, sharply arrested in 1885, as the prospect of Métis rebellion brought a chill to the air and, ultimately, the squelch of soldiers' boots through the mud on the Calgary–Edmonton Trail as they marched north for Batoche. In 1886, all danger passed, two Dominion Land Surveyors, George Roy and Charles Biggar, were sent to survey the Calgary–Edmonton Trail, the first designated highway to be legally surveyed in Alberta.

Beginning at the Red Deer River Crossing, George Roy and his party worked north, while Biggar went south. As Roy was the better writer of the two surveyors, his account of the survey was published as part of the annual report of the Department of the Interior. Roy surveyed a serviceable route following the travelled trail as closely as possible. Generally, the existing trail ran through suitable country, but he marked occasional diversions. Roy was keenly aware of the importance of the trail and the role it would later play in Alberta's history: "In view of the great traffic and immense travel which some day may be done [sic] this way, my intention was to make the road as straight as the actual direction of the trail between the two extreme points, Red Deer and Edmonton, would allow, without neglecting the advantages of a hard bottom, easy grades and good drainage." Roy attempted to reduce the number of deflections or bends in the trail, which was often lengthened by a curve around a soft spot, a small marsh, or a bluff. Where these were of little consequence, Roy straightened the trail route: "These obstacles my lines went through, for as long as the country is not settled the travel [sic] will run where it pleases, and after settlement farmers will improve the road to satisfy the public. However, except when of absolute necessity, all lines were avoided which would have caused any considerable amount of work to individuals, a little ditching, a small culvert, a slight cut, or a few branches thrown on a soft spot, being in most cases the only thing required to save a long turn of the road."

Roy suggested improvements, beginning with the crossing at the Red Deer River: "A hill will have to be cut on the bank of the Red Deer, and in such a way to allow the people who ford the river to use it as well as those who cross by ferry. A mile further a small bridge or a 6 by 6 culvert, with filling on each side to shorten the hill, would be useful." At Wolf Creek, Roy found that a ditch and corduroy boards needed to be laid for a distance of about a hundred feet. "After this," he continued, "all the way up to Bear Hills, the trail is crossed by numerous streams from 1 to 10 feet wide, through which a wagon goes easily enough, although they make the road a little rough." Roy pinpointed what would become an ongoing problem—the maintenance required for bridges on the trail. Roy had "little trouble with settlers," as he put it, but he did infringe upon the private inter-

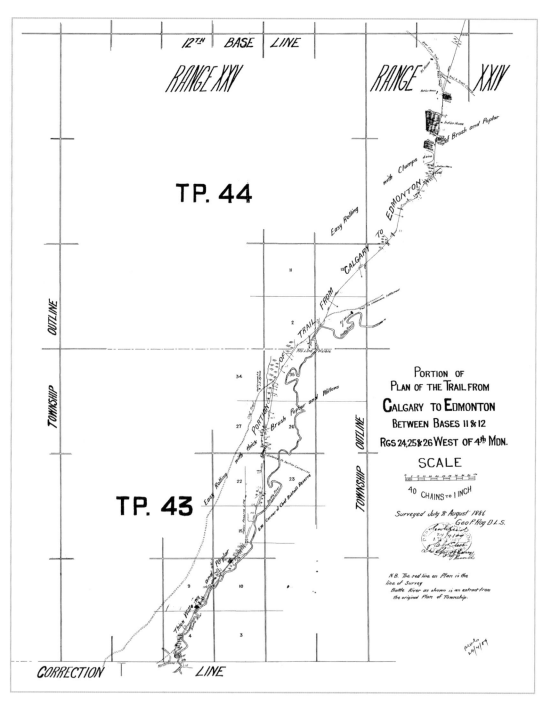

Registered plan of a portion of the Calgary–Edmonton Trail, 1886.
CANADA LANDS SURVEY RECORDS, 1723 CLSR AB

ests of one settler, Mr. Aylwin, who operated a post office at Holbrooke, just south of the Montana Reserve. Roy wished to reroute the trail to accommodate a bridge over the Battle River, west of present-day Ponoka, bypassing Aylwin's post office. The dispute ended up being referred to the Lieutenant-Governor of the North-West Territories for final arbitration. Roy won.[3]

## Surveyors and the Trail Commissioner

By the late 1880s, the survey of trails across the ranching country of southern Alberta caused problems as surveyors found the trails ran through townships where subdivision for settlement was beginning to take place, as well as through recently surveyed Indian reserves. Charles Biggar, DLS, began a survey of the well-established trail from Calgary to Fort Macleod in summer 1886. He soon ran into unexpected trouble: "From Calgary to Fish Creek the settlers have fenced the greater part of the old trail and left a road allowance, as a public highway. Upon examining this road I found that it crossed a slough, which at certain seasons of the year would be impassable."[4] Biggar decided discretion was the better part of valour and handed over the particulars of the potential quagmire to the Lieutenant-Governor. The settlers won their case—there were no diversions surveyed and the Lieutenant-Governor granted a sum of money for repairing the slough. The difficulties Biggar experienced in completing his survey prompted the surveyor general the following year to arrange for a trail commissioner to represent the Lieutenant-Governor in negotiations with settlers and made necessary arrangements for securing legal rights-of-way.[5]

John Stoughton Dennis Jr., Inspector of Surveys, was encouraged by this procedure. In 1888 the Dominion Land Survey tackled the survey of the trails from Calgary to Morleyville (Morley). Dennis accompanied Mr. McMillan, DLS, the trail commissioner to deal with disputed sections of trail, including both the north and south Morleyville trails. Although Dennis noted the majority of the set-

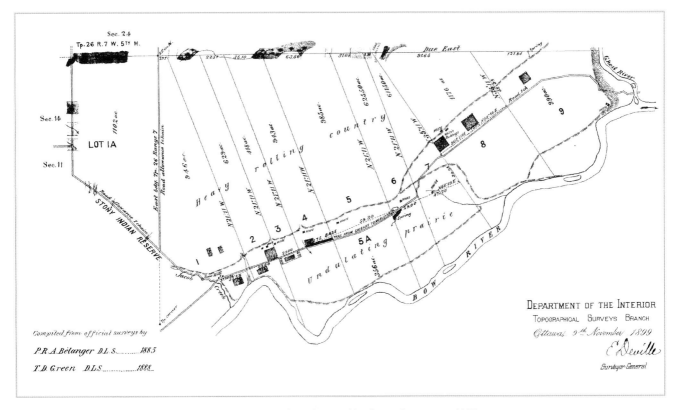

*Registered plan of Morleyville Settlement showing the trail surveyed by Thomas Green, DLS, in 1888.*
Land Titles Office, plan number 89B

## Lady Adela Cochrane's Assessment of Survey Requirements

In 1893 squatters fenced off a trail west of the settlements at Mitford [6] and Cochrane that then ran north through Grand Valley to Dog Pound Creek. The closure incensed the Calgary Lumber Company, who used the trail to access their timber berths in the Kanansksis Valley, as well as ranchers. A petition, signed by several prominent ranchers including Thomas Cochrane of Mitford, was duly sent to Ottawa in September 1893 for the survey of the trail as a public road. The matter became more urgent when a lawsuit resting on the question of the status of the trail was pending by November 1893, but the surveyor general wrote it was too late in the season to survey the trail.

When Thomas Cochrane showed the letter to his wife, Lady Adela, she took matters into her own hands. "I may mention that the trail is only $2^3/_4$ miles at the outmost, on a perfectly level piece of ground, so that it could be easily surveyed in one morning," she informed the surveyor general shortly before Christmas, with a strong flourish of the pen on "Mitford Emporium" letterhead. "The anxiety expressed for having this road opened," she continued, "is the fact that Mitford and Cochrane are both villages and it would prove most inconvenient if the land intervening were taken up by settlers."

She need not have worried, as the trail had already been recommended for survey four days earlier. Deville was highly amused at Lady Adela's estimated time for the survey; it, in fact, took nearly four days when it was surveyed to Dog Pound Creek the following year by Fred Wilkins, DLS, DTS. [7]

tlers in the Calgary area seemed satisfied with the location of the trails as then surveyed, he foresaw problems down the road as settlement progressed and improvement of the trails would be required. [8]

Thomas Green, DLS, then set out to survey two trails linking Calgary to the Stoney Indian reserve and settlement at Morleyville. One ran on the north side of the Bow River, approximating the route of today's Highway 1A. The second ran southwest from Calgary via Springbank, and Jumping Pound Creek to the CPR line and then west to Morley Station. His survey party spent five weeks surveying the north trail above the Bow River. It was showery on June 25 when he reached Cochrane. "A slight deviation from the original trail was made at Cochrane," he wrote in his diary, "so as to follow the present travelled trail and use a bridge constructed by the Cochrane Ranche Company over Big Hill Creek." Although the trail commissioner had already paved the way with settlers and provided a preliminary plan, Green was left to consult with the resident Indian agent about the route of the trail across the reserve. Once the survey of the north trail was complete, Green then worked his way back, surveying the trail from Morleyville to Calgary, south of the Bow. This trail was rough as far as Jumping Pound Creek, and Green found it was necessary to make many deviations from the old trail as recommended by the trail commissioner. [9]

The role of the trail commissioner seems to have been short-lived. In 1889 trails that linked the settlements at St. Albert and Fort Saskatchewan with Edmonton were formally surveyed. In early June, Phidime Belanger, DLS, surveyed the six and a half miles from Edmonton to St. Albert, through "settled country of nearly level prairie." He was able to carry his survey along the course of the established trail, making an occasional diversion to straighten out bad bends. "In one of these places, I ran the trail 5 or 6 chains off the old track and across a cultivated field owned by a Mr. Harnois, but the consent of the proprietor was obtained, and he was satisfied with the change." Belanger found the trail from Fort Saskatchewan to Edmonton a little more difficult to complete. Two trails, one referred to as the inner and the other the outer, had been identified, but the decision as to which would be surveyed was left to Belanger. Belanger promptly telegraphed the Lieutenant-Governor in Regina to appoint a trail commissioner to arbitrate the decision—to no avail! He was told to assume the responsibility and assess the pros and cons of each trail. Belanger read the petitions in support of each and spoke with settlers and travellers. "The people most interested, the travelling public of Edmonton and Fort Saskatchewan, were almost unanimous in favor of the 'inner trail,' he wrote, "and among the settlers whose claims are crossed by that trail I found only one who offered serious objection; therefore I proceeded to survey the inner trail."[10]

## Stakes and Picketmen

Surveyors followed the *Manual of Instructions for the Survey of Dominion Lands*, published in 1883, to connect the starting and closing point of a trail with an existing survey monument, as well as a section or quarter section monument on every surveyed section that the trail passed through. From an established starting point, the first station, the surveyor ran a line either along the centre of the trail to avoid having to clear bush, or along one of the limits, or sides, of the trail, using a transit to determine the trail deflections or bends. A "picket man" marked the position of these deflections with a wooden stake of some kind on the ground. A monument was then placed on the south or west limits at all points of deflection or every twenty chains. In 1887 John Stoughton Dennis Jr. recommended using iron bars and pits for monuments on trails, as posts and mounds were easily kicked out by horses and cattle moving over the trails.[11] All rights-of-way for trails that became public roads were one chain, or sixty-six feet, in width.

## SETTLERS DEMAND SURVEYS FOR NEW ROADS

During the 1890s, as the countryside began to fill up, a demand arose for new trails, known as "colonization roads," to be surveyed and constructed so that settlers would be linked to railway stations and centres of commerce. When the surveyors began township subdivision surveys, they found that settlers had developed a whole system of informal trails across country. Settlers' trails connected main trails with branch trails and trails leading to farms and post offices, as the settlement process unfolded. The surveyor sketched these settlers' trails as he found them on township plans, but did not actually survey them. Almost as soon as his work was done, trails became obsolete, and we would know little of where they once ran without the surveyor's work in recording their direction across a township. In lieu of these settlers' trails, which usually ran across private property, the surveyor marked out the road allowances, according to the provisions of the township grid system. In many cases, the surveyed road allowances passed through low or swampy land, as fresnoes and primitive graders only allowed limited reshaping of the topography. Road building took time, and meanwhile, people travelled the worn trails that followed the natural lay of the land to best advantage.

As homesteaders began fencing livestock in and putting up gates on trails that crossed their land, problems arose. The role of the surveyor broadened to public relations specialist as he found himself involved in disputes about closing trails, opposition to routes surveyed, and the negotiation and securing of rights-of-ways for road diversions where road allowances were unsuitable. Few issues divided settlers during the 1890s as much as the location and routing of trails and roads. Land surveyors were often caught in the middle. In 1898 the territorial government assumed responsibility for actually doing roadwork following the surveys—the improvement of public trails as the survey dictated. Individual territorial MLAs had the right to oversee the expenditure of money from Ottawa allotted to their districts. The work would be carried out through a range of agencies using local labour and contracts.[12]

Dominion Land Surveyors Ernest Hubbell, Phidime Belanger, and Joseph Woods surveyed most of the trails that were needed to facilitate settlement in the area around Edmonton during the 1890s. In 1894 Ernest Hubbell reported that settlers at Beaverhill Lake, several of whom had independently begun cutting a road as they saw fit, proposed a number of direct routes to Edmonton. Hubbell recommended the survey of a route desired by the majority of settlers from the lake either directly to Edmonton or via Fort Saskatchewan, noting this would include the shortest route from the Vermilion Valley, where settlement was rapidly taking place.[13] The next summer, Hubbell surveyed trails from Edmonton to Stony Plain and to Hay Lakes, where he was busy staking out a right-of-way in fall 1895. He had to negotiate with several settlers. "Saw Anderson, Crocket and Irvine and got their assignment of right-of-way," he noted in his diary on October 23. Five days later, however, Hubbell, out running his line on the trail, had an unexpected visit from a "deputation of Russian settlers . . . requesting that the road allowance be run." Then on November 1, Hubbell set out for Edmonton. He had a mission: to see if the local member of the Territorial Assembly, Frank Oliver, could persuade a Mr. Schatz to sign right-of-way papers. Such problems finally ironed out, Hubbell soon completed the survey of the trail.[14]

Settlers and surveyors wanted good roads for going about their business. The call for improved trails and colonization roads prompted the government to take action and survey roads in the Calgary, Pincher Creek, Innisfail, and Olds areas in 1893. In Calgary, Dennis, as Inspector of Surveys, found himself with the responsibility of determining what trails should be surveyed. He made investigations in the field and consulted with Mr. Haultain, the territorial MLA, Charles Magrath, DLS, land commissioner for the Alberta Irrigation Company, as well as with settlers in southern Alberta, as to where roads were required. Eventually, Dominion Land Surveyor Fred Wilkins was given instructions in the summer of 1894 to survey trails in southern Alberta.

Wilkins began by surveying thirty-three miles of trail from Lethbridge to Fort Macleod, connecting with a street within the town plot. From there, he surveyed the established trail to the international boundary.[15] He next surveyed the trail from Fort Macleod, tying into a monument on the town boundary on First Avenue, as far as the mouth of Pincher Creek. His instructions from the surveyor general for deviating from the travelled trail were specific: "At the crossing of Scott's Coulee on this portion of the trail the straight road from the bottom of the hill on the east side across the bottom of the coulee will be followed. When descending into the valley of Pincher Creek at La Grandeur's ranche the road should be made straight at bottom of the hill instead of following the present bend. After crossing Pincher Creek, and when ascending the hill out of the Valley, the straight road up the hill should be followed instead of going up through the ravine along the road as now travelled."[16] Settlers were less than pleased and Wilkins was left to deal with their wrath on his own. "Some landowners are in an awful way—everyone wants trail on his neighbours [sic] not his own land," he noted in his diary on September 3, 1894. Two days later he had completed the survey to Pincher Creek, where the projected trail was found to run across Anglican Church property: "English Church people wild about the trail being put on their land." Fred Wilkins ran into

*The trail into Pincher Creek surveyed by Fred Wilkins, DLS, DTS, as it appeared in 1899.*
GLENBOW ARCHIVES, NA-659-90

more trouble on September 18 while surveying a trail west from Pincher Creek to the coal mines: "About 40 settlers following us around each one to keep [us] off his land and go on any other bodies [*sic*] land." [17]

Surveyors in the field, particularly those working on township subdivisions, were often in the best position to judge where settlers needed trails or new colonization roads, and they reported their views each year to the surveyor general. Some trails became surveyed roads while others were closed, and new roads opened up. When road allowances were deemed unsuitable for travel, farmers and ranchers often wanted to fence them in for grazing, but could not do so without a surveyor's authorization. From 1897, settlers or ranchers had to hire a surveyor who was resident in the area to investigate and report on the situation before they could apply to fence in such road allowances. [18]

The demand for surveys of roads was directly linked with the pace of township subdivision and the political interests of the new towns along the railways. The announcement in 1900 of the subdivision survey of six townships west of Wetaskiwin immediately solicited a demand for "the survey of certain roads through these townships extending from Wetaskiwin to Pigeon Lake." It was suggested that they should be surveyed at the same time as the subdivision survey "so as to avoid complications with the large number of settlers" expected to immediately take up land. [19] "It is a well known fact," noted the *Ponoka Herald* on November 22, 1901, "that Ponoka is losing a large amount of trade and business in all lines which justly belongs to this place because of the condition of the road leading from here as far as Red Deer and Buffalo Lakes." The fact that business was diverted to Wetaskiwin and Lacombe came down to partisan politics, according to the *Ponoka Herald*. Surveyors' reports show that some areas certainly had better roads than others. As James

Wallace, DLS, reported to the surveyor general in June 1902, the north part of Pigeon Lake suffered for want of a good road, whereas the Battle Lake area was well served.[20]

The demand for roads kept land surveyors hopping. Angus McFee, DLS, surveyed new roads and road allowance diversions in the Lacombe and Alix area in 1898. In 1899 Alfred Driscoll, DLS, surveyed the main trails along the Medicine River in the Markerville area, while Allan Patrick, DLS, DTS, worked further south surveying an old trail as well as a new road from the northeast corner of the Sarcee Reserve to Millarville post office. George A. Stewart, DLS, surveyed roads connecting the High River townsite with the Macleod Trail in 1899.[21]

## DISTRICT SURVEYORS TAKE ON ENGINEERING RESPONSIBILITIES IN THE NORTH-WEST TERRITORIES

The twentieth century brought a more politically fraught atmosphere for surveyors working on trail surveys. In 1901 the NWT Public Works Branch appointed a number of district surveyors, all of whom were both Dominion Land Surveyors and certified engineers, to supervise both surveys and construction of roads. All these men would later bring their considerable administrative experience to public works in the new Province of Alberta. Tensions ran high at times between the district surveyors working for the North-West Territories government and the Topographical Survey Branch, which had the job of inspecting the surveys carried out by the Territorial Public Works Branch. Alfred Driscoll, District Surveyor and Engineer in Edmonton, expressed his impatience with Inspector William Pearce's criticism of the pits on a road survey for which he was responsible in 1903. "You say that your inspector has not mentioned the character of the soil, if he had done so it might have accounted for this matter, as it required a dynamite cartridge to get some of them down their proper depth, and I do not think the department would wish to chance the loss of a few surveyors while the supply is so small."[22]

The registration of survey plans for roads and road diversions could not keep up with subdivision surveys or the homesteaders seeking title to their land.[23] When, for example, a new road east of Ponoka was planned for 1905, the Department of the Interior informed the Department of Public Works of the NWT in April to speed up the plan, as a homesteader had applied for a patent on an affected quarter section. "If the roadway mentioned in your . . . letter is to be reserved, a certified tracing of the plan must be forwarded here at once. Otherwise the patent will be issued without any reservation for the said road."[24] Once roads became a provincial responsibility, the province compensated settlers whose land was surveyed and expropriated for public use.[25]

## TOWNSHIP SUBDIVISION: THE CALGARY AND EDMONTON RAILWAY SPURS SURVEYORS ON

The construction of the Calgary and Edmonton Railway (C&E), a subsidiary of the CPR, was a major catalyst for township subdivision surveys in central Alberta. During 1890, the CPR's railroad surveyors worked on location surveys. Their white canvas tents could be seen from the Calgary–Edmonton trail. Construction began in 1891, and by August the steel ended at Strathcona,

*T. Mather, Edmonton's well-known professional photographer, travelled south of the
Calgary–Edmonton trail to record the work of the CPR survey crews locating the route
of the Calgary and Edmonton Railway during 1890. This was the Nose Creek camp located in
McPherson's Coulee, south of Carstairs, named for well-known freighter Ad McPherson.*

GLENBOW ARCHIVES, NA-1905-6

on the south side of the North Saskatchewan River opposite Edmonton Settlement. The next year, the C&E continued its construction program south from Calgary to Fort Macleod. The route of the railway line, north and south of Calgary, followed closely the trails that had been surveyed in 1886 to Edmonton and to Fort Macleod. Across southern and central Alberta, township subdivision began in concert with the development of the railway line and its fledgling townsites, which sprouted along the line. The construction of C&E refocused the direction and work of the Topographical Survey Branch, and ensured that surveyors would be kept busy through the 1890s.

## SURVEYORS TACKLE PROBLEMS WITH SURVEYS IN THE EDMONTON AREA

The new C&E line brought underlying problems in the Edmonton area to a head. Surveyors watched in May 1892 as settlers arrived at Strathcona, now the end of steel, to discover that the immigration shed was still under construction. Hotel accommodation, if they could afford it, was limited—the Strathcona Hotel on Whyte Avenue was bursting at the seams. The Topographical Surveys Branch stepped in and set up tents as the only accommodation option available to many settlers.[26] Settlers were directed to cross the river from Strathcona by ferry to get to the Dominion Lands Office in Edmonton Settlement to apply for homesteads. A big map on the wall showed homesteads open for settlement, but many prospective settlers encountered delays and problems.

Not only had an insufficient number of townships been surveyed to date, but also the marks from the original grid layout from surveys in 1882 and 1883 had been obliterated, according to

## Defacement and Removal of Survey Marks

By 1890 a fifty dollar reward was offered for information leading to the conviction of anyone removing a survey marker. Conviction carried a seven-year prison term. Yet the problem persisted—settlers used the iron bars for pickets for tying horses, bolts for sleighs, pegs in stables, pokers, triangles for camp kettles, props in bake ovens—there were, it seemed, a hundred uses for a survey marker. In the Edmonton district, the majority of the posts marking the Beaver Creek to Victoria Road, put in by Joseph Woods, DLS, in 1896 had been pulled out a year later. Nobody ever seemed to be caught in the act, and nor had a fifty dollar reward been paid for securing a conviction of a culprit brought to justice. In 1898 the North-West Mounted Police suggested that possession should be added to the offence of defacing, altering, and removing a survey mark, and it has remained on the books to the present. In addition, fifty dollar reward notices printed in English, French, and German were posted. In 1903, following reports of missing posts, such as one filed by Corporal Watt of the NWMP in Andrew, a further one thousand copies were run off in Russian and Ukrainian. The Galician settlers, Watt claimed, were misinformed or did not understand that the removal of posts was a crime, compounded by the distribution of warning notices in English only. Nevertheless, the problem persisted everywhere in the province, and few cases seem to have been solved—with one exception involving a Didsbury settler.

In August 1907 the surveyor general informed the NWMP that he had received a communication from one S. Snyder reporting that H. B. Good of Didsbury had a survey post lying about his stable. Deville asked the NWMP to investigate. By October the Mounties had an answer. They searched Good's farm and indeed found a survey post in use on one of his gates. He was prosecuted and fined twenty-five dollars and costs. In his defence Good had declared he had his pony tied to the post; that the animal pulled it, and he and his brother put a pole on the mound where the stake had been, but forgot to replace the survey post. Further, he argued three of the quarter sections marked by the post were owned by the Good family, and fenced; there could have been no intention to mislead anyone. One wonders if Snyder got his fifty dollars.[29]

frustrated land guides who brought settlers out to their homestead claims. Some immigrants were obliged to strike out without applications and squat on the lands they picked out, pending the arrival of the surveyors and the opportunity to make a statutory declaration of their claim. Thomas Anderson, Dominion Land Agent in Edmonton, apprised John Stoughton Dennis Jr. of the situation when he arrived in Edmonton in early May 1892, and advised him as to where the survey marks needed to be replaced and where subdivision was most urgent.

The Edmonton district comprised a total of eighty-seven townships whose outlines had been run in 1879 and the early 1880s. In 1892, the pressure was to subdivide thirty-nine of these for immediate settlement. Dominion Land Surveyors James Gibbons, Arthur St. Cyr, Ernest Hubbell, and Charles Miles had their work cut out for them. They were charged with the "renewal" of survey marks, but soon discovered that most of them were obliterated. In order to re-establish the survey marks, they found it was necessary to painstakingly rerun each survey line and chain from post to post. This was time-consuming; in many cases, it took more time than the original survey. Charles Miles, working east of the Fort Saskatchewan area, noted that fires had changed the landscape from its appearance a decade earlier, and according to James Gibbons, the posts, if not burnt away, were submerged beneath dead grass. There was nothing to be done other than to resurvey the line.[27]

Settlers searching for their property lines also found posts and mounds in the Edmonton district that did not agree with the subdivision surveys. Dennis investigated and declared they were from survey lines run by Montague Aldous, DLS, DTS, from the Fourth to the Fifth Meridian under the First System of Survey in 1879. They were still in good condition, but "as neither their positions nor markings agreed at all" with the Third System of Survey, Dennis ordered their removal by the surveyors working on the re-establishment of survey marks in the area. The following summer, the re-marking of corners was extended to the Wetaskiwin area.[28]

On June 14, 1900, twenty settlers across two townships in the Ross Creek area, just east of

Edmonton, petitioned the surveyor general for a complete resurvey because they were not satisfied with the process of restoring survey marks underway. Charles DuBerger, DLS, was apparently only putting in new marks where he could actually find old ones, of which there were very few. Settlers were quick to pinpoint the problem: "It leaves us without any means of determining where our corners and section lines are, for doing local improvement works etc." Next there were complaints from a third adjacent township where DuBerger, prone to rheumatism, was expected but never turned up. In late summer, a Mr. Cryderman expressed the displeasure of the settlers: "There have been a good many claims taken in this district but they are all waiting for the surveyors to stake out the township so that they can build on them. If the Government don't soon get in here with the surveyors we will all leave here and go back to the States where they have the claim staked out as soon as you file on it."[30] While such problems were being resolved in the townships of the Edmonton area, theoretically open for settlement, initial subdivisions were also being made in central Alberta along the Calgary and Edmonton Railway from 1892.

## Township Subdivision East and West of the Calgary and Edmonton Railway

The number of settlers who arrived in central Alberta in 1892 was greater than anticipated. Only seven surveyors had been contracted to do subdivision work. As they raced to subdivide townships they found some townships already had up to twenty settlers. The surveyors' most urgent work lay fairly close to the railway line, particularly around Olds, as well as east of Bowden, and Innisfail. They subdivided townships in the Pine Lake area and east of Red Deer, as well northeast of Wetaskiwin, around Coal Lake, west and east of Bittern Lake, and in the Beaverhill Lake area.[31] By the end of the season it was clear that more surveyors would be needed.

As the trains rolled north from Calgary in 1893, they pulled settler cars containing the worldly goods and livestock of immigrants from the US to the central parkland. Half of the settlers in 1893 hailed from the US, one-third from Canada, and one-sixth from Britain and Europe; all aboard scrutinized the burgeoning towns along the route. R. L. Alexander, the government's official travelling immigration agent, made sixty-seven round trips on the Calgary and Edmonton line from the end of March, chatting with settlers, praising the soil's potential bounty, and giving out information he had gleaned while out driving around the townships adjacent to the rail line.[32]

In order to meet the anticipated demand for land in 1893, the Topographical Surveys Branch began work two months earlier than in 1892 and let contracts to subdivide an approximate total of one hundred townships of parkland. These townships were spread over a wide geographical range, forming three distinct areas. The first area lay east of Red Deer to the north and south of the Red Deer River into the Buffalo Lake area. Charles Magrath, DLS, DTS, taking a break from irrigation endeavours, subdivided a township in the ranchlands south of Erskine to the west of Ewing Lake, and townships north and south of the Red Deer River stretching from Haynes to Delburne. The second area lay north and south of the Battle River, in the area around the Red Deer, Battle, and Dried Meat Lakes. The third and largest area lay to the northeast of Edmonton, south of the North Saskatchewan River and along both sides of the Vermilion River.

In 1892 immigrants from Galicia and Bukovina, provinces in the Austro–Hungarian Empire, today located in Ukraine, formed a nucleus settlement at Edna northeast of Edmonton. Settlers gradually took up homesteads in the townships spreading east from Edna, reaching the Whitford Lake area by 1898. The survey of a large block of townships for Ukrainian settlers began in 1893. Six surveyors, including Thomas Chalmers and Charles Duberger, surveyed townships south and east of Vegreville in the Beaverhill Lake area, townships north to Whitford Lake, and east as far as the area north and south of Hairy Hill. In 1894 and 1895, only one surveyor, Ernest Hubbell, was subsequently needed to continue subdivision work in east central Alberta, to the east of Vegreville, as well as opening up land south of Lamont and north of Two Hills. This met the demand for homesteads until subdivision resumed in the area in the early years of the twentieth century.

By the mid-1890s, settlers were also braving the bush country of central Alberta, west of the Calgary and Edmonton Railway. Here the aspen parkland gave way to boreal–cordilleran forest. On the advice of the Dominion Land agent in Red Deer, surveyors went west to begin the work of township subdivision. In 1895 Joseph Woods, DLS, subdivided the first seven townships west of the Fifth Meridian in central Alberta. He worked west of Olds, Red Deer, and Bowden, as well as around Gull Lake. Along the Medicine River, Woods encountered immigrants from Iceland. He noted they lived "entirely by ranching and dairying, sending their milk in summer and winter to a creamery four or five miles east of the settlement." Woods was impressed by what he saw in this area, now known as Markerville: "There are good trails all through this settlement, the principal ones leading to the creamery and to Tindasoll post office, five miles distant." [33] Woods also subdivided townships west of Gull Lake and mapped the intersection of several trails, and a section of the old trail to Rocky Mountain House. [34] Later in the season, Woods paid off most of his party and built a homemade "jumper" or sleigh. He then set off to run a traverse survey of the Medicine River and of Gull Lake, in January 1896. [35]

Woods and other surveyors ran into settlers established in their townships ahead of the survey. In 1892 Dennis pointed out that while the survey should not get too far ahead of settlement—to avoid re-survey problems such as those in the Edmonton area—it certainly should not be following settlement. [36] Squatters, nevertheless, were always ahead of the survey, and dealing with them became part of the surveyor's work. Surveyors recorded statutory declarations, or squatters' statements on their land claims and improvements, in support of homestead application, thus preventing a homestead application by others.

When Arthur Wheeler, DLS, subdivided two townships around Whitford Lake south of Victoria Settlement in the fall of 1892, he encountered a total of seventeen settlers, some of whom had large families. Camped on the west side of the lake, Wheeler wrote in his field notebook: "The settlers seem to be a thrifty hardy lot, anxious to improve their holdings and well satisfied with the same. All state that they would have made greater progress but for uncertainty as to their location on even [numbered] sections." Wheeler noted that when he arrived, "new houses and house warmings were the order of the day and great plans were laid for future action." [37]

Although the Métis whom Wheeler encountered at Whitford Lake spoke English, language barriers could present problems in taking statutory declarations. Richard W. Cautley, DLS, working in 1903 in a township south of Vilna, found several settlers to be "improperly located." Unable to com-

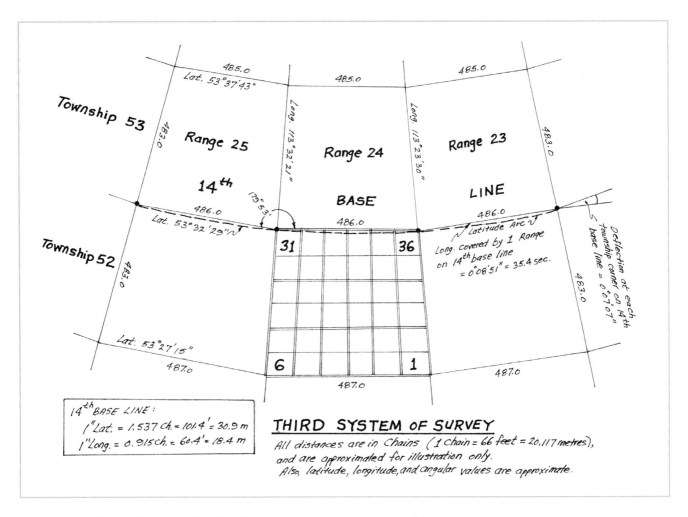

*Township 52, Range 24, West of the Fourth Meridian, showing the convergence of the meridians.*
DOUG BARNETT, "EARLY SURVEYS AND SETTLEMENTS IN CENTRAL ALBERTA,"
UNPUBLISHED MANUSCRIPT, 2001

municate with the settlers affected, he suggested that either an interpreter should be supplied or someone who spoke Russian should be sent out to take the declarations.[38]

Squatters took a risk in settling on land that was unsurveyed; most had no idea where they were in relation to the section and township lines or road allowances that would be laid out. They might have settled on an odd-numbered section reserved for the CPR or Hudson's Bay Company. Some squatters tried to be sure where they were in relation to a survey mark. In 1896, when Ernest Hubbell arrived east of today's Sherwood Park to do a subdivision, he found settlers had "gone to the trouble of running lines and taking measurements, so as to locate on the proper sections."[39] Others were not so careful. John Garnett, in the Pincher Creek area, watched a surveyor mark out section corners, realizing to his horror that his expensive house lay on the road allowance between two sections. Garnett applied to have the road allowance diverted, pleading considerable financial loss and arguing that it was not particularly suitable ground for a road.[40]

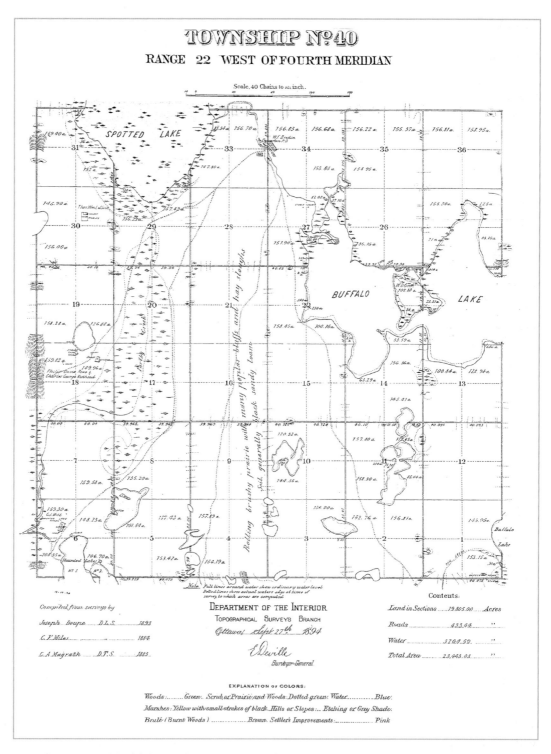

# TOWNSHIP Nº 40
## RANGE 22 WEST OF FOURTH MERIDIAN

Scale, 40 Chains to an inch.

SPOTTED LAKE

BUFFALO LAKE

Note. Full lines around water shew ordinary water level
Dotted lines shew actual waters edge at time of
survey, to which areas are computed.

Contents:

Compiled from surveys by

Joseph Doupe, D.L.S. .............. 1893

C.F. Miles .............. 1884

L.A. Magrath D.T.S. .............. 1883

DEPARTMENT OF THE INTERIOR
TOPOGRAPHICAL SURVEYS BRANCH
Ottawa, Sept. 27th 1894

E. Deville
Surveyor-General

Land in Sections .......... 19,805.00 Acres
Roads .......... 433.44 "
Water .......... 3209.59 "
Total Area .......... 23,443.03 "

EXPLANATION of COLORS:

Woods: ......... Green. Scrub or Prairie and Woods: Dotted green. Water .......... Blue.
Marshes: Yellow with small strokes of black. Hills or Slopes: .. Etching or Grey Shade.
Brulé (Burnt Woods) .............. Brown. Settler's Improvements: .............. Pink

*Joseph Doupe, DLS, subdivided this township in 1893, working from township outline survey marks established ten years earlier. By the early 1890s this was ranching country, served by trails from the Red Deer River crossing at Tail Creek to the south and from Lacombe to the west. All trails converged at a collection of log cabins at Lamerton. Here was William Bredin's trading post, where he sold flour and other provisions and distributed the mail hauled from Lacombe.*

*Township 40, Range 22, West of the Fourth Meridian.*
DIRECTOR OF SURVEYS OFFICE

## How Was a Township Subdivided?

Surveyors subdivided each township within an outline block of sixteen townships. It was a complex procedure that had to take the curvature of the earth into consideration in order to ensure closure of the survey. The subdivider generally began at the NE corner of Section 33, previously established on the baseline. Working from astronomical observations, he ran a true north-south line (i.e., 90° to the baseline) twelve miles north and twelve miles south of the baseline. He then laid out sections and quarter sections on that control meridian and placed the required monuments. Next he ran the other north–south lines off the baseline by turning the appropriate angle to create the proper convergence of each of the section lines, which were then chained out along with the road allowances and marked with monuments.

The surveyor also did a traverse survey of any lakes and rivers encountered. He carried a series of traverse lines forming a polygon around the perimeter of a lake, and eventually plotted the sinuous line of the bank by making offset measurements from the traverse to the bank. The portion of a lake in any given quarter section was subtracted from the approximately 160 acres of the patent to the quarter section. The surveyor also noted trails and settlers' improvements such as houses, barns, corrals, fences, and acreages under crop. As on all surveys, each surveyor kept a diary and a set of field notes, which were accompanied by a report on the character of the township—soils, availability of water and timber—in a regulation notebook.

The surveyor sketched all the prominent topographical features and marked the number of acres in each quarter section. All the information—diary, notes, and sketch map—was sent as his return of survey to the surveyor general's office in Ottawa to be checked and compared with the findings of the inspector of surveys, who would have visited the surveyor in the field. Finally, all corrections done, signed, and confirmed by the surveyor general, a first township survey map was printed in colour by the Topographical Surveys Branch and became the first official plan of that particular township.

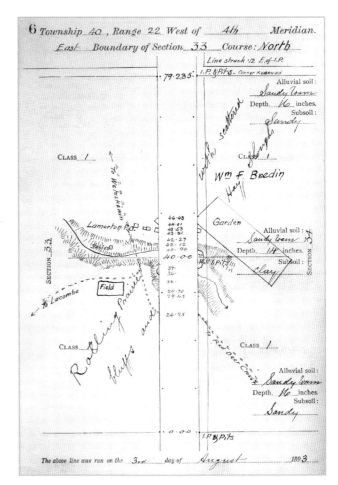

*Page from Joseph Doupe's Field Note Book 1347a, 1893,*
*for Township 40, Range 22, West of the Fourth Meridian.*
PAA, 83.376, FIELD NOTE BOOK 1347A, 1893, REPRODUCED WITH
THE PERMISSION OF THE SURVEYOR GENERAL OF CANADA LANDS

Surveyors recorded field measurements using split line field notes. The line that was surveyed in the field was split into two imaginary parallel lines when marked in the notebook. The split line notes are always along the east or north boundary of the section, and the direction of the line was marked on top of the page. The line always begins at chainage 0.00, on the bottom of the page. In this example, 0.00 is on the south or northeast corner of Section 28, from where the line was run north along the east boundary of Section 33. The distances between various features that intersected the line are marked in chains between the two lines. Thus, it was 6.43 chains from the half-mile point at 40.00 chains, to where the small corner of Bredin's garden was found to lie in northeast Section 33, while the rest lay in northwest Section 34.

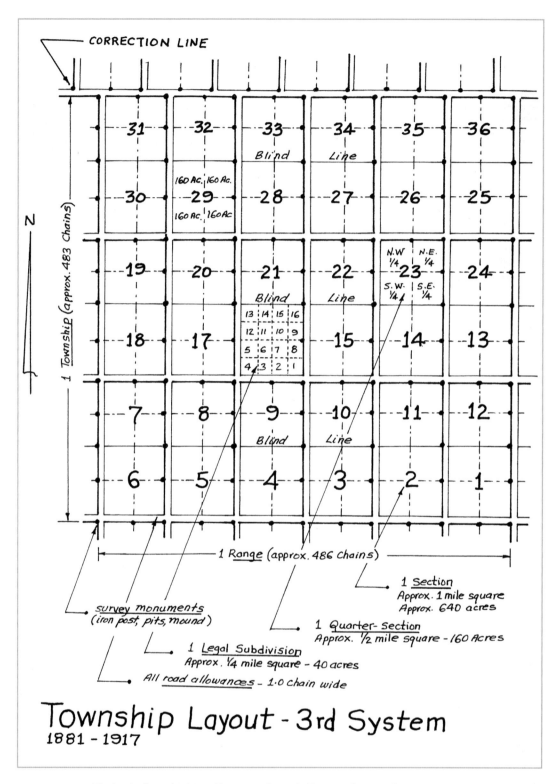

CORRECTION LINE

| 31 | 32 | 33 Blind | 34 Line | 35 | 36 |
| 30 | 160 Ac. 160 Ac. 29 160 Ac. 160 Ac | 28 | 27 | 26 | 25 |
| 19 | 20 | 21 Blind | 22 Line | N.W ¼ N.E. ¼ 23 S.W. ¼ S.E. ¼ | 24 |
| 18 | 17 | 13 14 15 16 / 12 11 10 9 / 5 6 7 8 / 4 3 2 1 | 15 | 14 | 13 |
| 7 | 8 | 9 Blind | 10 Line | 11 | 12 |
| 6 | 5 | 4 | 3 | 2 | 1 |

N

1 Township (approx. 483 chains)

1 Range (approx. 486 chains)

1 Section
Approx. 1 mile square
Approx. 640 acres

1 Quarter- Section
Approx. ½ mile square - 160 Acres

survey monuments
(iron post, pits, mound)

1 Legal Subdivision
Approx. ¼ mile square - 40 acres

All road allowances - 1.0 chain wide

# Township Layout - 3rd System
### 1881 - 1917

*The details of township layout. Every two miles, road allowances of sixty-six feet ran east–west,
intersected every mile by a road allowance running in a north–south direction.*

DOUG BARNETT, "EARLY SURVEYS AND SETTLEMENTS
IN CENTRAL ALBERTA," UNPUBLISHED MANUSCRIPT, 2001

*Ernest Hubbell, DLS, and crew in camp during a township subdivision survey, 1900.*
*There is a visitor in camp—a fox, visible in the left foreground.*
ALSA, MISCELLANEOUS COLLECTION

This formally created the boundaries, allowing patents to be issued and certificates of title subsequently obtained through a district Land Titles Office. Under the Torrens system of land registration[41] adopted in western Canada, the government acts as the keeper of land records, and by showing all interest in and changes of ownership the certificate of title ensures indefeasibility of ownership.

## SURVEYORS PROVE THEIR RESILIENCE

Surveying in the parkland or bush country to the northeast of Edmonton and west of the Calgary–Edmonton Trail was a more challenging operation than the townships of the open plains of southern Alberta. Axemen, hired to cut a sight line through the trees or bush, became an important component of any parkland survey party. It was common practice to hire axemen as needed in the area being surveyed. At Whitford Lake, Arthur Wheeler engaged Daniel Laboucon and Joseph Paul, who then moved with the survey party to the east side of the lake. The more heavily wooded country southwest of the lake required the services of additional axemen, including Métis homesteaders Charles Monkman and James Whitford.[42]

Many of the trails across the parklands were in such poor condition that even travel to the survey area was time-consuming. When Ernest Hubbell set out to survey some eighty-four miles of line in the area around Victoria Settlement on the North Saskatchewan River in 1893, it took two days to travel the first twenty-four miles. The trail south of the river to Fort Saskatchewan was in poor shape, so the wagons had to be unloaded, teams doubled up, then reloaded, to negotiate mud holes. From Fort Saskatchewan, the trail to Victoria was swampy and the mud was like glue. "To add to the harmony, the mosquitoes appeared in Myriads," Hubbell reported. "I do not exaggerate when I state that at times we could not tell the colour of a horse; the pests made the horses almost unmanageable, and at the end of every few miles we were compelled to stop and make smudges for them and ourselves. They were so bad in the vicinity of Beaver Lake we had to abandon travel for the greater part of the day, resuming our course during the cool of the night."[43]

Bush or grass fires were perhaps a greater hazard than mosquitoes. Two years later, in 1895, Hubbell was back in the area south of Victoria. A spring fire had swept through, obliterating survey marks, making it not only hard to survey, but to find fodder for his horses or even a patch of ground on which to pitch his tent.[44] On October 14, Hubbell's party completed the survey. Having just turned in for the night, they got a terrifying shock. "Fire came down on camp at 11:30 PM just in time to save camp and get out, entire country round burnt out," Hubbell tersely recorded in his diary as the shaken party set out for Edmonton.[45]

River crossings proved hazardous, as few bridges had been constructed before the turn of the century. When Joseph Woods forded the Red Deer River six miles west of Innisfail in 1895, he found the water was so high that he had to swim the horses across, while the supplies were safely brought over in a boat. The carts and buckboard were loaded down with stones to stop them overturning. Once out in the current, they could be guided with a rope from the boat, "for a great part of the distance they were entirely out of sight under water."[46] That same year, Hubbell had his heart in his mouth each time he crossed the North Saskatchewan River, north of present-day Two Hills, at Todd's Crossing in "a species of sieve, by courtesy termed a boat," borrowed from Mrs. Todd. "It was with a prayer of thankfulness we landed after each crossing, as it took at least one man bailing all the time to keep down the water which rushed in through the cracks in the boat."[47] Such moments of adrenalin were in contrast to hours of monotony slogging through bush and trees.

Wet summer conditions made surveying tedious. Being constantly wet did little for Charles DuBerger, who suffered from rheumatism to the point that he was unable to fulfill his subdivision contract in townships southeast of Edmonton in 1898.[49] James McLean, DLS, in the same area the next summer, noted it was too wet to survey as there were six to twelve inches of water in the marshes around lakes. "I therefore decided that I would gain time by returning and surveying them after the ice formed."[50] In the hilly bush country west of Gull Lake, William O'Hara, DLS, found that the wagon and horses he had were quite unsuitable. As three of the horses went lame and another died, he recommended the use of pack outfits with light horses or pack ponies for such conditions in the future.[51]

Surveyors in the west country soon ran into a different kind of trouble. Township block outlines had not been completed. Rather than being surveyed all at once, they were done piecemeal as required for township subdivision in the immediate vicinity. William O'Hara was sent out to run block outlines west of Gull Lake in spring 1900 to prepare for township subdivision. When O'Hara

## Surveying on Koney Island

In summer 1895 Ernest Hubbell was no doubt happy to do a traverse survey of Koney Island in Cooking Lake, not least as it broke the survey routine and offered some social interaction. Cooking Lake was a popular summer boating destination in the 1890s, and a group of Edmontonians had acquired a six-acre island retreat off its southwest shore. Here among the spruce trees, the Koney Island Club had built a fine clubhouse surrounded by several cottages. One of the members, Dr. Goodwin, lent Hubbell a club boat to land on the island. Although a tremendous storm brewed up the night Hubbell was there, he concluded it offered a "splendid rendezvous" for club members, and was a tranquil and exceedingly picturesque spot.[48]

got there, he discovered the baselines were almost entirely obliterated by fresh growth, and the old stumps of posts rotted away. Along the 12th Baseline, the country had been burned clean: "There are no mounds or pits and I find it absolutely necessary to re-survey and open the baseline to enable me to find the posts."[52] Hot on O'Hara's heels were his colleagues Angus McFee and Robert Lendrum, DLS, ready to subdivide the townships.

## SURVEYORS DEMAND MORE PAY

By the turn of the century an economic boom was getting underway in Alberta. James Wallace, DLS, found that men employed on his survey party in the west country of central Alberta refused to work in swamps for the traditional dollar-a-day. Wallace was given permission to pay his men $1.50 per day due to "exceptional circumstances."[53] The circumstances were not, however, so exceptional. Surveyors made repeated complaints on their inability to keep men on their parties. In 1902 Gerald Longeran, DLS, pointed out that in southern Alberta a man could get forty-five dollars a month during roundup, and during haying season from mid-July to mid-September a man could get about the same. Men who had spent half their life in a saddle, according to Lonergan, would "not work with a pick and shovel or swing an axe, which is the only work to be done on a survey."[54] By 1902 surveyors working in Alberta also felt that their own remuneration for township subdivision work done under contract, even as recently updated and fixed by order-in-council in 1901, was unfair.

The surveyor general sought the opinion of several surveyors. Charles Duberger, writing from Strathcona on November 7, 1902, commented that while the rate for prairie work at seven dollars per mile was reasonable, where prairie was thickly scattered with marshes, or in broken and hilly land with soils that were often hard, it was not. In his estimation, twenty-one dollars per mile was closer to fair in those conditions. Work in heavy bush, where a surveyor could hardly do more than one hundred miles in the space of twenty weeks, was another matter again. Duberger thought the fairest method of deciding payment was according to the classification of the land being surveyed, suggesting that in bush country, for example, payment should be as high as fifty-six dollars per mile.[55] James Wallace suggested the rate should be thirty dollars in heavily timbered country if level, and if hilly, thirty-five dollars per mile. Wallace spelled things out clearly: "Such things as rivers in flood, men deserting, roads being impassable, horses and men getting sick, and the surveyor's own health breaking down, are not at all remote contingencies in heavily timbered country, and such things may make the surveyor helpless to carry out his contract, through no fault of his own, except, perhaps, his want of foresight in taking such work under contract at all."[56]

The surveyor general succeeded in getting rates of pay increased for his surveyors in the field for 1903, to just short of double the rates paid a few years previously. Most surveyors preferred contract work to daily pay, despite the risk involved. In summer 1904, Archibald Ponton, DLS, agreed to subdivide townships on the edge of the foothills on contract. He soon demanded an extra allowance of four dollars per mile to cover the conditions encountered—mountain peaks, deep valleys, muskegs. Deville concluded that in the end, no matter "how high the rates of pay are some surveyors will always be found who will manage to lose money where others are making fair profits."[57] Nevertheless, the rates of pay were again readjusted in 1908. Dominion Land Surveyors had shown that they would continue to make demands about the conditions of their work and pay even before the challenges of surveying in Northern Alberta that were soon to come.

### Finishing the Job for the New Province of Alberta

After 1900, the maps that accompanied the instructions to surveyors showed an ever-increasing number of townships blocked out in pink, indicating that subdivision had taken place. In 1901 subdivision was being completed on lands east of Red Deer along the river. James Wallace ran township outlines, while Hugh McGrandle, DLS, subdivided several townships around Pigeon Lake. Angus McFee subdivided six townships west of Sylvan Lake in 1901 and, in 1902 took on another six that lay to the south of the lake and townships west of Olds. Townships south of Medicine Hat and in the Cypress Hills were surveyed next to meet a new demand for land there. The townships included in the land grant of the Alberta Railway and Coal Company's line south from Lethbridge were surveyed in 1900, allowing Charles Magrath, DLS, its land commissioner, to sell farmland to settlers.

In December 1902, Surveyor General Edouard Deville sought the opinions of the Dominion Land agents in Alberta as to where the next major push for township subdivision should be. In Red Deer, W. H. Cottingham, in anticipation of the arrival of a large number of people the next spring, suggested that as many townships as possible both east and west of Red Deer should be subdivided. In Calgary, the Dominion Land agent urged the subdivision of townships in the Sundre area and along the Little Red Deer River, among several other areas. The Dominion Land agent in Edmonton stressed the Strawberry Creek area because he had received many inquiries about it. The other area in demand was around Viking where over fifty homesteaders wished to apply for homestead entry. In addition, Cottingham pinpointed the new demand for townships north of Edmonton after the turn of the century, particularly those in a northwesterly direction, which would open up the country from Lac Ste. Anne to Fort Assiniboia and along the old HBC trail to Grande Prairie.[58]

In 1903, despite a word of caution from William Pearce, who believed that an "appalling amount of speculative homestead entry had taken place in certain localities,"[59] township subdivision pushed ahead in the North-West Territories in general. It reached a peak in 1903 and the first six months of 1904. The greatest number of townships subdivided—except the area west of Saskatoon—was in Alberta, and lay to the north and west of Edmonton and to the west of Red Deer. Never, since 1883, had there been so many townships subdivided. The acreage covered by surveyors was quite staggering: it was not much short of the area of Nova Scotia or about two-thirds of Scotland or Ireland.[60] As it turned out, more townships than were immediately needed had been subdivided in 1903–4. Finally, the surveyors were ahead of the settlers who arrived in unprecedented numbers after 1900. By 1905 huge tracts of land were marked out as the Alberta welcomed prospective farmers. Only the eastern reaches of the new province and the great expanse of Alberta's north remained to come under the surveyors' chains. The geographical focus of surveys for settlement was soon to shift as railway developers urged immigrants to turn their eyes to the Peace River Country—the next area to be surveyed for settlement.

## CHAPTER SIX

# A Region Apart
*Surveying in Alberta's North*

## EXTENDING THE GOVERNING LINES OF SURVEY INTO THE PEACE RIVER COUNTRY

William Ogilvie, DLS, and William Thompson, DLS, DTS, set out from Edmonton in 1882 to begin the survey of the Peace River country. Ogilvie ran the Fifth Meridian, which Montague Aldous, DLS, had established near Edmonton with so much difficulty in 1879, north as far as the Athabasca River. Thompson headed straight to Lesser Slave Lake. At the confluence of the Athabasca River and the Lesser Slave River—some distance west of where he judged the Fifth Meridian to lie—he blazed a tree, marking the station 'O.' Here, he left a note for Ogilvie requesting that he send the position of this point in relation to Ogilvie's Fifth Meridian line. Thompson ultimately hoped to tie this bearing into his own calculations for the Sixth Meridian to the west. From the head of Lesser Slave Lake, he ran a survey line as far west as the Sixth Meridian in the Birch Hills, south of the Peace River. From there, Thompson's axemen cut a line as the chainmen measured north across the Peace River and into the Whitemud Hills. Thompson continued the line north along the Sixth Meridian between the 21st and the 26th Baseline, and west to the unsurveyed boundary of British Columbia.

William Ogilvie travelled to the Peace River Country in July 1883, to run the 21st Baseline through the open country on each side of the Sixth Meridian. This established the basic governing lines of survey for initial township outlines and subdivisions. Ogilvie then ran the outlines for two townships in the Waterhole (today's Fairview) area. There several pioneer farmers from Ontario had settled, along with the brothers Brick—sons of Anglican missionary John Gough Brick at Shaftsbury on the Peace River. Ogilvie also marked out a boundary line between the HBC reserve and the Oblate mission at Dunvegan.

These early surveys showed the Topographical Surveys Branch that surveying in the North posed many challenges. Thompson and Ogilvie, each with a party of twelve men, discovered that Dominion Land Surveyors working in the North were completely dependent on local Métis guides for transportation—hiring dog trains for moving supplies over the snow. Game proved to be scarcer in the winter months than anticipated, and supplies available from the HBC were limited because the surveyors had not made prior arrangements. The two surveyors found communication with each other, and with Ottawa, difficult to maintain. These difficulties highlighted the fact that the Athabasca and Peace Rivers—and the forests and muskegs that lay between them—remained virtually unknown north of latitude 55°. After 1883, the surveyor general opted to undertake cheaper exploratory surveys along principal waterways in northern Canada prior to any future surveys and township subdivision work in northern regions. Exploratory surveys garnered information on the topography and the conditions that surveyors would encounter, including possibilities for transportation routes and availability of supplies and guides. With this information, surveyors could plan their work more effectively.

In 1884 the Topographical Surveys Branch dispatched William Ogilvie on the first exploratory survey. Ogilvie was charged with two objectives: he was to traverse the Athabasca and the lower Peace River, and comment on the agricultural potential of the Peace River country. He set out on the Athabasca Trail from Edmonton arriving at Athabasca Landing on June 9, 1884. Ogilvie opted to run his own canoes downstream from the Landing rather than employ HBC scows. At the Landing, Ogilvie's party waited out several days of rain before finally setting out on the swollen river with heavily laden canoes. One canoe overturned at Long Rapids and a man drowned. Ogilvie explained what happened: "The accident was entirely due to the choice and actions of the men themselves. They started without my orders or knowledge, and chose a place for descending the rapids, which was not that pointed out to me, by a man I sent to examine them, as the best place to run." The next day, Ogilvie ran the rapids at his suggested spot with no further mishap, and the party moved on, reaching Fort McMurray on July 12, and then from Fort Chipewyan ascended the Peace River against a strong wind.

Ogilvie made traverse surveys as the party travelled the rivers. Using a micrometer to determine distances in conjunction with a transit, and a picket man at a base on the riverbank, he made accurate measurements of 1,050 miles. Along the route, Ogilvie pulled in with his canoe to inspect gardens and crops and spoke with traders and missionaries to assess the potential for agricultural settlement. On his 1884 expedition, Ogilvie was enthusiastic. "From Dunvegan," he wrote, "on the north side of Peace River, down the river to Peace Point, and thence to Salt River, on the Great Slave, there is a tract of country about 600 miles in length and forty miles wide of which a large percentage is fit for immediate settlement, and a great deal could easily be cleared."[1] In 1891 Ogilvie returned on another exploratory expedition to the Peace River. This time he questioned the viability of the land on the plateau above the fertile river flats, and concluded that he could not advise anyone seeking a home in the North-West to think of the Peace River Country.[2] Ogilvie's findings did not foster faith in the region and led to the postponement of settlement surveys. The soil and vegetation conditions of land further from the river remained an unknown, and it would be more than two decades later that subdivision surveys began in earnest in the Peace River Country.

In the late 1890s, however, the lure of gold rekindled the Dominion government's interest in northern Alberta. The great Klondike gold rush brought prospectors overland through the Peace River Country on their way to the Yukon. The consequent signing of Treaty Eight in 1899 and the influx of Métis and white settlers into Alberta's North spurred the development of a regional frontier commerce based on freighting and supplying of goods.[3] Surveyors laid out Indian reserves, settlements, and surveyed trails, as the grid of the Dominion Land Survey gradually extended northwards towards Alberta's northern boundary on the sixtieth parallel.

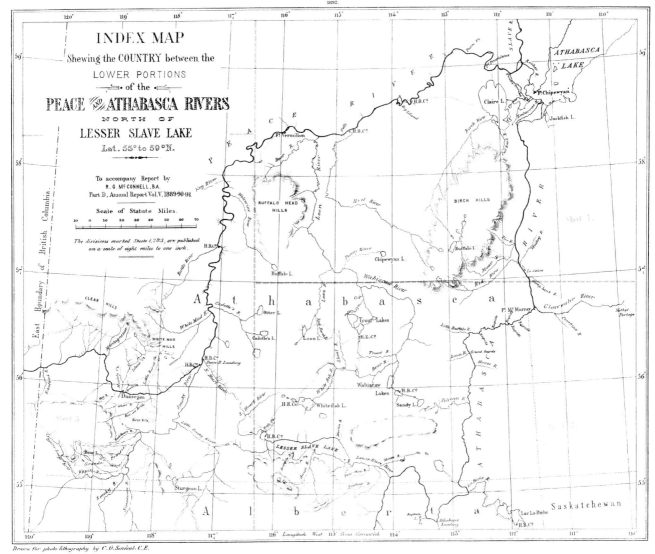

*This map showing the lower portions of the Peace and Athabasca Rivers north of Lesser Slave Lake,*
*was published by the Geological Survey in 1893.*

GEOLOGICAL SURVEY OF CANADA, ANNUAL REPORT, (NEW SERIES) VOLUME V, PART D, 1890–91. OTTAWA: 1893.

REPRODUCED WITH THE PERMISSION OF THE MINISTER OF PUBLIC WORKS AND GOVERNMENT SERVICES CANADA, 2004
AND COURTESY OF NATURAL RESOURCES CANADA, GEOLOGICAL SURVEY OF CANADA

In August 1896 George Carmack, Skookum Jim, and Tagish Charlie discovered gold at Bonanza Creek, a tributary of the Klondike River. The Dominion Land Survey was soon involved. When William Ogilvie, who had been surveying mining claims in the Yukon, sailed into San Francisco on a steamer from Alaska, newspapermen speculating on the value of its cargo mobbed the ship. News of Klondike gold spurred tens of thousands of men and some women—adventurers, dreamers, misfits, and the unlikely—from Canada, the United States, Britain, and a host of other countries to seek their fortune in the Yukon. It became the greatest gold rush the world has ever known. There were several ways of getting to the Yukon. One was the American route over the Chilkoot (Whitehorse) Pass, and another was the northern route via the Athabasca River and down the Mackenzie and the Peel or Liard Rivers. Another, and ultimately the most infamous route, was the overland route via the Peace River Country.

As the first groups of gold prospectors gathered in Edmonton, buying boats and supplies in early summer 1897, James McLean, DLS, surveyed the route from Edmonton to Athabasca Landing—the trailhead for the water route—for the North-West Territories government.[4] Frank Oliver, Edmonton's Liberal MP, endorsed the potential of Athabasca Landing as the jumping-off point for the Klondike. In April 1897, Oliver alerted Clifford Sifton, Minister of the Interior, to the pressing need for a settlement survey at Athabasca Landing where land disputes were hampering trade.[5] James McLean duly laid out river lots west of the HBC reserve as well as on its east side, where, in his view, a fine townsite could be located in the future. "The river landing for steamers is much better than at the H.B. Co.'s Reserve, and it is also less liable to ice jams."[6] By June 21, 1897, more than 130 boats had departed from the Landing for the Klondike, followed by every conceivable type of vessel that would float.[7]

In anticipation of profits to be made from the Klondike rush, the HBC had the reserve subdivided into forty 120-foot by 60-foot lots for sale in 1898. The small settlement at Athabasca Landing, consisting of HBC employees, independent traders, Anglican missionaries, and a NWMP detachment, mushroomed by spring 1898 into an often rowdy tent city of hundreds served by two hotels and a restaurant, four general stores, bakeries, a butcher and barber shop, along with half a dozen boat yards.

At the same time, Edmonton's merchants promoted an overland route via the Peace River Country—a route that would avoid US customs duties. On the map, it appeared a shorter distance than the northern water route; a desire to make the journey quickly, rather than surely, motivated the Klondikers who struck out overland early in 1897. Most parties who attempted it were ill-prepared and had little idea of the conditions: almost two thousand miles of frightful trails, timber, muskeg and mosquitoes, blizzards, snow blindness, frostbite, and hunger that lay ahead of them. Pressure to improve the overland route fell on the North-West Territories government in Regina, as it was responsible for surveying trails and roads. It sent two Dominion Land Surveyors on exploratory surveys to open up a road from Edmonton to Peace River and from there to the Nelson River.

The first section fell to Thomas Chalmers, DLS, who set out in September 1897 to survey a route from Fort Assiniboine (northeast of Edmonton on the Athabasca River) to Lesser Slave Lake.

He cut across the highest point in the Swan Hills to avoid muskeg south of the lake. Having surveyed a route, Chalmers assembled a road-cutting party and actually cut 240 miles of road in spring and summer 1898. Hundreds of prospectors who set out overland from Edmonton for the Klondike that year bypassed the traditional water route to Lesser Slave Lake via Athabasca Landing. Instead, many set out in winter 1898 in advance of Chalmers' road-cutting crew, to take the new Chalmers Trail through the Swan Hills to the south shore of the lake. An overwrought Chalmers, knowing prospectors were ahead of him as well as hot on his heels, hired whomever he could in summer 1898 to help cut the trail as they travelled its course. By July 28, he reached Lesser Slave Lake, leaving ten men working on improving the trail, which he declared was now passable all the way through for moderately loaded vehicles.[8]

Chalmers' opinion of his work proved wildly optimistic and tragically misleading. In July, Inspector Snyder of the NWMP described a treacherous part of the trail as it climbed about seven miles beyond the Salteaux River: "The rise up the mountain is long and not very steep, but the timber grew thickly and the trail is as yet very stumpy, making travel very difficult."[9] The trek to Lesser Slave Lake took months, not days, and the gold seekers ran out of feed for their horses. More than two thousand horses died on the Chalmers Trail because of poor packing techniques, exhaustion, and lack of feed. Prospectors avoided grazing their animals in the one stretch of country between Salteaux Creek and the Swan River where there was feed because of overzealous warnings of poisonous larkspur. Criticism of the trail,

### Transportation on the Great Rivers of Northern Alberta

The Athabasca River was the Hudson's Bay Company's link between Fort Edmonton, the rich fur resources of the Peace–Athabasca delta at the west end of Lake Athabasca and the far North. From Fort Chipewyan on Lake Athabasca, it was possible to navigate the Great Slave River north to Great Slave Lake, or the Peace River to the west. The HBC cut its own wagon road north from Edmonton to Athabasca Landing, upgraded its warehouse at the Landing to a trading depot, and in 1888 bought 640 acres of land around the post from the Dominion government at $2.00 per acre, plus $317.22 for the survey of the company reserve.[11] The Landing served as the point of departure for almost all survey parties and everyone else heading north from the 1880s to World War I.

Navigation on Alberta's northern rivers was a challenging undertaking. Men required strong backs for trudging the riverbanks harnessed to a towrope to "track" scows upstream, and steel nerves for shooting rapids and negotiating strong currents going downstream. On the Athabasca River, the Pelican and the Grand Rapids were the most exhilarating and dangerous areas of whitewater. During the 1880s, highly skilled HBC boatmen, who operated the company's scows, learned how to shoot these rapids. By 1882, the HBC managed to freight a boiler north to Fort McMurray for the S.S. Grahame, the steamer destined to ply the calmer waters between Fort McMurray and Smith's Landing (today known as Fitzgerald) just below the first rapids on the Great Slave River. The S.S. Grahame also steamed upstream on the Peace River from Lake Athabasca as far as the Vermilion Chutes north of Fort Vermilion. In August 1888, the S.S. Athabasca, a 160-foot steamer, was launched at Athabasca Landing to operate westwards upstream to Mirror Landing at the mouth of the Lesser Slave River.

touted by the government as a wagon trail, mounted. "The government should not have issued a map calling the blazed streak from Edmonton to Lesser Slave Lake a wagon road," Cornwallis King, DLS, of the Department of the Interior, wrote to William Pearce. King, horrified by the ugly scenes of dead animals and inept outfits he had witnessed on the trail, pointed out that an exploratory survey did not immediately result in a road. "A wagon road is a wagon road not a blaze on a tree."[10]

Angus McFee, DLS, of Innisfail, travelled over the Chalmers Trail through the Swan Hills in July 1898, heading for Peace River Crossing. McFee then took the trail from the Crossing to Fort St. John, which he reported was in good condition. His job was to explore a route for a wagon trail from Fort St. John on the Peace River to the forks of the Nelson River for the prospectors who had

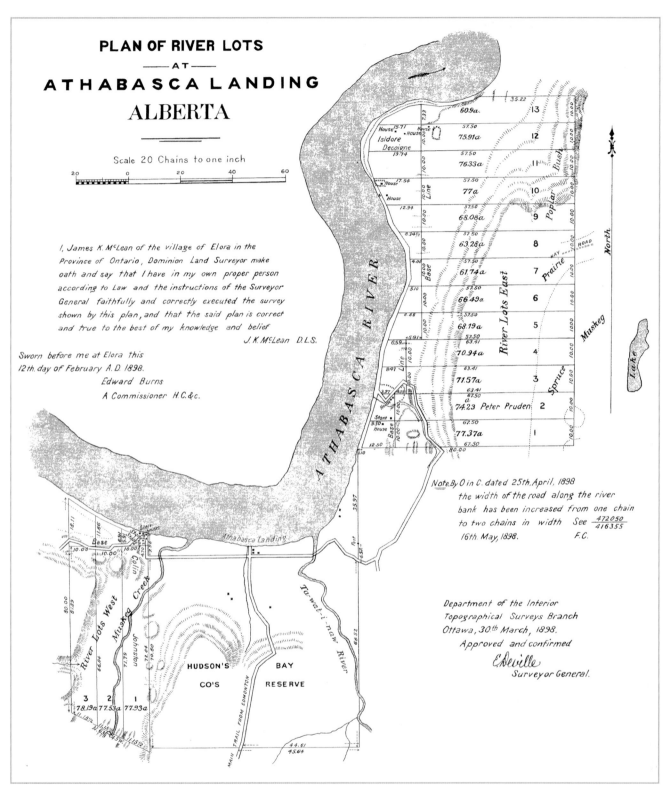

## PLAN OF RIVER LOTS
— AT —
## ATHABASCA LANDING
## ALBERTA

Scale 20 Chains to one inch

I, James K. McLean of the village of Elora in the
Province of Ontario, Dominion Land Surveyor make
oath and say that I have in my own proper person
according to Law and the instructions of the Surveyor
General faithfully and correctly executed the survey
shown by this plan, and that the said plan is correct
and true to the best of my knowledge and belief
                                    J.K.McLean D.L.S.

Sworn before me at Elora this
12th day of February A.D. 1898.
        Edward Burns
        A Commissioner H.C.&c.

Note. By O in C. dated 25th April, 1898
the width of the road along the river
bank has been increased from one chain
to two chains in width See 472050/416355
16th. May, 1898.                    F.C.

Department of the Interior
Topographical Surveys Branch
Ottawa, 30th March, 1898.
Approved and confirmed
        E.Deville
        Surveyor General.

*Official Plan of Athabasca Landing, 1898.*

made it that far.[12] In spring 1899, this time avoiding the Chalmers Trail to Lesser Slave Lake, McFee set out to survey a trail from Peace River Crossing to Pine River about ten miles from Fort St. John. As the *Edmonton Bulletin* explained, there was already a pack trail for part of this distance, "but Mr. McFee cut across the great bend of the pack trail north of Dunvegan, thereby shortening the distance considerably." McFee was impressed with the Peace River Country and declared there was "a grand field for development there when the area becomes more accessible."[13]

In the meantime, a railway line over the White Pass from Skagway to Bennett opened in August 1898. Prospectors no longer considered setting out on the overland route from Edmonton. The route that Chalmers had been instructed to survey had proved to be a disaster—the most horrific section of trail on the entire journey to the Klondike. The trail of death that bore his name was abandoned. Littered with horse skeletons, it was never to be re-surveyed or used again. Of the estimated fifteen hundred who ultimately attempted the overland route, fewer than half made it, and 10 percent turned back having gone less than a hundred miles.[14]

## SURVEYING OF LAND UNDER TREATY EIGHT AFTER 1899

The activity surrounding the Klondike gold rush affected Aboriginal peoples and disrupted traditional economic partnerships of the fur trade. In view of renewed interest in the agricultural potential of the Peace River area, the Dominion government decided it was time to seek a treaty with the Cree, Beaver, Slave, and later the Chipewyan, peoples of the north. In doing so, it also recognized that the situation in the North was quite different than it had been further south in the 1870s and 1880s. By 1899 there were so many people of mixed blood that all Aboriginal people, not just the Métis, were given the choice of taking reserve land or taking scrip, either in the form of certificates for 240 acres or $240 for the purchase of land. The Treaty and Half-Breed Commissions travelled north in 1899 to secure the signatories to Treaty Eight and to hear and investigate claims to scrip.

Treaty Eight was signed at Lesser Slave Lake in June 1899, with later additional signatories called adhesions in the years that followed. Unlike previous treaties, one clause specifically alluded to future surrender of reserve land surveyed under the Treaty for public works, buildings, railways, or roads. The first surveys for reserves under Treaty Eight were at Lesser Slave Lake, where small Native groups had located north of the lake, all claiming reserve lands. Dominion Land Surveyor Archibald Ponton surveyed two new reserves, Driftpile No. 150 and Sucker Creek No. 150A on the south shore. Ponton's hope that Natives in the area would move to one spot where there was better agricultural land was dashed as the Department of Indian Affairs continued to survey isolated small reserves around the lake in years to come.[15]

John Lestock Reid, DLS, spent the summer of 1905 in the Peace River area. He surveyed a series of small reserves for a Cree band at Peace River Crossing, near Shaftsbury Settlement, dividing Reserve No. 151 into several parcels.[16] Reid, who arrived at Sturgeon Lake on June 6, 1905, did not appreciate what he perceived as prevarication on the part of Indian bands in selecting their reserve lands. "These people, as usual, have a most inflated idea of the amount of land they are entitled to, after many meetings, and no end of explanations and talk, they finally told me they would not take any reservation."[17] Three years later, Reid finally ran the initial boundaries for Reserve No. 154 at

Sturgeon Lake. Only 5 percent of the land in the Peace River area was eventually set aside for reserves. Reserves were later relocated, or surrendered, as settlement progressed, keeping land surveyors busy for years.[18]

In view of the likelihood of many Aboriginal people opting for scrip rather than treaty benefits, the government set up the Half-Breed Commission to deal with the administration of scrip.[19] Working from their tent, the commissioners assessed claims accompanied by written documentation and checked lists to make sure that the claimants had not previously received scrip, before issuing certificates. There was, however, a major problem with scrip for land in the North. Surveyors had not yet subdivided the townships nor were there land offices established where settlers could make an application for homestead or purchase. The holders of scrip, then, could not immediately convert it into land. Many Aboriginal people sold their scrip certificates, impressed with the worth attached to them by the infamous "scrip buyers" who followed the commissioners north, ready to pay cash for the certificates. Although scrip was initially non-transferable, the demand for its sale mounted. In the field, the commissioners, in consultation with David Liard, Treaty Commissioner, made the decision to issue the scrip to bearer, thus allowing transfer. Ottawa subsequently accepted this decision.[20]

Anyone, Aboriginal or not, who occupied land with buildings in the North prior to Treaty Eight was entitled to a land grant of upward to 160 acres. Many of the settlers in tiny settlements along waterways wished to have this land as river lots. Albert C. Talbot, DLS, and his survey party arrived at Lesser Slave Lake in the very wet summer of 1901 to survey the land occupied around the lake into river lots. Talbot began his survey on the south side of the lake and then set out in his scow, rigged with a sail, across the northwest bay to the northern part of the settlement. Here he found that three successively wet summers had caused the water level to rise—flooding the hay lands under two or three feet of water. On June 1, the level of the lake stood four feet higher than usual, and it continued to rise another foot over the next two months. The Métis settlement had suffered, and at Willow Point, where a small village had sprung up during the rush to the Klondike, nearly all the houses surrounded by water lay abandoned. "It is doubtful," Talbot concluded, "if any of the original squatters in the village will ever ask for a grant of the land applied for, as everyone has left the

### Surveyor Searching for Rail Route Saves Scurvy Stricken Prospectors

Even the Canadian Parliament caught gold fever, taking the extraordinary step of voting monies in 1898 and 1899 for an exploratory survey for a railway route to the Yukon from Edmonton. Dominion Land Surveyor C. F. K. Dibble was placed in charge of the survey, which the *Edmonton Bulletin* declared, was really only necessary from Peace River Crossing to British Columbia, as the land in between was known and presented no obstacle to a railroad! Dibble and V. H. Dupont, DLS, who headed up a second party, went upstream from Peace River Crossing to Hudson's Hope and then parted company at the forks of the Parsnip and Finlay Rivers. Dupont worked back, seeking a rail route along the south side of the Peace to the British Columbia Boundary, while Dibble pressed northwest to find a route that would join the Peace and Stikine valleys. The *Bulletin* reported the progress of the survey at length, providing further information on the state of trails leading to the Yukon and generally fuelling interest in the Peace River Country.

In spring 1899, surveyor Dibble saw the worst tragedies of the frightful overland routes to the Yukon when his party encountered about fifty men wintering at Fort Graham in BC. Scurvy, an invisible scourge caused by a lack of vitamin C, had left many there sick. Several had already died. Dibble took a week to bring some of those stricken back to Peace River Crossing. On the way down, they found a cabin on Clearwater Creek where five men from Ontario lay dying from scurvy, too weak to bury their leader, who had died nearly two weeks previously. Horrified, Dibble's party interred the remains and carried the sick men with them to Peace River Crossing, where one later died. Dibble's rescue mission alerted the outside world to the horrors of scurvy among prospectors.

place and many have gone out of the country altogether." To receive the grant, the squatters would have been required to be in occupation before the Treaty.

Talbot then moved to the Roman Catholic Oblate mission to the north at the Lesser Slave Lake Settlement. Fortunately for Talbot, the survey party was able to take shelter at the mission during a nine-day storm of sleet and snow. When he had laid out lots there, including four for the Oblate fathers, Talbot surveyed north of Buffalo Lake (today known as Buffalo Bay, the west arm of Lesser Slave Lake) and laid out lots within the Heart River and Salt Prairie Métis settlements.[21] Talbot's survey revealed that the focus of Métis settlement had shifted further north to the Peace River Country, as well as to Fort McMurray on the Athabasca River. All eyes, it seemed, turned to the North, where settlement was to follow the extension of the Dominion Land Survey.

## SURVEYING NORTHERN BASELINES

Although Ogilvie and Thompson established the location of the 21st and the 23rd Baselines in the Peace River district in 1883, baselines lying to the south had not been surveyed. Dominion Land Surveyors, beginning in 1904, extended the grid of baselines in manageable sections north from the 14th Baseline that runs through Edmonton along Jasper Avenue. Arthur St. Cyr, James Wallace, and Henry Selby undertook the largest proportion of this costly work. In 1904 alone, the cost of baseline survey work amounted to fifty thousand dollars. Surveyor General Edouard Deville estimated in February 1905 that the following summer's work should not exceed $20,000, as surveyors were now aware of the difficulties and their survey outfits or camp equipment had been paid for.[22]

In 1905, while running the 19th Baseline west of the Sixth Meridian, Arthur St. Cyr made a startling discovery. The Sixth Meridian was in the wrong place. In 1883 Thompson had miscalculated the latitude, putting all the baseline posts about eleven hundred feet too far south and the whole line about five chains too far east. Rather than rerun the line, Deville instructed surveyors to allow for the error in their calculations and to move the posts to the correct latitude when the subdivision surveys got underway.[23] By 1906, consecutive baselines from the 16th through to the 20th Baseline that ran through the country just north of Lesser Slave Lake, connected the Fifth and Sixth Meridians.

Surveyors extended these lines in sections over the next couple of years. Archibald Ponton, extended the Fifth Meridian north to the southwest corner of what is today Wood Buffalo Park on the 27th Baseline in 1908. In 1910 James Wallace, ran the Fourth Meridian north as far as the 21st Baseline.[24] By 1915 surveyors had extended baselines into unexplored territory. As Deville explained, each party on a baseline or meridian survey had twenty-three men, enough to send additional men to explore the country for twelve miles on each

*Axemen hard at work, n.d.*
PAA, A.5543

side of the survey line, and their reports were used to produce maps showing topographical features, timber, and soil types.[25] These reports were then available in advance of the initial township outline and subdivision surveys, which followed close on their heels.

Baseline survey work was a gruelling exercise in axe work and endurance that demanded a high level of accuracy, and leadership to organize various parties of men working along the line. It was hard to secure enough surveyors with the superior abilities required to take on the rough demanding work. In 1907 Deville warned that subdivision could not proceed until the required baselines were marked: "The whole system of Dominion Land Surveys hangs on the baselines; if their accuracy is not perfect, every subsequent survey is bound to go wrong."[26] Despite Deville's concerns, the baseline surveys continued, first in the northwest to facilitate any further subdivision along the Peace River.

## TOWNSHIP SURVEYS FOR SETTLEMENT IN THE PEACE RIVER COUNTRY

As the baseline surveys crept ahead, they revealed the problems of transportation to the Peace River Country, its limited number of trails and lack of ferries—all a drawback to settlement. Officials in the Department of the Interior, including William Pearce, continued to question the extent and suitability of the area for farming. They worried about frosts, and above all, the lack of a railway to carry grain to market. Without a rail line, the scale of farming would remain at subsistence level. The promise of the Peace Country became a political issue and the voices who cautioned against it, including naturalist James Macoun—son of botanist John Macoun, who had extolled the virtues of the Peace Country in 1875—soon ran into opposition spearheaded by Edmonton's Frank Oliver, Minister of the Interior.[27] In Edmonton, where the festivities for the inauguration of the province were barely over, the Liberal Government, led by Alexander Rutherford, also set out to champion the development of the Peace River Country.

During 1905 the immigration agent in Edmonton received many inquiries about homesteading in the Peace River Country. However, as he pointed out, he could not recommend it, as township subdivisions had not begun.[28] There was one exception. In 1901 Charles Fairchild, DLS, subdivided a tract of land south of the fork between the Peace and the Smoky Rivers granted to the Peace River Colonization and Land Development Company. The plans of the poorly financed company came to naught, as in 1907 the first francophone settlers from Quebec found the land too wooded to clear for farming, and the grant was soon cancelled.

By 1908 baseline surveys were finally far enough along for township outline surveys to begin, along with some township subdivision around the previously surveyed settlements at HBC posts and missions at Spirit River, Dunvegan, Shaftsbury, Peace River Crossing, Fort Vermilion, Griffin Creek, and Little Prairie, where new settlers were expected to begin farming. Dominion Land Surveyors Henry Selby, Herbert Holcroft, and Jean Baptiste St. Cyr (brother of Arthur St. Cyr), began the next stage of surveying in the Peace Country. Speed was of the essence and surveyors were urged to use their discretion in subdividing. Surveyor General Deville grew impatient with delay in the completion of the survey of river lots at Dunvegan that was hindering subsequent subdivision of the land around. "You are not to leave surveys unfinished because of the objection of the

Royal North-West Mounted Police, the Hudson's Bay Company or other claimants," he admonished Holcroft in spring 1908. "If the lots laid out by you are not satisfactory to any of the claimants the matter can be fully adjusted afterwards. What is important is that the survey be finished so that the lands can be dealt with."[29]

The year 1909 marked the beginning of the real push for township subdivision in the Peace district, as the Canadian Northern Railway secured a charter to build two lines north; one only got as far as Sangudo, and the other reached Athabasca in 1912. Three years later Premier Alexander Rutherford made a flamboyant announcement of financing for J. D. McArthur's Edmonton, Dunvegan and British Columbia Railway. The Peace River County, it appeared, would have direct market transportation. Settlers would, however, have to wait for years, as the line was only constructed as far as Lesser Slave Lake by 1914, and it would be another two years before it reached Spirit River, with a branch line extending south to Grande Prairie. By 1916 the Central Canada Railway would serve the area between McLennan and Peace River town. In the meantime, township subdivision progressed in anticipation of the day it would be needed.

Walter McFarlane, DLS, a mathematics graduate of the University of Toronto, was fascinated with the idea of going to the Peace River Country. In 1909 he approached Deville for a two-year contract to do subdivision work. It was good timing, as in late 1908 Deville struggled to find surveyors willing to undertake the arduous contract work at the current rates of pay. McFarlane had thought his proposal through, noting that high wages would be required to get experienced men for his party. In early 1909 Deville offered McFarlane a thirty-thousand dollar contract for the subdivision of eighteen townships, partial subdivision of eleven others, and a ten-township outline survey in the Grande Prairie area between Smoky River and Beaverlodge. McFarlane left Edmonton on February 22, 1909, with thirty men, twenty-four horses, twenty tons of supplies, and four tons of iron posts—the largest survey party ever to head north from the city. By the time he returned in

## James Nevin Wallace, DLS, ALS, Placed in Charge of Levelling

In 1908 a system of taking levels on baselines and meridians began to furnish more accurate topographical details on the country being surveyed, and it was extended in 1915 to apply to all township subdivision lines.[30] James Wallace assumed charge of the new Levelling Office set up by the Topographical Surveys Branch in Calgary. While it was not required that a leveller be a Dominion Land Surveyor, it was necessary to have the precision skills levelling required. In 1915 Wallace instigated the "leveller's examination." Although in 1919 it came under the jurisdiction of Dominion Board of Examiners, Wallace continued to prepare and mark the examinations until 1925. Wallace wrote an account of early levelling operations that was published in 1916. His later *Benchmarks established along certain meridians, baselines and township outlines in Alberta*, published in 1924, was used extensively by surveyors working in Northern Alberta through the 1950s.

*James Nevin Wallace as a young man [ca. 1900].*
WALLACE FAMILY PAPERS

*Managing a scow on the Athabasca was no small feat.*
ALSA, RICHARDS COLLECTION, EDGAR MUMFORD ALBUM

December 1909, his survey had revealed that the extent of open prairie country was greater than formerly believed in Ottawa. McFarlane was so impressed with the Peace Country that he later took out a homestead, as did several of his survey crew, in the Buffalo Lakes area.[31]

Dominion Land offices opened in Grouard in June 1909 and in Grande Prairie in July 1911. Intending settlers could study a map for the areas surveyed to date and consider their prospects for filing a homestead in the Peace River Country, thrown open for homesteading in 1910. The pace of survey picked up in 1912, as eight parties worked in the Peace River region, some on ongoing baseline surveys to ensure the subdivision could be done as soon as possible. Among the surveyors who subdivided townships over the next few years were men beginning a surveying career in Alberta—Alex G. Stewart, Henry Soars, George Tipper, John A. Buchanan, Austin L. Cumming, William Waddell, and Harry S. Day. These men had an additional set of initials after their name, ALS. It stood for Alberta Land Surveyor. The Alberta Land Surveyors' Association, established in January 1910, was mandated under the Alberta Land Surveys Act of 1910 to regulate the profession of land surveying within the province of Alberta. Surveyors who set up surveying firms in Alberta also had the option of working for the Dominion government in unsurveyed territory or on Dominion Lands.

The surveyors' description of each township in the Peace River Country found its way into a guide to townships in the Peace River Country, published by the Department of the Interior in 1912. An expanded version entitled *Description of Surveyed Townships in the Peace River District in the Provinces of Alberta and British Columbia* was published in April 1916 as Bulletin No. 35 of the Topographical Surveys Branch. Surveyor General Edouard Deville noted in the preface: "The object of the 1916 publication was to place in the hands of prospective settlers, reliable, up-to-date

*Loaded sleighs edge their way north over the ice on the Peace River.*
ALSA, WEIR ALBUM

information, which will enable them to form a correct idea of the country in which they wish to take up land, and of the easiest and most economical method of reaching it." [32]

At the same time, the south Peace River Country, now served by railway lines, became the focus of a wild speculative real estate boom. Surveyors must have scratched their heads in disbelief as numerous companies advertised townsite lots for sale where they had just run their lines on virgin ground. Most outrageous was the speculation at Dunvegan, described as "the great Mecca of the North," where lots were for sale on the steep hillside that plunges to the river below. Nevertheless, the Dominion Land Survey had provided a guide for genuine settlers on the land, who were limited in number during the years of the Great War.

## THE CHALLENGE OF TRANSPORTATION AND SUPPLIES FOR SURVEYING IN THE NORTH

Surveyors bound for northern Alberta consulted with one another, reaping the experience of those who had made the trip before, or read the reports of those who had gone in previous years, often on the instructions of the surveyor general. Peace River Country surveyors had a choice in making their travel plans: for a short season's work they could go downstream on the Athabasca by scow, but for a long season they had to go in and out on the ice. Timing, in any arrangement, was therefore crucial. "A survey party should leave Edmonton as early as February 15 to be sure of the ice," Surveyor General Edouard Deville informed Henry Holcroft, DLS, in December 1907. "At most of the stopping places there is only enough hay to last the earlier part of the freighting season," Deville added. [33] Warnings such as this may have influenced the first six surveyors offered contract work in the Peace River area for the season of 1908—they declined the opportunity. [34] The logistical difficulties of northern surveys ensured that only the most intrepid surveyors took them on.

Generally, surveyors bound for the North arrived in Edmonton in January, put up in a hotel, and began organizing their parties and supplies. There were many things to arrange. The surveyor had to interview men for fitness and suitability. He had to calculate how many iron posts were required and hope that a sufficient number of them were available. He had to check all his equipment and instruments before going into the field, and calculate how much grub the party would need for months on end. Surveyors had to order, purchase, and load all the supplies required for the first leg of a journey that would last hundreds of miles.

Outfitting a survey party had a political dimension. The Hudson's Bay Company lost favour under a federal Liberal government from 1896 and no longer had a monopoly on supplying survey parties or transporting them north. Several general supply companies in Edmonton were on approved "patronage" lists and included Ross Brothers, McDougall and Secord, Gariepy and Brosseau, and Larue and Picard. From 1911, when Robert Borden and the Conservative party defeated Laurier's Liberal government, most surveyors, as dutiful civil servants, switched their outfitting to the merchants on the new patronage list for Edmonton and Strathcona. In 1913, Fred Seibert, DLS, and Guy Blanchet, DLS, caused a controversy when they bought supplies wherever they chose rather than from merchants on the government patronage list. Local barrister and politician A. H. Greisbach was quick to complain to Edmonton's Conservative MP in Ottawa of a

## The Heyday of Athabasca Landing

In spring 1907, settlers arrived every day at Athabasca Landing only to find all the available land taken up. Pressure mounted to have townships around the Landing subdivided quickly. Dominion Land Surveyor Jean Leon Côté, who had his eye on the work since the previous year, sought a contract to subdivide six townships in the immediate vicinity.[35] In November 1908, the Athabasca Landing Board of Trade passed a resolution calling on the Dominion and the provincial government to hasten the construction of a railroad between Edmonton and Athabasca Landing, which would eventually extend to Lesser Slave Lake and the Peace River district.[36] In the meantime, Athabasca Landing grew as the gateway for the North. The Hudson's Bay Company sold off the lots it had surveyed in its reserve for a townsite, and business expanded rapidly. The Canadian Northern Railway steamed into the Landing from Edmonton for the first time on May 25, 1912, and Athabasca Landing was advertised as the place "where rail and water meet."

Surveyor Jean Leon Côté was one of Athabasca's promoters. He entered politics in 1909, winning a seat in the legislature for the riding of Athabasca, to promote the development of Alberta's North. Côté opened a branch office together with his business partner, engineer Frank Smith. They prepared a map of the townsite for incoming settlers as well as real estate companies. In November 1912, the Athabasca Board of Trade petitioned the Department of the Interior for the survey of seventy more townships around the Landing.[37] The town of Athabasca, as the Landing was by then known, boomed. By 1913 approximately 2,000 people called it home. Then disaster struck—a flicker of flame turned into an inferno in the early hours of Tuesday, August 5, 1913, and almost half the business section of Athabasca turned to ashes. While its commercial boom came to an abrupt halt, Athabasca remained a gateway to the North for everyone heading for the Peace River Country or down the Athabasca River to Fort McMurray.

loss of "prestige and influence that the late government did not hesitate to secure to itself and friends." Not only do survey parties "outfit themselves with merchants hostile to us," he wrote, but also "they employ their gangs of men without any reference to us locally." Finally, he accused, "under the late administration survey parties had an awkward habit of turning up at remote polls and voting solidly for the late Government."[38]

The letter outraged Surveyor General Edouard Deville. While he would ask Seibert and Blanchet for an explanation, he informed the Minister's private secretary, the idea of not hiring surveyors previously employed under a Liberal government was impractical. Surveyors recommended by Greisbach, in fact, had been hired, he noted. However, it was Greisbach's request that he should be consulted as to the men employed in Edmonton for survey parties that really angered Deville. "The men wanted on surveys are common labourers; the work is hard and the life not pleasant. The kind of labourers surveyors are likely to obtain from the patronage committee will not feel inclined to work under such conditions when they are aware they hold political appointments and consider themselves independent of their chief." Never, he concluded, had surveyors been subjected to interference in the selection of their men.[39]

Surveyors finally had to make freight arrangements, arranging for scows at Athabasca Landing and teams of horses and sleighs or dog trains for later winter work. From 1902 Revillion Frères garnered a good deal of the freighting business for surveyors going north. Surveyors also had the choice of competitive prices offered by the Northern Transportation Company, whose steamers plied the waters of Lesser Slave Lake from 1902. By 1915 both the Northern Transportation Company and the HBC had steamers on the lower Athabasca and Peace Rivers.

It was impossible to carry all the supplies needed for the season for a northern survey with the main survey party. Surveyors arranged to have quantities of food, iron posts, and other supplies

*Cecil Hotel, Jasper Avenue, 1906.*
PAA, B.4339

### The Cecil Hotel

Among Edmonton's hotels, the Cecil, whose doors opened in October 1906, was a favourite among land surveyors bound for the North. Surveyors often noted they were staying at the Cecil, or used its letterhead in their correspondence with the surveyor general in Ottawa. There was a reason for the strong affinity land surveyors showed for the Cecil—the manager was C. Belanger, son of Phidime Belanger, DLS. The younger Belanger, whose name was most likely Cecil, had initially embarked on a career as a Dominion Land Surveyor, but decided to turn his attention to the hotel business. He understood the special requirements of surveyors—from storage of equipment to telegrams coming and going. In 1909 Belanger bought out a remaining third share in the hotel and expanded the premises, building forty new bedrooms fitted with baths, no doubt appreciated by weary surveyors, and enlarging the dining room. The improved Cecil Hotel became a central meeting point and reliable communication centre for surveyors in Edmonton through World War I.

## Grand Rapids on the Athabasca River

The talented pen of William Ogilvie first described the Grand Rapids. "Mid-way in the rapid is a large timbered island around which the waters sweep, and, converging below, rush through a channel not more than a 100 yards wide, while above the island the river is from 500 to 600 yards in width. The rush of water through this channel is tremendous, and reminds one forcibly of the rapids below Niagara Falls . . . one sees a spectacle that inspires with awe and wonder, and one that an artist would love to look upon and feel to be worthy of the best strokes of his brush."[40]

Freighters saw the rapids with a less romantic eye and were particularly wary of the three rocks in the east channel—the only way through. Heavy loads were a problem and the Hudson's Bay Company invested in a portage for the Grand Rapids by building a narrow gauge tramway on the island that divided the river into two channels. The scows unloaded at the head of the island, where freighters placed goods on flatbeds, which they pulled along the railway to the foot of the island. There the scows, able to negotiate the worst of the rapids while empty, were repacked. The scows then tackled the remaining rapids through the east channel. A pilot on the river, named Clark, used dynamite to blast two of the infamous rocks out while the river was frozen in spring 1898, making the channel less hazardous.[41]

The Grand Rapids, however, remained dangerous and time-consuming, as scows had to be tracked upstream through the rapids. It became quite a bottleneck on the Athabasca as the North opened up and traffic increased. Surveyor John Pierce, describing the scene in May 1915, noted the Grand Rapids had a temporary population of two hundred travellers in transit! By 1915, however, the settlement in the Peace River Country and the construction of the Edmonton, Dunvegan and British Columbia Railway as far as Peace River Crossing gave a new route to the north. The HBC moved its transport office from Athabasca Landing to Peace River Crossing and moved the tramway at Grand Rapids to the portage at Fort Fitzgerald.[42]

cached at convenient points to be accessed during the survey and brought into camp. Their assistants were often sent out ahead to arrange for hay to be cut during summer, and to see to the freighting of the goods. They also often arranged the building of caches. Sometimes caches were placed on stilts and then covered, but generally they were left in a small log cabin built for the purpose.

Accessing the caches later was not always easy, as Guy Blanchet discovered while working on the 23rd Baseline in 1911–12: "Snow storms on the 6th and 7th November marked the beginning of winter, the thermometer dropped to 30 degrees below zero. On November 9th I divided the party sending six men and four horses back to the Athabasca River, now 30 miles away, to open the pack trail into a sleigh road and bring up two sleigh loads of oats and supplies. Meanwhile, with remainder of the men and horses, I left to open up a trail to a cache at the Brule Rapids on the Athabasca and to locate, if possible, some hay which an Indian was to put up. Both parties encountered many difficulties and it was not until November 25th that the two parties united at the end of the line arriving within a few minutes of each other."[43]

Every surveyor's nightmare was to arrive at his cache during the survey to find the supplies missing. Predatory animals, particularly bears, were always a threat. In 1914 flooding on the Smoky River swept away a cache left by Austin Cumming, DLS, who was at pains to point out the high water level was an aberration, the

*One survey crew put the cookstove to work while waiting at Grand Rapids, 1915.*
ALSA, RICHARDS COLLECTION, EDGAR MUMFORD ALBUM

highest for twenty years according to "old-timers" in the area.[44] More alarming was the possibility of theft. While rare, it did happen. In 1911 Guy Blanchet sent one of his party ahead with a dog team to move supplies from one cache to another. When the man arrived at the cache, he was shocked to find it had been broken into. The thief had cut one of the pin logs, undone tie ropes, and removed part of the roof. The theft appeared to have taken place before the snow flew and there was evidence of a camp some distance away. A bear had also been there, he reported, but after the cache had been broken into, as the dirt he had dug out was on top of the removed parts of the cache. All he found of the fifteen hundred pounds of supplies left the previous summer

*Mud being carried for the roof of a cache for a survey party working on a section of the Fifth Meridian in 1909.*
GLENBOW ARCHIVES, NA-3471-14

was one box of baking powder, a box of butter, two pots, two empty boxes, an axe handle, and two bundles of iron survey posts.[45] Blanchet reported the robbery to the NWMP police detachment at Wabasca, who, not surprisingly, never caught the culprit.

Not only did the loss of a cache mean no food and other supplies, it also meant the surveyor was out of pocket for the cost of those supplies. In several cases involving trusted senior surveyors, it took about two years and a thorough investigation before the government would ante up the financial loss to the surveyor. In Blanchet's case, it was noted he had taken every precaution "to make the cache safe except leaving a cache keeper; had one been engaged, his wages would have amounted to more than the cost of the supplies."[46] In January 1916 the matter of the $187.34 owed to Blanchet was still before the Treasury Board. After a delay of sixteen months, Deville grew impatient; he warned the deputy minister that they would have to abandon the system of ration allowances as no surveyor could be expected to run the risk of such large expenses. This provoked an almost immediate and positive decision from the Treasury Board.[47]

## SURVEY CAMP LIFE

Survey parties in the North established a main camp, usually as close to the river they travelled along as possible. The first task was to unload the scow, or sleighs, depending on the season. Along with the tents, fragile surveying instruments, iron posts, and the party's personal belongings—blankets and clothes in a "dunnage" bag—were huge quantities of dry bulk food. While cached supplies were forwarded later to the camp at the survey location, considerable quantities of cases, boxes, and bags had to be packed up and moved each time the survey party moved camp. It was vital to keep the food dry, piled high inside large canvas tents. Each survey party had a camp range stove complete with pipes, pots and pans, plates, knives, forks, cups, and serving dishes. Everyone,

*Occasionally, someone had a musical instrument to start a band.*
ALSA, WEIR ALBUM

chainmen, mounders, axemen, labourers, and the surveyor's assistant—sometimes an articling student, sometimes a recently commissioned Dominion Land Surveyor—pitched in when on the move, each with an assigned task.

Surveyors knew of the danger of scurvy and carried dry vegetables such as split peas and beans, as well as dried fruit—evaporated apples, figs, prunes, and cases of currants. Cornmeal, rice, and pot barley were staples, along with dry salt pork, tea, and coffee. Baking ingredients included flour, baking powder, yeast, condensed milk, molasses, sugar, and salt. Some survey parties enjoyed semi-luxuries such as canned tomatoes and jam, depending how deep the pockets of their employer were. Survey parties carried guns to protect themselves and to ensure a supply of fresh food. They often hunted, and as numerous photographs taken in northern survey camps attest, wild game and fowl certainly graced the table of many a cook tent. Fried fresh fish was another treat, and sometimes all that lay between the surveyors' next meal and a long wait for cached supplies to arrive. As Fred Seibert recalled, his men caught jackfish with the help of pork fat.[48]

Some survey parties ate better than others did. Robert Logan, who worked as an articling pupil with Phidime Belanger, DLS, in 1910, had vivid memories of the food or lack of it. "We had good reason to believe," Logan later recalled, "that it cost my chief at that time just twenty cents per man per day for food. We had stewed beans, sow-belly . . . stewed dried apples, bread, boiled beans and stewed evaporated apples, and tea, three times a day, plus good old pea soup . . . there is nothing better than pea soup after ten to twelve hours out on the line, or walking to and from

*Fred Seibert's crew on the 26th Baseline take a dip, 1914.*
ALSA, MICHAEL COLLECTION, ATHABASCA RIVER SERIES

the line, unless it is a quart or so of good strong tea." He recalled that the menu differed slightly on alternate Sundays, with the addition of a small portion of cake smeared with a modicum of jam or fruit. "Every other Sunday, at the mid-day meal, each man found in front of him a little white enamel saucer with five prunes on it—five no more no less."[49]

For members of the survey party, the luck of the draw lay not only in their employer, but also in the cook. Claude McLaughlin, on a baseline survey crew in 1916, was happy with the grub served up, which included bear meat, venison, and even the occasional porcupine. What he liked best was the bread, and sixty years later, he recounted how the cook baked it. "He used to build a fire in the sand along the river, the bank, he had a good hot fire and then he put the bread in a closed-in dish, it was entirely a round dish, and he'd bury it in the sand then leave it–oh boy, was that ever . . . you can see a pile of it there . . . everything's in it," he said, pointing to a photograph of the cook tent in his album.[50] McLaughlin and a couple of others were sometimes in such a hurry to get back to camp for supper they would scramble aboard a log, straddle it, and put out into the current. As the river was so high that year, they would soon appear opposite the camp and holler to the cook to help them get to the bank, where they awaited the rest of the party to come after a long walk through the bush.[51]

On long summer evenings, a surveyor might find it pleasant to sit outside his tent, pipe in hand, to write up his official diaries and progress reports to the surveyor general in Ottawa. He checked field notes, prepared township progress sketches, kept records of observations of various kinds, and perhaps wrote home. On the other hand, he might not—so much depended on the mosquitoes! Smoke from the fire might provide sufficient relief for the men to occupy themselves playing cards or cribbage. Everyone was ready to sleep early at the end of a long day on the line. In winter, the outdoor life was less idyllic and keeping warm was an occupation in itself—and photos of survey life were restricted to recording survey parties on the move!

Survey parties had to become bush smart. A man learned to rely on signs of the forest—how moss grows on the north side of a tree where the bark is always darker—to avoid losing his way. [53] The surveyor was always relieved to see his men return safely from a trip to collect supplies at a cache. He had to rely on his men to act appropriately in the event of bush fires. Claude McLaughlin never forgot the day in 1916 when fire descended on the survey crew. "We had to get into the swamp, and get down because the smoke was coming right over the top of the trees and it . . . leaped from spruce top to spruce top across the whole thing and even the animals came into the swamp to get away from the fire." [54]

Accidents or illnesses were a constant concern and a heavy responsibility for the surveyor in charge with only rudimentary first aid. Medical attention was a long journey away. Surveyors dealt with arthritis, rheumatism, or malaise as best they could. In August 1908, reporting that the Peace River Country did not seem to agree with him, Jean Baptiste St. Cyr peevishly added that he had no intention of returning. Nevertheless, he did, admitting water might have been the cause of his malaise. [55] Drinking water was always a problem. James Wallace, working on the 19th Baseline, noted that everyone in his camp at a small pond was sick with diarrhea, probably because of bad water. [56]

Sunday was traditionally washday. "That was a Sunday Job, wash your clothes and clean up," as Claude McLaughlin recalled. All survey parties carried a quarter washtub and a washboard for scrubbing clothes; plenty of soap was brought north with other supplies. Sometimes the washtub was used as a sitting bath. Another way to clean up was to take a plunge in icy river or lake water, the latter being more alluring in the high heat of summer. Shaving was a shared ritual and seemed to be a favourite subject of photographers who captured many a creamed face hamming it up.

Whoever had barber skills cleaned off the week's stubble, especially necessary just before coming out of the bush for home.

The surveyor, as Fred Seibert noted, had to be a good bush supervisor. "He had to lead his men, not drive them. The men had to respect him, not only for himself and his training, but also for what he himself could do in a practical way in the bush. He had to be one of them, and yet not one of them."[57] The surveyor, who had the alarm clock, pitched his tent close to the men, ate, and generally worked alongside them, but every man knew who was boss. In the North, discipline problems or disenchantment among the survey crew were rare: isolation was inclined to keep everyone on track, literally and figuratively.

## PETROLEUM SPECULATION AT FORT MCMURRAY AND THE DEMAND FOR SURVEYS

While subdivision was in full swing in the Peace River Country, the Topographical Surveys Branch was suddenly under pressure for surveys in northeast Alberta, on the Athabasca River. In 1910 the fledging settlement at Fort McMurray, at the confluence of the Athabasca and Clearwater Rivers, was a centre of wild speculation. Not only was there a rumour afloat that the Alberta and Great Waterways Railway would construct its line all the way north from Lac La Biche to boost salt and other mineral development, but there were hopes that the development of petroleum reserves would usher in an economic and real estate boom. The tar springs, noted by John Macoun in 1875 and by Robert Bell in 1882, while on exploratory trips for the Geological Survey, were studied more closely by Robert McConnell in the 1890s. The Dominion government consequently funded an experimental oil well drilled at the confluence of the Athabasca and Pelican Rivers in 1897. While it failed to gush petroleum, the primitive rig hit a large gas field, which, uncapped, raged like a beacon until 1918. From 1906, a number of private investors, including German immigrant Alfred von Hammerstein and Jim Cornwall, local entrepreneur and promoter, began a push to tap the tar sands by conventional drilling.

As oil well drilling equipment was shipped north by scow it led to a good deal of speculative hype, and claims were made all along the riverbank. Claims, however, meant little, as many prospectors discovered when they tried to hire a surveyor to survey the boundaries of their claim. It was necessary to apply in person for a lease to the petroleum and gas rights, which remained the property of the Crown. The regulations governing oil and gas issued by order-in-council in 1910 stipulated that the leases were for twenty-one years and were for no more than 1,920 aces.[58] In December 1912, Albert Tremblay, DLS, surveyed several leases for the Athabasca Oil and Asphaltum Company, which had acquired Alfred Von Hammerstein's claims on the banks of the Athabasca River, south of Fort McMurray. Lot 1 comprised 1,894 acres, and Lot 2 contained 1,972 acres. The Dominion government placed the oil sands region of the Athabasca and Clearwater Rivers under a reserve in 1913 as part of a policy of government controlled petroleum development.[59] By 1914 the speculative fever and hopes of a giant pool of oil had cooled.

At Fort McMurray, the initial flurry of excitement over petroleum caused settlers, many of whom were involved in freighting and provisioning, to stake their lots hurriedly and guard squatters' rights to the land carefully. In 1909 they demanded a subdivision of the vicinity into quarter

## The Tragic Death of Henry Selby

On August 31, 1910, a telegram arrived in Ottawa from Athabasca Landing. Henry Selby had drowned in the Athabasca River on his way south from Fort McMurray. Selby, impatient with the speed of the heavily laden HBC scow, transferred to an empty scow that had overtaken them. Selby later got off the scow to walk along the river-bank ahead of the trackers. He disappeared and a search party began to follow his footprints: he was the only pas-senger not wearing moccasins on the scow. Only his cap was found. Perhaps Selby, who had earlier mentioned he was not feeling well, had become dizzy or had heart trouble and tumbled down the riverbank. The boatmen left a rough cross and a message for the HBC scow coming behind with Selby's survey party and equipment.

When he received the news, J. H. McKnight, DLS, Selby's assistant, mounted a search, but to no avail. McKnight eventually proceeded to Athabasca Landing, where he paid off the survey party and took charge of the survey equipment and Selby's belongings and papers. McKnight then engaged a scow and resumed the search for Selby's body in the company of a NWMP constable and a local fire ranger. Finally, on September 18, they found Selby's remains, which had come to rest near the Cascade Rapids some twenty miles south of Fort McMurray. They built a coffin from lumber they had brought with them, and dug a grave close to the riverbank. "The grave is marked," Knight reported on October 6, "and if the body is removed it would have to be brought out by dog trains in winter."

Henry Selby's grief-stricken widow faced a predicament. The insurance company would not pay out Selby's life insurance until his body was brought to Ontario. The Association of Ontario Land Surveyors, of which the late Selby was president at the time of his death, offered to pay the considerable costs involved, but Mrs. Selby would not hear of it. She insisted the Dominion government should assume the responsibility. Frank Oliver, Minister of the Interior, finally stepped in to ensure the final cost of transporting Selby's body and interment, $714, would be paid. [60]

sections. However, as the surveyor general pointed out in June 1909, this was not possible until the 23rd Baseline was run between the Fourth and Fifth Meridians. By December, things had become more pressing, as a trader by the name of William Gordon fenced off three thousand acres and was attempting to eject his Métis neighbours from the land. Deville argued that a survey of the settlement at Fort McMurray was the only possible solution, given that James Wallace could not survey the Fourth Meridian as far north as Fort McMurray until the fall of 1910. Frank Oliver, as Minister of the Interior, took a personal interest in the situation evolving at Fort McMurray, where he noted "the possibility of conflict arising from overlapping claims for tar sands, petroleum and quarriable stone." Oliver took the unprecedented step of personally interviewing the Dominion Land Surveyor chosen for the job of laying out lots at Fort McMurray—Henry Selby. Selby was to survey occupied lots as was the general practice for settlement surveys, "but also those of the adjoining lands for which a demand may be seen in the future." Selby had a tough time documenting and sorting out the many disagreements when he arrived in Fort McMurray in July, but succeeded in adjusting all claims including those of William Gordon, who had invested in con-structing a considerable number of buildings.

The developments at Fort McMurray required that the 23rd Baseline, located directly south of the settlement, be run immediately, although baselines further south had not yet been run. In

May 1911, Guy Blanchet left from Edmonton to survey the 23rd Baseline between the Fourth and Fifth Meridians. By October, Blanchet ran out of iron posts. He managed to get a telegram from Fort McMurray through to Jean Côté, who owned and operated the warehouse in Edmonton leased by the Topographical Surveys Branch to store supplies and outfits. Côté sent 250 small and 20 large iron posts by special team to Athabasca Landing to catch the last scows of the season heading downstream before the ice came in. The posts missed their scow "by some unavoidable mishap," as Côté informed Deville. The fact that Deville subsequently approved the dispatching of the posts by "special canoe" at a cost of $250 indicates how important it was for a baseline to be established in this area.[61]

## FRED SEIBERT SURVEYS THE 26TH AND 27TH BASELINES, 1914–15

In 1914 baseline surveys north of Fort McMurray finally began. The further north the baselines were, the harder the terrain was for the axemen, not just to cut the baseline, but to make trails through muskeg country to get to the baseline itself. In 1914 Fred Seibert, a veteran of northern baselines since 1911, set out in May 1914 to survey the 26th Baseline west of the Fourth Meridian, located approximately 114 kilometres north of Fort McMurray. Seibert was a man with high energy and prepared to take risks to get things done. He planned his spring travel to the line carefully and made the unusual decision to purchase his own scows, hire steersmen, and use his survey party as crew, rather than take passage with a freighting company. As he explained to Surveyor General Deville, it was not possible to find freighters in May, and even if he could, he noted, the cost to Fort McMurray was prohibitive—about twenty-four hundred dollars for twenty tons.

Seibert was taking a chance and he knew it. His worst fears were realized when they lost a scow en route. In his diary for Tuesday, May 12, 1914, Seibert merely recorded: "Broke scow on Long Rapids." Seibert's party salvaged what they could of the sodden supplies and "exchanged loads, leaving a cache of hay and oats to be gotten later." Undeterred, Seibert argued they were still ahead. They had got away earlier in the season than regular freighters would have done, and had made the trip in one week—less time than would have otherwise been possible. It was important, Seibert maintained, to get to the 26th Baseline as early as possible in the season to ensure completion in the fall. He was unlucky: the river was lower than usual in 1914, and they encountered considerable difficulties on all the rapids and had to portage the Little Cascade. At Fort McMurray, they procured horses and another scow and loaded everything—horses, a canoe, food, and the whole outfit—on the four scows.

When he thought they were near the 26th Baseline, Seibert took an observation for latitude, and the party built caches for supplies needed for the work on each side of the river. Seibert then set out on May 20 to blaze a trail east to the Fourth Meridian. "I kept the trail as close as possible to the latitude of the line so as to be able to use it when producing the line on our return to the river. A pocket compass was used for direction. I was able to observe for latitude once when about half way to the meridian and our latitude was found to be within one half mile of where we estimated it to be." Seibert split his party in two; the axemen went ahead to cut the trail, while his assistant took charge of the second group doing further cutting and packing supplies. Seibert explored five to ten

*Benchmarks were placed along the baselines at half-mile intervals. A 'T' and the number of the benchmark, cut with a cold chisel, denoted a benchmark. Where boulders or rocks were not available, benchmarks were cut on a tree in conjunction with three-foot iron posts with a five-inch plate clamped to the bottom. The benchmarks were used to run check levels to avoid errors creeping in as the line progressed. Seibert's crew on the 27th Baseline cut this benchmark in 1915. Fred Seibert is on the far right leaning against the tree.*
LIBRARY AND ARCHIVES OF CANADA, C018570

miles ahead of the axemen, and the party reached the Fourth Meridian on June 4 and began the survey of the 26th Baseline.

By July 9, Seibert had run the line west to the Athabasca River. The remaining ninety-six miles of the survey on the west side of the river proved more difficult, running through swamps and muskeg and land flooded by beavers. Seibert had been advised not to use pack horses in the fall west of the Athabasca, but rather to wait to complete the survey in winter when he could use teams with sleighs instead. He nevertheless pressed on through the fall, but lost fifteen of his thirty-one horses to swamp fever and had to resort to man-packing.

Seibert's party managed to cross the Birch Mountains and rafted supplies from their cache on the Birch River that ran parallel to the line at one point. By September 14, they had to face winter conditions. They finally reached the Fifth Meridian on October 7. Then they had an arduous journey south along the meridian, before following the Wabiskaw River south to the settlement at Wabiskaw Lake. On November 11, Seibert and his party arrived at the railhead at Sawridge, just east of present-day Slave Lake, to discover war had broken out in Europe.[62]

In the spring of 1915, Fred Seibert was back in the North to survey the 27th Baseline west of the Fourth Meridian. Ever independent, he hired an additional explorer and assistant explorer without permission, much to the irritation of the surveyor general. When his explorer, Douglas, failed to materialize in Edmonton, he hired Wilson as a replacement and set off. It turned out that Douglas, due to a jumbled telegram, had gone to Peace River Crossing. When he realized his error, he travelled to Athabasca Landing, and from there all the way down the river past Fort McMurray,

*Seibert's crew transferring a cache of supplies along the 26th Baseline.*
ALSA, MICHAEL COLLECTION, ATHABASCA RIVER SERIES

to join Seibert. He miraculously located Seibert's cache on the riverbank and followed his trail overland until he caught up to the party. Seibert felt he could hardly send him or his replacement, Wilson, back south again! Disturbed by the loss of fifteen horses the previous year, Siebert also hired additional packers to manage the horses, which were shipped by train as far as Lac La Biche. "My reputation as a baseline surveyor would not be worth much if I had so many losses among my horses as I did on the twenty-sixth base, even if I did bring what was left out in better shape than any other surveyor in that country," he explained to Deville. "I might say," he added, "that my horses show the result of good management this year and I have not lost one." [63]

Other unforeseen difficulties, however, arose. On June 1, a fire in the proximity of the survey line forced the axemen to return to camp while Seibert and his assistant remained on the line with the survey instruments for the night. Shortly after daybreak, having got past the fire, the crew arrived back at the line. Later in the summer, fire got far too close for comfort and nearly killed his horses packed with supplies.[64] Despite such delays, Seibert averaged forty miles of line a month for the whole season, ten miles more than the average.[65] He completed the survey and again trekked back south along the Fifth Meridian to the terminus of the Edmonton, Dunvegan and British Columbia Railway at Sawridge on October 18, and took the train to Edmonton.[66]

## JOHN PIERCE'S SUBDIVISION OF THE MOST NORTHERLY TOWNSHIPS ON THE ATHABASCA

Once the governing lines of survey were established in northeast Alberta, township subdivision quickly followed north along the Athabasca River from 1913. In 1915 John Pierce, DLS, led a survey party to survey several townships lying north of the 25th Baseline on the banks of the Athabasca

River. Today, they remain the most northerly subdivided townships in the northeast part of the province. Pierce spent a week in Edmonton organizing his survey party and purchasing provisions. Leaving the Cecil Hotel on the morning of May 21, he joined his crew at the railway station, loading supplies on the train for Athabasca Landing. When they arrived in the afternoon, Pierce was pleased to find that his able assistant, Mr. F. W. Beatty, had organized scows and crews for immediate departure downstream—"we were thus able to avoid many of the troubles often encountered by having idle men in town."[67] By June 1 they had reached the location of the survey.

Pierce had done some strategic planning in approaching the survey, using its proximity to the Athabasca River to full advantage. About two-thirds of the work could be done walking in daily from camps along the riverbank, which meant that pack horses and their costly feed were not needed. Pierce issued the entire survey crew with pack straps and pack sheets and everyone pitched in when they had to take the camp outfit inland.[68] Instead of spending money on horses, Pierce brought an outboard motor to use on the back of a canoe. In Edmonton, he also picked up an eleven-foot folding canvas boat "for traversing small bodies of water," along with three canoes he had purchased the previous year from the HBC.[69] "Our scows and cache are always along the river and when the inspector comes, should we be working away from the river, he will be able to find where we are," Pierce wrote to Deville in Ottawa.[70]

### The Tumpline

Survey parties used tumplines in the North to World War I. In 1892 William Ogilvie noted, "the old-fashioned tumpline, by which the weight is supported principally by the neck, is simple and convenient, but requires a lot of practice to develop the necessary 'stiffneckedness.'"[71] It was tough work packing goods and an acquired skill; beginning with about 30 pounds, a man could generally work up to carrying about 150 or 160 pounds.[72]

As the survey party began its subdivision work, ominous plumes of smoke to the northwest caused Pierce and his men to put down their survey instruments. For two and a half days, they helped the fire rangers from Fort McMurray battle the flames. The surveyors then resumed work, which progressed well through the summer. In fall, travelling on the river as the leaves changed colour, the survey party watched Indian families set their nets in every available eddy to catch jackfish for the coming winter. They also noticed the outcrops of tar and asphalt deposits along the banks, and Pierce noted that the mounders occasionally encountered asphalt when digging their pits.

The Athabasca River ran through the townships surveyed, so a traverse survey of the riverbanks was required. At the end of July, Pierce noted, the river was still "very high and the shores are all flooded back into the bush, so that I am not attempting to traverse until later on in the fall when the water is low."[73] By November the ice was strong enough to begin the traverse work, which included the islands in the river. At the

*One of John Pierce's survey crew demonstrates the carrying of a load with a tumpline and straps, 1915.*
ALSA, RICHARDS COLLECTION, EDGAR MUMFORD ALBUM

*Straining in their harness, John Pierce's survey crew had to help the horses out in deep snow.*
ALSA, RICHARDS COLLECTION, EDGAR MUMFORD ALBUM

beginning of December, the survey was completed. Pierce had arranged for two freight teams to come in over the ice and take them to Fort McMurray. The town impressed Pierce during their stopover: "It is now connected with the outside world by government telegraph service and regular mails, and has a local telephone system, several well-stocked stores, good hotel accommodation and schools and churches. While it has suffered from the evils of an earlier real estate boom, due to the prominence given to the oil and natural gas prospects of the adjacent country, it still presents a healthy thriving appearance." From McMurray, they travelled via Gregoire Lake to the end of steel on the Alberta and Great Waterways Railway. They clambered aboard a construction train that took them down to Lac La Biche, where the scheduled train had them in Edmonton on the evening of December 16—in plenty of time for Christmas.[74]

These northern surveys were the greatest challenge yet faced by land surveyors in Alberta. It was a demanding, rough life shaped by the discomforts as well as the satisfaction and camaraderie of men living in camps, meeting the vast landscape and punishing climate on their own terms. The surveyor became an integral part of the northern landscape—loading his supplies on scows, paddling his canoe or crossing tributary rivers on rafts, and running his survey lines through rough country hailed as the land of promise. Other areas in Alberta also held out promise, but for their beauty as well as for their bounty.

## CHAPTER 7

# The Beauty & the Bounty

*Surveying in the Rocky Mountains and Foothills*

MANAGEMENT OF THE WILDERNESS: A DELICATE BALANCE

As the Canadian Pacific Railway built its band of steel through mysterious mountain valleys, those that followed unearthed their secrets—coal, hot springs, and spectacular vistas. Dominion Land Surveyors extended surveys into the Rocky Mountains, which provided new challenges and pleasures for the profession. Land surveyors played a significant role in the creation of the world-renowned park around Banff, followed by parks at Waterton and Jasper. They served in administration and policy development, as well as surveying forest reserves, parks, and facilities for tourism. The demands of surveying in mountainous areas meant surveyors also played a major role in the evolution of alpine pursuits in the Rockies.

Along with western Alberta's beauty, much of her bounty lay within the eastern Rockies and foothills, where there were extensive coal deposits. By the turn of the twentieth century, immigration and industry created a huge demand for domestic coal, and the railways required ever more coal as an increasing number of locomotives rolled across the West. Dominion Land Surveyors kept apace with the railway construction that preceded the development of mines, completing township subdivision in the vicinity, and surveying mining claims and then mine properties and associated company-owned townsites.

Conservation of the wilderness meant something a little different before World War I than it does today. Pre-war conservation was more about managing the wilderness where tourism and industry could coexist, than about preserving its pristine state. The concept of what a national park should be evolved slowly. Although parks were primarily intended as public pleasure grounds, industrial activity was permitted in both reserves and parks.[1] Coal mines operated in the Bow Valley and the Athabasca Valley, which lay within dominion park boundaries. Mines were also established within forest reserves in the Crowsnest Pass and in the Brazeau River area, where commercial harvesting of timber paralleled the drive for preservation of the wilderness landscape. Natural resources did not heed theoretical boundaries, but land titles and provincial and the Dominion government did. As activity in the Rockies grew, so too did the need to establish the boundary between Alberta and British Columbia along the watershed of the Rockies.

## EXTENDING THE DOMINION LAND SURVEY INTO THE MOUNTAINS

The first Dominion Land surveys in the Rocky Mountains were made in connection with coal mining claims in the Bow Valley, soon to develop into busy mines at Canmore and Anthracite. In spring 1884 Thomas Fawcett, DLS, DTS, shortly after the death of his wife, set out from Ottawa to survey the Bow Valley beginning from the 7th Baseline near Padmore (Canmore) and going as far as the summit. Deville spelled out the goal clearly: "The object of this survey is to afford a base for the location of mining claims. You are to plant the proper section and quarter section corners; locating them either by a careful traverse survey along the railway line or by running along the section lines, or by triangulation, or any other method which seems advisable to you."[2]

By the end of July 1884, Fawcett had completed the survey to the Continental Divide on the railway grade. He was then ready to work away from the line northwest up the Bow Valley. "My methods of prosecuting this survey was by traverse," he reported, "carrying out my azimuths to four places of decimals and the distance to three—while I applied the correction to my bearing resulting from the convergence of Meridians at the commencement of each range so as to conform as near as possible to the system of producing the Base Lines."[3] While he was in the mountains, Fawcett kept a record of temperature, barometric pressure, and precipitation—including snowstorms on August 15 and September 3, an indication of the future challenges of working in the mountains. His final returns of survey, however, did not meet with full approval: Fawcett was informed that "micrometer measurements were not satisfactory on work of such importance that he was engaged in."[4]

Accurate surveys would be needed all along the railway line, and the issue was how to establish accurate reference points to delineate future boundaries and produce maps for administrative purposes. In such mountainous terrain, magnetic declination—the difference between true north and magnetic north—made it difficult to establish accurate positions. In 1886 Dominion Astronomer Otto J. Klotz, DLS, DTS, ran a declination survey of the railway line west from the Continental Divide to Revelstoke, making a series of latitude and longitude, and declination observations. These were to establish a true location for the railway line and provide an accurate base for future surveys within the railway belt that ran twenty miles on either side of the line.[6]

The same year, Surveyor General Deville sent James J. McArthur, DLS, to the Rockies to initiate a topographical survey along the railway line. McArthur began his triangulation work at Canmore, establishing survey stations on mountain summits and locating their positions from the railway survey marks. At each station, he took readings on the surrounding peaks and the stations previously occupied, establishing their position and altitude in relation to the levels previously

### The Challenge of Mountain Rivers

Surveyors had little experience with streams coursing from the mountains. On the morning of August 6, 1884, Thomas Fawcett attempted to cross the Bow River and almost met with disaster. He penned a despondent letter from his tent that evening to the surveyor general, reporting the loss of his six-inch transit that was valued at $220. "The boat (with two men, myself, the instrument and axes) proved insufficient for the strength of the current which doubled it up and caused it to fill with water," he wrote. "The current being very strong and the channel full of rocks—after struggling for a time to take the instrument ashore I became exhausted and found enough to do to get ashore myself. One of the men injured himself by being dashed against a tree."[5] Eventually, searching along the bank, one of Fawcett's men found the instrument, but it was damaged and missing pieces.

## James J. McArthur, DLS

James J. McArthur, a native of Aylmer, Quebec, was an inveterate explorer and Canada's first alpinist in the days before climbing became a pleasure pursuit. Many would follow in his dogged footsteps in ascents of the Rocky Mountains. In fall 1887, McArthur, at the end of a second long season surveying along the CPR line in the Selkirk Mountains, climbed northwest up the Bow Valley through which the Icefields Parkway now runs. Together with his assistant and a packer who was also cook, McArthur struggled through the snowstorms to reach a camping spot "mid-way between the Bow Lakes," that are today named Hector Lake and Bow Lake, and hunkered down to weather out a four-day blizzard. When it cleared up, McArthur set out with his transit packed in its box to climb the peaks around the valley.

"I occupied three stations:" he wrote, "one on a high point on the ridge leading up the pass from Mount Hector, another on the mountain overlooking the first Bow Lake, and the third on the west side and further up the pass. The great quantity of snow rendered these ascents very disagreeable and dangerous, the loose rocky *débris* being almost entirely covered and rendering it necessary to feel every step without alpenstalks, whilst the descent of fresh snow, when cutting our way up the steep parts of the glaciers, rendered our position sometimes very precarious. When on the summits we suffered greatly from cold. Climbing through the fresh snow, sometimes waist deep, wet our feet and legs above the knees, and on reaching the top and exposed to the cold wind, our boots and pants froze stiff and we were sometimes in great danger of freezing." From those mountaintops, McArthur could see the immense icefield on top of the world and the glacier that fed the streams flowing into the lakes below.[7]

established by the CPR. McArthur also sketched the topography between stations.[8] This work allowed subdivision surveys along the railway line to begin the following year. The Dominion Land Survey had begun the task of establishing its own survey marks—independently of the CPR—from which mining claims, townsites and other boundaries could be laid out.

### Photo-topographic Surveying Begins in the Canadian Rockies

By 1888 Edouard Deville was ready to try photo-topographic surveying in the mountains, working from triangulation stations on mountain peaks, in the hope it would be quicker, more accurate, and less expensive than sketching. In summer 1888 McArthur was sent west with a camera to begin the experimental work. When his plates arrived in Ottawa in July, there were exposure problems with many of them. Deville put the fogging down to light getting in while the plates were being changed and suggested McArthur examine all his holders for holes. He was right, and McArthur noted he would endeavour not to expose the holders to light. By November 15, 1888, McArthur had successfully completed twenty-three triangulations using thirty camera stations covering the railway belt six miles either side of the line, between Vermilion Pass and Banff, as well as the entire Rocky Mountains Park.[9]

The era of photo-topographic surveys had begun, and during the decades to come the new technique would be perfected in the mountains and the foothills of Alberta, British Columbia, and the Yukon. The following year, 1889, a systematic triangulation survey of the railway belt began. The intent was to link a system of triangulation all through the Rockies. Although McArthur's work was severely hampered by smoke from forest fires and a snowstorm on September 6, he nevertheless managed to survey from the boundary of the Rocky Mountains Park, along the Bow River to a point eight miles east of the Kananaskis River. He made fifteen triangulations and twenty-five

*A survey party on the Bow River, below Bow Falls, Banff, [ca. 1890].*
WHYTE MUSEUM OF THE CANADIAN ROCKIES, NA 66-1347

mountain ascents to establish camera stations and took 250 photographic views from the peaks. During the season of 1890, McArthur surveyed from Simpson Pass to Vermilion River.[10]

In 1891, the pace picked up from the summit of the Rockies when William Drewry, DLS, joined McArthur. The two surveyors began to use a double chain rather than a single chain of triangles as they progressed west. As Drewry explained, this involved a short-term loss of time for a long-term gain. "In a single chain, the first two signals being set, every additional signal set gives an additional triangle: while in a double chain, the first three signals being set, every three additional signals give four additional triangles." The Selkirks became the focus of attention as the two men worked west to Field in British Columbia by 1892, having surveyed a total of two thousand square miles. Drewry noted that a map of the Selkirk Mountains would be "very desirable" because the geography had proved to be very different than they had imagined.[11]

It would be another decade before surveys in the Selkirks would resume. In the meantime the surveyor general applied photo-topographic surveying techniques along the international boundary between Alaska and the Yukon, and then along Alberta's foothills for irrigation. The challenges of ascending the Selkirks were left to international mountaineers until 1902, the year Arthur Wheeler, DLS, arrived with his survey camera. Wheeler, a master of photo-topographic surveying techniques developed in the foothills in connection with irrigation surveys, was ready to begin surveying at alpine rather than foothill elevations. He established a reputation as an avid climber during his photo-topographic survey work in the Selkirks and on the Alberta side of the Great Divide. In the summer of 1903 he followed in James McArthur's shadow up the Bow Valley to Bow Lake. Wheeler's brother Hector, and his son Oliver, were members of his survey party. Morrison Parsons Bridgland, another young man in the party, would later distinguish himself as one of Alberta's prominent mountain surveyors.

## BEAUTIFUL BANFF: SURVEYORS AND THE EARLY DAYS OF TOURISM

Tourism in the Rockies began in 1883 as the CPR gangs pushed west through the Bow Valley into the mountains, chopping trees into railway ties and laying the rails. Three CPR labourers, William and Thomas McCardle and Franklin McCabe, exploring south of the Bow River, followed their noses to discover sulphur hot springs to which they laid claim. Soon the Cave and Basin was a favourite relaxation haunt of men in the valley eager to relieve their aching limbs. Before long, one of the visitors, William Van Horne, president of the CPR, reportedly announced, "These springs are worth a million dollars!" Indeed they were, and the Dominion government seized on their potential commercial value. Dominion Land Surveyor William Pearce was dispatched to Banff to conduct an inquiry into the hot springs, which effectively wiped out all private claims to the waters of both the upper and lower hot springs.

In 1885 Dominion Land Surveyor George A. Stewart pitched his tent at the CPR station. He then surveyed the grounds around the springs for a public reserve approximately ten miles square, of which he was promptly put in charge. Stewart tackled the formidable challenge of serving as superintendent of what became Canada's first national park, from 1885 to 1896, as he continued to survey the area. He laid out Banff townsite on the flat on the north side of the river, at a place he described as "well suited for the business transactions of the future inhabitants of the park." Stewart worked hard to control the rapid development of the townsite that followed, including the building

*James J. McArthur and William S. Drewry demonstrate climbing methods while carrying equipment for photo-topographic surveys in the Rocky Mountains.*

of a bridge across the Bow and a road to the lower hot springs at the Cave and Basin. Having surveyed tracts of forest and waterways all the way to the end of Lake Minnewanka, he pushed the government to increase the area of the reserve.[12]

In 1887 the Rocky Mountains Park Act created a national park whose boundaries stretched in a large rectangle on a northeast–southwest axis through the area of Banff and Lake Minnewanka, ten miles wide by twenty-six miles long. Dominion Land Surveyor Arthur St. Cyr organized a survey party in Calgary in September 1887 and began a survey of the western boundary of the park. He soon found he could only produce a line for five miles before he was unable to penetrate into the mountains to the west. He then switched to the northern boundary.[13] In January 1890 the Department of the Interior produced the first map of the Rocky Mountains Park, compiled from the surveys done by George Stewart, and Arthur Saint Cyr, as well as James J. McArthur's photo-topographic surveys.

During summer 1888, Stewart watched park visitors disembark from the CPR at the new Banff railroad station, now relocated closer to the townsite. They were eager to take to the waters at the two bathhouses at the hot springs. The wealthiest tourists were conveyed up the long winding road on the south side of the Bow River to the recently completed CPR Banff Springs Hotel. The hotel, a granite fortress with a chateauesque copper gabled roof, stood three stories high, overlooking the confluence of the Bow and Spray Rivers in the valley below. For half the price, visitors could stay at Dr. Brett's Sanitorium, a combined hotel and hospital, with bathhouses supplied with water from the upper hot springs.

In the summer of 1889, George Stewart found himself organizing firefighting crews to cope with huge forest fires that threatened the valleys of the park. He immediately demanded the appointment of a forest ranger to prevent forest fires and implement the hunting regulations that he was too busy to enforce. The first ranger, John Conner, died in 1890, leaving Stewart on his own for the rest of his tenure. There can be no doubt that the skills learned in the outdoors as a surveyor served Stewart well as superintendent when he had to face a range of administrative and practical challenges in Canada's pioneer park.

Nevertheless, the challenges were greater than one man's energy could meet and Stewart complained that his responsibilities were too broad. Not only was he surveyor and engineer, but also ranger, justice of the peace, architect, and administrator who had to draw up leases and policy for the park. Stewart rattled a few people in the course of his many duties, and when the Liberals came into power in 1896, he found himself rather ignominiously thrown out of work.[14]

Superintendent George Stewart, his successor Howard Douglas, the Canadian Pacific Railway, and enthusiastic entrepreneurs all worked hard through the 1890s to develop Banff. It became a resort for the affluent of Europe and the eastern seaboard of the United States. They flocked to take curative waters and sample the delights of the wilderness in luxurious comfort, while convivially amusing themselves in what became a rustic garden in the wilderness, complete with attractive bridle paths and a natural history museum. All recreational facilities at Banff required surveys, from the CPR's golf course to the lease for a "pleasure park and picnic ground" at William Mathers' motor launch on the Bow River. All these surveys were tied into the Dominion Land Survey's monuments that extended into the park.

## SURVEYING ROADS FOR THE ROCKY MOUNTAINS PARK

The twentieth century saw an expansion of the park and a demand for a surveyed system of trails and roads for visitors to explore the wilderness. The forest reserve set up at Lake Louise in 1902 was included within the Rocky Mountains Park in 1911. The scenic waters of Lake Louise graced by a CPR chalet became a tourist destination, and the Brewster brothers, the CPR's livery contractors, had stables there to provide horse-drawn transportation or guided saddle horse excursions on the mountain trails. By 1912 it was clear that the increasing number of tourists required a better transportation network. Captain A. W. Gray of Toronto was appointed as road location engineer, and the Topographical Surveys Branch instructed Claude M. Walker, DLS, of Banff, to carry out the survey work required, in co-operation with Captain Gray. James B. Harkin, Commissioner of Dominion Parks, provided Gray with road location plans from the Alberta Highways Branch. Surveying in the park therefore involved both interdepartmental and dominion-provincial cooperation.

Surveyor General Deville travelled to Banff in summer 1913 to discuss road construction. Walker, correctly guessing he was going to be busy as a road specialist for some time, was eager to receive *Byrne's Treatise on Highway Construction* and plans from Ottawa for building wooden and concrete bridges. In late June 1913 Walker reported his party was engaged in surveying a road from Banff to Lake Louise, "establishing centre line, taking profile and cross sections of same."[15] Walker kept up a detailed correspondence with the surveyor general for the rest of the summer, making progress reports and outlining the challenges posed by the landscape. By September, he had tied his road survey in the Vermilion Pass to the recently established provincial boundary monuments and begun work on other surveys for the season in Yoho Park, and at Field and Glacier on the British Columbia side of the Continental Divide.

In 1913, William Pearce, now working for the CPR, was also directing his attention to the issue of motor access to the Rocky Mountains Park. Pearce, believing a rapid increase in automobile travel was imminent, envisioned today's major routes though the mountains—including the Icefields Parkway—in the interests of tourism, fire protection and transport of forest products. He thought it would be advisable to survey the best routes while there were no complications in setting land aside. He suggested that care should be taken to improve present trails or locate new ones so that they could be easily and cheaply surveyed and laid out for future roadways. Surveyor General Deville, although in sympathy with Pearce's vision, thought the plan a little too ambitious for public opinion.[16] The surveys of roads went ahead but on a lesser scale.

In January 1914, Deville asked Claude Walker for a progress update. Walker offered preliminary suggestions as to what was required, including a re-survey of the Canmore townsite and miscellaneous surveys for private individuals. He listed a number of road location surveys: a road leading from Spray River Road around the southern end of Sulphur Mountain and joining Canyon Road, near to or in the canyon; a road on the eastern side of Tunnel Mountain diverging from a point on the south Anthracite Road, crossing Bow River and joining Loop Road near the golf course; a road from Lake Louise to Field and from Field to Ottertail; a traverse of the road to Yoho Valley from Field, of which two miles had already been surveyed; traverse of a road from Laggan station (the CPR station for Lake Louise) to Moraine Lake; from Laggan station to Lake Louise itself; and a traverse and relocation of the new "Calgary Auto Route" from where it ended in 1913 near Canmore to the park boundary. Walker also noted the necessity for cross-sectioning, levelling for bridges, and setting grade stakes for construction camps. He took a thorough approach and expressed his disapproval of the method of doing preliminary surveys practiced in 1913, stating a preference for having sufficient time to go over the whole stretch of road before running the final location survey. Walker's suggestions were acted upon and road surveying began in earnest in 1914, only to be interrupted by the outbreak of war in August that year.[17]

## SURVEY OF VILLA LOTS AT WATERTON PARK

In 1886 surveyor William Pearce suggested that a public park for the nation should be established at Waterton, following the success of the reserve at Banff. Two townships were eventually set aside as Waterton Lakes Forest Park in 1894, only to be redesignated Kootenay Lakes Forest Reserve in 1906, under the care of ranger George "Kootenai" Brown, the legendary Irish-born frontiersman and former NWMP officer who settled in the area in 1891. The Lakes had become

## The Survey of Banff Cemetery

Superintendent Howard Douglas called for a survey of the cemetery plot in Banff in 1899. "Up to the present time the graves have been placed in all directions and no trace kept of any of them and no office record kept," he explained. About one hundred people had been buried there—"many of them tourists and strangers and when their friends come here they find it difficult to locate them." Douglas suggested that lots be surveyed. People would pay a small charge for them and be encouraged to make improvements and grow plants.[18] Bryce J. Saunders, DLS, already working in Banff, undertook the survey and proposed to lay out a path in front of certain plots where families had gone to expense and trouble. In 1913 Claude Walker, DLS, surveyed an extension to the cemetery.[19] Surveyor and alpinist Arthur Wheeler is one of the legendary figures buried in the Banff Cemetery.

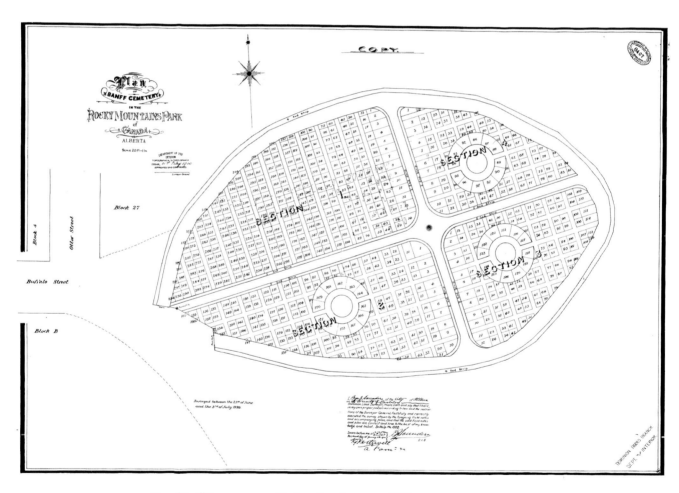

*Plan of Banff Cemetery, surveyed by Bryce Saunders, DLS, in 1899.*
CANADA LANDS SURVEY RECORDS, 8407 CLSR AB

*Survey crew's pack horses leaving Banff, ca. 1912.*
GLENBOW ARCHIVES. NA-3544-1

a popular camping spot by 1909. The Forestry Branch decided that the reserve should be protected for recreational enjoyment and pass to the jurisdiction of the Dominion parks. It was
immediately proposed to survey the land around the lakes into residential or "villa" lots for private
lease. A grand total of five thousand lots was proposed, but when Surveyor General Deville indicated that it would be a whole summer's work at a cost of between nine and ten thousand dollars,
it was decided to cut down on the number of lots.[20]

As the leaves changed colour in fall 1910, William O'Hara, DLS, was sent out to survey the first
lots. On arrival he met with James B. Harkin, Commissioner of Dominion Parks. Harkin pointed
out the favourite spots of campers at the Upper Lake, which O'Hara then laid out as villa lots, leaving a hundred feet from the water's edge in front of the lots, to afford some protection against the
violent gales that swept the area on occasion.[21] O'Hara was as enthralled with Waterton as the
international boundary surveyors had been more than thirty years earlier. "There is no locality in
western Canada," he wrote, "which I have seen or heard of, which can compare with the Waterton
Lakes as a summer resort, there being a rare combination of climate, mountain scenery, large bodies of fresh water and trout fishing."[22]

By spring 1911 there was a good deal of pressure on the Topographical Surveys Branch to confirm the survey. Those who had kept "tent hotels" in the past now sought permission from ranger
George Brown to put up temporary buildings on the surveyed lots. Others clamoured to be
allowed to begin construction of cottages. Without a plan of survey, they could not do so. An undis-
closed problem in O'Hara's field notes was holding things up but the plan of survey was finally
approved and confirmed in September 1911.[23]

In 1907 the Grand Trunk Pacific Railway (GTP) began building a line west from Edmonton, following the route proposed by Sandford Fleming for the CPR thirty years previously. The Jasper Forest Park Reserve, soon to be Jasper Forest Park, was established the same year to protect timberlands on either side of the GTP route through the Yellowhead Pass. In November 1909, surveyors began laying out the park boundaries.[24] By the summer of 1911, the GTP was providing a daily passenger service from Edmonton as far as Fitzhugh, to be renamed Jasper in 1912. The *Edson Leader* reported that the quality of the service, featuring the first electrically lit cars in Western Canada, made the trip popular with tourists. Surveyors heading into the mountains also used the GTP to get to their survey locations quickly and in comfort.

In late May 1911 George Herriot, DLS, disembarked at Pocahontas with instructions to carry out a contour survey of the land adjoining the hot springs on Fiddle River. The previous summer R. C. Lett, Colonization Agent for the GTP, travelled over the proposed route of the line from Edmonton to Victoria. Having left the completed section of the line far behind at Wolf Creek, Lett arrived in Jasper Forest Park and took the trail up Fiddle River. Lett was a fine photographer, and the GTP brass was smitten by the beauty of the Fiddle River area.[25] Plans were soon underway to develop a townsite at the mouth of the Fiddle River as a tourist resort. A scheme to pipe the water down from the hot springs was incorporated into preliminary plans drawn up by architect Francis Rattenbury for a hotel estimated to cost about half a million dollars to be situated overlooking the impressive canyon on Fiddle River.[26]

Herriot began a survey that the GTP planned to use for laying out roads and a system of water distribution connecting the springs to the proposed hotel below. "Your first work will be to extend the subdivision lines of the DLS southerly from the 13th Baseline along the valley of the Fiddle Creek [*sic*] as far as the hot springs and as far as seems advisable," Herriot was informed by Deville.[27] In such a valley, it would prove impossible to reach the corners of all quarter sections, so Herriot was instructed to indicate them with witness monuments. Then he began the contour survey, using stadia measurements, a more convenient method to establish distances and elevations than running chained traverses in such mountainous terrain. Herriot explained exactly how he proceeded. "The field party consisted of an instrument man, a sketcher or topographer, a recorder, and three rodmen. The instrumentman operated the transit, read all rod intervals, bearings and vertical angles. The recorder entered all these readings in the field book, and computed the horizontal distances and vertical heights by means of the stadia slide rule. The sketcher plotted the points and sketched in the contours as well as possible. The three rodmen were kept fairly busy on account of the steep hillsides and the heavy windfall."[28]

Herriot suggested the route for a scenic road up Fiddle River. "Picture yourself a journey over such a trail," he wrote in his final report. "You seem to be hanging on the edge of things—where you look to the one side only to stare into the blank rock face, and on the other side you turn with a gasp of surprise to see four hundred feet below the tiny ribbon of Fiddle Creek [*sic*]. The sensation would be even as Milton has described it when he writes—'Before their view appear, the secrets of the hoary deep.'"[29] Deville omitted such misquoted flights of fancy in the final version of this report published in the Department's *Annual Report*. Clearly, the beauty of the mountains moved the young surveyor from Ontario, as it would later surveyors of the park, including Hugh Matheson and Morrison Bridgland.

Although the GTP hotel at Fiddle River was never built, and the townsite survey was put aside in the interests of economy, the park authorities developed access to Fiddle River. By spring of 1912, a Dominion Land Survey party was busy locating a scenic carriage drive to the hot springs.[30] A bridle trail was also cut to the Punch Bowl Falls at which several rustic bridges had been built by 1913. Despite the interest shown by several parties to develop the hot springs before World War I, the park only provided a temporary bathhouse by 1913. The rustic hot springs pool, built by miners in 1912, remained their local preserve.

Development at Jasper was more successful than at Pocahontas. Preliminary plans drawn up in 1911 for a townsite were scrapped as it was realized that the survey plan would need to facilitate both the GTP and the Canadian Northern Railway (CNOR). The CNOR, pushing west from Edmonton in 1912, was destined to run parallel to the GTP through the Yellowhead Pass. A townsite was envisaged west of the GTP line, while the bench above the rivers was reserved for the CNOR, which finally decided to establish its divisional point at Lucerne on the BC side of the Yellowhead Pass. Jasper, with the railway station strategically located at its centre, became the short-lived divisional point on the Grand Trunk Pacific line. By 1916 the wartime demand for steel meant sections of both the CNOR line and the GTP line were torn up, leaving one single line through the Yellowhead to Jasper. In 1919 the new Canadian National Railway took over the GTP section of track through Jasper.

*A surveyor with the Grand Trunk Pacific Railway writes up his reports in his tent.*
GLENBOW ARCHIVES, NA-915-2

## Stadia Measurements

Stadia measurements of distance were made with a transit and stadia rod. The collapsible rod was generally twelve feet high and four inches wide, and graduated into feet and tenths of a foot. The transit telescope was equipped with additional horizontal stadia hairs above and below the intersection point of the centre cross hairs. The interval of readings on the stadia rod between the top and bottom stadia hairs allowed the surveyor to calculate the slope distance to the rod. The vertical angle read on the transit vernier would allow the surveyor to correct this slope distance to a horizontal distance. The surveyor could then read the angles on the horizontal vernier and plot the traverse.

Meanwhile, in Ottawa, the surveyor general was concerned with modern views on the desirability of town planning. Deville had grand plans for Jasper, but his hopes to hire William Bernhard, a Chicago landscape architect, were thwarted by his political bosses and the Parks Branch. In April 1913 he bitterly observed that the plan proposed by the parks commissioner was "a common grid-iron pattern of the real estate man, made to face on 95 acres of railway yards. It is devoid of any characteristic or attractive feature and ignores every principle of town planning."[31]

Dominion Land Surveyor Hugh Matheson stepped off the train at 9:30 AM on May 22, 1913, ready to begin work surveying the government townsite on the general plan proposed by the parks commissioner, following specific instructions from the surveyor general.[32] By June 27, he had completed the survey of 210 lots. It had been very difficult to place the iron posts due to the gravel layer on the soil and numerous boulders that had to be moved. Furthermore, there were a number of buildings across the lot lines. "However," Matheson noted cheerfully, "only two corner posts happened to fall inside [a] building, one of these being the barracks of the Northwest Mounted Police."[33] By 1914 Jasper was beginning to take shape, with gravelled and graded streets, shops, a school and two churches serving a population of 125, most of whom worked for the GTP or the park.

Following the pattern already set in the parks, Matheson surveyed villa lots on the shores of Patricia and Pyramid Lakes fronting on the access road that was built alongside the water in August 1913. However, he encountered problems because the townships around Patricia and Pyramid Lakes had not been surveyed. "Consequently," he pointed out to Deville, "I had nothing on which to conveniently tie the end of my traverse of the road to Pyramid Lake . . . I concluded that the best method was to run the east boundary of section 29 and as much of the east boundary of section 32 as was necessary for the purpose." Matheson laid out 150 lots at Patricia and another 80 at Pyramid Lake. Each had the road allowance running between their front property line and the lake. He reported to Ottawa that the park authorities had already received applications for them.[34] The plan of survey, finally approved in 1914, made provision for only 80 lots at Patricia Lake and 70 at Pyramid Lake. There was, however, no spree of building summer residences. Disposal of the lots at Patricia Lake did not go ahead. At Pyramid Lake, the lots, despite the initial enthusiasm reported by Matheson, moved slowly, and by 1928 only eight had been sold.[35]

## TOPOGRAPHICAL SURVEYS BEGIN IN JASPER PARK

A topographical survey of the Jasper area was urgently needed to prepare maps for the forestry and park branches, as well as to encourage tourism. It was decided to begin in the lower Athabasca and Miette valleys, before moving to mountain elevations. In late fall 1913, Hugh Matheson began topographical work five miles above Jasper, and then moved to an area approximately five miles south of the townsite. Although winter set in, he persevered, despite a substantial loss of belongings and supplies destroyed in a hotel fire in Jasper on December 9. He finally ended his season on January 6, 1914.[36] That April Matheson returned to Jasper to continue the topographical survey at elevations that allowed for the use of transit and stadia rod and a plane table for plotting. Matheson explained to the surveyor general exactly how he carried out the work: "My topographical surveys were controlled by the section lines of the township subdivision. The sections were divided into smaller areas by transit stadia traverses. The section lines and traverses were plotted on the plane table sheet in camp, and the elevations of the stations marked. The stations were then occupied by

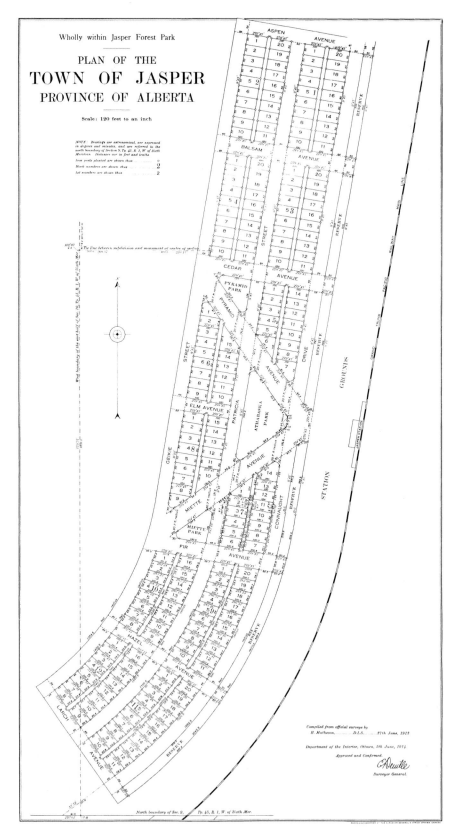

*Plan of Jasper townsite as surveyed in 1913.*
CANADA LANDS SURVEY RECORDS, 21221 CLSR AB

the plane table. Stadia readings were taken on suitable points with the telescopic alidade, and the points plotted on the plane table. The table was orientated by means of the magnetic field."

Matheson noted that he had used the Grand Trunk Pacific Railway benchmarks as data for his levelling. "From these[,] lines of levels were run along roads and trails throughout the area surveyed, and bench marks were established on which I checked my traverse whenever convenient or necessary." The work required four men—a topographer, a recorder, and two rodmen.[37] The benchmarks, however, later required a correction to reduce them to mean sea level.[38] If the topographical work at Jasper was to be extended into the mountains, Matheson noted, the surveying camera could be used very effectively.[39]

On a wet morning in June 1915, Morrison Parsons Bridgland arrived in Jasper Park to begin a photo-topographic survey. Bridgland, by all accounts, was a quiet, patient, and unassuming man. He was very different in temperament to his former survey boss, Arthur Wheeler, with whom he had worked in the mountains from 1903 to 1907.[40] Eager to tackle new territory, he was forced to wait out the rain. He calibrated his camera and checked the focal length of the lens as he awaited the arrival of his pack horses by train from Edmonton. Eventually twelve arrived, and were packed up. Bridgland was ready to go. His assistant, A. E. Hyatt, had worked with him before and was expert enough with instruments and cameras that Bridgland split the six-man party in

**The Plane Table**

The plane table is a device that allowed the surveyor to plot large-scale detailed topographical maps. It consisted of a table equipped with level bubbles and a compass for orientation and an alidade—a telescope attached to a ruler—mounted on a tripod. The surveyor dispatched a rodman to each point on the ground that was to be measured. As the rodman held the calibrated rod vertically on the ground, the surveyor took measurements on the rod from the plane table station. These were then easily plotted on a piece of paper attached to the plane table using the alidade ruler. The result of each observation is a record of the horizontal distance and direction to the rodman, along with the change in elevation. When enough points were plotted, a contoured map could be drawn.

two. He and Hyatt each had a labourer and cook to assist as required. During the summer the two parties occupied ninety-two stations overlooking the Athabasca and Miette valleys. Bridgland discovered that the highest peaks were not always the best place to take photographic views. From a very high peak, the surrounding features appeared dwarfed and less defined. Another consideration during the changeable weather conditions of July 1915 was the frequent sudden onset of storms at high elevations—not just a threat to the survey but a life-threatening hazard.[41] Nevertheless, Bridgland did take photographs from many peaks, including Mount Aquila, of which he made the first recorded ascent from Portal Creek in early July 1915.

A day of well-deserved relaxation for his survey party, July 29, 1915, turned into one of tragedy. While Bridgland prepared for the next stage of the survey, his men went swimming in Lac Beauvert. Hyatt drowned. Bridgland, having dealt with a police inquiry, left the rest of his party in Jasper to accompany Hyatt's body on the train from Jasper to Edmonton, then to Calgary and Revelstoke, where he assisted in funeral arrangements. On his return, he spent some time in the Topographical Survey's office in Calgary developing glass plates, and requested another assistant from Ottawa. He returned to Jasper and entrusted Norfolk, one the labourers in his party, with some photographic work. Bridgland's party moved east along the Athabasca Valley during the remainder of August. The inclement weather of July had changed to sweltering heat as they tack-

*This photograph was taken in 1915 looking north from a shoulder on Mount Edith Cavell at 7,995 feet. In 1998 researchers at the University of Alberta launched an interdisciplinary project to chart changes in the landscape of Jasper Park. The photo-topographic survey work of Morrison Bridgland was put to new use as researchers retraced his steps to take photographs from each of the ninety-two stations on the mountain summits in the Jasper area.*
M. P. Bridgland, 1915. Digital image copyright 2000, University of Alberta

led the peaks of the Ashlar and Miette ranges above Fiddle Creek. Bridgland continued the survey into October, taking the last of a total of 759 photographs on October 13, on the north side of the Miette River overlooking Jasper townsite.

As it turned out, the tragically interrupted survey set a record: Bridgland's party had mapped 920 square miles and had done so at about half the cost—$4.20 per square mile—of similar surveys previously undertaken by Wheeler. For Bridgland, there was also satisfaction in having made the first recorded ascent of eight peaks in the park, including Mount Tekarra and Mount Clitheroe. Bridgland spent 1916 meticulously contouring the first topographical map of the central part of Jasper Park. Deville informed the Director of Forestry that Bridgland was his best topographic surveyor in the spring of 1917, as Bridgland set out to begin a series of surveys in the Bow River and Clearwater Forest Reserves.[42] Following Bridgland's survey, little else was done in Jasper Park, other than a survey of the western boundary. Then, in 1927, Bridgland returned for three field seasons to continue his photo-topographical surveys.

### Surveyors Prepare Maps for Tourists and Climbers

The photographic surveys carried out in the Rocky Mountains by James J. McArthur, Arthur Wheeler, and Morrison Bridgland were used to produce topographical maps. People working and visiting in the mountains and mountain guides wanted maps to find their way rather than relying on dead reckoning. The fact that Palliser's account of the passes through the mountains continued to be in demand into the twentieth century is a reminder that, outside the main passes opened up by the railways, the Rockies remained virtually unknown. In 1900 Surveyor General Deville noted that the Topographical Surveys Branch had no spare copies of Palliser's journals.[43] By then, however, some maps, based on the work done by James J. McArthur, were available. Eighteen map sheets were published at twenty-five cents per sheet. The demand for maps from mountain guides leading climbing parties mounted steadily after 1900.

In 1914 Arthur Wheeler urged the surveyor general to have maps prepared for the central Rockies. Wheeler suggested making use of his own lithographed map of the foothills, prepared over a decade earlier as part of the Canadian Irrigation Surveys which had never been publicly released as it had been badly produced by the printer. He requested sets of four sheets for mountain guides at Stephen House in British Columbia, Lake Louise Chalet, and Glacier. "It really is of great importance that these men should have reliable maps in the interest of the tourist business that is being done in the Canadian Rockies."[44]

Deville eagerly linked the work of surveyors with promoting tourism in the Dominion parks, and worked closely with the Parks Branch. He initiated the collection of topographical data to compile a map of the vicinity of Banff. His idea was to publish popular topographical maps of the most interesting areas with information of interest and benefit to tourists, all of which would finally be included in a general map of each dominion park.[45]

In 1917, despite a hiatus in tourism due to the war, the Department of the Interior published Bridgland's *Description of & Guide to Jasper Park*. It was a glossy, well-designed booklet that contained information on the flora and fauna of the Park and detailed sections on trips north, west, and south of Jasper, including trails to Mt. Edith Cavell, the Tonquin Valley, and Maligne Lake. The guide, which outlined the early history of the area, including David Thompson's discovery of the Athabasca Pass, was illustrated with a selection of the photographs Bridgland had taken from his survey stations on mountain summits around Jasper. Parks Commissioner Harkin had expressed one small criticism of the draft of Bridgland's guide. "I notice that Mr. Bridgland states the accommodation at the tented city is excellent. I do not think we would be justified in taking this attitude in an official publication."[46] Bridgland was a fine surveyor and writer, but his idea of suitable accommodation was perhaps a little more rustic than Harkin wished to promote for Jasper. The problem of accommodation was solved in 1922 when the Canadian National Railway built Jasper Park Lodge.

*Ley Harris, DLS, ALS, who worked with Bridgland from 1918–1931, positions his camera from a mountaintop station, n.d.*
REPRODUCED WITH THE KIND PERMISSION OF HELEN HARRIS

## Surveyors and the Alpine Club of Canada

By the twentieth century Dominion Land Surveyors had company in the Rockies—Swiss guides and experienced international alpine climbers.[47] All this activity sparked the idea of forming an alpine club, like those of Europe and the United States. In 1905, publication of Wheeler's *The Selkirks Range*, the first book on Canadian mountaineering, further raised public interest. Winnipeg journalist Elizabeth Parker reviewed Wheeler's work in the *Manitoba Free Press*, and promoted the ideals of a Canadian alpine club. An enthused Wheeler; his assistant, Morrison Bridgland; mountaineer A. P. Coleman; outfitters and guides from Banff, including Jim Brewster; Elizabeth Parker and her daughter Jean; and Calgarian minister Rev. J. C. Herdman formed the Alpine Club of Canada (ACC) in Winnipeg in 1906. Wheeler was elected president and Bridgland chief mountaineer. Edouard Deville was made an honorary member and Sandford Fleming, veteran surveyor of the mountain passes, was appointed honorary president.[48]

The close connection between surveyors and the ACC continued as the Topographical Surveys Branch supported its employees in promoting the club's objectives for the study of alpine regions and the preservation of flora and fauna. Wheeler and Bridgland were both given time off government survey work to launch the first of the annual ACC camps that were held each year to train climbers and inaugurate members in graduating categories of membership. The two men guided all

*Arthur O. Wheeler, surveyor and alpinist, posed with his alpenstalk, ca. 1906.*

GLENBOW ARCHIVES, NA-4376-10

day and spent evenings that became legendary around the campfire, where the day's exploits were recounted. Alpine adventure attracted hundreds of members of both sexes. In 1909 a permanent headquarters for the club was constructed at Banff, just in time for the annual camp that a contingent of British climbers was slated to attend that year.

Wheeler went off the deep end in 1908 when informed by the surveyor general—on the orders of Frank Oliver, Minister of the Interior—that he was not to take time off to attend the camp with his assistants. Not afraid to play hardball, Wheeler immediately enlisted the support of club members and raised hell in the press: "What an ugly advertisement for Canada if word goes forth that we can not receive you as our guests; there will be no camp this year because the Government refuses the minimum of assistance required." It worked. Wheeler and his men were given permission to supervise the ACC camp. Wheeler conducted his survey work that May in a frenzy, tearing back and forth from the field location to Banff to oversee preparations, and it was with some relief that he ran up the Union Jack for the opening ceremonies.[49] Wheeler got his way again in 1909, but from 1910 on, neither Wheeler nor his assistant Morrison Bridgland got time off to pursue ACC activities. Wheeler was so angry he quit his government position two years later to go into private practice, and also set up his own mountain guiding business, based in Banff. Bridgland continued his love affair with the mountains as a government employee as he climbed peaks for his survey of the Crowsnest Pass Forest Reserve in 1912–13.

The Alpine Club of Canada went from strength to strength, publishing articles through the *Canadian Alpine Journal*, and building small huts for overnight stays. Wheeler obtained a contract to survey the ACC lot at Lake O'Hara in 1913. "While making the traverse I practically surveyed the lake," he informed the surveyor general. "It will be of interest to you to notice that in shape and position it is almost identical as laid down on my map of a portion of the Rocky Mountains by photo-topographical methods." [50]

## SURVEYORS GO TO WORK IN THE INTERESTS OF KING COAL

By the late 1890s, the first mines developed in the Bow Valley could not keep up with the demand for coal, and eager prospectors turned their attention to other areas, especially the Crowsnest Pass, the Brazeau area west of Rocky Mountain House, and the Athabasca Valley. The construction of the CPR line through the Crowsnest Pass in 1898 fostered the success of the Crowsnest Pass Coal Company on the British Columbia side of the pass, and soon smaller entrepreneurs and investors looked to the undeveloped reserves on the eastern side. Prospectors were busy staking coal claims in the Crowsnest as the Department of the Interior set out to survey the Pass following the construction of the CPR line in 1898. In 1900 Dominion Land Surveyor Joseph E. Woods extended the survey lines at one-hundred-foot intervals from the railway right-of-way up the Crowsnest Pass. His job was to survey a sufficient number of sections to cover any claims made over the next few years as far as the Continental Divide—the boundary between the soon to be Province of Alberta and British Columbia. Deville ordered Woods to pay close attention in running his section lines to the location of the Great Divide. [51] Woods surveyed the townships on either side of the rail line though the pass in 1900 and 1901, and his assistant Gerald Lonergan finished the job in 1902.

Woods' extension of the township grid of the Dominion Land Survey system into the Crowsnest Pass meant that coal claims could be staked within quarter sections and tied to a Dominion Land Survey monument. This, in turn, made it easier to describe the prospectors' claims

---

### Labour Problems on Surveys in the Pass

After 1900 it became increasingly difficult to hire men to work on survey parties in the Crowsnest Pass for the traditional one dollar a day. In August 1901 Joseph Woods informed the surveyor general that he would be unable to get any labourers to work on his party at that rate. "Around here labourers receive two dollars and a half a day, miners three dollars to three and a half per day, mechanics four to five dollars per day. Around Pincher Creek farm hands are receiving fifty dollars a month and their board." [52] Unable to compete with these rates, Woods went east to look for men at Fort Macleod. He had other problems in the Pass: "I was much annoyed and delayed whilst making the survey through the pass by men getting intoxicated; liquor was easily obtained along the railway." Men on survey parties in the Pass were not dependable because they knew they could easily get other work if fired. In the end Woods was unable to do the survey needed to locate the lands leased by the British American Coal Company. [53] In 1902 Gerald Lonergan pointed out that in southern Alberta a man could get forty-five dollars a month during roundup, and during the summer haying season a man could get forty to forty-five dollars a month. Most men who spend their life in a saddle, Lonergan noted, "will not work with a pick and shovel or swing an axe, which is the only work to be done on a survey." [54]

and sped up the process of licensing leases. The leases were usually sold to mining magnates able to raise the capital to develop the mines and build spur lines from the tipple to the CPR main line. Prospector C. A. Little persuaded H. L. Frank, a mining magnate from Butte, Montana, that his coal lease near Burmis was worth developing. It turned out Little was wrong, but Frank and his partner, W. S. Gebo, were undeterred and purchased better prospects east of Blairmore. By 1901 their Canadian American Coal and Coke Company was operating. Both the mine and the associated townsite became known as Frank.[55]

The Canadian American Coal and Coke Company hired Joseph Woods, the Dominion Land Surveyor who knew the Crowsnest area best, to lay out the townsite at Frank in 1901. Woods laid the village of Frank out on a square block form with a station on the CPR line. Soon two dozen cottages and a boarding house were up. The village had a thriving population of three hundred in time for the grand official opening on September 10, 1901, attended by none other than Clifford Sifton, Minister of the Interior.[56]

Coal mining was off to an optimistic start in the Crowsnest Pass. Joseph Woods lived in Frank during 1902 and then moved to Pincher Creek in 1903, where he went into private practice, surveying full-time for the coal companies in the Pass, laying out townsites (Burmis, Bellevue, Hillcrest, Lundbreck), and townsite extensions (Coleman and Blairmore). Woods laid out the Western Oil and Coal Consolidated townsite at Beaver Mines, located southwest of Pincher Creek on the Kootenay and Alberta Railway that branched off the CPR line just west of Pincher Creek. The last townsite Woods laid out in the Pass was the new town of Frank in 1914, some distance from its 1901 location, amid fears of another slide like the disaster of 1903, which could erase the remaining part of Frank in its path.

North of the Crowsnest Pass, the survey party of D. B. Dowling with the Geological Survey of Canada discovered new coal strata in the basin of the upper North Saskatchewan River in 1906. Dowling's reports caught the attention of Martin Cohn (who changed his name to Nordegg in April 1909), a German immigrant who arrived in Canada as manager of the German Development Company, financed at a million dollars. During the summer of 1907, Cohn, in conjunction with further investigations by the Geological Survey, staked out coalfields—the south Brazeau, the Bighorn, and the Saskatchewan. Bringing a 30-pound lump of coal with him, Cohn returned to Germany to raise an extra 7 million dollars required to set up a mine.[57] Word of the coal resources in west central Alberta spread, and soon a Toronto syndicate, having hired Bryce Saunders, DLS, was busy staking rival claims in the same area. It was, however, a long time before all this activity would result in coal mining.

In 1907 the Department of the Interior ruled that coalfields had to be tied into and described within the Dominion Land Survey system of township, range, and meridian. The problem was the Dominion Land Survey had not been extended far enough west into the foothills in the upper North Saskatchewan River area. The 12th Baseline was extended sufficiently far west by 1908, but the 11th Baseline had not been run. The surveyor general was once again under pressure to keep the survey ahead of demand for resource exploitation. In summer 1908, he dispatched Bryce Saunders to survey the 11th Baseline west and Thomas Green, DLS, to survey and tie the subdivided townships in the vicinity of the coal claims on the Brazeau River into the 11th Baseline as it progressed west. The season was, however, doomed to failure, causing further delays for the prospective mine developers. Green arrived by train at Laggan station near Lake Louise and proceeded north to the Brazeau River to begin the survey of township outlines to be tied into the 12th Baseline. He then moved south to begin the work in the vicinity of the 11th Baseline, only to find Saunders had not yet run the line.

Green spent two days trying to ascertain the whereabouts of Saunders to no avail. Meanwhile, his search party located G. S. Malloch of the Geological Survey working in the vicinity. "On Monday 28th [September] I took a couple of men with the transit telescopes and we went eastward some five miles and climbed the highest peaks of the Big Horn Range of Mountains in this vicinity, that is, of the 11th baseline, and carefully and minutely scanned the country to the east but could see no traces of said base line or any operations in connection therewith."[58] Green faced a dilemma: how could he finish his subdivision work? He felt that he could not wait around in the face of approaching winter. He decided to quit for the season and start south for home. As it turned out, Saunders had only been less than twenty miles away from where Green had halted his survey, but as Green later pointed out, the fact that it took Saunders two months to get that far west indicated "the roughness of the country and why, after two days attempting to get through the mountains and the timber, I abandoned the search for the 11th baseline and Mr. Saunders."[59]

While recuperating from a fall from his horse at the hot springs baths at Brett's Sanatorium, Green filled in the surveyor general as to how he had ended the season. En route south, Green stopped at the Big Horn River, where he spent ten days surveying the coal lands of the German Development Company, located on the Sand River. "I did this as a private speculation, and I may say that Mr. Martin Cohn had communicated with me and requested me to survey said coal lands . . . Mr. Cohn is Managing Director of said company. I fully realize that it is not a good precedent to establish, but under the circumstances I feel I was justified in doing the work," he explained to Deville.[60] Deville was incensed to receive this letter from Green, revealing the details of the season's survey, so anxiously awaited by the Minister of the Interior, Frank Oliver. "I believe the best we can do now," Deville informed Oliver, "is to send out another party just early enough to reach the Brazeau over the winter roads and to be ready for commencing work as soon as the snow is gone."[61]

Township subdivision surveys were carried out in the Brazeau district for the next four years. By February 1912, $87,200 had been spent on them and another season was just about to get underway. The coal lands scheduled to be surveyed in 1912 were located within the Rocky Mountains Forest Reserve, and surface rights could therefore not be sold. The Department of the Interior finally ruled it was not necessary to have coal leases surveyed within the township system, but merely staked out. In 1913 Austin Cumming, DLS, surveyed the outlines of a tract of land to be leased to the Brazeau Collieries. Here the company built a town that would become known as Nordegg.[62]

Mining was also well underway by this time in the Athabasca Valley east of Jasper, where there were a number of mines. In 1908 Frank Villeneuve and Alfred Lamoureau staked coal claims four miles long and one mile wide in the valley. Here they found coal seams thick enough to mine at the eastern base of Roche Miette and on the opposite side of the Athabasca River in Moosehorn Creek Valley. Canadian and American financiers were immediately interested and bought out the claims of the two men as well as those of four others who held adjacent claims, and they then built the first mine.

Jasper Park Collieries, a public company with 2,500,000 shares outstanding valued at one dollar, was soon poised to exploit the property at the location that became known as Pocahontas. During 1910 Dominion Land Surveyor Charles Grassie began a survey to consolidate the coal leases into one parcel, but without Dominion Land Survey monuments in the specific area to tie into, it was difficult to describe the land grant applied for under a license of occupation. It was not until 1913 that Grassie was able to describe the parcel of land to his satisfaction. Meanwhile, the mine continued with its business, the matter of a land title seemingly secondary to the production of coal.

Dominion Land Surveyor Jean Leon Côté, along with his partner mining engineer Frank Smith, saw potential in the new mine at Pocahontas. The Edmonton pair acquired major share holdings in 1911, and soon Smith was on site as the company's consulting engineer.[63] In the last week of September 1911, the first carload of coal was shipped. By 1912 several hundred men were working at the mine. Jasper Park Collieries had a two-thousand-foot siding joining the GTP line at each end so coal could be loaded directly at the tipple.[64] Over forty-five thousand tons of coal had been mined by March 1912 for fueling the Grand Trunk Pacific, which no longer had to haul coal from the Crowsnest Pass for its western sections.[65] Later that year, a huge injection of capital in the Jasper Park Collieries saw further construction and mine development, and in 1913 the company opened a second mine, known as the Miette mine, at Bedson across the Athabasca River. Corporate restructuring in 1914 catapulted Côté to the position of vice-president of the thriving Jasper Park Collieries.[66]

The company surveyed and laid out a townsite on its property. The townsite was located on an upper and lower bench joined by a steep flight of steps. Thirty houses had already been built, and ten more were under construction in 1912. A post office and store and the mine manager's house were located at the lower townsite. Although the company laid out its own cemetery, when it needed an extension by 1918, the rules had changed and it was required to engage Dominion Land Surveyor Arthur E. Glover to do the survey. The cemetery subsequently came under park jurisdiction.

By that time, however, the heyday of Jasper Park Collieries had waned. When two miners died from gas poisoning in the mine, Côté took the train from Edmonton to deal with the inquiry. The deaths coincided with union demands for increased wages. Then, in April 1918, Alberta's Chief Inspector of Mines was less than impressed with safety practices when he arrived at the mine, and Côté was again on the train from Edmonton to investigate.[67] By 1919, as labour unrest was widespread in Alberta, the Collieries were in serious financial trouble. The mine finally closed in 1921. As Côté's son recalled, the family had little to show for their five-digit loss other than a coal lamp that hung on the veranda of their Edmonton home for many years.[68]

## SURVEYING TIMBER RESOURCES

Dominion Land Surveyors had considerable involvement with Alberta's timber resources prior to World War I, as they assessed and surveyed timber berths—tracts of crown land leased for commercial timber cutting. The Department of the Interior, through its Timber and Mineral and Grazing Lands Office, set up in 1882, controlled cutting of timber. A license to cut timber was issued by crown timber agents and was governed by departmental regulations.[69] Initially, a lumberman chose where he would like to operate, sent out a timber cruiser to estimate the potential yield of a given area, and then submitted an application for a license accompanied by a sealed tender. The berth was then offered to the public at the highest tendered bid. Where township subdivisions had been carried out, the berths were allocated as township sections, but in unsurveyed territory the lumberman was expected to hire a Dominion Land Surveyor to survey the berth. Once the surveyor general had approved the field notes and plan, the license was issued subject to the payment of rent, stumpage fees, and taxes.

Much to the delight of Alberta's pioneer lumbermen, everyone needed lumber, from coal companies to steamboat companies. In Calgary, the largest operation was the Eau Claire and Bow Valley River Lumber Company, set up in 1883, which secured title to ten timber berths—a total of approximately 483 square miles.[70] Louis Stewart, DLS, DTS, surveyed the identified berths. Two lay west of Banff, two up the Spray River, four in the Kananaskis Valley, one at Lac des Arcs, and one east of Canmore.[71] The company mill floated logs down the tributaries of the Bow River and downstream to their mill in Calgary. By 1887 the mill had sawn piles of lumber for sale. In Edmonton, John Walter and David R. Fraser, whose business took off in the early 1890s at the end of steel at Strathcona–Edmonton, were busy acquiring timber rights along the tributaries of the North Saskatchewan River southwest of the city in the Breton area.

In 1899 the Dominion Forest Branch was set up, for forest conservation and management under forest rangers. The Branch heeded the calls of Dominion Land Surveyors William Pearce, John Stoughton Dennis Jr., and Arthur Wheeler, concerned with conservation of trees on the foothill slopes of the eastern Rockies in the interests of water retention for irrigation. The surveyors raised the alarm about repeated summer fires and suggested that the location of timber berths for cutting trees required careful study. They worked in liaison with the Forest Branch. In 1900 Arthur Wheeler furnished the Forest Branch with photo enlargements and a map showing "what timber it is desired to reserve in connection with the irrigation water supply in Alberta."[72] The Dominion government then reserved timberlands along the southeastern slopes of the Rockies as far as the international boundary, to ensure the water supply for the irrigation projects.

Surveyors became involved as the lumber industry became central to a debate on conversation versus exploitation of forests as a natural resource, an issue compounded by the competing interests of two different branches within the Department of the Interior in the years 1899 to 1906. It was a sign that production won out over conservation when Frank Oliver replaced Clifford Sifton as Minister of the Interior. Oliver threw forest reserve lands along the foothills open for timber berths. "The usual plaint [sic] of the lumberman and political exigencies resulted in the cancellation of the reserve," lamented John Stoughton Dennis Jr. in a paper read before the Canadian Forestry Convention in 1906. Dennis warned that, "should the forests be destroyed, the streams, irrigation systems would meet a similar fate."[73] Although further reserves were established by subsequent legislation, the legacy of allowing timber berths within reserves retarded forest management, not least as it increased the risk of fire.

*Allan Patrick at work in the foothills, n.d.*
GLENBOW ARCHIVES, NA-88-1

### Allan Patrick, DLS, DTS Escapes the Rap for Forest Fire

Fires in the forest reserves were a constant threat. Although locomotive sparks or lightning strikes caused some, others were caused by man's carelessness. One of the worst forest fires during Alberta's dry summer of 1910 swept through the valley of the High River, destroying mature spruce for a swath of thirty miles by five or six miles wide. The fire was started by a smudge fire for horses lit by a survey party under the direction of Allan Patrick, DLS, while surveying a timber berth. Everything in the valley was tinder dry at the time, but the survey party nevertheless built a fire close to their camp. It was obscured by a ridge and could not be seen. According to the Superintendent of Forestry, "The fire got away, and with a gale behind it, swept the valley. No fire ranger or staff of fire rangers could stop its progress." Allan Patrick was charged and the local magistrate fined him twenty-five dollars. Patrick appealed the conviction and won. The appeal judge deemed the fire an act of providence, much to the outrage of the Superintendent of Forestry, who was convinced "the case was one of pure carelessness." [75]

In 1907 new timber regulations came into force that brought tighter controls but were designed to maximize revenue. Timber berths, both within reserves along the eastern slopes of the Rockies and outside them, were now offered for sale by public auction as demand dictated. The government hired surveyors and timber cruisers to measure and assess the value of the trees in a berth. The surveyed berths then went on sale when there were sufficient speculators to raise a high price, rather than waiting for a lumberman to make an application.

Dominion Land Surveyors in private practice in Alberta were invited to tender for contract survey work on timber berths on a rate per mile of line. The bids were sent off to Ottawa in a sealed envelope, and the job went to the lowest bidder. In 1912 a contract was available for a berth covering fourteen sections. Charles Fairchild bid on the contract at $75 per mile for a total of $750, but John Stocks, who bid $45 per mile not to exceed a total of $456, got the job. [74] By 1914, as the economy slowed down, surveyors were prepared to underbid each other substantially. In April 1914, seven Alberta Land Surveyors responded to a call for bids on a timber berth.

Oluff Inkster and Henry Soars bid the highest, $70 per mile, while George Pinder was prepared to do the job for $45 per mile. Richard Knight, however, put in the lowest bid, $27 per mile, and was awarded the contract.[76]

Surveyors followed a general set of instructions first issued in 1910 for surveying timber berths, but were also given a special set of instructions for each berth, which included how the berth was to be tied into any previous survey in the area.[77] Surveyors cut well-blazed boundary lines through the bush and set marked wooden posts, with bevelled tops to let the rain run off, every half mile. On the side facing the berth, the post was marked with the number of the berth, and if the berth was divided into blocks, also with the block number. Once the surveyor general approved the survey plan of the berth, a government timber cruiser estimated the value of the timber, and an upset price was then placed on the berth

*Survey crew loading pack horses in the High River valley, 1910. Note the cookstove. Surveyors all had to learn to load pack horses for working in the mountainous back country—the diamond hitch was the key to success.*
GLENBOW ARCHIVES, NA-3471-41

before it went for public auction.[78] Although the cutting of timber could then finally begin, it was often years before a timber berth would be worked, and in fact, many were cancelled as the lumber industry hit hard times by the middle of World War I.

## SURVEYORS TACKLE THE ALBERTA–BRITISH COLUMBIA BOUNDARY SURVEY, 1913–1924

In 1913 a boundary commission was appointed to survey the boundary between Alberta and British Columbia along the Continental Divide. The Continental Divide is a natural watershed that runs from Alaska to the Strait of Magellan. From the Great Divide, as it was known in the nineteenth century, waters from the Canadian Rocky Mountains drain to three oceans, west to the Pacific, north to the Arctic, and northeast to Hudson Bay and the Atlantic. Part of the Divide forms the southern portion of the boundary between British Columbia and Alberta, a sinuous line on a map but marked by no monuments when it was defined in 1871. The discovery of rich coal seams straddling the provincial boundary posed jurisdictional problems, more particularly after Alberta became a province in 1905. Forest reserves also straddled the boundary. Monuments on the ground would assist surveyors and others, including fire wardens, who needed to know in which jurisdiction their work lay. Industry, settlement, and transportation routes through the mountain passes demanded more accurate maps and appropriate registration of survey plans.

The Boundary Commission was a tripartite arrangement between the director of surveys for

*Monument 4A in the Kicking Horse Pass. Arthur Wheeler designed the boundary monuments, concrete pyramids two feet high set on a concrete foundation, the gravel for which had to be packed in over rough trails. The monuments (twenty-seven pounds) were very solid. Each had a brass plate with Alberta on one side and British Columbia on the other, as well as a letter identifying the pass and a number that signified its position in the pass.*
DIRECTOR OF SURVEYS OFFICE,
ALBERTA–BRITISH COLUMBIA BOUNDARY ALBUM

each province and the surveyor general. Deville issued instructions for how the work was to be done, beginning from an established monument at the summit of the Kicking Horse Pass and working south. Richard W. Cautley, DLS, ALS, Boundary Commissioner for the Province of Alberta, laced up his boots ready to tackle the preliminary surveys in the mountain passes where the positions of the boundary monuments would be established at set intervals. Veteran mountaineer Arthur Wheeler, DLS, ALS, contracted to represent the interests of British Columbia, was charged with mapping the watershed line on the peaks adjacent to the passes by means of a photo-topographical survey, tied to the boundary line established in the passes. Not only did he climb for hours to find suitable locations for this work, but he built rock cairns at each triangle apex or selected camera station. James Nevin Wallace, DLS, ALS, the third commissioner, assisted in determining the boundary location, inspected the surveys in the passes, and acted as mediator in the event of any disputes.

In June 1913 the boundary survey began in Kicking Horse Pass, and by the fourth season the various survey parties had established the boundary south to the international boundary. It was indeed a challenging task. Axemen first had to cut sight lines between monuments. Then the distances and angles between monuments, and the difference in elevations, were measured. Distances were measured by steel tape, or by triangulation where the terrain made it impossible to chain them out. It was difficult to establish the exact line of the watershed in swampy conditions in the passes.

The survey parties faced cold, adverse weather, exhaustion, and encounters with grizzly bears. On one occasion a grizzly bear showed his displeasure with the survey by trying to tear down Monument 8H: "he sat up on the base of the monument and endeavoured to wrench the top off, failing which, he bit it and left deep tooth marks grooved in the metal covering."[79] The commissioners brought the first phase of the Alberta–British Columbia Boundary survey to a close in 1916.

There was little time, however, to rest. The second phase of the survey was launched the next year because settlement in the Yellowhead Pass and in the Peace River district required boundary demarcation. In June 1917, the boundary surveyors surveyed both the Howse Pass and the Yellowhead Pass, eventually completing the mountainous sections inbetween during 1921. In late July 1921, Richard Cautley began the survey of the summit of the Athabasca Pass. Cautley was well aware he was following in the footsteps of David Thompson, whose diary recorded the loss of five pounds of musket balls in a leather bag carried off by wolverines in January 1811. On July 13, 1921,

*A moment's rest at monument 11A in the Kicking Horse Pass. At higher elevations above the timberline, Wheeler used cairns and bolt monuments—a hole drilled in solid rock with a brass bolt cemented into it.*

*R.W. Cautley with his eye on the line in the Kicking Horse Pass*
*on the Alberta–British Columbia Boundary Survey.*
<small>Director of Surveys Office, Alberta–British Columbia Boundary Album</small>

## Mount Cautley

In 1917 Mount Cautley, with an elevation of 9,450 feet, located on the south side of Assinboine Pass, was named for Richard W. Cautley. "In theory, I know that it is perfectly absurd that one of the Creator's stupendous mountains should be named after any man. But I was awfully pleased at this particular negation of my theory," he admitted.[80]

a member of Cautley's survey party found 114 old musket balls within a half mile of the location of Thompson's camp. "There can be very little doubt," Cautley concluded, "that they are the same which Thompson lost 110 years earlier."[81]

By 1924 the Alberta–British Columbia boundary had also been extended northwest from Yellowhead Pass to the 120° longitude meridian, and north for forty-one miles. The survey was assisted by a triangulation survey undertaken by the Geodetic Survey[82] as far north as Torrens Mountain, which provided a tie between the township system established in the Yellowhead Pass and the townships further north in the Peace River area. The work of the Boundary Commission in the mountains, particularly in the Jasper area, and the topographical maps subsequently produced, carried interest in park development for tourism and alpine climbing into the 1920s.

A special memorial monument was erected in Robson Pass in 1924 to mark the end of the boundary survey in the Rocky Mountains. Arthur Wheeler assumed charge of the event, which coincided with the meeting of the Alpine Club, whose annual camp was in the area. "Will arrange for special monument ceremony on morning July 31, he triumphantly telegrammed the surveyor general. "Guests, he continued, "should bring bed rolls or sleeping bags we can arrange blankets for the Minister of the Interior."[83] The Minister did not attend; nor did Richard Cautley, Alberta's commissioner. Still busy in the field, Cautley could not be contacted in time, but James Wallace spoke alongside Wheeler. The unveiling went well until the heavens opened, dispersing the small crowd of alpinists along with representatives from the CPR and the Canadian National Railway, who had climbed up from the Mount Robson station.[84] A photograph of the ceremony appeared in Toronto's *Saturday Night* on August 30, with a well-satisfied Arthur Wheeler sporting a jaunty hat with a feather. For Arthur Wheeler, like many of his colleagues, the interests of work and pleasure were one and the same, as they surveyed in both the interest of the beauty and the bounty of the Rockies.

## CHAPTER 8

# Surveying in the Glory Days
*Urban and Professional Affairs to the End of World War I*

## SURVEYORS AND ALBERTA'S URBAN LANDSCAPE

Surveyors played a significant role in forming the urban landscape as villages and towns bustling with businesses arose on the frontier. Alberta's great expanses had revealed a land of agricultural opportunity, and the work of surveyors in laying out townships was central to the realization of that dream for settlers. As new rail lines snaked their way over the landscape, towns grew up alongside them. From the 1890s, railway construction and new townsites went hand in hand, simply because railway companies surveyed townsites on their property and sold them. In fact, three-quarters of the province's towns were built on railway lands.

For the railways, townsite development was all about real estate promotion and making a profit, either through direct sales or through a subsidiary land company in conjunction with a myriad of land policies geared to promote business. Each siding designated for a station was also marked for a future townsite to ensure both freight and passenger traffic through the station points. Townsite locations, therefore, had more to do with economics than geography, and reflected a need for grain elevators at strategic distances apart along any given line. Furthermore, townsites were not necessarily immediately surveyed, but as demand for lots arose due to burgeoning settlement.[1]

After 1910 the Department of the Interior took tighter control of the land that railway companies acquired for townsites. A railway company could not acquire more than one quarter section of land at any given townsite, or four quarter sections at a townsite that was destined to be a railway divisional point. Any potential acquisition of land for townsites was submitted to the department for case-by-case approval.[2] Furthermore, the Department of the Interior insisted that Dominion Land Surveyors survey all railway townsites. Surveyors either were employees or worked on contract to the railway companies.

## SURVEYING ALBERTA'S RAILWAY TOWNS

The extent to which individual surveyors influenced the variation in townsite plans found in Alberta is a matter of some conjecture. Ann Holtz, in her study of the formation of Alberta towns, pointed out that railway companies were more flexible in their town designs than is often believed,

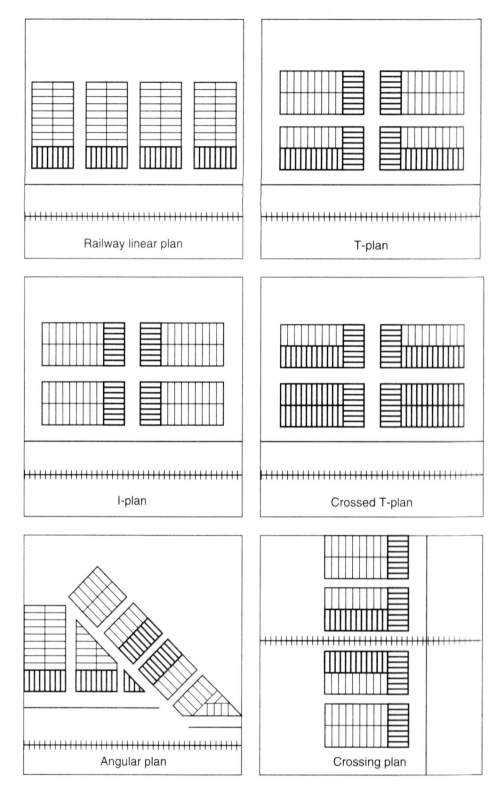

*Townsite Designs, Alberta.*

ADAPTED FROM ANN HOLTZ, "SMALL TOWN ALBERTA: A GEOGRAPHICAL STUDY OF THE DEVELOPMENT OF URBAN FORM,"
MA THESIS, UNIVERSITY OF ALBERTA, 1989, AS DEPICTED IN DONALD G. WETHERELL AND
IRENE KMET, TOWN LIFE: MAIN STREET AND THE EVOLUTION OF SMALL TOWN ALBERTA, 1880–1947
(EDMONTON: UNIVERSITY OF ALBERTA PRESS AND ALBERTA COMMUNITY DEVELOPMENT, 1995), 152.

indicating that they used a variety of plans over time and did not seem to have established policy for townsite design.[3] A surveyor, as Holtz suggests, may well have decided to lay out townsites as he saw fit. This may have been according to his personal preference, in the interests of speed and economy, or because of input from interested local parties. Only one thing was certain: all the plans centred on the railway station. The terrain and the size of the townsite also have influenced the surveyor's decision to adopt one of several basic designs: the Linear plan, the Crossing plan, the T-plan, the Crossed T-plan, the I-plan, or the Angular plan.

Regardless of the plan adopted, surveyors working on townsite subdivision had no detailed formula as to how to proceed. The *Manual of Instruction for the Survey of Dominion Lands,* beginning with the 1905 edition and then the revised edition of 1913, provided only the most basic guidelines. For example, the *Manual* suggested that an angular layout, while not the norm, was allowable: "The streets and avenues of a townsite generally cross each other at right angles, but different angles may be adopted whenever they are considered preferable." Surveyors were reassured that streets and avenues could be made more than sixty-six feet wide if future traffic seemed to warrant it. The *Manual* defined a town block as the land between two adjacent streets and two adjacent avenues, but the dimensions of a block could vary according to the width and number of lots it contained. As the 1913 *Manual* noted, "the method of laying out townsites is modified to suit circumstances as appears desirable." Only one thing was standard—iron posts were to mark all lot and block corners unless the surveyor was otherwise instructed.[4]

The Calgary and Edmonton Railway (C&E), constructed in 1891–92, hired a number of land surveyors to survey townsites on a variety of layouts. In 1892 Richard J. Jephson, DLS, surveyed a townsite at Siding 16, now Wetaskiwin. He laid it out on the Crossing plan, with town blocks on each side of the tracks. This design posed a safety hazard, and the Linear plan or the T-plan became more common. At Innisfail in 1892, George Bemister, DLS, employed a layout that included angular streets. On the other hand, he adopted the Crossing plan when he surveyed the townsite at High River in 1893.

Allan Patrick was the first Dominion Land Surveyor resident in Alberta to undertake contract townsite surveys for the CPR along its C&E line. Beginning with Didsbury and Bowden in 1900, he subsequently laid out townsites at Millet, Olds, Morningside, and Penhold. His surveys at Blackfalds in 1902 and at Airdrie in 1906 were done for a private land developer who had purchased the land from the CPR. South of Calgary, Patrick surveyed Cayley and Stavely in 1903 for the CPR, and also Granum the same year, for a private land developer. Patrick was hired in 1905 to survey a townsite at Claresholm, where the CPR had built a C&E station in 1891 but sold the adjacent land for private development. Patrick laid out the majority of the townsites he surveyed on the Linear plan.

As the number of immigrants increased and settlers took up the subdivided townships near the main lines, the CPR embarked on branch line development. In 1904 construction began on lines east from Wetaskiwin to Camrose and from Lacombe to Alix, and both were completed by fall 1905. The Camrose line was extended as far as Hardisty by the end of 1906 and the Alix line extended to Stettler. Little time was wasted surveying townsites. Dominion Land Surveyor Alexander Taylor laid out fourteen, generally on the T-design, while Ernest Bartlett, DLS, of Medicine Hat, laid out several others including Czar, Hughenden, and Provost, as soon as the tracks were laid.

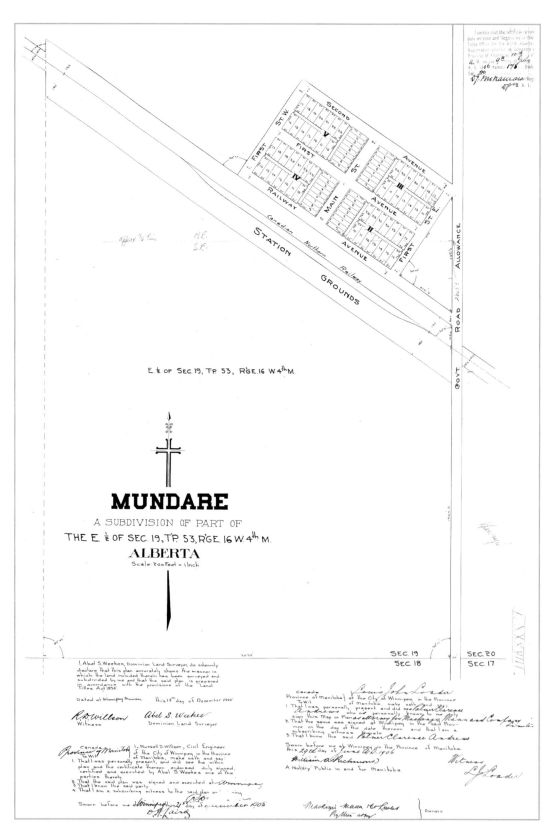

*Registered CNOR townsite plan on the T-plan at Mundare, surveyed in 1905 by Abel Seneca Weekes, DLS.*

LAND TITLES OFFICE, PLAN NUMBER 178P

In 1908 the Canadian Pacific Railway decided to stop contracting surveyors and hired David T. Townsend, DLS, as company surveyor. Townsend was kept busy before World War I surveying towns that barely made the boom: Acme, Consort, Fleet, Veteran, Bindloss, Champion, Chin, Coutts, Empress, and Enchant. Townsend continued to lay out townsites on CPR branch lines across Alberta to 1940, his output rivalling that of his counterpart Abel Seneca Weekes, DLS, at the Canadian Northern Railway (CNOR).

The CNOR, from the beginning, preferred to hire rather than contract land surveyors. In 1905

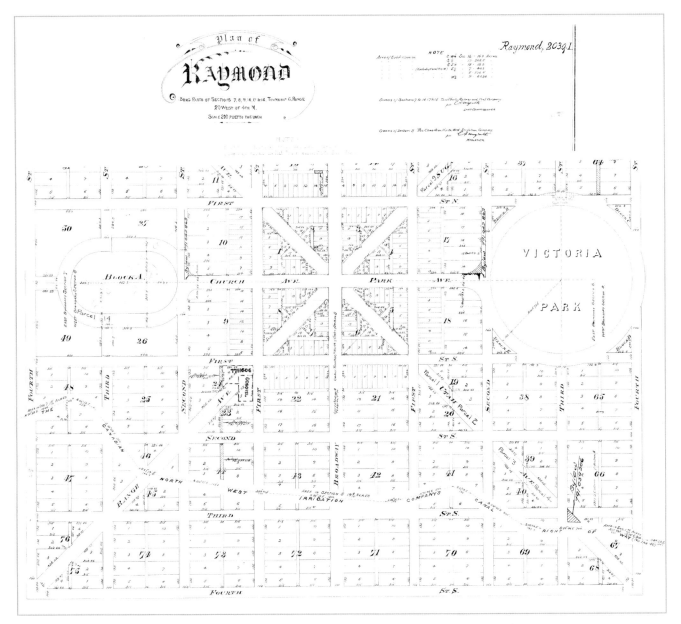

*"Plat of Zion" at Raymond. The Church of Latter-Day Saints hired Dominion Land Surveyors to lay out townsites in southern Alberta based on the traditional Mormon "Plat of Zion," which was a mile square, divided into blocks of ten acres. Charles Magrath, DLS, laid out the first square townsite at Cardston in 1893, and surveyed this one at Raymond in 1901.*
LAND TITLES OFFICE, PLAN NUMBER 23091

## Lacombe: A Town with Angular Distinction

The Calgary and Edmonton Railway decided to develop a townsite south of Ed Barnett's stopping place on the Calgary–Edmonton Trail. Barnett, along with two partners, purchased the quarter section adjacent to the quarter section where the railroad planned its townsite and station. In 1894, when Jacob L. Doupe, DLS—son of Joseph Doupe, DLS—arrived to survey the C&E townsite, he duly laid it out in blocks parallel to the rail line. The location, however, meant that the blocks abutted the road allowance adjacent to Barnett's quarter section, cutting off its full layout. Barnett hired Doupe to subdivide a portion of his adjacent quarter section into townsite lots also. Doupe laid out blocks with streets perpendicular to the dividing east–west road allowance for Barnett and his partners. The overall result was to give Lacombe two adjacent townsites, meeting at the east–west road allowance. It immediately took the name Barnett Avenue and evolved as the main street—now part of Highway 12. Barnett later hired Allan Patrick to survey an extension of his subdivision to the north. The joining of two townsites affected the angular aspect of Lacombe's street plan.[5] It remains distinctive today, accentuated by the impressive triangular flat iron building that the Merchant's Bank constructed in 1904.

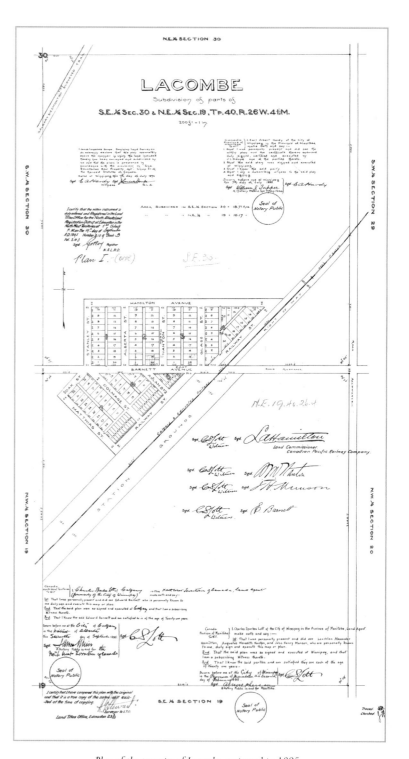

*Plan of the townsite of Lacombe, registered in 1895.*
LAND TITLES OFFICE, PLAN NUMBER 2109B

the company employed Abel Seneca Weekes to survey townsites along the line being constructed from Lloydminster to Edmonton, including Vegreville and Mundare. As settlement had already taken place in many districts along the line, the CNOR did not have the luxury of picking its locations as arbitrarily as the CPR had in earlier days. Location of townsites often required negotiation with landowners, and many of the company's townsites were developed on a half-interest basis with landowners.[6] As a CNOR line to the south was constructed west from Saskatchewan through Drumheller and into Calgary just before World War I, Weekes was sent out to survey the townsites including Sibbald, Oyen, Delia, and Hanna. Weekes laid out almost all of the sixty-five townsites he surveyed over twenty years—the majority of them prior to 1914—following the I-plan.

The Grand Trunk Pacific Railway (GTP) completed its line from the Alberta boundary near Wainwright to Edmonton in 1909. In contrast to the CPR and the CNOR, the GTP had decided the previous year to sell its lands through a development company. This approach soon caused problems. According to press reports, the GTP bonds were secured by trust mortgage that covered the whole railway, and therefore developers could not be given a clear title to the townsites. In response to the problem, in January 1908, the rail company created the Grand Trunk Pacific Town and Development Company, to sell lots in townsites surveyed along its line.[7] The GTP also developed many of its townsites in conjunction with private owners. The land surveyors hired to lay out GTP townsites used a variety of designs. S. L. Crerar, DLS, for example, used the I-Plan at Wainright and Irma. Alfred E. Farncomb, DLS, laid out Alix on the T-plan, but adopted the I-plan at Delburne.

Despite variations in design and a lack of specific instructions, the overwhelming use of a basic rectangular townsite plan determined most of Alberta's streetscapes, enlivened only occasionally by angular vistas. Occasional exceptions to the rule were usually part of a latter addition or subdivision of the original townsite. In 1905 at Red Deer, where George Bemister had initially surveyed the townsite on the T-plan in 1891, Alfred Farncomb subdivided exclusive river-view lots for development on land owned by S. F. Gaetz. Farncomb dismissed straight lines in favour of a crescent shape; Waskasoo Crescent today overlooks the Red Deer River. When Richard Knight, DLS, ALS, surveyed the Lakeside subdivision within the townsite of Wabamun on the GTP line in 1912, he laid out parks with crescents following the contours of the landscape.[8] In general, however, the economy of the grid overshadowed aesthetic considerations in determining most of Alberta's urban landscape.

## SURVEYORS AND THE URBAN REAL ESTATE BOOM IN THE "GREAT ALBERTA"

"*I am the Great Alberta*," proclaimed an advertisement in the *Calgary Herald* in June 1910. It profiled a woman's face in the rugged Rocky Mountain boundary of the province. "*I am prosperity to him who would enter my gates.*"[9] It seemed the world believed it as thousands flocked to Alberta's towns and cities, which were newly surveyed by an ever-growing number of land surveyors who set up flourishing private practices. Edmonton's phenomenal growth began in 1905, and Calgary followed suit from 1909. A fierce rivalry grew between the two cities, perhaps because of what they had in common—"a frontier boosterism that promoted frantic real estate speculation and glorified individualism, business success and materialism."[10]

*Lineup for land sales on Eighth Avenue SW, Calgary, outside offices of Toole, Peet
and Company, real estate agents for CPR suburban lots.*
GLENBOW ARCHIVES, NA-2641-1

The year 1912 marked the peak of the real estate boom. In Edmonton alone, it seemed that every second firm in the city dealt in real estate—some were big, some were small, some had a well-established reputation, while others were fly-by-night operations. The Radial Realty Company advertised Edmonton as the capital and the central point, offering city property, farmlands, and townsite properties. H. Y. Burne and Company of Jasper Avenue handled every type of real estate—business property, warehouse sites, mortgages, residential property, suburban lots, farmlands, and agreements for sale, as well as coal lands and timber limits. Penhale, Smith and Cormick informed their prospective customers: "Edmonton is filling up rapidly and the rush in 1912 is expected to be unprecedented."[11] Unprecedented indeed was the scene in Edmonton in 1912, when the HBC put the northern half of its reserve, surveyed into lots, up for sale by public lottery.[12] Over fifteen hundred people lined up for the chance to draw a ticket to buy a lot at an exorbitant price.

In Calgary, the turnover in real estate was equally staggering. By 1910 the city had fifty-four real estate companies. Two years later, there were 441, and twenty-two hundred people were working in the real estate business. Buy! Buy! Buy! was the call. Speculators that got in early did well, buying up entire subdivisions for resale. The rise in prices was fantastic—a lot in the Hillhurst subdivision that had cost thirty to forty dollars in 1904 sold for eight hundred to a thousand dollars in 1910.[13] In November 1911, a "land show" was held at the city's Sherman Rink. The first of its kind ever held in Canada, it offered a property exposition where the prospective buyer could

### Herbert Harrison Moore, DLS, ALS

The field notebooks kept by Herbert Harrison Moore of Calgary open a window on a surveying practice during the boom. Moore received his Dominion Land Surveyor commission in 1904 and immediately moved from Ontario to Calgary, where he set up an office in the Herald Block that he was to run for fifty-one years. One of his first jobs in 1904 was to subdivide part of a section of land south of the Bow into blocks for landowner R. W. MacDonald. He was kept busy doing subdivisions during 1906, including an extension for the Sunnyside subdivision and surveying the outlines of Elbow Park late that year. He also undertook smaller jobs such as re-staking lots for landowners. He was working on such a job on Sixth Avenue in 1909 when Allan Patrick, his colleague and main competitor, arrived to survey the adjoining lot to the west. Moore noted that Patrick found the original posts, and there was a discrepancy of two and three-quarter inches between them and the ones he was putting in. They split the difference, each moving the posts an inch or so. Later that year, Moore was hired to survey the baseball diamonds at the Exhibition Grounds. He surveyed the new subdivision of Rochon Park between February and March 1912, and also undertook townsite surveys for private developers on the CPR line at Camrose, Airdrie, and Midnapore before World War I.[14]

*Herbert Harrison Moore, 1917.*
ALSA, WEIR ALBUM

see what the city had to offer all at once, as well as take in daily auctions. Heralded by the fanfare of marching bands, floral and art displays, the show attracted big crowds.[15]

Prospective buyers consulted maps of each city, updated every couple of years, showing the surveyed subdivisions that every real estate agency had hanging in its office. In Calgary, the Great West Drafting Company compiled a map in 1910, which included the subdivisions of Mount Royal, Hillhurst, Sunnyside, Rosedale, and Sunalta, as well as others such as Belfast and Kitsilano.[16] In 1913 the owner of the Connaught subdivision in southeast Calgary distributed a map of expanded Calgary subdivisions, which featured miniature engravings of some of the city's prominent new commercial and industrial buildings around the edge.[17] In Edmonton, land surveyors Driscoll and Knight produced a series of maps of the city subdivisions.[18]

Land surveyors embraced the entrepreneurial spirit that swept Alberta. Since the formation of the province in 1905, they were no longer dependent on limited employment opportunities offered by the Dominion government. For those surveyors who did not care to be far from home, there was now plenty of work in the cities. Owners of quarter sections in the areas around the cities eagerly had a surveyor come out to subdivide the land into streets and lots to place on the market. There was a huge demand for urban survey work of various kinds. As well as urban subdivisions and occasional new townsites, surveyors also did surveys of lots that required a verification of the location of existing buildings, and surveys in relation to infrastructure including roads and sewers.

The idea that the real estate market was overextended and a crash was inevitable was lost on

Albertans. When the bubble burst and thousands were out of work, they blamed it on the world economic slump, and land surveyors were tempted to do so also. Lionel Charlesworth, in his presidential address to the Alberta Land Surveyors' Association (ALSA) in January 1914, referred to the thirteenth year of the century as the "hoodooed year," with which members of the ALSA had a close acquaintance. Charlesworth noted the decline in activity in 1913 was due not to local conditions, but to a downturn in the world economy. "I am sure we all have the utmost faith in the future right here in Edmonton."[19] Not all of his colleagues shared Charlesworth's somewhat misplaced optimism.

Land surveyors were busy meeting the demands for subdivisions, but many of their clients were indulging in "wildcatting" or offering townsite lots for sale that would never be built on. This reckless speculation in real estate caused unease among many land surveyors. During 1912, the situation prompted a member of the legislature to introduce a bill to prohibit a landowner from subdividing land before it was needed, to prevent wildcatting and accumulation of profits on the part of real-estate sharks. Although the bill did not proceed, it raised questions as to the responsibility of surveyors employed by land developers. One land surveyor in Calgary was reputed to have subdivided forty quarter sections in the Calgary area.[20] Lionel Charlesworth, speaking to members of the ALSA in January 1913, stressed the possibilities the surveyor had "in influencing his client towards a reasonable system of subdivision, taking into consideration future requirements of the public."[21] As Richard W. Cautley noted, "most of us have known in our hearts that land values have been enormously inflated for years."[22] For Cautley, the issue was not that the government had the power to direct how such surveys were to be made, but that it took no responsibility as to if or when they should be carried out.[23]

### ALBERTA'S LAND SURVEYING FIRMS TO WORLD WAR I

Archibald McVittie was the first Dominion Land Surveyor to recognize the opportunity for full-time survey work in Alberta, when he laid out the government townsite at Calgary in 1883. He promptly set up an office in a log building and went into private practice with a partner called Wolf.[24] Alberta's first survey firm had been born. Over the next twenty years, a number of Dominion Land Surveyors worked in Calgary intermittently, including James McMillan, T. R. Vaughan, Richard Jephson, and Arthur Wheeler. Allan Patrick had an office on Stephen Avenue by 1895.[25] Their number also included John W. McArthur, who by 1899 apparently found more prospects in Lethbridge. Between 1906 and 1909, three Dominion Land Surveyors, Herbert Moore, Allan Patrick, and Albert C. Talbot, advertised in *Henderson's Directory* of businesses in Calgary. In 1912, at the height of the real estate boom, Calgary boasted seven surveying firms. They included brothers Frederick and Lambertus Heuperman, Benjamin. F. Mitchell, Allan Patrick, Walter Scott, and Herbert Moore. In 1913 Clayton Bush, and in 1914 John S. Leitch, joined the fraternity of Calgary land surveyors just as the boom times were about to end.

Edmonton's demand for resident land surveyors came later than in Calgary. By 1899 only one Dominion Land Surveyor, Thomas Chalmers, had an office in Edmonton, while across the river in Strathcona, C. E. Dawson, DLS, advertised as "surveyor and real estate." The effect of the Klondike gold rush on Edmonton's prospects was evident. By 1900 three more Dominion Land Surveyors,

## The Heuperman Brothers

Frederick and Lambertus Heuperman came to Canada from the Netherlands. Fred Heuperman was an artist; his ink sketches done in the Tawatineau Valley in 1908 depict survey camps complete with a wagon for supplies and cook tents. The Heuperman brothers moved to Calgary in 1909 to article to Allan Patrick, becoming commissioned Dominion Land Surveyors and Alberta Land Surveyors in 1911. The brothers opened their own office in the Leeson and Lineham Block in 1912. They offered drafting services, and at the height of the real estate boom, produced a copyright map of Fort Macleod, sold at $2.50 per one hundred sheets. Their practice, however, did not last long, as Lambertus moved to Oregon and Fred joined the engineering staff at Canadian Western Natural Gas Company in 1914.

*Surveyors at work in the office of Patrick, Heuperman and Heuperman, 1911.*
Glenbow Archives, nc-24-152

Alfred Driscoll, A. G. Harrison, and J. D. Hutton, had set up offices. In Strathcona, Dawson had competition from Robert Lendrum, who would later lend his name to a city subdivision. By 1905 Driscoll had gone into partnership with Bryce J. Saunders. Jean L. Côté, who had been in partnership with Richard W. Cautley, in 1906 joined forces with engineer Frank B. Smith.[26] Four firms had cornered the Edmonton market for surveying by 1909. The two Cautley brothers, Richard W. and Reginald H., both Dominion Land Surveyors, had an office in the Jasper Block, while Côté and Smith were located at No. 8-9 Cristall Block. Partners Alfred Driscoll and Richard Knight, the surveying firm of Kimpe and Heathcott, and Horace Seymour set up an office in Edmonton as the frenzy of subdivision got underway. The number of survey firms quadrupled by 1912. By 1913 Benjamin Frederick Mitchell had offices in both Calgary and Edmonton. Driscoll and Knight had branch offices in Calgary and Camrose, and worked in British Columbia, employing up to fifty men.[27]

Surveyors set up practices in other burgeoning centres in Alberta. In Fort Macleod, the Ottawa

*Hugh Pearson, DLS, ALS, third from left, outside the branch office of Côté and Smith, at Athabasca Landing, 1912.*
GLENBOW ARCHIVES, NA-2788-10

firm of Wolf, Cotton, and Company had opened an office by 1887.[28] In Lethbridge, where Charles Magrath cornered the market for surveying from 1889 for over a decade, James (Fred) Hamilton and William Young established themselves by 1907. By this time, Archibald McVittie, while maintaining a practice with his brother in Cranbrook, BC, returned to southern Alberta. He opened offices in Lethbridge and Medicine Hat, where Lionel Charlesworth had opened an office a few years earlier. When immigration to central Alberta increased after the turn of the century, Alfred Farncomb based his practice in Red Deer, while Angus McFee was based in Innisfail.

Many of Alberta's land surveyors set themselves up in the handsome new sandstone blocks that symbolized the optimism and confidence of Alberta's glory days. Setting up a practice required some capital, leasing an office, and possibly hiring a draftsman. Surveyors in private practice had to purchase office supplies, tracing linens, and pencils, along with whatever surveying instruments were required. By 1912, several companies specializing in survey supplies and instruments served Alberta's surveyors. In Edmonton, there was the Douglas Company, Young and Kennedy, and the Davies Company, which supplied tents, tarpaulins, and bags along with clothing, boots, and canoes. The firm of Finnie and Murray, of Winnipeg, had an agent and sample room in Edmonton filled with the same sort of gear. Any surveyor in Edmonton without drafting facilities had the option of having drafting done by the Munday Map and Blue Print Company, which also did map mounting and sold surveyors' instruments, as did the Calgary Drafting Company in the southern city.

Surveyors also had other expenses. The Dominion government demanded surety through personal guarantors of all surveyors working on contract since the 1870s. By the beginning of the twentieth century, surveyors working for the Dominion paid for a surety bond through a major

*Land Titles Office, Calgary, 1909. This was where Calgary's land surveyors came to register their survey plans and request plan searches as needed.*
GLENBOW ARCHIVES, NA-203-2

insurance company. Jean Côté, for example, in 1904 paid twenty-five dollars for his annual bond issued by the American Surety Company of New York, while Alfred Farncomb took out a bond with United States Fidelity and Guaranty Company in Toronto for liability up to five thousand dollars.[29]

Part of setting up a practice often involved hammering out partnership arrangements. In May 1912, Jean Côté formed a new partnership with his nephew Albert J. Tremblay, recently commissioned as a Dominion Land Surveyor, and Hugh Pearson, DLS, ALS. They had equal shares; each drew a monthly salary of one hundred dollars and shared the annual profits.[30] Surveyors and civil engineers formed partnerships in the period of rapid expansion of infrastructure and frantic building construction in Alberta. Côté and Smith paved the way, integrating closely allied professional skills in one office to provide a full service for developers. In 1912 a civil engineer named Parker joined surveyor Edward Harrison and mining engineer Gerald Ponton in Calgary. A number of Alberta's land surveyors were university graduates in civil engineering as well as qualified Dominion and Alberta Land Surveyors. In Lethbridge, Fred Hamilton offered his services in 1911 as a civil, irrigation, and hydraulic engineer, while advertising his willingness to undertake surveys for townsites, cemeteries, and farmlands. In Medicine Hat, Ernest Bartlett and Charles Grasie, advertised in *Henderson's Directory* for 1914 as engineers and surveyors who specialized in townsite and subdivision surveys as well as irrigation surveys.

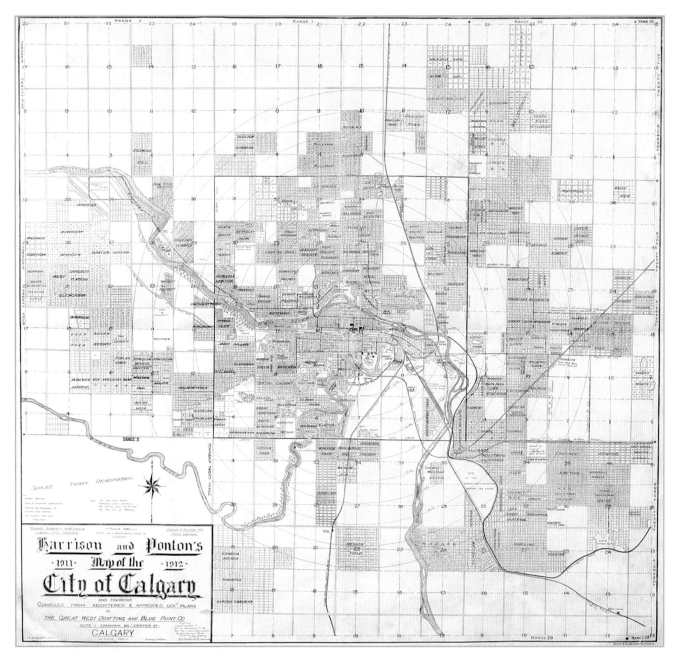

*Harrison and Ponton's Map of the City of Calgary, 1911–1912.*
PAA, 80.145/1659

*Survey instruments on the street railway tracks during the construction of Portage Avenue, now Kingsway, in Edmonton, 1912.*
GLENBOW ARCHIVES, NA-1652-15

## SURVEYORS AND EARLY TOWN PLANNING INITIATIVES

In the midst of all the subdivision frenzy, there was some dissatisfaction with the mundane layout of Alberta's grid streetscape and public discussion of town planning measures. The concept of town planning first came to public attention in Alberta in 1910, when Henry Vivian, a British MP, spoke in Calgary on the subject.[31] He must have made an impact, as the City of Calgary passed a motion in 1911 calling for a comprehensive town planning commission, which was soon set up. In Edmonton, the City Engineer Arthur Joseph Latornell, who was a land surveyor, made town planning an issue in the years before World War I.

In early 1912 Latornell emphasized the necessity for care and accuracy in the subdivision of land that would become part of the cities of tomorrow. "The undivided acres are to the planner as the canvas to the painter on which he will paint the daub, the common place picture or the masterpiece." The subdivision of land, Latornell pointed out, affected features of the city including traffic, installation of utilities, no less than the appearance of the city and the lives of its citizens. The appearance of the automobile on streets elsewhere had caused problems, and Latornell wished to pre-empt them in Edmonton. Traffic, he emphasized, was the most essential consideration, as street layout determined the traffic flow and direction of arteries to the city centre. He noted there was "very little danger of being too liberal in providing ample width of streets." Surveyors, he suggested, had a role in the economy of utilities—gas, light, telephone, and sewage systems—by avoiding expensive jogs and turns in their layout, but not at the expense of street layout to facilitate traffic.

Latornell also emphasized that planning should take advantage of natural landscape beauty and think ahead for the provision of artificial beautification. "The park system, the playground and the community park, should be part of the original plan," he warned. Failure to envisage a civic plan—requiring later re-subdivision—could be averted by the establishment of a planning board to plan the broad outlines of the city, leaving the details to the individual developer and surveyor subject to the approval of the board.[32] Later in 1912, perhaps due to Latornell's influence, the City of

Edmonton, which had set up a parks commission, sprang into action. It hired Morell and Nicholls, landscape architects from Minneapolis, to produce a visionary plan for Edmonton that included a civic centre and green spaces.[33] Edmonton enthusiastically embarked on its grand civic plan fit for a capital city, soon to be cut short by war and never resumed.

Thomas Mawson, a noted British landscape architect and adherent of the international City Beautiful movement, visited Calgary in spring 1912. He held out a vision for the city to a rapt audience whose enthusiasm for the future held no bounds. The city council, dominated by real estate interests, promptly hired Mawson to address the problems of uncontrolled growth.[34] In April 1914, Mawson finally delivered his impressive report, which stressed the necessity for open spaces, parks and recreational facilities, and radial transportation corridors, but it was too late to ride the wave of optimism and spending.[35]

Concern for the appearance and public health issues in Alberta's burgeoning cities prompted passage of the Alberta Town Planning Act, based on the British Town Planning Act of 1909, through the legislature in summer 1913. It introduced town planning schemes at the municipal level authorized by the Minister of Municipal Affairs. It covered planning issues such as streets, open spaces, the preservation of beauty spots, utilities, and easements.[36] While timely, the moment was not auspicious for success. As the economic bubble burst and land values suddenly depreciated, there was little incentive to implement the Act. In the middle of a war, little happened. The Act, although comprehensive, remained, in the words of Alberta Land Surveyor Horace Seymour, a "may" Act and not a "must" Act.

In January 1916, Horace Seymour, who worked with Thomas Adams, the Dominion Town Planning Advisor,[37] brought his experience in the east to the Annual General Meeting of the Alberta Land Surveyors' Association, where he outlined the part the surveyor might play in town planning. He warned "that the relation of the surveyor to town planning in the Province of Alberta will be largely what the surveyor himself and this Association make it."[38] Seymour, over a decade later, became the first Director of Town Planning in Alberta, but it would take another thirty years before town planning came into its own in Alberta.

## PROFESSIONAL AFFAIRS OF ALBERTA LAND SURVEYORS

Once Alberta achieved provincial status, discussion arose as to who could survey within her boundaries. Any surveys on land not previously surveyed, generally referred to as unsurveyed territory, required the services of Dominion Land Surveyors. However, there was no provision for legal subdivision or the survey of smaller parcels of land within land already surveyed as part of the Dominion Land System. Moreover, the situation lent itself to loopholes and allowed surveys to be done by men who were not Dominion Land Surveyors. In 1906 John B. Bright and F. Crean advertised in *Henderson's Directory* as surveyors in Fort Macleod, but they were not qualified Dominion Land Surveyors.

William Pearce was quick to see the implications of a clause in the Public Works Bill introduced in the legislature in early 1906, which allowed engineers to sign road diversion plans for registration at the Land Titles Office. While the Minister of Public Works pointed out this was an inadvertent error and was already rectified, it put Pearce on the offensive. He attempted to rally surveyors in

Alberta into action. "Don't you think," he wrote in a letter that went to more than twenty surveyors in the province, "we had better get together and engage someone to look after the necessary legislation?"[39] Pearce argued surveyors in Alberta must not allow anyone to undermine their professional status due to loopholes in provincial legislation, and thus in turn protect the public. Surveying, he insisted, should be a self-governing profession empowered by the government of the day, to ensure competence and high standards. Alberta passed such legislation for the medical, dental, veterinarian, and architectural professions in 1906. Land surveyors would be next.

Pearce led a crusade among his colleagues for professional legislation for surveyors, but to little avail; the problem became obvious—everyone was simply too busy to address the issue. Pearce thought someone in private practice should spearhead it. Finally, in December 1909, he managed get a number of Alberta's busy surveyors to meet in his CPR office in Calgary. Several days later, Pearce travelled to Edmonton to meet with another group under the leadership of Director of Surveys Lionel Charlesworth. A committee was soon studying acts in other provinces. Charlesworth and Richard Cautley, Surveyor to the Land Titles Office, shaped a draft bill for discussion prior to submission to the Alberta legislature.[40]

## The Formation of the Alberta Land Surveyors' Association

The Alberta Legislative Assembly passed the Alberta Land Surveyors' Act on March 19, 1910. It clearly stated that no one could survey lands within Alberta—other than Dominion Lands—unless he had been duly authorized as a registered member of the Alberta Land Surveyors' Association, which was to be set up as "a body politic and corporate with perpetual succession and a common seal." A group of surveyors immediately met to discuss setting up the Alberta Land Surveyors' Association. This preliminary council then lobbied for amendments to the Alberta Land Surveyors' Act, passed on December 16, 1910. This clarified that Dominion Land Surveyors, resident in Alberta on the passing of the Act, were entitled to pay the membership fee and simply register within a year as Alberta Land Surveyors before January 1, 1912. Any other Dominion Land Surveyor, or those who applied after January 1, 1912, would be required to sit the examinations provided for in the Alberta Land Surveyors' Act.[41]

On January 17, 1911, the Alberta Land Surveyors' Association was formally inaugurated at a general meeting in Edmonton, attended by twenty surveyors.[42] William Pearce was elected President, Lionel Charlesworth Vice-President, and Richard W. Cautley Secretary-Treasurer. Joined by six able council members—Jean Côté, Arthur Latornell, Allan Patrick, Maurice Kimpe, Richard Knight, and Benjamin Mitchell—they sat down later in the day to draft the bylaws of the Association.[43] The ALSA wasted no time in exercising its powers. All Alberta Land Surveyors, before they received their commission, had to provide two sureties for a bond of one thousand dollars registered against failure to fulfill their duties.[44] In February, the examining committee met at the home of Dr. Henry Marshall Tory, President of the University of Alberta, to discuss the ALSA examinations.[45]

Dominion Land Surveyors not granted the privilege of ALSA membership through the grandfathering clause in the Alberta Land Surveyors' Act had to take a provincial examination in order to practice in Alberta. This caused professional offence across the country. The question received

## Reciprocity Within the Commonwealth

In 1910 the idea of reciprocal privileges for surveyors practicing in the British Empire, first raised in 1900 at a colonial conference in New Zealand, was on the table for discussion at the colonial conference in London. Canada's surveyor general was slated to attend and speak for Canada's surveyors, although, in fact, he represented surveyors working for the Dominion government only. Deville later laid out in detail the whole history of reciprocity in relation to surveyors in Canada.[50] Alberta's Director of Surveys Lionel Charlesworth, sought clarification: would the reciprocity under discussion be extended to Alberta Land Surveyors? Deville responded that it pertained to Dominion Land Surveyors only. Deville stated his position on the reciprocity proposal: "The system of surveying in this country is recognized as the finest in the world, and is entirely different, I believe, to anything in existence in other parts of the Empire, and the conditions under which work is done in this country are entirely dissimilar to those in other countries, and I think that Canada and Canadian surveyors would possibly have much to lose and practically nothing to gain." He added that, while he would "be glad to see surveyors in Canada bound by close ties and acting in unison," there was little practical value in reciprocity within the Empire.[51]

In Alberta, there was support for this view. Benjamin Mitchell, on behalf of the temporary committee struck prior to the first annual meeting of the ALSA, informed Deville that surveyors in Alberta trusted he would look after their interests in London. There was a strong feeling in the province, he reported, "that it would be wise to have reciprocity among the surveyors of western Canada if not the whole Dominion."[52] The London conference, however, was postponed, as the delegates from South Africa did not want to be abroad during the official Union of South African States in 1910. Deville, who held out little hope for reciprocity among land surveyors, even within Canada, was somewhat relieved.[53] The whole issue went into hibernation, not to re-emerge until 2001.

quite an airing at the annual meeting of the Association of Dominion Land Surveyors in 1912. As the era of township subdivision waned, there was considerably less work for Dominion Land Surveyors. Surveyor General Deville waded in on the issue. Speaking at the 1913 meeting of the Association of Dominion Land Surveyors, Deville declared Dominion Land Surveyors put out of private business in the western provinces by the legislation.[46] This was a slight exaggeration, as a surveyor holding an Alberta Land Surveyor's commission, regardless of other commissions, did not have to live in Alberta. In 1912 almost one-third of the ALSA members lived outside the province.

The annual meetings of the Alberta Land Surveyors' Association quickly became the forum for discussion of issues affecting land surveyors and for suggestions for the smooth operation of the profession in Alberta. In 1912 the ALSA proposed that the government produce a manual of survey for Alberta Land Surveyors that included a compilation of the various provincial acts that dealt with surveys or plans, including the Railway Act. Debate ensued as to procedures for preserving survey monuments. The members adopted a resolution to amend the Land Titles Act to ensure that surveyors could recover their fees from clients who did not pay.[47] Council met on February 21, 1913, to hear its first complaint brought against a surveying firm—by another member of the profession. After the meeting, a notice went out to corporations on the question of unauthorized surveyors practicing in the province.[48] Heated debate arose in 1914 when Richard Knight formally proposed a tariff of charges and Lionel Charlesworth vehemently opposed it, as the law did not require it. The motion eventually passed and was approved at the next annual meeting in January 1915. A tradition of presenting technical papers of interest or of pressing concern to land surveyors was also established at the first annual meetings of the ALSA.

Along with business came pleasure. The annual banquet of the ALSA, complete with speeches and lively toasts, was an important social event. At the first dinner, held in Cronn's Rathskeller in Calgary in 1912, "the table was beautifully decorated, the service excellent and the fare a temptation."[49] Plans were immediately made for dinner the next year in Edmonton, and funds allocated to include "musical numbers" as well as to cover the entertainment of visiting members of other survey associations and select invited guests from among allied professions. In 1913 ALSA members enjoyed their meal to the strains of Richardson's Orchestra, and invited guests included James Henderson, Vice-President of the Alberta Architects Association, and A. T. Fraser, District Engineer of the Canadian Northern Railway. Not even the war was able to dampen spirits at the 1915 dinner held in the CPR's Palliser Hotel in Calgary. Two of the invited guests raised their voices in "splendid song" in between toasts and the programme offered by the Palliser Orchestra.[54] A tradition had been struck that would endure: an annual collegial gathering of Alberta Land Surveyors.

## ALBERTA SURVEYS ACT, 1912

As the real estate boom peaked and the demand for surveys for land subdivisions and lots rose sharply, surveyors in Alberta faced a quandary. They now were mandated to survey in Alberta, but unlike Dominion Land Surveyors, who followed the instructions of the Dominion government, they had no manual of procedure for surveys. Questions kept arising as to what procedures would be best to follow. What recourse did they have if the original township monumentation could not be found? Who should approve the signed survey plans prior to registration with the Land Titles Office? How should they describe land accurately and succinctly that lay outside the township system? Alberta Land Surveyors decided to take the matter into their own hands and address these issues. They were fortunate that one of their members, Jean L. Côté, sat in the legislature as the MLA for the riding of Athabasca. Côté introduced the Survey Bill in December 1911 and it received a final reading in January 1912.

Côté explained that the survey of parcels smaller than a legal subdivision of the Dominion Land Survey system did not come under the control of the Dominion. The objective of the bill was to establish

### Director of Surveys Office, 1905–1915

In September 1905, a Surveys Branch, headed by a director of surveys, was set up within the new Alberta Department of Public Works, and was responsible for the survey of infrastructure such as roads, ditches, and sites for new provincial buildings. Lionel Charlesworth, DLS, was the first director of surveys, and he steered the course of the office for its first ten years. The director of surveys ensured that land surveys in Alberta were performed under the law, initially the Land Titles Act. In addition to supervising survey parties, Charlesworth was kept busy in his office, issuing instructions to the nine district surveyors and engineers, and examining their returns. He was responsible for filing plans with the Land Titles Office, which was transferred to Alberta's Department of Public Works in 1906. He also examined lands required for provincial public buildings, as well as settling compensation claims for lands required for rights-of-way.[55] On the passage of the Alberta Land Surveyors' Act in 1910, the director of surveys was responsible for making sure surveys met provincial requirements. Following the Alberta Surveys Act of 1912, he became responsible for approving all plans of survey undertaken by the provincial government and for the preservation of survey monuments.[56]

*Lionel Charlesworth, DLS, ALS, Director of Surveys, 1905–10, and President of the Alberta Land Surveyors' Association, 1912–13.*
ALSA, WEIR ALBUM

uniform procedures for townsite subdivisions, and for the inspection of such surveys through the director of surveys in Alberta to ascertain whether surveys had been made according to the requirements of the Land Titles Act.[57] The bill gave surveyors authority to enter private property to measure and restore lost corners, and to compel witnesses to give evidence, and made it possible for cities, towns, or villages to make a re-survey of any obliterated boundaries. Côté declared that it was "a matter of concern to the Public that before any permanent work on roads, public highways, or in the cities, is undertaken, the boundaries should be permanently established."[58] Surveyors were now to keep field notebooks, ready to supply evidence of the survey in court if necessary. The bill made the marking of corners of blocks compulsory, established regulations for the survey of lots where the corners had been lost, and included provisions for the proportional divisions of blocks of uneven size.

The Surveys Act went on the statute book in February 1912. Surveyors were now required by law to re-establish and survey whatever original monuments and boundaries necessary to establish the boundaries of land to be further subdivided. The director of surveys was empowered to make inspections of surveys at the request of either the Council of the Alberta Land Surveyors' Association or the Registrar of the Land Titles Office. Surveyors had protection in the course of their duty from any person who might "interrupt, molest, or hinder." Such offense was liable to a fine of fifty dollars or imprisonment for up to two months.[59] Legislation enshrined the significant role that the profession would play in the control of land as a legal entity.

RESOLVING THE ISSUE OF RAILWAY RIGHTS-OF-WAY

One of the practical problems faced by land surveyors in Alberta was the manner in which railway surveys were carried out, as this affected subsequent survey work in the vicinity. The Canadian Pacific Railway had been an irritation to the surveying profession from the start, claiming the privilege to have right-of-way surveys made by employees of the railway company who were not Dominion Land Surveyors. From 1886, the Association of Dominion Land Surveyors repeatedly petitioned the Department of the Interior not to accept such plans. Finally, in 1890, railway surveys required the signature of a DLS. However, sometime around 1900, the practice of sending these plans to the surveyor general's office for approval was discontinued. Deville himself seemed at a loss to explain this change. In October 1907, Deville admitted that, although once again railway surveys were turning up in his office for approval, Dominion Land Surveyors had not certified them.[60]

By this time, a proliferation of railways was at issue. In 1909 Deville reminded the CNOR that right-of-way surveys were to be made by Dominion Land Surveyors, and that the plan must bear the affidavit required by Section 31 of the Dominion Surveys Act, as amended in 1909. Railway plans, certified by a DLS, filed at the Land Titles Office in the district, and approved by the surveyor general, finally went to the Board of Railway Commissioners, who approved railway plans in Canada.[61] Yet it appeared that there was a distinction drawn between railways with a dominion charter and those with a provincial charter. A. D. Cartwright, one of the commissioners, returned "as constructed plans" of a section of the Canadian Northern Western Railway Brazeau Branch line in west central Alberta to Deville in April 1912. "This [rail]road, having a provincial charter," he noted, "does not come within the jurisdiction of this board."[62]

Such anomalies and confusion dogged railway plans. Since the 1880s, title was granted to railway companies on provision of railway location or sometimes construction plans. This had posed myriad problems, as it did not necessarily provide the proper basis of a survey marked on the ground and tied into surrounding lands surveyed according to the Dominion Land Survey system. As the pace of railway construction picked up after 1905 in Alberta, surveyors became aware of the problem. Richard W. Cautley was horrified at what he found when appointed surveyor to the Land Titles Office in Edmonton in 1909. Right-of-way plans, he told surveyors gathered in Edmonton for the annual general meeting of the ALSA in January 1912, were not in fact registered at the Land Titles Office, merely filed on record, which did not effect a title. Further, he pointed out, "location plans are never signed by authorized land surveyors, and construction plans are not necessarily so." He noted that although an authorized surveyor may sign railway right-of-way plans, the same names appeared so often on corporation plans that they meant little as an affidavit of personal execution. "Such men seem to have been maintained by railway corporations as part of the office furniture, in the same way as one may keep a rubber signature stamp on one's desk," Cautley dryly concluded.

As railway rights-of-way were not registered, owners on either side of railway lines had problems with the accuracy of their own title as a result. Surveyors who were subdividing land adjacent to a railway for townsites also faced problems dealing with discrepancies between the location plan and the actual rail line. Cautley advised surveyors to insist on being paid by the day, for the time required to redefine the boundaries of such railway rights-of-way on the ground, and for making all necessary searches in the Land Titles Office or elsewhere. The potential for litigation was obvious, and the Canadian Pacific Railway began surveying and posting their rights-of-way some years later, before they were legally required to do so. "They have also recognized the fact that describing land is surveyors' work, rather than lawyers' [work]," Cautley reported. He praised Jacob L. Doupe, ALS, DLS, as Assistant Land Commissioner, and then as Chief Surveyor for the CPR, for the role he played in organizing their land titles.[63]

In 1912 the Alberta Legislature amended the provincial Land Titles Act to require an actual plan of survey for a certificate of title for a railway plan. At the same time, the Alberta Surveys Act demanded the marking of railway rights-of way. Rights-of-way surveyed without any marking were not allowed, and surveyors no longer had to guess whether they were dealing with errors in measurement or whether the right-of-way had been changed from the plans.

## SURVEYORS, WORLD WAR I AND AFTER

War between Germany and Great Britain broke out in August 1914 and Albertans watched young men go to war. Several Alberta Land Surveyors were among the early enlistments. Five were commissioned officers, largely because of their professional standing as surveyors.[64] By January 1916, nine Alberta Land Surveyors were on active service. Others continued to join up as the situation in Europe looked increasingly grim. By 1918 twenty-four were serving King and country. Three were never to return. They were William Carthew; Albert J. Tremblay of the Royal Air Force, who met his end in an accident in the skies over Britain shortly before the war ended; and Arthur

## Honour Roll

| | | |
|---|---|---|
| Bush, Lieut. Clayton E. | 1st contingent, CEF | Calgary |
| Carthew, J. T. | Coldstream Guards, BEF | Edmonton |
| **Carthew, Lieut. W. M.** | **49th Batttalion, CEF** | **Edmonton** |
| Condamine, C. de la | French Army | Calgary |
| Cumming, Capt. Austin L. | Canadian Engineers, CEF | Edmonton |
| Garner, Lieut.-Col. A. C. DSO, OC | 12th Battalion Railway Troops, CEF | Regina |
| Gemmell, Lieut. H. W. R. MC | 43rd Battalion, CEF | Winnipeg |
| Heathcott, R. V., Capt. | Canadian Engineers, CEF | Calgary |
| Heuperman, L. F. | Siberian Expeditionary Force | Calgary |
| Inkster, Oluff MM | 202nd Battalion, CEF | Edmonton |
| Knight, Lieut. Sidney | Royal Air Force | Edmonton |
| **Latornell, A. J., Lieut.-Col.** | **75th Battery, CEF** | **Edmonton** |
| MacLeod, Lieut.-Col. G. W. DSO & Bar | 49th Battalion, CEF | Edmonton |
| McDonald, Brig.- General, H. F. CMG, DSO | Headquarters, 1st Infantry Brigade | Calgary |
| Pearson, Capt. Hugh E. MC | 138th Battalion, CEF | Edmonton |
| Pinder, Capt. George Z. MC | 49th Battalion, CEF | Edmonton |
| Robertson, Lieut. E. D. | Canadian Engineers, CEF | Edmonton |
| Saunders, Major B. J. | 1st Contingent, CEF | Edmonton |
| **Scott, Walter A. MM** | **256th Battalion, CEF** | **Medicine Hat** |
| Seibert, F. V. | Royal Air Force | Edmonton |
| Stewart, Lieut. A. G. | Canadian Engineers, CEF | Edmonton |
| **Tremblay, Lieut. Albert J.** | **Royal Air Force** | **Edmonton** |
| Waddell, W. H., Lieut. | 202nd Batallion, CEF | Edmonton |
| Wilkin, Lieut.-Col. F. A. MC | 1st Motor Machine Gun Batt., CEF | Winnipeg |

Those in bold were killed in action or died as a result of service overseas.

Latornell, who died of wounds sustained at the front in 1917. Walter Scott made it back to Alberta, but never recovered from tubercular peritonitis, and died suddenly in Calgary in August 1919. Three Alberta Land Surveyors received the medal for Distinguished Service Overseas, four received the Military Cross, and two were recipients of the Military Medal.[65]

The war almost killed the spirit of Alberta boosterism—but not quite. In 1915, even after sixteen months of war, Albert Talbot, President of the Alberta Land Surveyors' Association, urged endurance, energy, and optimism. "Our profession in common with others has suffered. We are, however, not without hope that when victory crowns the allied arms, the surveying and engineering professions, will enjoy their own again. While it may appear a somewhat narrow view to take of a war, that has so far left nothing but misery and devastation, it is surely not unnatural to expect that many of the tired peoples of Europe will turn their eyes towards this western land. Our own soldiers fraternizing with their British and French comrades in arms will not remain silent concerning the attractions of the Country where they have planted their homes."[66]

On the home front, however, the profession had undeniably taken a beating. New members for the Alberta Land Surveyors' Association were scarce during the war, two in 1916 and three in 1917. The collapse of Alberta's boom times for surveyors is evident in *Henderson's Directory* for 1915. There were only three land surveyors listed for Calgary—Allan Patrick, Herbert Moore, and Seabury Pearce. In Edmonton, attrition was not obvious until the following year. In 1916 only five firms advertised in *Henderson's*, while in 1917 there were only three firms operating—Côté, Tremblay and Pearson; Richard W. Cautley; and Driscoll and Knight. In Calgary by the last year of the war, things were at an all-time low; only the two Alberta Land Surveyors established before the boom were still in business—Allan Patrick and Herbert Moore. When the war ended, things revived somewhat in Edmonton, and five firms were in business by 1919.

Alberta Land Surveyor James Wallace, as president of the Association of Dominion Land Surveyors, addressed its members in Ottawa in January 1919. He had an optimistic vision of the future of Canada and the potential of the surveying profession: "If the Country is growing up, can the surveyors not grow up too? . . . The men are here. The organizations are here. And surely anyone who has been in the West knows . . . there is work enough waiting to be done. But a better organization of the surveyors themselves is urgently needed. We are few in number compared with other professions, and the weight of everyone is required. We should broaden our training to meet the requirements of different branches, so that the Association may include surveyors engaged on many different classes of work. . . . Let us stand on the dignity of being members of a profession worthy of that great country that gave our profession its birth."[67] Alberta Land Surveyors put the best face on things, for their profession and for their country, stressing the role they could play as Canada got back on her feet.

CHAPTER 9

# Surveying in Transitional Times
*New Challenges, 1918–1939*

SURVEYORS FACE IMMEDIATE GRIM POST-WAR REALITIES

Once the jubilation of Armistice Day passed, a pall of gloom settled; veterans came home slowly as the cold winter set in, matching the province's depressed economy. Albertans addressed the grim realities of post-war adjustment, laced as it was with further loss caused by the pandemic Spanish influenza. At first, reports of influenza did not alarm Albertans, who thought it to be no more serious than "la grippe." Panic set in as tens of thousands came down with the flu, which eventually claimed the lives of 3,259 Albertans. By the end of October 1918, schools, libraries, theatres, and court-houses, among other public gathering places, had closed, as the Provincial Board of Health imposed quarantine measures.[1]

Business life in the province virtually halted, but land surveyors tried to persevere with their work in the field. Throughout the fall of 1918, however, the flu threatened its progress or made it impossible to carry on. Percy Johnson, DLS, ALS, cancelled work in the Stony Plain area, finding it impossible to arrange a camping spot or care for his horses due to the chaos engendered by the flu.[2] Athos Narraway, DLS, became ill and confined to bed for three weeks, and although he recovered, he was unable to continue his inspection work in the field for the remainder of the season.[3]

One luckless survey party in Alberta experienced death from the Spanish influenza.[4] In late October 1918, anxiety ran high in a survey camp in northern Alberta, led by Sydney Fawcett, DLS. One of his assistants, William E. Lumb, DLS, awaited news of a sick child. When a train arrived on the track close to their camp on Sunday, October 27, Fawcett gave Lumb permission to ride to the nearest telegraph station at Spirit River. Lumb returned on Monday, mentioned that two men on the train were sick, and went to work. On his return to camp Tuesday evening, Fawcett found Lumb lying beside the cookstove with a fever. He quickly took the man's pulse—120 per minute! Alarmed, Fawcett wrapped Lumb up in an overcoat and got him up on a horse to travel the four miles to Belloy, where the train was due in one hour. He delayed only long enough to tell his second assistant, J. E. Roy, DLS, what was happening as they left. They caught the train and Lumb was soon heading south for medical attention. By the next day, Fawcett was feeling sick but recovered by Saturday of that week, when Roy joined him at Belloy. To Fawcett's dismay, Roy was now unwell, able to take only soup and milk. By Monday, Fawcett had relapsed,

Roy was deteriorating, and T. A. McElhanney, DLS, another assistant surveyor in the party, was sick. Clearly, it was time to get Roy out, but a chain of misfortune was to follow.

The train due to leave on Tuesday was cancelled. A doctor, due to drive up from McLennan by Packard car, never arrived—he collapsed over a patient. No medical attention was possible. There was nothing to do except wait for the train due on Friday. "Poor Captain Roy was carried aboard and the doctor also ordered Mr. McElhanney and myself to go to the hospital at Spirit River," Fawcett related. "Even to the last mishap assailed us and the train ran off the track and was hours late running into Spirit River. When we got there only one bed could be had and Captain Roy was placed in it." Fawcett and McElhanney had little choice except to continue to Edmonton, where they recovered. On November 11, Fawcett received a telegram—Roy had passed away. "Sir, it grieves me sorely to think that poor Captain Roy endured all the hardships and privations of the battlefields in France," Fawcett wrote to Deville, "only to fall victim to this dreadful plague."

On November 7, 1918, Surveyor General Deville telegrammed to William H. Norrish, DLS: "If on account of epidemic or quarantine or illness on your party you are unable to carry on operations efficiently, you may discharge party and return home." Norrish responded that there had been some cases of influenza in the Red Deer area, but the worst appeared to be over. "No sickness has occurred on my party and every precaution has been taken to protect the men," he assured Deville. Norrish, evidently better prepared than many Albertans, had kept his men virtually isolated since the beginning of September 1918. They had not been allowed time off to observe Labour Day or Thanksgiving Day. When the war finally ended, Norrish's survey party was not among those who celebrated the signing of the armistice on November 11.[5]

Many of the men on survey parties were veterans who bore the scars of warfare in Europe. Even before the conflict ended, Dominion Land Surveyors had instructions to employ returned men whenever possible for the 1918 summer season. In March 1918, Ernest Hubbell, DLS, Chief Inspector of Surveys, argued that returned men should be paid sixty dollars a month for survey work while they waited for land to settle on.[6] Returned men did not always thrive on survey work. As Richard Cautley, DLS, ALS, observed, combat experience did not turn salesmen, clerks, or tailors into good men for a survey party.[7] In April 1918, Frank Heron had returned from the front, shell-shocked and with shrapnel wounds. His doctor deemed that survey work would be beneficial. William Norrish took on the eighteen-year-old Heron, who had previously worked in the cutting room at Great West Garment Company in Edmonton, as a labourer on his survey party. Norrish thought the young man would be mostly working as a rodman, but his instructions later included work that demanded "hard chopping." It turned out Heron was reluctant to do axe work. Although Heron got extra pay—the $2.25 a day accorded to returned men—he soon quit.[8]

Richard Cautley almost exclusively employed returned men on his party in 1919, but as he noted, they were all woodsmen and some of them had been with him before the war. "I never had a better outfit in my life, or one that was more pleasant to deal with," he wrote later. "There were three sergeants in one tent who had all won decorations. One of them was notified to come down to Edmonton to be decorated by the Prince of Wales, but he wouldn't go." The grim reality of his men's wartime experience was apparent to Cautley when the party stopped to cool off in Rea Lake on a hot June afternoon. "When the boys stripped, I was a bit staggered," he admitted.

"Every man had been wounded, except one, and their wounds had healed so recently that they still looked angry."[9]

Many of these veterans were not in the best of shape for the rigours of travel to northern Alberta. Several surveyors heading north to the Peace River Country in 1920 on the infamous Edmonton, Dunvegan and British Columbia Railway purchased sleeping berths for their men. The journey to Grande Prairie was scheduled to take twenty-nine hours. But, as many discovered, this was a bare minimum, as the train often arrived days, rather than hours, late. Departmental rules only allowed for berths for the chief and his assistant. When William Norrish faced loss of two days' wages for breaking the rules and spending $1.80 on a berth for each man in his party, he made an impassioned plea to the surveyor general for common sense. Noting that his party were returned men, he wrote: "It seemed to me imperative that the men should be assured of sleep as far as the sleeping cars go."[10] At Spirit River, the sleeping cars remained behind, and Norrish's party spent three and a half hours pacing the platform, trying to keep warm until the train to Grande Prairie arrived. They then lurched their way along in an unheated, antiquated day coach, arriving in Grande Prairie forty-three hours after they had left Edmonton—thankful that they had not been derailed!

By one o'clock the next day, they were at work loading up the wagons and were ready to pull out by evening. "Do you think we could have done this if the men had lost two nights' sleep or say three or four nights' sleep if we hadn't been lucky enough to hit the best trip in several weeks?" Norrish asked Deville. "I maintain," he argued, "that the government received ample value for $18.00 expenditure and were further rewarded by sending out a happy party of men."[11] Deville certainly looked into the matter, and although it is not clear what the outcome was, one can hazard a guess that Norrish retained his pay.

By spring 1919 unemployment in Alberta was rising as thousands of returned men were looking for work, along with people thrown out of work by the termination of wartime employment positions. Surveyors, nevertheless, found it difficult to recruit suitable crews on the pay the Dominion government offered. The labour situation became volatile in Alberta, as widespread dissatisfaction grew. Henry Soars, DLS, ALS, began organizing his party in mid-May that year, but the General Strike in Edmonton delayed his start.[12] In 1920 Cyprus Hotchkiss, DLS, ALS, noted there were inexperienced men aplenty but few experienced survey hands or men with other bush experience available.[13] The same spring, his colleague, R. C. Purser, DLS, had particular difficulties employing a qualified instrument man for his survey party. "After exhausting various means, newspaper advertising, visiting the G[reat] W[ar] V[eterans] A[ssociation] Employment office, the Alberta Government employment office, the University of Alberta and so on, I was forced to give up the idea, the salary being in general considered too low for a man of the qualifications asked for." Purser finally hired an "engineering helper."[14]

The war left, as its immediate legacy, a period of economic doldrums, and surveyors had difficulty finding employment. A number of Alberta Land Surveyors had to look for other work, as indeed some had already done during the war. William Milton Edwards, ALS, gave up on his private practice in Lethbridge in 1915. From 1917 to 1922, he left the surveying profession altogether to manage a lumberyard and then put his mathematical skills to work doing business accounts. Eventually he was able to return to surveying in 1923.[15] Horace Seymour, DLS, ALS, went abroad to Venezuela, where he embarked on a survey of Lake Maracaibo for a petroleum oil company developing the surrounding oil field. Seymour then put his town planning experience to work for the city of Maracaibo.[16]

Others sought positions with the Alberta civil service, to which they brought some considerable experience. Alex G. Stewart, DLS, ALS, worked on the Canada–Alaska Boundary, surveyed township subdivisions in the Peace River area, and worked as a district engineer with Alberta Department of Public Works. He was briefly in private practice in 1912, and then served overseas during the war. On return to civilian life in Edmonton, he rejoined the Department of Public Works, but soon had an offer he could not refuse. As he later recalled, the Land Titles Office sent an SOS to Mr. Charlesworth, Director of Surveys, to send a surveyor over, as they had been without one for some time—seemingly since 1913! "I went and apparently the Registrar liked me all right. He would have liked anybody I guess, who would get him out of the difficulty he was in there. He had transfers, mortgages, liens, and every other thing piled high on the desk."[17] Stewart was surveyor to the Land Titles Office through much of the interwar period, from 1920 to 1936.

When the war ended, the profession did not draw young men in Alberta as it had done during the boom years. Only two men sought ALS commissions in 1919, and two more in 1920. The post-war years proved to be uncertain, and the cloud lifted slowly. It was only in 1921 that membership picked up with six new members. In fact, only ten more men became Alberta Land Surveyors before 1932.[18] Yet post-war hope for economic recovery shaped a positive attitude towards the future among surveyors, who were bolstered by the immediate implementation of a land grant scheme to enable returned soldiers to go into farming, which would require further township subdivision.

## Soldier Settlement and Land Classification Surveys

As thousands of men returned from the horrors of the trenches in Europe, the Canadian government attempted to make the transition to civilian life easier by offering free homestead lands in northern Alberta to those who wished to farm. All unclaimed land in the Peace Country within fifteen miles of a railway line was reserved for soldier settlements. Although a description of townships in the Peace River Country had been published in 1916, the Soldier Settlement Board evidently did not consider it specific enough for picking out a prime homestead location. As a result, two survey parties were dispatched to the Peace River and Grande Prairie area to advise how much land in each quarter section was suitable for agriculture, and what type of soil it contained. The whole idea was that a soldier settler would be able to select an open quarter and make a fair start at farming the first year.

In 1918 Dominion Land Surveyor Louis Brenot was in charge of the land classification surveys.[19] Brenot led the first survey party, and Sydney Fawcett, the second. Brenot worked on either side of the Edmonton, Dunvegan and British Columbia Railway between Smoky River and Lesser Slave Lake. He had three assistants, all of whom were Dominion Land Surveyors. When he arrived in Edmonton in May 1918, he applied at the Great War Veterans Association to hire returned men for his survey party. He then set out north. Brenot's parties were able to cover between four and nine townships a day depending on the terrain. They found a considerable number of quarter sections suitable for tillage among the bush areas. As each survey party progressed, it measured elevations with a barometer and noted all topographical features at frequent intervals. Every half mile, or more frequently where a change in soil type was evident, the party did a soil test. Assessment of the quality and quantity of water, as well as the projected cost of clearing the land, ultimately helped to estimate its value. Brenot produced a lengthy report that provided a profile of the history of development in the area, and rated all quarter sections from one to nine, to indicate whether they were open for immediate cultivation or required clearing before the land could be broken.

Further north, Sydney Fawcett led the second party, examining some seventy-nine hundred quarter sections along the Edmonton, Dunvegan and British Columbia Railway from Smoky Lake to Spirit River and the proposed railway route from the town of Peace River to Dunvegan. The party located two large tracts of land suitable for immediate settlement. One was a district northeast of Spirit River, known locally as the Blueberry Mountains, and the other lay northeast of the burgeoning town of Sexsmith. Unfortunately, there was not enough land surveyed and opened for settlement in these areas to offer the prospective veteran homesteader a fair chance of successful settlement. Despite the shortage of available surveyed land, over eight hundred veterans had consulted a colour-coded map to pick out a homestead in Alberta's north by the end of 1919.[20] Demand for land continued to mount. In 1920 the number of survey parties in the field increased to four as the area to be considered for soldier settlement was extended to an area north of Edmonton, between the Athabasca River and Lac La Biche, as well as north of Peace River.

The Soldier Settlement Programme highlighted an urgent need for township subdivision surveys in many northern districts. As the land deemed suitable for settlement along the Keg River had not been surveyed, a Topographical Surveys Branch party set out to subdivide the area in 1919. John Buchanan, DLS, ALS, of Edmonton, who had surveyed in the Peace Country before the Great War, was in charge. On May 22 his survey party loaded their supplies and climbed aboard a steamer at Peace River. By day's end, they disembarked on the riverbank at the location point for beginning the survey. By the third week of October seven townships had been surveyed—but not without some difficulty in positioning the survey posts due to large boulders and gravel.[21] In 1919 Fred Seibert, DLS, ALS, led a subdivision survey to facilitate soldier settlement in an area north of Peace River. Meanwhile, west of Dunvegan, Richard Knight, DLS, ALS, extended the township subdivision where several soldier settlers impatient to begin farming had squatted. They could then begin

## Radio Breaks the Silence

The advent of radio in the late 1920s made an impact on surveying, not least in northern areas, in providing a time signal for determining longitude. In 1927 Knox McCusker was able to pick up the 6 PM time signal through CFCN radio station in Calgary, while he was working in the Peace River area. In April 1928 he gave an address over CNRO radio in Ottawa: "Last summer, while out on an exploratory survey many miles and a week's journey from the nearest railway, we were listening in to the orchestra at Cramers' Chateau from Portland, Oregon. Between numbers we could distinctly hear the hum of voices, the tinkling of glasses, and all the sounds of a big summer dance pavilion, while outside our tents, surrounded by the intense stillness not fifty paces away stood an old grizzly bear sizing up this to him, new and strange layout."[23]

*Knox McCusker tests his reception. A two-tube regenerative set was specially designed for survey work;*
*it weighed fifteen pounds and occupied a space of 18 x 12 x 12 inches.*

building and clearing land, confident of the boundaries of their homesteads.[24] In 1920 similar parties set out to subdivide townships southeast of Spirit River and northwest of Grand Prairie.

A party under the direction of Cyprus P. Hotchkiss, DLS, subdivided land in townships east of Fort Vermilion in the lower Peace River district.[25] The river split one of the townships where Hotchkiss was working, and he used a scow as a cook tent and cache for their camp on each shore. Unlike the reports of earlier surveyors subdividing in the Peace River district, Hotchkiss's carefully typed photo-illustrated report included details that revealed the changes settlement had brought to the Peace area generally, such as the appearance of wild mustard and other noxious weeds, and he noted the urgent need for a doctor in the area.[26]

Between 1919 and 1921, surveyors subdivided parts of fifty-six townships in northern Alberta, most in connection with the Soldier Settlement Programme. A sprinkling of later survey parties were employed on subdivision work until 1931, marking the end of township subdivision in northern Alberta for two decades.[27]

The post-war demand for farmland, especially for soldier settlement, was urgent further south also. Surveyors went out specifically to investigate soils and record the acreages of soils of different grades, while also assessing lands for selection as forest reserves. This was important work as land was opened up on the fringes of established agricultural districts. A classification survey required actual soil samples and a more scientific approach that would help the settler in knowing what type of land he was getting. Soil samples initially went to Ottawa, but by 1922 surveyors working in Alberta were able to send their soil samples to a laboratory at the University of Saskatchewan in Saskatoon.[28] The description of the soil was then included in the final classification report.

Surveyors embraced land classification work during the 1920s. They interviewed local settlers as to climatic conditions, growing season for crops and vegetables, as well as suitability for livestock operations, and market conditions and opportunities, including roads and distance to the nearest rail point. New technology helped as photographs became a significant aspect of recording for land classification surveys. They clearly illustrated developments and conditions outlined in the report. By the 1920s, Kodak produced cameras that were light, small, and convenient for surveyors in the field. Surveyor General Deville favoured the Vest Pocket Kodak with a Zeiss Anastigmat and recommended its use for the soldier settlement surveys in the Peace Country. "Although the size is small, the definition is very fine and the negatives will stand considerable enlargement, if deemed necessary. The developing outfit is very compact and the whole equipment takes very little room."[29] By the early 1920s, all surveyors involved in land classification surveys used these cameras. Stanley Livingstone Evans, DLS, ALS, investigating lands west of Edmonton in 1920, took a Vest Pocket Kodak TS 2224 along with twelve rolls of film, instructions for use, a developing tank, ten packets of developing powder, and all the accessories required for developing the film in the field.[30] As the 1920s progressed, settlers were able to consult the land classification surveys at Dominion Land Office agencies or sub-agencies across Alberta. At the Dominion Lands Office in Rocky Mountain House, for instance, intending settlers could pore over maps and plans accompanying the surveys done in the Sylvan Lake area in 1923.[31]

## CHANGE IN OTTAWA AND THE ANTICIPATION OF THE TRANSFER OF NATURAL RESOURCES TO ALBERTA

The interwar years brought changes to the organization of the Topographical Surveys Branch. In Ottawa the new Surveys Bureau, set up in 1922, amalgamated three different branches within the Department of the Interior involved in surveying—the Geodetic Survey, the Topographical Survey, and the ongoing Canadian section of the International Boundary Commission.[32] Cutbacks were almost immediate. Athos Narraway, Controller of Surveys, informed Austin Cumming, DLS, ALS, who was working in Alberta in September 1922, that all surveyors were to finish fieldwork by October 31 to keep expenditures within the appropriation voted by Parliament. "Our programme of surveys for 1922 was first arranged on the basis of expenditure of $760,150, which was later reduced by the Minister to $600,000 and when before parliament was further cut to $570,000. Consequently we find ourselves faced now with a probable overdraft unless we curtail operations considerably."[33]

The days of the Calgary office of the Topographical Surveys Branch seemed numbered. By 1925 Frederic Peters, the new surveyor general following the death of Edouard Deville in 1924, was planning on moving Morrison Bridgland, DLS, ALS, and his assistant Ley Harris, DLS, ALS, to Ottawa. Peters changed his mind about the necessity of the move by September 1926, postponing it for a year. As Bridgland was in the middle of preparing four map sheets around Calgary, it was more convenient to maintain the office in Calgary.[34] Bridgland's arguments to stay in Calgary were obviously as strong as his desire to do so; in February 1927 Peters recommended that Bridgland and Harris remain in Calgary, as there was still a great deal of photographic work to be done in the mountains.[35]

After the reorganization, Dominion Land Surveyors no longer worked on contract. Some received a salary and became civil servants. Knox McCusker, DLS, ALS, reflected in his diaries on these changes as they affected many surveyors working for the Dominion government in Alberta: "Out in the spring to do a survey, then home again to make up the notes and plans. In the early 1920s this was changed. The boys became civil servants with all the advantages pertaining thereto. An era free from worry then followed. No wondering in the spring whether we were to go out or not. No worrying about old age, the pension would ensure a peaceful old age complete with golf, chicken ranch or what have you, and above all we couldn't be fired without reason."[36] For others, the life of a civil servant held no attraction. Fred Seibert looked for survey work elsewhere. He took a position as Superintendent of the Natural Resources Division of Canadian National Railways in Winnipeg, where he worked for the next forty-eight years.[37]

During the summer of 1927, the Topographical Survey made a reclassification of its employees. Morrison Bridgland was affronted when he did not get a promotion along with others who had been employed for less time. Bridgland had spent twenty-six years in the west and was an active member of the Alberta Land Surveyors' Association. His response had a western ring: "I fear . . . that there is always a tendency to overlook members of the outside service and to give preference to those who are nearest headquarters and in a better position to urge their claims."[38]

By the late 1920s, the professional status of Dominion Land Surveyors was under some pressure. In Ottawa, Frederic Peters upheld the necessity for Dominion Land Surveyors to be involved in surveys under his control: "In the past practically all the work carried on by the Topographical Survey of Canada had to do with subdivision of land and consequently its field staff consisted entirely of Dominion Land Surveyors. Of more recent years the work of this survey has gradually changed from subdivision surveys until a large portion of its field operations now consists of topographical mapping and land classification." This was no reason for change or an undermining of standards, he argued, pointing out that the late Dr. Deville had insisted that the field men of the Topographical Survey hold DLS commissions.[39]

Underlying the tensions within the Surveys Bureau in Ottawa was the anticipated transfer by 1930 of western natural resources from the Dominion to the prairie provinces. In 1905, when Alberta and Saskatchewan became provinces, the Dominion government agreed to hand over control of natural resources to the provincial governments. However, in Alberta, the Liberal govern-

## A Dissenting Voice

In January 1921, Richard Cautley expressed his views as to how the transfer of natural resources would affect surveyors practicing in Alberta. The province, he said, would have trouble finding sufficient money to pay for the surveys that were still required. The many other demands on the available funds—nowhere close to what the Dominion government had been pouring into Alberta—would, he argued, shape the provincial government's survey policy. He did not think it would set aside funds for long-term needs, comparing surveying land ahead of settlement "to the business of a French wine merchant who puts down a million dollars worth of new wine each season which will not be matured—or saleable—for fifteen years." Cautley was distrustful of a provincial government takeover of survey operations in the proposed areas of provincial jurisdiction, believing a federal system with high standards worked well for the whole country. [40]

ment, despite vigorous protest from the Conservative opposition, was happy to accept an annual cash subsidy instead. The election of the United Farmers of Alberta in 1921 changed the status quo, and the issue of natural resources was once again on the table.

Preparation for the transfer was well underway from the mid-1920s and land surveyors in Alberta sought to make the best of it. In January 1924, Charles M. Hoar, President of the Alberta Land Surveyors' Association, stressed the opportunities that transfer of natural resources would mean for the Alberta Land Surveyor. "He is best fitted to carry on the various reconnaissance, exploitation, and development surveys for the determination of the best method of developing these resources." Hoar stressed that surveyors needed to become more specialized, but also that they must be prepared to accept new responsibilities that would come with new undertakings. [41] Furthermore, he argued, the opportunity for Alberta Land Surveyors would increase as those for Dominion Land Surveyors decreased.

A large drop in funding for the Topographical Survey's work in Alberta was apparent in 1924–25. Then there was a sudden rise in expenditure in 1928–29, [42] as the Survey wrapped up ongoing projects and embarked on last-minute surveys requested by other government branches, to ensure a smooth transition of responsibility. The Canadian National Parks Branch, for example, lost no time in getting surveys done that would be more difficult to arrange once the transfer had taken place. In fall 1928, the Parks Branch, believing that the Eau Claire and Bow River Lumber Company was cutting trees on land that was inside the Rocky Mountain Park boundary, decided to survey the south boundary of the company's berth for a definitive judgement on the question. Knox McCusker went out to the timber berth, originally surveyed by Louis B. Stewart, DLS, DTS, in 1884. After completing the survey, McCusker met with representatives from the Parks Branch, the lumber company, and the Dominion Lands Office in Calgary, to ensure all agreed to the south boundary as he had surveyed it. [43]

Finally, the transfer of natural resources from Ottawa came into force in 1930. It would be many years, however, before all the paperwork connected with surveys in Alberta would be completed, and all the field notebooks, diaries, and correspondence of surveyors who subdivided the townships of Alberta were sent west in cardboard boxes.

## RETRACEMENT AND MISCELLANEOUS SURVEYS

Special surveys instigated during the war years to correct and extend work associated with original township subdivision surveys continued into the 1920s. It became evident as early as 1914 that many sloughs and lakes shown on township maps had dried up since the surveyors had mapped them. Shores often receded to such an extent that the acreages calculated for adjacent quarter sections were no longer accurate. Problems in connection with the disposal of such land were becoming more frequent. In central and southern Alberta, as elsewhere across western Canada, Dominion Land Surveyors embarked on surveys, using a stadia rod and transit to check distances between points in subdivided country previously accepted as correct.

They carried explicit instructions as to how to examine blocks of townships and how to survey all bodies of water. Those recently examined and marked on the updated township plans were acceptable as correct. However, when a township plan did not show a body of water, surveyors were not to presume this was correct. Instructions for stadia surveys noted: "It is to be borne in mind that all townships are to be investigated and reported upon whether they contain water bodies or not." The stadia survey was to tie into established adjacent monuments according to the latest *Manual of Instructions*, published in 1917. Surveyors were to report all corners that were under water at the time of the original survey, but that were now on dry ground and could therefore be marked by monuments in their true position. The surveyor in charge was to decide whether his stadia party would build the monuments or whether a mounding party should do them later.[44]

In 1918 stadia surveys were carried out in the area northeast of Calgary, east of Red Deer, and south of Edmonton,[45] south of Medicine Hat, and northeast of Edmonton in 1919.[46] While undertaking stadia surveys, Dominion Land Surveyors also reported on the condition of all monuments in the township, and whether a re-survey of the township was required, as well as giving information on the grading of roads and other improvements, including fences. When it was clear to a surveyor that the resurvey of a township was both necessary and desired by settlers, he left a petition form for retracing obliterated survey lines. Signed by at least one prominent settler, it then went to the surveyor general.[47]

Land surveyors also carried out various retracement surveys and the building of missing or misplaced monuments to complete surveys under the township system. They generally rectified any errors that had previously been made by surveyors, or by mounding parties, during the initial great push to get townships subdivided. In spring 1917, Arthur E. Glover, DLS, ALS, did a retracement survey to determine the correct location for a monument and to erect a proper monument.[48] He spent all summer 1917 working on similar surveys, sorting out issues that had arisen with conflicting documentation or duplicated monuments. One of these involved reassessing the position of the Red Deer River in a township subdivided in 1904. Glover's resurvey ensured that the position of the river could be shown correctly in the next edition of the plan of the township.[49]

Surveyors undertook numerous other surveys categorized as miscellaneous in Alberta during the 1920s, including the investigation and retracement of school lands for sale. Increasingly, other government branches requested specific kinds of surveys. In 1919, for example, the Dominion Water Power Branch required a benchmark in the Peace River area south of Fort Vermilion where several townships were to be subdivided. "A first class bench mark as near the water of Peace River as safety from flooding will allow should be established somewhere within your subdivision," Surveyor General Deville informed James King, DLS. "It might be a mark on some huge boulder if available on either side of the river." King subsequently had a leveller, George Banister, DLS, assigned to his party, as there were almost no levels previously established in the area.[50]

In 1920 Ralph C. Purser, DLS, arrived in Alberta from Ottawa. His first job was to survey two parcels of land for a mining lease for which the Cadomin Coal Company wished to apply. Purser's survey party then spent the summer on the move, travelling from one survey location to the next, often some considerable distance apart. Purser's survey instructions were for a mixed assignment that included investigating a road allowance that was not the standard width of one chain, as well as investigating and surveying the lands around Shoal Lake. The homestead inspector in charge of that area reported that settlers were now eyeing land that had been under water at the time of original survey. Without a survey, they could not take it up. Purser returned to Alberta the following summer of 1921 with instructions for similar investigations and stadia surveys, along with a survey of the surface rights for the Harlech Mine in the Brazeau district.

Fred Seibert undertook the most unusual of miscellaneous surveys in 1921. His task was to investigate the area where the "wild wood buffalo" ranged along the 60° parallel that marked the northern border of Alberta. As a result, five hundred square miles were set aside as a sanctuary in 1922. Seibert published articles about the bison of northern Alberta in several Canadian magazines, including *Maclean's* and the *Canadian Forestry Magazine*.[51]

## SURVEYORS GET BEHIND THE WHEEL

Surveyors embraced the automobile, for however bumpy the road was, it beat a long day on foot moving from one location to another, or rattling along in a buckboard or a democrat. As road allowances opened up in Alberta, surveyors, like everyone else, were eager to make use of them. Although Dominion Land Surveyors first used automobiles in 1915, it took some time to prove their worth on the job, and meet the requirement to prove the necessity of purchasing government vehicles to the War Purchasing Commission. Surveyor General Deville was initially less than enthusiastic about the automobile. It took some time for him to accept the car's cost-effectiveness, judging from a wrangle between himself and Dominion Land Surveyor William H. Norrish.

On arrival in the Buffalo Lake area to undertake a stadia survey, Norrish quickly saw what an advantage the automobile would provide. He bought a 1917 Ford Model T from a local farmer for $465. As he later admitted to Deville, because he purchased it with his own money, he had refrained from mentioning it in his progress reports or even in his diary. At the end of the season, however, he made his pitch for reimbursement for the use of the automobile. "There were several days when the car saved half a day's time for the whole party and in the last week it saved about a day and a half at least by allowing us to camp at the town of Mirror instead of making a much longer move to the north side of the arm of Buffalo Lake and then have to move back again." Norrish noted the car was highly efficient for transporting supplies from the closest town. "Groceries, vegetables and mail were always brought to camp with the car and very often this was done in the evening. If one of our slow teams was sent to a town fifteen miles away with the wagon, they would take all day, thus keeping a rodman off the work and cutting the mileage in half."[52] He pointed to his exploratory survey around Cygnet Lake, where the use of the car had saved at least two days of his time as well as livery charges, which could have amounted to twenty-five dollars and the train fare that would have amounted to five dollars. He ultimately persuaded Deville that the Topographical

Surveys Branch should purchase the car and reimburse him for running expenses. Despite Norrish's self-proclaimed best efforts to put it up properly, the Ford did not survive the winter very well. By the following spring the tires had disintegrated, even though the car had been up on blocks and drained of water.

In spring of 1918, William Norrish, embarking on stadia surveys along the Red Deer River, was outraged to find himself without motorized transportation and the car allocated to another surveyor! He was to make use of the four horses, supply wagon, and democrat allocated to him. Deville added insult to injury: "Last season the appropriation of your surveys was $6,250.00 whereas the total of your expenditure was $7,044.29; you accordingly exceeded the amount set aside for your surveys by $794.29 which excess covered the cost of your car and running the same."[53] The feisty Norrish, by now used to the convenience of the car, refused to take no for an answer and once again simply purchased a used 1917 Model T! He asked Athos Narraway, Controller of Surveys, to intervene with Deville. Narraway, who was for the first time using a car for his own work in central Alberta, sided with Norrish. "There are very few surveys in prairie or semi-prairie country where the use of a car would not justify the paying of reasonable running expenses," he declared to Deville in June.[54]

Deville was not amused. He calculated what Norrish had achieved both with and without the car, and, on July 18 concluded, "It does not seem that an automobile is necessary on your surveys, nor would we be able to justify its purchase before the War Purchasing Commission." Norrish stubbornly would not let the matter rest, pointing out that the mileage figures cited

*Surveyors edge their automobiles along the bank of the Red Deer River, 1922.*
LIBRARY AND ARCHIVES CANADA, PA 019091

by Deville "do not begin to show the work accomplished and that the period during which the automobile was used was too short to use for a comparison."[55] Deville finally did agree to pay the gas costs, but not the depreciation or repair of Norrish's car.

The automobile was definitely here to stay. Athos Narraway was delighted to feel the miles slip away with relative ease as he travelled south from Edmonton to inspect surveys underway in southern Alberta and southern Saskatchewan in 1919. The whole trip took only fifteen days. Only a few years earlier, he would have wearily climbed up onto a democrat for this journey of hundreds of miles. Gerald Lonergan, DLS, ALS, was also behind the wheel that summer in Alberta, covering up to two hundred miles a day as he drove to inspect one survey after another.[56]

In Ottawa, the Topographical Survey ordered a number of Ford Touring cars in 1920. Stanley

Evans picked up his from the Lines Motor Company in Edmonton before setting out northeast of the city with his lands classification party. Land surveyors, however, continued to use a variety of means of transport. As Ralph Purser noted, his transport for miscellaneous surveys north of Edmonton for the season of 1921, "was arranged locally and consisted of whatever means was best suited for the district and was most readily obtained. It included motorcar, team and democrat and wagon. Long distances across country were, in general, travelled by train."[57]

By 1925 the Topographical Survey operated thirty-nine cars.[58] Surveyors with the Alberta Department of Public Works also had automobiles. As early as 1919, William Howard Young, ALS, used a motorcar while surveying in the Youngstown area. So did Homer P. Keith, ALS, while surveying a new road in southern Alberta across the Blood Indian Reserve to Hillspring.[59] But the automobile, even as the 1920s unfolded, was not stress-free—it broke down, got stuck in the mud, required quantities of gasoline to keep it going, and its tires punctured more frequently than one might wish on one's worst enemy. Certainly, the surveyor added a few new skills to his repertoire, as the automobile became his best friend.

## SURVEYORS AND NEW ROADS FOR ALBERTA

Alberta Land Surveyors were soon at work doing right-of-way surveys for the new roads that were demanded by automobile drivers in Alberta. The Good Roads Board, set up by Alberta businessmen in 1919, promoted the construction of roads to encourage tourism in the province. Meanwhile, the farming community argued for better market roads for rural areas that included raising road beds and building bridges and culverts. A final plan for road construction in Alberta produced in 1920 included a web of roads that meshed with major routes projected through Saskatchewan and British Columbia. In 1922 passage of the Alberta Public Highways Act gave the Good Roads Board hope.

*George Pinder's survey crew loading up in Lethbridge, 1927.*
ALSA, WEIR ALBUM

The Alberta Highways Branch gradually embarked on an ambitious road-building program, begun by the cost-sharing program set up through the Canada Highways Act passed in Ottawa in 1919 to encourage the construction and improvement of highways. Alberta, along with other provinces, then produced a map showing proposed roads to stimulate trade and commerce.[60] Local roads within municipal districts remained the responsibility of local authorities, who hired their own surveyors.[61] The municipal district of Wostok in east central Alberta, for example, hired Alfred Driscoll, DLS, ALS, of Edmonton to survey for road improvements and diversions in the late 1920s.[62]

Land surveyors with the Surveys Branch, working under the provincial director of surveys, undertook the rights-of-way survey work required for provincial road building. However, as Homer Keith, District Surveyor and Engineer for the Lethbridge area, noted in 1922, they also gave assistance in highway construction, primarily staking grades and road centres during construction.[63] The real action, however, did not begin until 1924, when funds kicked in from the Main Highways Loan Act, passed by the federal government. The Highways Branch then had to hire numerous surveyors and engineers to use the eagerly awaited funds from Ottawa to build roads that were to meet national standards. Surveyors who also had engineering qualifications assumed the highest positions of responsibility. In 1924 Homer Keith became chief construction engineer for Alberta, and over-

*George Pinder, DLS, ALS, 1928.*
ALSA, PINDER COLLECTION

saw 420 miles of main highway construction that year.[64] By 1928 there were four district surveyors and engineers with the Surveys Branch. They oversaw surveys for main highways that included routes from Wetaskiwin to Camrose, Mundare to Vegreville, Drumheller to Munson, and from Cardston to Waterton Lakes.[65]

Alberta Land Surveyor George Pinder became district engineer and surveyor for the Lethbridge area in 1926.[66] His papers reveal much about the nature of his work in southern Alberta in the late 1920s. Each spring, he organized his crew, loaded up a truck with equipment and supplies for the season, and set out. His main objective was to re-survey the road from Cardston to Mountain View, and on to Waterton. The Good Roads Board wished to see this road constructed to aid development of the tourist industry in the Park.

Pinder ran into a good deal of opposition from local settlers who found themselves cut off from previous routes, disputed bridge locations, and questioned the required diversions. All of this required negotiating a solution before the work could begin. To travel about during the survey, Pinder used his own 1926 Ford car, then the Chevrolet truck he purchased in spring 1927. The new road also necessitated the construction of a railway crossing west of the Peigan Reserve, and it took some time before the Canadian Pacific Railway would agree to the plan. Pinder spent a considerable

*Pinder's survey crew takes a lunch break, August 1931.*
*Pinder's assistant Carl Lester is seated on the far left.*
ALSA, WEIR ALBUM

amount of his time in penning copious correspondence on the details of these matters to his boss, Director of Surveys Percy Johnston. In addition, Pinder had to tackle the ever-increasing number of forms covering the details of his work that he was required as a civil servant to fill out every month. Nevertheless, he enjoyed the work. "Am having a great time down here," he wrote in June 1927, "working in beautiful country, excellent cook, and congenial crew, am living in a house and expect to be here for another month at least."[67] Pinder, however, generally slept under canvas and moved with his crew as required. He was a widower, but when he remarried in 1930, his new wife, and his young son from his previous marriage, spent the summers in camp with him. The days of staying in hotels had not yet arrived for most Alberta Land Surveyors, and Tom Pinder recalls trundling around with his father in a springless old Chevrolet one-ton truck between 1930 and 1932.[68]

In the summer of 1928, along with surveying road diversions and other stretches of highways in the south, Pinder's crew surveyed the Lethbridge to Pincher Creek Highway. Pinder also finally completed the survey of the highway to Waterton. Then, in 1930, he surveyed the highway through the Crowsnest Pass to the British Columbia boundary. In 1931 his work took him east of Lethbridge, surveying the new highway from Taber to Bow Island. In his report that year, Pinder drew attention to the problem of establishing permanent monuments in an area prone to soil drifting. Another problem was also emerging—the loss of monuments due to reconditioning of highways. Reconditioning involved using fresnoes to clean out the ditches that had filled with soil. This left few iron posts in place. Consequently, any later instructions to road construction crews based on monuments would be of little use. "The question of these monuments," Pinder concluded, "is in my opinion of very great importance to the Government, Landowner, and Surveyor, and it must be borne in mind that the amount of reconditioning of roads and the destruction of monuments will increase as the Province is developed and roads built."[69] Two years later Alberta was in the throes of the Depression and the provincial highway building program ground to a halt until after World War II.

## TOPOGRAPHICAL SURVEYS FOR NEW SECTIONAL MAPS

The end of World War I was a watershed in the focus of the Topographical Surveys Branch. The basic job of mapping land boundaries accomplished, Dominion Land Surveyors turned their attention to producing topographical maps urgently needed for the proper administration of natural resources, and for the use of engineers, foresters, fire rangers, geologists, and miners. In 1919 they began the revision of the three-mile-to-one-inch sectional maps that the Topographical

Survey had produced for the prairies since 1892. Surveyors in the field collected information about roads, buildings, and improvements, took elevations, and detailed all topographical features. Ultimately, the sectional map sheets that previously only showed land boundaries, water areas, and elevations at railway stations, transformed into topographical maps.

One of the first section maps revised in Alberta was the Blackfoot Sectional Map No. 115. A levelling party with the Canadian Irrigation Survey had already established contour lines over a large part of the map area. Dominion Land Surveyor James R. Akins and one of his assistants spent almost four weeks collecting information about the area. He visited the Land Titles Office, the Levelling Office in Calgary, the Office of the Commission of Irrigation, and the Canadian Pacific Railway Irrigation Office, before going out into the field. All of this preparation meant the work was accomplished quickly, helped by the fact that only small streams had to be traversed, as the larger rivers and streams had been done in the original survey.

In the Edmonton area, which was comprised of heavily timbered land dotted with lakes, John W. Pierce, DLS, was in charge of the survey for the revision of the Edmonton Sectional Map No. 315. The map showed several lakes that had not been included on township plans, along with the corrected courses and connections of streams previously plotted in error.[70] During the next season of 1920–21, surveyors revised the Rosebud Sectional Map No. 165 as well as the easterly part of the Calgary Sectional Map No.

*Surveying on the road through the Crowsnest Pass, 1930.*
ALSA, Weir Album

114, where the party led by James Akins had to fight its way through thick willow scrub. On the Sarcee Indian Reserve, the work was difficult because there were a lack of surveys for the area within the reserve boundaries on which to base the revision.[71]

Sectional maps were in great demand—particularly for the settlement and development of rural areas, but also as road maps. By the mid-1920s, surveyors worked on surveys for map sheet revision in conjunction with other surveys that were required in the area covered by the map sheet. William Christie, DLS, led a survey party to revise the Victoria Sectional Map No. 365 and at the same time carry out a land classification survey. In addition, he subdivided a surrendered portion of the Saddle Lake Indian Reserve.[72] Topographical mapping also become linked with a whole new survey method—aerial photo surveys.

## SURVEYING FROM THE SKIES

High on Alberta's mountaintops, land surveyors had introduced photo-topographical surveying during the 1890s. Thirty years later, surveyors took to the skies to take photographs to survey what was on the ground below. The war years had pushed the frontiers of flight and revealed possibilities of utilizing aerial photography to establish ground positions. Canada began experimenting with aerial survey work immediately after the war, and an aerial surveys program was soon organized to assist the Geodetic Survey undertaking reconnaissance flights into the Arctic, northern Ontario, and the western provinces. In Alberta, aerial surveying grew out of the fire patrol service provided for the Forest Service by the Air Board. The Air Board oversaw civil aviation immediately after the war, operating from newly created air bases. There was tight cooperation between the Royal Canadian Air Force (which in 1924 passed from the jurisdiction of the Air Board to the Department of Defence), the Dominion Forest Service, and the Topographical Survey. The first airbase in Alberta was established at High River. There was much excitement among the local population, by now intoxicated with the postwar exploits of civilian pilots and their barnstorming feats. A landing strip was prepared and offices built. By spring 1921, several large canvas hangars were ready to house the first open-cockpit De Havilland aircraft. The pilots were soon in the air, heading out over the forest reserves of southwest Alberta.[73]

Surveyor General Deville immediately took a hand in aerial work. He provided the specifications for photographs and gave instructions as to the angle of the camera mounted in the cockpit of the aircraft, the altitude of the aircraft, and the frequency with which photos were to be taken. Deville researched cameras, lenses, and film and had the Air Force experiment with them. While the Air Force flew the fire patrols, Deville worked to perfect a camera. Although in 1921 there were no instruments capable of plotting maps from air photos, Deville wanted to use aerial photography to assist surveyors working on the ground to revise sectional map sheets in the province. In 1923 he ordered low-level oblique views of the ground features within the Edmonton area. The idea was to use the roads visible in the photographs to map the limits of timbered areas. "In order to complete the grid on the photograph," Deville stated, "it is essential that at least two north and south roads and two east and west roads be shown clearly."[74] Unfortunately, the RCAF planes never got as far as Edmonton that year, but they did some experimental work in the Red Deer area, taking photographs at five thousand feet, seventy-five hundred feet, and at ten thousand feet, to assess the results. The results of early oblique work at low altitudes were somewhat disappointing, but the surveyor general was confident the program was worthwhile.

Vertical photographs taken at 90° to the ground at higher altitudes proved more successful in Alberta. They were used in conjunction with a number of surveys in the province from 1924. While the RCAF was in charge of flying—supplying aircraft and equipment, pilots, and photographers, as well as paying for the developing and printing of the photos—the Topographical Survey directed the survey itself. It received requests from various government departments for aerial photographs, and then issued instructions on location and specific techniques, directions, altitudes, and speeds at which to shoot the photos. Experienced Dominion Land Surveyors, well versed in mapping and aerial photography, accompanied each flight. Like the pilots, they padded up with sheepskin jackets and goggles. The surveyor's job was to guide the pilot along the route and advise the photographer as to where, when, and how to take the photographs. When adverse weather conditions, or frequent engine troubles, interfered with flight plans, it was the surveyor's job to reorganize the instructions. He was also charged with the safety of the crew should a forced landing be necessary in a forested inaccessible area. The role of the land surveyor, Surveyor General Frederic Peters noted in 1924, "is therefore of the greatest importance as to the success of this undertaking. Pilots and photographers are not navigators or mappers, nor is it desired that they should be, as their full attention is required to their own particular duties."[75]

The Topographical Survey was also responsible for the subsequent filing, indexing, and plotting of the photographs. A good deal of work had to be done with the photographs before they could be distributed to the various government departments and organizations that

*Cook tent on the move, survey party near Vegreville, 1922.*
LIBRARY AND ARCHIVES CANADA, PA 018354

requested them. This included the calculation of measurements and the preparation of proper plans. Land surveying and aerial surveying became closely linked. As Peters stressed, using aerial photographs required certain measurements on the ground; "that is to say aerial surveying and ground surveying go hand in hand."[76]

Richard H. Knight, DLS, ALS, was the first surveyor in Alberta to use aerial photography in conjunction with surveys on the ground. In the summer of 1924, he undertook a land classification and topographical survey of seventy townships, comprising 2,592 square miles around Vegreville, Vermilion, and Lloydminster. He worked with vertical aerial photographs taken in late May and early June at an altitude of 11,500 feet, which rendered each quarter section two inches square. Knight's instructions were to gather topographical information for each quarter and classify it according to seven main classes of land, four of which had two sub-classes; classify the roads and run soils tests; and then contour the total area at fifty-foot intervals for publication on a scale of three miles to one inch. During the summer of 1924, despite adverse weather conditions, compounded by rain and snow in September, surveyors completed a number of other aerial surveys, including the Edmonton area. It took thirty-two hours over fourteen separate flights to photograph the entire area covered by the Edmonton Sectional Map, 3,224 square miles.[77]

In Knight's opinion, aerial photographs were a godsend. No longer did he have to walk to the centre of the quarter section to sketch the adjacent topography; without photographs it is not generally possible to see or estimate distances beyond a quarter mile. He reckoned this aspect alone meant the survey party could do twice the amount of work in a given time. Further, the photograph was more accurate than sketching in the field. Surveyors could now compile township plans in the office during the winter months. For land classification, the aerial photograph gave the surveyor a complete view of the quarter section. He could see at a glance, as Knight explained, "how each tract of land is cut by streams, watercourses, valleys, ridges, lakes, sloughs, swamps, low lands, timbered lands." With some experience, Knight maintained, certain types of soils could be determined from aerial photographs: "On sand areas the trees and bluffs show a lighter colour. Parallel features denote a drifting sand soil or beach deposits. Sandy clay and clay soils always show white when under cultivation therefore in improved districts the photographs aid in outlining the extent of such soil." The only disadvantage Knight could think of was the cost associated with all aspects of the aerial work itself. He warned that the quality of the photographs was vital for their usefulness.

Knight experienced problems with photograph quality during the summer of 1924. It was very dry in Alberta, and forest fires hampered the work in the air. Smoke and the rush to get the work done in time for his ground survey actually rendered a large number of the photographs useless. It was also necessary to develop the film quickly, as it was unstable and did not develop well after about a month.[78] These initial surveys had other teething problems that included malfunctioning altimeters in the planes and problems with the dust debris raised on stubble field landing strips. Loose straw damaged the varnish on the doped wings of the De Havilland aircraft, and water remained lodged in the wing fabric. The cockpit of the De Havilland was too small, and a blind spot caused by the lower wing led to directional error.[79] Some of these problems were alleviated as the aerial survey program accelerated through 1925 and five new Avro aircraft arrived at High River for use along with the De Havilland aircraft.

*Richard H. Knight, DLS, ALS, 1921.*
ALSA, WEIR ALBUM

Early in the 1925 season, Richard Knight embarked on a land classification survey and revision of the Victoria Sectional Map. He carried a book of aerial photographs in the field as he examined 7,368 quarter sections northeast of Edmonton. The photographs provided a plan of each quarter section as he assessed the soil in order to divide the lands into seven classifications. Working directly on the photograph using black ink, he marked whether the surface topography was rolling, gently rolling, level, and so on, as well as whether it was prairie, cultivated land or hay lands, muskeg or bush. He marked roads in red along with farm buildings, schools, and churches, while using a blue pencil to shade all water areas. His survey party of five labourers, an instrument man, a soils expert, and an assistant, moving rapidly across the country in a Ford truck and three Ford touring cars, carried out the two objectives of his survey season simultaneously.[80]

The Alberta Department of Public Works noted the efficiency and economy of subsequent aerial surveys between 1925 and 1927 for the revised Calgary, Red Deer, and Peace Hills Sectional Maps.[81] In 1928 Premier Brownlee wrote to Charles Stewart, Minister of the Interior to request that aerial surveys be undertaken in northeastern Alberta adjacent to the junction of the Clearwater and Athabasca Rivers near Fort McMurray, and north along the Athabasca to the McKay River. "We understand there is a considerable stand of timber there available for pulpwood purposes, and if this could be demonstrated by aerial photography we would be prepared to supplement it by the necessary cruises to estimate more definitely its actual value and the possibilities of a pulpwood industry being established at Fort McMurray."[82] The Topographical Survey agreed to do the survey in conjunction with surveys over Wood Buffalo Park. The project went on hold—indefinitely as it turned out—as there were no suitable planes available, and the Air Force was waiting on new aircraft that would be safer over such hazardous terrain.

By the early 1930s, advances in both aircraft and aerial cameras, and the development of more highly sensitized film, made for considerable improvement in aerial photography. In 1933 the Royal Canadian Air Force replaced the open-cockpit planes with high-wing monoplanes that had enclosed cabins. The first of these was the Fairchild FC2W.[83] The new airplanes extended the possible range of flight over difficult terrain, especially problematic in Alberta, where higher altitude made landing on water a difficult proposition. These cabin planes could be equipped with three cameras rather than one to allow for synchronization of exposures. This, once technicians ironed out the initial problems with mounting the cameras, became the norm. For oblique photography, three cameras, mounted as a unit in the aircraft, pointed obliquely toward the ground in the opposite direction to which the airplane was travelling. The three cameras collectively produced a fan of pictures, the side photographs overlapping the centre one. The three exposures were made simultaneously, as each camera was electrically connected with the others. As the plane flew along strips of territory eight miles apart, an automatic clock was set to make contact at the desired number of seconds interval between exposures; one fan exposure could be made at every one and three-quarter miles. In 1935 Surveyor General Frederic Peters explained how it worked in a paper written for the *Financial Post*. The *Post* turned it down as old news and suggested a story on surveying for the burgeoning mining industry in the Northwest Territories![84]

By 1938 aerial photographs of many areas of Canada were available for surveyors at a nominal cost from the National Air Photographic Library established in Ottawa in 1925. An editorial in *The Canadian Surveyor* noted in July 1938, "An increasingly large number of surveyors in private practice are finding that the use of air photos is of the greatest value in their work. Such photographs can be used to advantage in all sorts of property surveys and practically used as evidence in litigation. The photograph has the obvious advantage of being more easily interpreted by the layman than a surveyor's plan, and it is often possible by its help to explain a situation to a client which otherwise he would have difficulty in grasping." Aerial surveying had become an integral part of modern surveying and mapping methods that were part of a land surveyor's practice.

## The Passing of a Generation

The 1920s marked the passing of several surveyors who had been early leaders in their profession and who left their mark on the story of surveying in Alberta. Their deaths marked the closing of an era. Among them was James J. McArthur, who died on April 14, 1924. He received his commission as a Dominion Land Surveyor in 1879, and instigated the first photo-topographical surveys in the Rocky Mountains in 1887. Then, on September 21, 1924, Edouard Deville, Surveyor General of Canada died after an illness of some months.

Tributes to Deville were many, both during his lifetime and in the months following his death.

## The Canadian Surveyor

In 1922 the *Dominion Land Surveyors' Journal* made its appearance. Editor Ralph C. Purser, DLS, ran articles and reviews of technical textbooks, and provided a platform for the exchange of views and experiences across the county. Surveyors who were members of provincial survey associations recognized its value in connection with other professional organizations and educational institutions in Canada, as well as the many technical surveying organizations across the British Empire that received copies. The provincial associations were soon eager to cooperate in the production of the journal, which changed its name to *The Canadian Surveyor* to reflect its inclusive nature of all surveyors across the country. It tended to publish papers read at the annual meetings of surveyors, which focused on the latest developments in surveying, such as aerial mapping or surveying instruments. When the Association of Dominion Land Surveyors changed its name to the Canadian Institute of Surveying in 1934, The Canadian Surveyor retained its name, only changing to *CISM Journal* in 1988 and then to *Geomatica* in 1993.

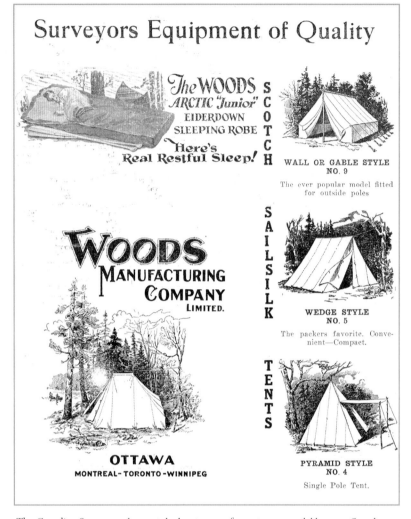

The Canadian Surveyor *also carried advertisements for equipment available across Canada.*
The Canadian Surveyor, July 1928

Two years before his death, the Engineering Institute of Canada bestowed honourary membership on Deville. On that occasion, Thomas Shanks, his colleague as Assistant Surveyor General, spoke of Deville's scientific genius, his unflagging industry, patient and humble devotion to duty, and "his mastery of essential details as the executive head of a rather complex organization." Shanks referred to "the incorruptible integrity of his administration; to his honourable and fair dealing with subordinates and to his loyalty to superiors in office; to his scrupulous and painstaking research into every phase of any subject which he was called upon to study; and to the consequent accuracy and finality of his decisions."[85]

Deville led the Topographical Survey for thirty-nine years, a period known as "the Deville era." Alberta Land Surveyor James Wallace paid his old boss in Ottawa a tribute. He hailed Deville as a figure of world significance: "Edouard Deville must be considered to have held the record in having had charge of the greatest system of surveys for settlement of all times and in all countries, and whose life was a struggle to create and maintain an accuracy hitherto unknown in such surveys."[86]

Frederic H. Peters, Irrigation Commissioner in Calgary from 1911 to 1921, had the difficult job of stepping into Deville's shoes as surveyor general.

Three days after Deville's passing, Alberta lost one of her most prominent surveyors, Jean L. Côté, who was also a member of the Alberta Legislature. Appointed to the Canadian Senate in September 1923, he underwent surgery for gallstones and appendicitis in the same month. Côté never fully recovered, although he sat in the Senate through the winter of 1923–24. On September 24, 1924, at the end of a summer spent with his young family at Les Eboublements, his native village in Quebec, he had a sudden and fatal attack of peritonitis. Two days later, the family buried Côté in the village churchyard—far from his home in Edmonton and the province he had served as surveyor and politician.[87]

By the late 1920s, William Pearce, honoured with the first life membership in the Alberta Land Surveyors' Association in 1924, was frustrated to find his famous robust health declining. Pearce put the stiffness in his knees down to having jarred his joints by riding thousands of miles in buckboards. But in 1927 doctors diagnosed this as "an aneurism of the artery." Pearce, the great walker, was ordered to curtail his activities.[88] William Pearce died on March 3, 1930, just before Alberta acquired control over her natural resources that he had so vigorously promoted. His passing, however, also marked the beginning of the Depression, and a difficult era for the profession.

## Surveying During the Depression

The onset of the Depression in 1930 sharply curtailed the range of work carried out by the Topographic Survey in Alberta. In May 1930, however, Surveyor General Frederic Peters noted that he intented to continue the Dominion mapping service in the west. In fact, according to Peters, the transfer of natural resources to the province of Alberta increased the demand for mapping work: "Presently the demands from the provincial authorities, from prospectors, from commercial companies, and from many other sources, are increasing far beyond the facilities which the Survey has to meet them."[89] Nevertheless, the layoff of a number of staff affected the work carried out in Alberta.

Knox McCusker was one of twenty-six Dominion Land Surveyors laid off as the Depression struck. He decided in 1931 to return to the Peace River Country where he had enjoyed working so much, homesteaded, and started a business as outfitter and guide for tourist and hunting parties. In 1933 the Alberta government let several surveyors with Public Works go. Among them was George Zouch Pinder. As his son, Tom Pinder, recalled, "Dad got the chop with nearly everyone else and the best they could offer him was a job "in charge of six pick-and-shovel men at 45 c[ents]an hour." Pinder, now fifty-three, bought five acres just south of Calgary and devoted much of his energy to gardening. He did continue to take on survey work as it came along on a part-time basis, often with Herbert H. Moore in Calgary.[90] Turning to private practice offered limited hope of business.

In 1933 and 1934, economic gloom settled over Alberta and over the surveying profession as building and other development projects went on hold. Furthermore, the much-touted benefits of the transfer of natural resources to Alberta in 1930 were not as bountiful as some had hoped.

Membership in the ALSA dropped even further and attendance at the annual meetings those years was poor, drawing only about fifteen members. Those that did attend were usually surveyors still employed by the Dominion or provincial government or by railway companies. Only seven new Alberta Land Surveyors received commissions between 1933 and 1939. Once again, surveyors had to turn to other work; surveying could only be a sideline.[91]

Ironically, the Depression years allowed for the survey of the "Highway in the Clouds," the Icefields Parkway between Banff and Jasper, which took eight years to construct. Undertaken as part of dominion government relief works in the parks in 1931, the survey reached Bow Summit by winter. Claude Walker, DLS, ALS, along with Ley Harris, DLS, ALS, led the survey parties that chained their way north as far as the Columbia Icefields by spring the next year. Walker, who had been surveying with the Parks Branch for twenty years, also had the role of supervising engineer for the highway. He was the oracle when it came to the conditions and challenges of building a mountain highway, and all involved sought his advice on every aspect, including snow removal equipment![92] Dominion Land Surveyor Thomas Stanley Mills was the chief engineer for the highway. Surveyors had to do considerable exploratory work to find the best route and subsequently undertake right-of-way surveys. They had many things to consider at such high altitude—alignment, grades, and curves through terrain that required river crossings and passed through areas of quick runoff that posed drainage requirements. In the Sunwapta area, sixty-five miles southeast of Jasper, surveyors decided on a series of switchbacks to gain elevation safely.[93]

The elaborate opening ceremonies planned for July 1, 1940, were cancelled. As Canada was at war, it was considered unseemly to spend money on celebrations as the Allied defence deteriorated on the European front. Tourists, however, still eagerly awaited the completion of the road, and on June 15, it unofficially opened to motorists eager to travel the 149 miles of gravel road whose route skirted the Columbia Icefield and on to Jasper.[94]

## The Alberta–Saskatchewan Boundary, 1938

By the late 1930s, as the Depression finally began to lift, there was considerable interest in mineral development on Crown Lands north of Lake Athabasca. Since the transfer of natural resources in 1930, and without a boundary north of Lake Athabasca, jurisdiction in the area had become an issue between Alberta and Saskatchewan. The Fourth Meridian, originally established as a governing line of survey for the Dominion Land Survey system, served by default as the boundary between Alberta and Saskatchewan from 1905. The difficulties experienced in 1879 in initially establishing its location—the resulting discrepancies, along with adoption of the Third System of Survey in 1881—had continued to haunt Dominion Land Surveyors who surveyed townships along the meridian. By 1915 many township plans along the Fourth Meridian had to be revised. Although corrections in latitude were made during retracement surveys, the positions of township corners were wrong along the meridian.[95] By 1918, despite problems caused by early surveying inaccuracies, Dominion Land Surveyors James Wallace, Guy Blanchet, and John MacFarlane had extended the Fourth Meridian from Township 62 as far north as Township 115 on the south shore of Lake Athabasca. A boundary commission was set up to finish the job. Accordingly, in 1937, under

*Survey crew on the Alberta–Saskatchewan Boundary Survey wait patiently
for the arrival of the float plane, summer 1938.*
ALSA, WEIR ALBUM

provincial and dominion orders-in-council, Frederic Peters was appointed Chairman of the Alberta–Saskatchewan Boundary Commission, with Commissioners M. B. Weekes, a Saskatchewan Land Surveyor, Controller of Surveys for Saskatchewan, and Albert P. C. Belyea, ALS, Director of Surveys for Alberta.

On March 8, 1938, Bruce Waugh, DLS, arrived in Edmonton to take charge of the field party to extend the Fourth Meridian north of Lake Athabasca. He sent his assistant, Joe W. Doze, DLS, ALS of Edmonton, to open up the line to the lakeshore from the south. They went out by air—possibly the first time an airplane was used in transporting surveyors in northern Alberta. Doze and another member of the party clambered aboard a plane at the Edmonton airfield and were soon aloft, heading for Fort Chipewyan. Here they hired horses and sleighs and set out for the Fourth Meridian. Waugh and the rest of the party soon followed by train as far as Waterways, and then flew the rest of the way to the line. On March 18, they began work running the line north across the rough encrusted snow-covered ice on the lake. The drawback of air travel became apparent when bad weather delayed their flight back to Edmonton. They were kept waiting at the lake until the pilot could land his ski-equipped plane on the ice to pick them up and fly them to Fort McMurray. After a short rest, they were on their way home to Edmonton. One can only imagine how they felt—this was a truly efficient way to get to and from a survey location.

Waugh returned to the north shore of Lake Athabasca that summer to run the remainder of the boundary. He had a larger crew and two additional assistants, Oluff Inskter, DLS, ALS, and Oscar W. Martyn, DLS, SLS. The party travelled by water to the starting point on the north shore of the lake. The line ran through rough and rocky terrain interspersed with muskeg and lakes. Intervening lakes had to be crossed by canoe, but they also offered an opportunity to land a float plane to drop

*Float plane tied up at shore, ready for loading during the Alberta–Saskatchewan Boundary Survey.*
ALSA, WEIR ALBUM

supplies on a regular basis and move camp as required. The dates for moving were pre-arranged, which put an additional stress on the rate of progress and required working through wet weather to ensure pickup at the appointed time and place.

In July 1938, Dominion Land Surveyor C. H. (Marsh) Ney of the Geodetic Survey flew to Miles Lake, establishing a camp from where he set out to make precise astronomical observations for the latitude and longitude of a point near the end of the line. Using a radio, he arranged for the pilot to pick him up and drop him thirty-five miles south. Leaving the results of his observations, along with surplus groceries for Waugh's party, he then flew back to Miles Lake, picked up his assistant, camping equipment, and instruments, and flew on to Fort Chipewyan. Such logistics would have been a dicey proposition only a decade earlier.

As the boundary survey progressed, mounders erected two sets of monuments—one to mark the township corners and one to define the provincial boundary. Frederic Peters arrived in camp at the end of the survey in time for the raising of the final monument on Labour Day. The next day, the men listened as the sound of engines drew near—two airplanes skidded across the water and the whole party and their equipment were loaded on board bound for Edmonton.[96]

Just as an exciting new era of air travel for surveyors began and the gloom of the Depression was beginning to lift, war broke out in Europe in September 1939. Albertans found civil life disrupted once again as mapping, road building, and urban development came to a halt. The course of land surveying in Alberta went on hold, as wartime demands diverted survey work into support of the war effort in defence of Canada.

# Eye on the Line
*World War II and Surveying for the Defence of Canada*

THE SURVEY OF WARTIME AIR BASES AND ALBERTA'S ROLE IN THE SKIES

By early September 1939, Albertans were once more at war. Many surveyors in the province had gone through a long period of economic doldrums. They numbered fewer than forty and most were no longer young. The vast majority of them were, in fact, past enlistment age for the armed forces. Alberta Land Surveyors supported the war effort on the home front using transit and field notebook rather than guns. Some worked on military projects such as surveying wartime air bases built in Alberta.

Canada's Prime Minister, Mackenzie King, after protracted negotiations ensuring a sovereign role for Canada, signed an agreement for the British Commonwealth Air Training Plan (BCATP) in December 1939. There had been rapid advances in aircraft technology, along with some cooperative Canadian and British air training during the interwar years. It took some time, however, for the wartime air-training plan, whose logistics were staggering in their scope, to become operational. The fall of France in April 1940 gave it a shot in the arm. Young men from all over Canada, Britain, New Zealand, and Australia came to the open clear skies of Alberta to learn to fly. They arrived at hurriedly selected and constructed air training schools run by the RCAF, on existing and new air bases. Two Alberta Land Surveyors served with the RCAF in Alberta. Oluff Inkster, ALS, dropped his private practice in Edmonton and joined the RCAF—not to serve in the air, but to lend his survey skills to the war effort as works officer on the construction and maintenance of airfields.[1] In May 1941 Robert McCutcheon, ALS, joined up and served as a navigation instructor in a number of training schools.[2]

Speculation as to where the BCATP schools would be located in Alberta was rife. Communities hoped for lucrative short-term construction work as well as the money the facility would generate in town for non-military staffing at the base, supplies, and the dollars spent in restaurants, sporting facilities, and cinemas by air force recruits. Established airports and airstrips used by local flying clubs who were to be involved in training pilots were among the most likely locations and had a head start on getting up and running. Only days after Canada signed the BCATP agreement, the *Lethbridge Herald* reported with alarm on December 21, 1939, that three survey parties had been spotted near Medicine Hat, Fort Macleod, and around Calgary. Did this mean that authorities intended on passing over the existing airfield at Lethbridge?[3]

The location of BCATP facilities was a matter of rivalry for Alberta's communities. Edmonton claimed superior conditions over Calgary for training pilots.[4] No. 3 Manning Depot was located in Edmonton, along with an initial training school, a flying school, and, by 1941, an air observer school. However, the Western Command of the BCATP located in Calgary, and the city had a service flying training school and a wireless school. Among other communities favoured for BCATP sites were Vulcan, Claresholm, Pearce, Dewinton, High River, Bowden, Fort Macleod, and Medicine Hat, with the only central Alberta facility at Penhold. Alberta ultimately had seventeen of Canada's 105 training schools, which produced 130,000 men for allied aircrews.[5] Two new military bases were also constructed in Alberta during the war, one at Wainwright and the other at Cold Lake, in addition to air bases for the RCAF that predated the war.

The selection of locations for BCATP aerodromes, which included flying, bombing, gunnery, and navigation schools, made following the input of civil aviation authorities, was not an easy task. It required careful consideration. The first essentials were good drainage, approaches that were clear of obstacles, easy access by road and/or rail, ample water, and power supply.[6] Certain types of terrain were also need for training—water for navigation exercises and unpopulated areas for bombing exercises.[7] Many aerodromes were completely new air bases on expropriated land, either purchased or leased by local agents with the Land Department of the Canadian National Railway, through a wartime cooperative arrangement.[8] It was the responsibility of the Canadian Department of Transport (DOT) to instigate detailed surveys prior to final approval by the Department of National Defence for development of proposed sites.[9]

Wartime cooperation between the Canadian and provincial governments meant Alberta Land Surveyors with the provincial Highways Department undertook the work. It began just as they

*Tarmac runways at the BCATP base at Pearce were surveyed and built for training pilots for bombers.*
GLENBOW ARCHIVES, PD-342-190

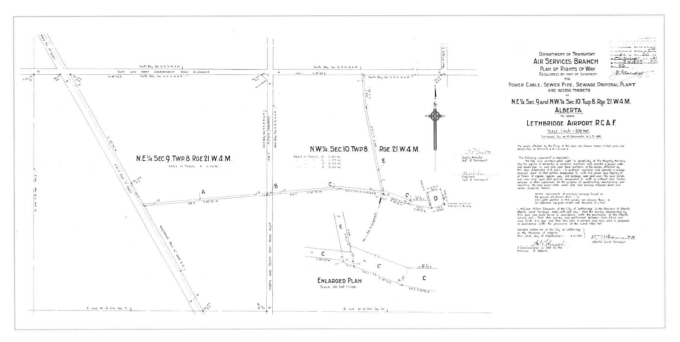

*Registered plan of rights-of-way, Lethbridge Airport, 1941.*
LAND TITLES OFFICE, PLAN NUMBER RW 429 FC

were laying off their survey parties in the fall of 1939, and was completed at high speed before the snow fell that year.

Surveyors in Alberta worked according to a national plan of operation. They studied topographical maps of districts and marked areas where land agents could obtain a level area of approximately one square mile. A reconnaissance then followed from the air, noting approaches, accessibility, and drainage patterns. Next, they examined potentially suitable sites on foot and prepared investigation reports. The reports then went to Ottawa by airmail, where the most favourable were approved for detailed ground surveys in the preparation of contour plans for the aerodrome. "All winter long as the surveys plans were received, work went on in laying out the aerodromes to take the best advantage of the natural features of the site."[10] Elementary flying schools that used light aircraft required all-turf runways, while the remainder, including the bombing and gunnery schools that used heavier aircraft, required hard surfaces. Detailed engineering surveys followed immediately, so that construction plans and specifications could be drawn up in time for construction in early spring 1940.[11]

There is a marked lack of discussion in the historical sources on certain kinds of details related to the war effort in Alberta. The normal channels of federal–provincial jurisdiction no longer applied for the duration, and things were often done with speed, urgency, and secrecy. The evidence suggests that in cases where the facility was starting from scratch, such as at Claresholm and Vulcan, DOT expropriated entire quarter sections, precluding the necessity for legal surveys of boundaries. Existing registered plans for wartime airfields in Alberta date from the 1950s, and therefore reflect the post-war boundaries. Where legal surveys were required for expansion or improvement to existing facilities, local Alberta Land Surveyors in private practice did them. In

September 1941, for example, William Milton Edwards, ALS, surveyed rights-of-way for a power cable, sewer pipe, and sewage disposal unit at the RCAF airport at Lethbridge. This development was presumably tied to the number of expected recruits for the bombing and gunnery school that opened in November 1941.

Taking photographs was for the most part forbidden and the adage of 'loose lips cost lives' applied to civilians, including surveyors, employed on war-related projects. The truth is that the line between military and civilian endeavours blurred during wartime cooperation. Jack Holloway, ALS, summed up the work of the Alberta Land Surveyors on the home front: "[They] did their best to cope with the tremendous demands for survey work which were generated principally by wartime needs and military projects that materialised in Alberta and more northern areas, especially after the United States entered the war."[12] Alberta Land Surveyors also played a role in the mega-projects undertaken in conjunction with the United States military—the North West Staging Route, Alaska Highway, and the Canol project, all of which had Edmonton as their supply base.

## The Defence of the Northwest: The North West Staging Route

In the summer of 1935, Alexander McLean of Canada's Civil Aviation Board climbed aboard a small plane with the famous bush pilot Punch Dickens of Edmonton and flew on a reconnaissance survey across northern Alberta, Northwest Territories, Yukon, and northwest British Columbia, to investigate a potential civil aviation route through Siberia to China. Although this idea never got off the drawing board, airmail service was operating between Edmonton and Whitehorse by 1937. The intrepid pilots, Alberta's famous Ted Field and Grant McConachie, equipped their aircraft with pontoons in summer and skis in winter, to land in remote communities. Nevertheless, ultimately the inability of pre-war aircraft to undertake long-distance high-altitude flights precipitated the construction of a series of landing strips to be known as the North West Staging Route. Location surveys were underway by 1939 for airfields at Grande Prairie, Fort St. John, Fort Nelson, Watson Lake, and Whitehorse.

In 1940 the Joint United States–Canada Permanent Board of Defence recommended construction of a line of airfields from Fort St. John to Fairbanks, extending the route already established by Canada, and the American government agreed to pay for all facilities that were not already part of Canada's system. It proved a challenge to get supplies to these isolated airfield locations from the Northern Alberta Railway's terminus at Dawson Creek. From Fort St. John just across the river, Dominion Land Surveyors had surveyed a winter trail in 1922, to Horse Guard on the Sikanni Chief River. In early 1941, Department of Transport bulldozers widened the road and extended it north to Fort Nelson. Dominion Land Surveyor Knox McCusker, of Fort St. John, freighted tons of supplies for DOT from Fort St. John to Fort Nelson in the spring and summer of 1941 for the construction of the new Fort Nelson airport as part of the North West Staging Route. From Horse Guard on the Sikanni Chief River, McCusker used scows to transport heavy equipment as well as 1,500,000 gallons of fuel for airplanes and trucks downstream to Fort Nelson.

Then, in December 1941, came the Japanese bombing of Pearl Harbour, and the United Sates declared war on Japan. The US geared up for an all-out total war effort from 1942, and the spotlight focused squarely on the defence of Alaska and the necessity of upgrading the North West Staging Route. This meant building longer landing strips, improving communications and air traffic control, and upgrading meteorological information for safely getting American aircraft to Alaska. Thousands of American personnel, military and civilian, descended on a somewhat beleaguered Edmonton during 1942 to work with their Canadian counterparts in the RCAF. Planes landed by the hundreds on a daily basis at the expanded Blatchford airfield, ferrying supplies and troops north to defend Alaska and the continent against a Japanese attack that never materialized. Airfields along the staging route expanded further, including the one at Grande Prairie, where five hundred American and Canadian personnel were stationed.[13] Additional airstrips were built, as the United States Air Force used the air route to shuttle almost eight thousand bombers, fighters, and transport planes on the Lend–Lease Program, to Fairbanks, where Russian crews waited to ferry them to the Soviet Union.[14]

Land surveyors played a role in all this frenetic activity. Oluff Inkster, who had earlier worked in the north, played a vital role with the RCAF in locating suitable terrain for airstrips in 1942.[15] Among the men on the Department of Transport's crews doing preliminary surveys was Theodore Neumann, who worked for five and a half years throughout Alberta and in the Northwest Territories, and later became an Alberta Land Surveyor.[16]

## THE ALASKA HIGHWAY

No history of Alberta during World War II can be without reference to the Alaska Highway. Edmonton was the staging post for the extraordinary story of its construction and remains linked to its legacy of northern access and development. The highway was not, in fact, an idea conceived in response to war, but marked the execution of an idea that had been around since the 1920s, when British Columbia first promoted a road to Alaska. Possibilities had been explored and bandied about—a coastal route (route A) or an interior route (route B) via Prince George—but it all remained talk, even after war broke out. In summer 1941 a Canadian Highway Commission came out in favour of route B, but meantime, a third route, route C, was promoted by interests on the prairies and the plains of the Midwest south of the forty-ninth parallel. Edmonton's relentless municipal council led the way in arguing for a highway from Edmonton heading northwest to parallel and service the North West Staging Route airfields. All remained in the planning stages until Pearl Harbour. The US military made an instant decision to build a road, more or less following the North West Staging Route from the end of steel at Dawson Creek to Fairbanks, Alaska.

The urgent demand for the surveying and construction of a highway on Canadian soil by a foreign army, albeit through allied cooperation, caused major concerns about Canada's sovereignty. Canada signed an agreement in March 1942: the Americans would pay for the road, and the sections running through Canada would be turned over to Ottawa six months after the war. Canada would provide a right-of-way, waive import duties and taxes, and offer, among other concessions, free timber and gravel. Both the US military and the civilian US Public Roads Administration (PRA) would be involved. The army was responsible for all negotiations with Canada, funding the PRA, and the logistics of transporting men and supplies north from Edmonton by truck, train, and plane.

*One of Knox McCusker's dog teams in action, March 1942.*
ALSA, WEIR ALBUM

The PRA was responsible for reconnaissance surveys, plans, and specifications for the location of a civilian road as close as possible to the army's 'pioneer' road.[17] All this offered little to Canadian land surveyors, as the United States Army began by moving in survey battalions, one working south from Whitehorse and the other north from Fort St. John, to survey the route for the pioneer road.

Dominion Land Surveyor Knox McCusker did not worry about such matters. He was "Johnny-on-the-spot" at Fort St. John, and played a significant role in the location of the highway. In February 1942, McCusker was at Horse Track on the government road north from Fort St. John when he noticed an army visitor in camp. The new arrival proved to be none other than US General William Hoge, commander of the US Corps of Engineers, in charge of building the proposed Alaska Highway. The Canadian Department of Transport had flown him north from Edmonton. Hoge soon became acquainted with McCusker, whose reputation as northern bushman and guide was legendary. General Hoge, according to newspaper reports, spent the night at McCusker's ranch near Fort St. John, poring over the maps that McCusker had drawn over the years. They included a remarkable scaled record of at least half the country between Fort St. John and Whitehorse and rough maps of the remaining area of northern BC and Yukon. However, most importantly of all, it was McCusker's knowledge of muskeg conditions, so misleading in the depth of winter, which dictated a route to Fort Nelson that skirted the Rockies, rather than one following the more direct winter route across muskeg.

McCusker signed on with Hoge and became, in his own words, chief packer and guide for the US army. By March, he was leading American engineers across country in dog-team parties to confirm aerial surveys of the area. McCusker completed an initial reconnaissance survey of 450 miles as far as Toad River in under a month. The story placed McCusker on the pages of *Saturday Evening Post*—the only Alberta Land Surveyor to achieve such notoriety. McCusker then

*A typical stretch of corduroy on the pioneer road to Alaska, 1942.*
GLENBOW ARCHIVES, NA-2819-1

guided the construction party up to Fort Nelson, leading a stadia survey party. A single bulldozer cutting along the centre line followed them, with more bulldozers coming up behind to widen it out on either side and level it for grading. Men laid corduroy to prevent vehicles from slipping into the mud when the permafrost thawed. It proved to be a race against time, but by mid-April they made it. McCusker, ever the storyteller, related with relish how, having received seventy-five engineering students as labourers, he duly requisitioned seventy-five diapers. The US army responded that it could not supply these items but would forward the request to Washington. McCusker later received the certificate of merit for his contribution to continental defence from the Commissioner, US Public Roads Administration, for the role he played on the Alaska Highway and in connection with the airports of the North West Staging Route.[18]

From Fort Nelson, progress on the road was rapid. Much of the route followed existing trails known to Native guides. Path finding was also combined with preliminary surveys done from the air.[19] The road pushed ahead at breakneck speed, urged on by a Japanese invasion of the Aleutian Islands in June 1942. By November 1942, the pioneer road to Alaska was completed. Ten thousand soldiers and eight thousand civilians had combined their energies over eight months to build fifteen hundred miles of road.[20] The civilian PRA developed the Alaska Highway in 1943, building bridges and culverts and widening the road, ultimately incorporating more of the pioneer road into the final civilian road than had been planned.[21] On one of the summer crews was Alberta high school student Jim Clark, whose experience served him well for his later career as an Alberta Land Surveyor.[22] Later, in summer 1944, the recently married McCusker set out from Fort St. John with his wife, Gwen, and survey crew in two new two-ton trucks to begin the first of the legal surveys of the now completed Alaska Highway through the Yukon for the Canadian government. Gwen McCusker wrote an account of the trip, noting they generally stopped at army camps for the night, where meals and gasoline were available. "I might mention . . ." she wrote later, "for a person coming from a rationed area the tables at the camps presented an utter disregard for ration points."[23]

## CANOL PIPELINE PROJECT

In 1942 the Americans had yet another joint military–civilian plan for the defence of Alaska. They proposed bringing a supply of oil for the Alaska Highway, airfields, and military bases in Alaska through a series of pipelines from Norman Wells through Whitehorse. Imperial Oil (Canada) had drilled a successful oil well at Norman Wells on the banks of the Mackenzie River in the 1920s. Two decades later, the company found itself involved in the fast-track planning of further drilling and the construction of refineries at Norman Wells and at Whitehorse. The refineries were to be linked by an above-ground four-and-a-half-inch pipeline across some 550 miles of mountainous wilderness. Numerous pumping stations would be required to force the oil over high passes. Simultaneously with all the other activity of the North West Staging Route and Alaska Highway, the US military set out to build or upgrade another series of airstrips, including Fort McMurray, and Embarass, linking Edmonton with Norman Wells, as well as a series of roads. Meanwhile, the railhead at Waterways, near Fort McMurray, became the loading point for shipping heavy-equipment, trucks, bulldozers, and US troops on the fantastically long water route northwest to Norman Wells.

Guy Blanchet, DLS, who had surveyed in northern Alberta before the Great War, sorted out a route for the rough service road from Norman Wells to Whitehorse that was to be built beside the projected pipeline to allow for its regular inspection. Rapid air reconnaissance was used to plan an initial route, but attempts to confirm it on the ground proved disastrous, as the vehicles sank in the mud of the Mackenzie Valley. Blanchet decided on alternative measures. He set off in early October

*Knox McCusker's survey crew, 1942. McCusker is standing on the far right.*

1942 with guides and five dog teams to do an old-style track survey through a mountainous pass on an obscure trail recommended by area Natives. One hundred miles in, Blanchet was convinced of the suitability of the route, and sent word back with two dog teams. Soon a tractor train was hot on his heels. Blanchet continued with his three dog teams, and finally they broke through the mountains. By spring 1943, the reconnaissance survey was complete. Although further surveys were necessary where engineering obstacles required a diversion from the route, Blanchet's track survey determined the highway route. He himself marvelled as he drove over the almost completed road in September 1943.[24] In mid-January 1944, welders made the final connection on the long sinuous pipeline.

Meanwhile, oil output from Norman Wells had tripled by December 1942, due to the drilling of nineteen new wells by Imperial Oil crews working for the US army. The Canol project, as it was known, was formally opened on May 1, 1944, long after the Alaskan military emergency passed. Imperial Oil and the Canadian government took over the project on a two-to-one share basis, as the Americans wrote it off as wartime expenditure. By the end of the war, two companies, Imperial Oil and Noble Drilling Corporation of Edmonton, had drilled eighty-three new wells in the area around Norman Wells.[25] After the war, the tiny Canol pipeline, which had no economic feasibility for shipping oil south to Alberta and the prairies, was soon terminated. Yet even in its folly, and despite the closure and the dismantling of the pipeline and the Whitehorse refinery at the end of the war, it had shown that pipelines were a possibility, a possibility that would become reality in the 1950s.

The wartime activity brought out the ambiguities of land ownership in the north. The whole question of surveys, or lack of them, in northeast British Columbia, Yukon, and northern Alberta, and the issue of legal title, remained a confused matter until after the war. The Americans, in fact, were leasing the land for airstrips and highways, as well as parcels of privately owned land needed for military use, such as in Edmonton. The threat of expropriation of land for the highway and airstrips by the PRA caused so much resentment among landowners in the Dawson Creek and Fort St. John area that responsibility for land acquisition was taken over by Canada. Then, in 1943, an agreement between the US and Canada called for the Canadian government to henceforth buy the land required by the US military, and take over leases already signed for the duration of the war. As the American airstrips were built without proper surveys, there was no way to produce the leases against which a title could be registered.[26] Right-of-way and other legal and control surveys would eventually come later, when the completed road and airstrips were turned over to Canada in 1946.

## ALBERTANS AND CANADIAN SURVEY REGIMENTS ON THE EUROPEAN FRONT

The use of surveying techniques by the artillery to locate enemy guns was a Canadian contribution to modern warfare. In Europe, as the allied artillery guns boomed, surveyors systematically located enemy targets using basic surveying methods. General A. G. L. McNaughton, First Commander of the Canadian Forces during World War II, developed the technology. Canadian troops first employed it during World War I at the Battle of Vimy Ridge in 1917, and it contributed to the Canadian victory. During World War II, Canadian surveyors did air photo interpretation work, laid out airstrips, and operated a mobile mapping unit complete with a printing press run off a generator. Most surveyors were attached to the artillery, each artillery unit having regimental and battery surveyors. There were two survey regiments in the Royal Canadian Artillery. Their job was to give support to the artillery as required.[27]

In September 1939, the First Survey Regiment, Royal Canadian Artillery, was mobilized in Montreal and went overseas in 1940. It later split into two, forming the Second Survey Regiment in 1943. The First went to Italy and the Second to northwest Europe, landing in France in 1944. While the grim realities of their work were far from the conditions of land surveying in Alberta, the experience of young Canadians in those survey regiments or with surveying in the artillery had a direct link with Alberta. After the war when they returned to Canada, they qualified as land surveyors and practiced in Alberta. Among them were George Walker and Dalton Martin, who served as surveyors with the Third Division of the Canadian Artillery. Dave Usher and Armstrong MacCrimmon served in Canadian survey regiments.

Dave Usher signed up in Calgary in April 1941, and by November left Montreal with the First Survey Regiment for two years of overseas training in England. In 1943, he sailed for North Africa, and from a staging point near Algiers was soon headed for Sicily and the Italian campaign to provide survey information to the field regiments in the First and Fifth Divisions of the Canadian Army. From Ortona, where the worst of the offensive was over by the time the Canadian survey troops arrived, the First Survey Regiment followed the infantry, ahead of the artillery, into the Liri Valley, prior to the Canadian breakthrough to Rome. As the Germans retreated north to the Hitler line, the Canadian troops advanced, eventually as far north as the Po River.

Each survey regiment was divided into three units—the survey troops, the flash spotters, and the sound rangers. As a team, they used survey methods to pinpoint the exact location of enemy guns, which in turn allowed Canadian gun battery officers to adjust their gun positions for accurate fire on the enemy. They provided coordinates derived from established Universal Transverse Mercator (UTM) coordinates,[28] which in the Liri Valley were often located on mountaintops. Usher recalled they sometimes used pre-war Italian maps as they carried the survey forward from these monuments to the gun positions.

Usher was with G troop, who had the additional special task of assisting the artillery in calibrating its guns for greater accuracy. He recalled the first time they did the calibration work on the flatlands just north of Naples. As they retreated, the Germans flooded the land that had been drained for farmland. Along the coast there were sand dunes where G troop set up a calibration base for allied regiments where the artillery could shoot out to sea. They set up three observation posts at intervals along the dunes positioned well above sea level and determined coordinates for them. They ran a triangulation survey to the various gun positions some distance inland behind them. "The gun positions, our observation posts and our computing centre were all connected by a field telephone," Usher recounted. Each gun then fired a round to a predetermined coordinate target out at sea. When the airburst came just before the shot hit the water, the surveyors took an observation. From this, through triangulation of coordinates, they could determine whether the gun range was long or falling short and adjust the calibration accordingly. G troop set up another calibration base near Rimini on the Adriatic coast. A third base was later set up on the coast of Belgium, when they had joined allied troops on the move to Holland and Germany for the final liberation of Europe in 1945.[29]

Armstrong MacCrimmon served with the Second Survey Regiment in northwest Europe, 1944–45. In 1942, when he was on parade drill during training at Petawawa, an officer asked anyone who had any training in surveying to step forward. MacCrimmon had worked with his father, who was an engineer—so he took the step forward that determined the rest of his working life. Soon Euclidean geometry was the focus of his training for guiding the allied guns on the European front. He sailed on the *Queen Elizabeth* in December 1942 and resumed training in southern England. In July 1944, he landed on Juno Beach—exactly one month after D-Day—on his twenty-second birthday with X Troop of the P Battery in the Second Survey Regiment. For six weeks, they moved inland from the beach head with the Canadian artillery troops. They slept in shallow trenches they dug each night, and encountered heavy enemy fire and bombing. Following the bombing of Caen by the Royal Air Force on July 20, the allied troops eventually broke through the so-called Falaise gap, and, supported by the survey troops, advanced all the way across northwest Europe.

The survey troops moved from one artillery position to another by Jeep, primarily to assist in determining the location of enemy guns and establish a target for their own guns. The flash spotters operated ahead of the guns, from observation posts with known coordinates. When a flash from enemy gunfire came, the spotters took a bearing. If at least three bearings were recorded, information was rushed behind the lines to a computing or plotting centre. When it was possible, sound ranging and mortar location troops used microphones connected to a recorder in the plotting centre to relay the same information. At the plotting centre, surveyors pinpointed the position of the enemy guns, which they relayed to their gun battery. In order to fire on his target position, the gunnery officer had to know the precise position of his guns.

The surveyors with a survey troop established coordinates for a point in the immediate vicinity of the guns' emplacement. This was marked by a stake referred to as a bearing picket, set in the ground by the gunnery officer. They then measured and recorded angles from the bearing picket to several visible points—such as a church spire—with known coordinates, which were chosen by the gunnery officer. A dispatch rider rushed the calculated angles back to the plotting centre behind the lines, where true bearings from the bearing picket to the selected points were calculated. This information, along with the coordinates for the bearing picket, was relayed back to the gunnery officer by field phone. He was then able to coordinate each of his four guns. He was able to determine the position of the enemy target from the information given by the flash spotters, the location of his pivot gun, and its distance and bearing to the target.[30]

Surveyors carried out their work at high speed and often under fire. It was certainly hazardous work. Dalton Martin recalled that, while doing survey work with the artillery, they had to leave their helmets and rifle in the Jeep—any steel would deflect the compass readings. Sometimes the enemy got too close for comfort. A German plane spotted Martin while he was climbing over a fence. It opened fire, missed him, but blew up a tank behind him.[31] Sometimes the speed of advance was such that it was not possible to produce regular survey work.

In northern Holland three men with the survey regiments, including Armstrong MacCrimmon, were sent forward to do map spots and sun shots—one sun shot was observed and computed in a record twenty-four minutes. This produced just enough data to keep the guns in line.[32] MacCrimmon's troop moved, producing survey data, for the final advance on Oldenburg. The ceasefire eventually came. Before he returned to Canada, MacCrimmon, along with many other Canadians, attended a survey school at Zeist in Holland.


## SURVEY CHALLENGES ON THE HOME FRONT

In January 1942, Alexander Cormack, outgoing President of the Alberta Land Surveyors' Association, noted, "The past year, I believe, has been more prosperous for the members of our profession than for many years previously. This activity arises largely through the vast expenditure of public funds occasioned by the war, but while taking full advantage of it, the prudent man will reflect that such a prosperity, founded as it is upon the destruction of wealth, can never be of an enduring nature."[33] The civilian survey work in Alberta that continued during the war seems to have been most particularly aimed at keeping provincial infrastructure in step with wartime production and transportation needs. Calgary Power undertook location surveys for power lines. The Survey Branch of Alberta Public Works had field parties out doing surveys connected with the maintenance of Alberta's roads, rights-of-way, and telephone lines. Three of the four surveyors on staff were Harry Day, Paul Hargrove, and Alexander Cormack.[34] Alberta's roads were taking a pounding with wartime traffic, and availability of asphalt was limited from June 1941. By 1944 the heavy traffic bound for Grande Prairie and the Alaska Highway forced Public Works to undertake surveys in connection with stretches of highway between Valleyview and Debolt.[35]

As the war progressed, wartime controls imposed under the War Measures Act meant that Ottawa increasingly governed by decree. Everything focused on Canada's war effort, as raw materials, people, and the country's financial resources were turned towards industrial production of military equipment and ammunition. Not only price controls, but also labour regulations, were imposed through a series of orders-in-council. Surveyors, along with everyone else, had to conduct their business under these constraints, including shortages of coal for heating fuel, higher personal taxes, and the added difficulties of rationing introduced in April 1942, when many food items became unavailable or had to be procured by coupon. There were shortages in gasoline by the summer of 1941, and from spring 1942 surveyors had to plan carefully and conserve rationed gasoline for necessary trips. There was no longer a chance for surveyors to buy a new vehicle or radio, as production of such items for civilian use halted.[36] Most trying of all was the rationing of tires, which made it difficult to take on work that required extensive travel. There was no respite as the war dragged on. In December 1944, the setback suffered by allied forces in Belgium had its repercussions on the home front—tires continued to be unavailable for anything other than military needs.[37] The one bright spot for surveyors was that, although hard liquor was rationed, beer was not!

Seemingly unwilling to go back to horseback days, the Canadian Institute of Surveying petitioned the War Time Prices and Rationing Board on behalf of the profession across the country to make sure that surveyors would receive supplies for essential work. By September 1943, a land surveyor had to arrange with the Alberta Land Surveyors' Association to make an application to the nearest Rations Administration Branch for a temporary rations card for his survey party. Details of how many men were in the party, the length of time in the field, and the location of work had to be specified. Each member of the party was then expected to surrender coupons from his own personal ration book for the number of days he was expected to be in the field.[38] By the end of 1944, it was becoming difficult to hire men for survey crews. As Wilfred Humphreys, President of the Alberta Land Surveyors' Association, pointed out, "This combined with the difficulties of car transportation resulted in the situation where the surveyor was not only busy—he was over-busy and often unable to cope with work offering [sic]." Humphreys noted that changes in the war production program, and the release of certain categories of workers, was expected, and hopefully this would ease the situation over the coming months of 1945.[39]

## Alberta Land Surveyors and the Cold War

When the war finally ended in 1945, the horror of the preceding years did not fade quickly. The terror of nuclear annihilation focused on fear of communism, manifested as anti-Soviet rhetoric. Many Albertans were prepared to believe there was a communist under every bush. In the legislature, Alf Hooke, the Socred Minister for Economic Affairs, went so far as to hazard a guess that one in five hundred Canadians were communist sympathizers.[40] The power of communism in China and the first nuclear test by the Soviet Union seemed more alarming after the outbreak of the Korean War in 1950 as Canadian troops once again engaged in battle. Canadian–American co-operation for the defence of North America against a perceived Soviet threat resulted in the development of three early-warning radar systems to warn of air attacks during the 1950s.

## Surveying for Early Warning Radar Systems Across Northern Alberta

The Pine Tree Line, initiated in 1951, was the first early-warning radar system. Military strategists proposed a continent-wide network of forty-three long-range radar stations. By 1957 thirty-nine had been built. The line ultimately included three stations in Alberta: Beaverlodge, Cold Lake, and one built in 1964 at Penhold.[41] By November 1953, Canada approved, in principle, the establishment of another early-warning radar line along the fifty-fifth parallel from Alaska to Newfoundland. The issue of Canadian sovereignty underlay Canada's insistence that the new Mid Canada Line would be built in Canada by Canadians. Canadians would also staff the section control stations. Soon the RCAF was planning the enormous undertaking known as Operation Backlash.

Along with eight manned sector control stations, ninety unmanned Doppler Detection Stations thirty miles apart on a double staggered line across Canada were to provide radar cover between three thousand and sixty thousand feet. The Alberta sector control station number 800 was at Stoney Mountain, near Anzac, twenty-four miles southwest of Fort McMurray. Surveyors working for the Department of Transport surveyed the sector control sites for the Department of Defence. The radar installation was to be supplied by the civilian rather than the military sector, and the Bell Telephone Company was selected to also manage the construction.

In early 1955, survey firms across the country were contracted by the Bell Telephone Company to survey the unmanned detector sites on the Mid Canada Line. The Alberta survey firm of Stewart, Little, Stewart and Weir organized four crews to locate the western sites along the line from Fort St. John to Lac La Ronge in Northern Saskatchewan. Alberta Land Surveyors Charlie Weir and Earl Little were also engineers; Little was a commissioned BC Land Surveyor and Weir held a Saskatchewan commission, which enabled the firm to carry out the survey of stations across three provinces.

The surveyors plunged into an international operation dealing with both the RCAF and the USAF, while doing a job that was both urgent and secret. By the time they arrived on the line, the planning for the logistics of the undertaking had been underway for nearly two years, and detailed specifications for buildings and equipment were ready. In 1954 aerial photograph flights undertaken by surveyors with the RCAF, the Surveys and Mapping Branch of the Department of Mines and Technical Surveys, and the Geodetic Survey of Canada resulted in a series of topographical maps covering a fifteen-mile wide strip the length of the fifty-fifth parallel for preliminary siting purposes. The contouring interval was close on these maps—25 feet—to ensure inter-visibility between the towers for the microwave signals.[42] Grande Prairie was the Alberta centre for one of the four RCAF detachments of 108 Communications Flight. The RCAF supplied pilots and helicopters to ferry men and equipment around.[43] American helicopter teams provided additional support for the Canadian pilots. Land surveyors assisted the siting engineers. Their first job involved flying in a helicopter held in a straight line at a constant altitude between two proposed sites to prove there was an unbroken line of sight, as the contour mapping indicated.[44] Then the surveyors began detailed field surveys.

The land surveyors' instructions contained a sketch of each site, many of which were on hills. The sites had offset locations, which ultimately would form two radar curtains.[45] The four survey crews flew to the radar sites by helicopter, and they were often lowered down on a winch rope if muskeg prevented the helicopter from landing. Sometimes they were able to clear a spot in the trees to allow the helicopter to land where the ground was firm. Once on the ground with their equipment, including transits, bundles of axes, steel tapes, tents, and supplies, they had to pitch camp. In some areas, clean water was difficult to find, and they had to boil slough water. Then they set to work.

The whole job at each site took about a week or so, as the weather did not always cooperate to allow for good sun and star shots to ascertain the azimuth and exact latitude and longitude in the absence of established baselines. The axemen cut out the site, which was two hundred to three hundred feet square, and the survey crews determined its legal boundaries. They marked the location of the tower for the construction crews to follow.[46] They also indicated the precise direction the antennae should be orientated so that the transmitters and receivers would be connected by wave signal. For the surveyors in charge, Charlie Weir and Earl Little, there was a lot of extra flying involved, as they spent one or two nights with the crews at each site. They had to check the work at each site before the American helicopter team picked up the crew and moved them to the next site.

RCAF aircraft checked on the survey crews every day. In the initial stages, an Otter flew overhead and the crew made ground markers—set numbers of white strips—to indicate a move was needed or an emergency. By the time they had reached the McLennan area, the RCAF had switched from Otter to Canso aircraft equipped with VHF radios, which made communication more accurate and saved time. The helicopters could be sent exactly when they were needed to pick up the crews for a move. Despite the excellent radio communications, all did not always go according to plan. The airstrip at Lesser Slave Lake was so bad that the Otter pilot kept landings and take-offs to a minimum, following a close escape on June 10, when he "narrowly missed a horse on landing and cleared through a barbed wire fence into ploughed field."[47] Meanwhile, at a site north of Lesser Slave Lake, Charlie Weir's survey crew was running out of food. They mixed up a can of bully beef and a can of beans with rolled oats to survive. "It stayed in your stomach for two or three days!"[48]

It was not always easy to meet the schedule of the American chopper crews, and Weir recalled they had a bit of an attitude, but eventually shaped up in their treatment of the survey crews. In a beer parlour in Fort McMurray, he reminded them they were the taxi drivers![49] The American crews were not experienced in bush country and sometimes left insufficient minimum clearance. One of them struck trees near Lesser Slave Lake on June 13, damaging the chopper's blades. Then a second one crashed. No surveyors were on board. Although everyone was eventually rescued, it delayed the whole schedule by seven days in the Fort McMurray area. The incident resulted in a decision to repaint the five helicopters remaining in the fleet. Their colour was changed from green camouflage to bright yellow for easier search and rescue.[50]

Charlie Weir noted that despite the secrecy of the whole project, the legal survey plan for each site was ultimately filed with the provincial Department of Forestry and Lands, and recorded in the *Alberta Gazette*. The construction of the sites quickly followed the surveys, during the summer of 1956. It involved the nightmare of moving huge quantities of construction materials, supplies, and food, as well as the electronic equipment, much of it hauled by helicopter from marshalling sites, which in Alberta included Slave Lake and Anzac. By April 1957, the four western control stations were manned and ready and the whole line was operational by January 1, 1958.[51] The sites on the Mid Canada Line were never put to the test, nor were they destined to last for very long. Canada capitulated to pressure from the United States to allow them to build the Distant Early Warning (DEW) line across Canada's Arctic Circle by 1957. The US paid for the twenty-two stations, but Canadians surveyed and built them, and Canada retained ownership of them.

By the early 1960s, the Mid Canada Line was obsolete. In January 1964, the Mid Canada Line sites west of the Manitoba–Ontario border were closed down, followed by those to the east of it in 1965.[52] Peter Lypowy, ALS, with the federal Department of Transport, was later responsible for disposing of these sites.[53] There is little sign on the ground that they ever existed.

*Earl Little, ALS, BCLS, in camp on Mid Canada Line. Note the bundles of axes and a shovel.*
ALSA, WEIR ALBUM

## SURVEYS FOR MILITARY BASES

Surveyors were also required in refurbishing and laying out new military bases in Alberta as part of the nation-wide preparedness against Soviet long-range bomber missile attack over the pole. The RCAF across Canada grew from eleven thousand in 1947 to fifty thousand by 1955—numbers that required a major construction programme known as "Operation Bulldozer." Ottawa budgeted $14 million for the establishment of the Primrose Lake Air Weapons Range in Alberta, where Canadian and NATO pilots could test and practice the deployment of guided missiles.[54] In 1952 the Alberta and Saskatchewan governments leased 3 million acres of provincial land, tracts of bush and muskeg that straddled the Alberta–Saskatchewan boundary, to the government of Canada.

Surveyors with the Department of Transport undertook the location and surveys for Department of Defence projects in each province. In this case, the work involved the expropriation of land. DOT staff based at the western regional office in Edmonton, including Peter Lypowy, ALS,

*Survey crew disembarking from helicopter. Charlie Weir, ALS, SLS, is standing second from the left.*
ALSA, Weir Album

secured the perimeter of the weapons range. This included locating and compensating trappers and fishermen who were forced to move outside the range. Surveyors then laid out the boundary over the course of two winters.

Lypowy worked on the northern boundary of the Air Weapons Range, beginning on the 19th Baseline that ran south of the boundary. Lumber and equipment for the survey was freighted in by rail on three flat cars, then hauled through the bush from the rail line to the survey location. When the two crews arrived at the survey location, they had to build their own bunkhouses out of quarter-inch plywood, which they set on skids. Each crew had six men along with a cook and two cat-skinners to cut out the line. They maintained radio communication with the forestry tower in Lac La Biche, which turned out to be handy when Lypowy fired a party chief and had the RCAF fly in a replacement. Along the line bulldozed out by the catskinners, the survey crew drove big steel posts into the ground, eight of them to a mile. "We had truck loads of these G—d posts," as Lypowy recalled. Each post had an aluminum plaque with "Air Weapons Range No Trespassing" on it.[55]

At Cold Lake, a new air base that extended over ten square miles was developed simultaneously. This required surveys for the location of airstrips, buildings, the layout of roads, and utilities, which were all designed for later expansion. The Department of Transport hired Underwood McLellan and Associates of Saskatoon to do the surveys needed for ground installations, as they had undertaken surveys for other RCAF bases in Saskatchewan and Manitoba in 1951. Roy A. McLellan accompanied DOT officials on a mission to find a suitable location for the airbase. In spring 1952, they did preliminary reconnaissance from the air and then on the ground to locate a site.

Dave Ferguson, an Alberta Land Surveyor with Underwood McLellan and Associates, had two surveys parties working with the department's survey crews to speed up the contour mapping of the site. Ferguson's crews then carried out all the site surveys required for construction of facilities on the ground.[56] Ev Carefoot, ALS, also employed by Underwood McLellan, recalls that the very first legal survey plan he signed was for the control survey and boundaries of the radar site at Cold Lake, one of the Pine Tree early-warning stations. The radar site was located high on a hill to the southeast of Cold Lake airport, and it took two months to survey it during the bitter-cold months of December 1953 and January 1954.[57]

Soon afterwards, civilian contract surveyors, once again from Underwood McLellan and Associates, did surveys in connection with the expansion of the Namao airbase and the Currie Barracks in Calgary. At Namao, while Peter Lypowy, with the Department of Transport, surveyed the one-and-a-half-mile mile airstrip extension,[58] Dave Ferguson and Ev Carefoot carried out the surveys needed for the additional four hundred houses to be built in the late 1950s. Carefoot established a control grid for the whole site, which included a munitions dump, while Ferguson did the subdivision layout. Their survey crews also did all the engineering surveys required for utilities. Underwood McLellan and Associates undertook similar survey work for the upgrading of the Currie Barracks in Calgary.[59] Other firms also found work surveying military bases. When Ev Carefoot joined Associated Engineering in 1955, the firm's surveyors, who included Len Grover, ALS, did surveys for the Griesbach Barracks in Edmonton.[60]

For the most part, surveys for Canada's military during World War II and the Cold War were done out of the public eye, as military surveys involved secrecy. The war years gave many young men their first taste of surveying work and techniques as members of survey crews on the home front or in the military—serving with the Royal Canadian Air Force or the Royal Canadian Artillery. Their exposure to surveying in the military often determined their career choice after the war. By the early 1950s, the next generation of Alberta Land Surveyors was charting a course in the brave new world of modern Alberta.

CHAPTER 11

# New Horizons
*Surveying for the Emerging Oil and Gas Industry*

## SURVEYORS TAKE ON A CRUCIAL ROLE

The discovery of abundant oil reserves at Leduc in 1947 was the single most important factor in the evolution of the land surveying profession in Alberta in the second half of the twentieth century. Although little heralded in the heroic narrative histories of the oil industry in Alberta, land surveyors played a crucial role in its development. Early drilling locations were based on surface geology, such as in the anticlines (visible folds in the bedrock) of Turner Valley. In the late 1940s, the new technology of seismic exploration, which used sound waves to determine the geology of the earth beneath the surface, was employed in Alberta. For the first time the oil industry was able to obtain information on the subsurface geologic makeup by means other than mapping the surface geology. This was particularly significant on the plains and in northern Alberta, where there were no surface geologic features such as anticlines upon which to base a choice of drilling location. Seismic operators, however, needed surveyors to locate the survey lines, determine and chart the precise location of the seismic line shots so that a drilling rig could accurately find the target shot hole again. Surveys for the exploration and production of oil and gas were tied into the land survey system as marked on the ground. The surveyor's job was to tie the land survey system and the well position coordinates together, and to mark an 'X' on the ground for the drilling crews.

## LEGACY OF EARLY OIL EXPLORATION IN ALBERTA

Alberta Land Surveyors always had their eye to the ground when it came to the potential of natural resources. It was a land surveyor who first brought an oil well into production in Alberta. Allan Patrick, DLS, became aware of oil seepages along Cameron Creek in the Waterton Lakes area in the 1880s. Bolstered by a report on the oil's potential made by Alfred Selwyn of the Geological Survey, Patrick confidently filed a claim on 640 acres in 1889, and then set out to raise capital for drilling.[1] In the meantime, two prospective oilmen, William French and William Fernie, managed to get their hands on some old drilling equipment from Ontario and had it shipped west. All for naught—in 1891 they struck water at a depth of 230 feet. Undaunted, Patrick eventually joined rancher John Lineham and Arthur Sifton, brother of Clifford Sifton, Minister of the Interior, in the formation of the Rocky

216

Mountains Development Company in 1901. They hired experienced drillers from Ontario and put them to work at the end of the wagon road into Cameron Creek Valley.[2] Soon three hundred barrels a day were gushing to the surface—Alberta's first oil strike!

Patrick and Lineham thought big. Patrick surveyed a townsite to be called Oil City on a bench above Cameron Creek. The plan, registered at the Land Titles Office in Calgary in 1908, contained 450 lots in sixteen blocks.[3] The Rocky Mountains Development Company's success, although limited to one well bore that was abandoned in 1907, touched off a speculative wave that crested in 1905 when more than half the land in Waterton Park was reserved for petroleum exploration.[4] The hope for commercial oil and gas production in Alberta had been sparked.

The discovery of gas in Turner Valley in 1914 followed by a major strike that caused a mini-boom in 1924, brought big players into the field. The British American Oil Company and Imperial Oil Company backed a small Calgary Company, Turner Valley Royalites, in their quest for crude oil. In 1936 the "Turner Valley Royalties No. 1" well proved to be a gusher. The basic techniques and instruments required for the oil industry had proved themselves, and regulation by the Government of Alberta soon followed. In 1938 the Alberta Oil and Gas Conservation Board was established to regulate haphazard and wasteful production, which often saw one company encroaching on

*A typical scene on a country road in the Leduc oil field, near Kavanagh, 1954.*
CITY OF EDMONTON ARCHIVES, EA-122-173

the edge of the lease of another. From 1942, only one well could be drilled in each forty acres, and a well could not be drilled within 330 feet of the boundary of a section.

The year 1942 also marked the requirement for surveys to ensure the correct location and spacing of well sites within the township system. A well was to be located at the centre of a legal subdivision, with the option of an offset location within a square of 330 feet.[5] In that same year, Imperial Oil hired Alberta Land Surveyor Alex G. Stewart to survey its oil and gas well sites at Turner Valley—a significant turning point for the involvement of Alberta Land Surveyors in the industry.

Turner Valley's production bolstered the war effort to 1945, but was falling off by 1946, and Canada still imported 90 percent of its petroleum.[6] Exploration in Alberta yielded little hope of immediate petroleum riches. Imperial Oil had drilled 133 dry holes by early 1947. Yet the hopes that the next wildcat would be another gusher never died. In 1946 Imperial acquired the rights to leases covering two hundred thousand acres in twenty-four townships around Edmonton, and instigated a massive seismic operation. As drilling then proceeded, the geologists eventually honed in on a quarter section near Leduc.

## Leduc: Alberta's Mecca

On February 13, 1947, the much-anticipated Leduc No. 1 came in and Albertans were transfixed by the image of a roaring column of burning oil and gas. Then on May 7, Leduc No. 2 came in at 5,370 feet—revealing deeper reserves in the Devonian-era reefs. Within two months there was an oil field. Drilling rigs proliferated like weeds as all the major oil companies—including California Standard, British American, Shell and McColl Frontenac—rushed to Leduc. Seismic work and exploration continued in cloak and dagger style, with oil spies on every road allowance. By the end of the year, thirty-one of the wells proved to be producers, and everyone in Alberta wanted to invest in oil or start an oil company. The famous blowout environmental disaster in September 1948 at Atlantic No. 3, near Leduc, which resulted in oil spewed over a wide area, did

*Philips, Hamilton and Associates courting clients at the oil show at Devon, 1951. Geoffrey Hamilton is standing on the right.*
J. H. Webb Collection

little to dampen Albertan enthusiasm for oil. 1948 also marked the discovery of oil at Redwater and the output of the quickly developed Redwater field was forecasted to double that of Turner Valley.[7] More excitement followed at Joseph Lake and Golden Spike in 1949.

As one successful discovery well after the other dotted the landscape, further well sites followed for each company. All these well sites required surveyed leases and access roadways. The telephones in land surveying offices were soon ringing off the hook, and surveyors scrambled to get crews together and buy new equipment. They packed their panel trucks or their large comfortable sedans with instruments on the back seat and a rack on the roof to carry rods, and headed out into the frenzied world of the oil fields. Well site surveys were followed by surveys to mark out flow lines, and a need for survey plans for battery sites followed. The battery sites contained tanks, valves, and separators to collect oil from several wells. From the battery sites surveyors marked out a right-of-way for a pipeline to carry the crude to its destination—ultimately one of the refineries constructed in Calgary and Edmonton.

## Light at the End of the Tunnel: the Post-Leduc Boom

By 1950 Alberta Land Surveyors in private practice were kept hopping, as by then Alberta boasted 2,025 oil wells and 401 gas wells.[8] The demand for surveys accelerated, but survey companies did not have enough qualified men for the work due to a post-war lull in training new land surveyors. By 1943 most of Alberta's surveyors had been in their late fifties or sixties. From the outbreak of war in 1939 to 1946, eleven Alberta Land Surveyors died, depleting their numbers.[9] In early 1945, there was a flurry of enquiries from men in the Canadian armed forces about a career in surveying at the end of the war. The Alberta Land Surveyors' Association produced three pamphlets: "Qualifications for Admission to Practice," "Land Surveying as a Career for Ex-Service Men," and "Future Prospects in the Surveying Profession." These were mailed out to individuals, to the Faculty of Engineering at the University of Alberta, and to the offices of the Department of Veteran Affairs that had been set up in Edmonton and Calgary.[10] In January 1948, the secretary of the ALSA noted that despite many ongoing enquires about surveying from young men, the number to embark on qualifying remained small.

There were two traditional avenues of training in Alberta. The first was to take basic survey and drafting courses, offered from the 1930s at the Alberta Institute of Technology and Art in Calgary, and then article before sitting the ALSA exams to qualify for an ALS commission. The second was to get an engineering degree and then article. In both cases, a considerable amount of learning was through on-the-job experience. Part of the problem was that Alberta Land Surveyors were still operating as one-man outfits, employing field assistants as needed. Without a clear increased demand for surveys, they were reluctant to take on articling pupils.[11] Leduc would change all this. The development of the oil industry spurred the evolution of larger firms, providing many more places for articling pupils.

By early 1947, some ex-service men who had gone into engineering at the University of Alberta sat DLS preliminary examinations. R. M. Hardy, Dean of the Faculty of Engineering and President of the Alberta Land Surveyors' Association, reported there was hope for expansion of the land surveying profession over the next three or four

*First-year drafting class at the Alberta Institute of Technology and Art in 1952. Standing at the back, wearing a tie, is instructor Jim Clark, and on his left, Lyle Ford. In the middle row second from left, is Neil Coy, third from left Don Duffy, fifth from left, Doug Barnett. All later qualified as Alberta Land Surveyors.*

D. BARNETT COLLECTION

years.[12] However, only three of these first nineteen passed the preliminary examination. Mathematics proved to be the obstacle, not helped by the fact that the DLS Examination Board had just raised standards in mathematical proficiency. The ALSA decided to set its own examinations, easier to pass but still with a high enough standard for its provincial requirements. Such a move involved setting a new syllabus in conjunction with engineering faculty members at the University of Alberta, and an amendment to the Alberta Land Surveyors' Act in 1949.[13]

Then in 1950, the Alberta government, alarmed by the shortage in many professions—teachers, accountants, engineers, and doctors—questioned the level of qualifications imposed by professional associations as Alberta's post-Leduc economy took off. Proposals to lower the bar, and even to remove the statutory powers of professional associations, were met with alarm by land

## Surveying with the Imperial Oil Company

Some of the oil companies decided to hire their own surveyors rather than contract out the work—a practical scheme given that they had extensive and seemingly never-ending exploration locations to check out. Imperial Oil established its own land surveying department and in fall 1947 was looking for more skilled manpower. Gordon Turnock, a young engineering graduate who had spent the summer in the NWT on a baseline survey, signed with Imperial on November 13, 1947. He recalls that the first well site he surveyed was No. 29—Imperial was really on a roll. Doug Stevenson also joined Imperial's surveying team. Every morning they climbed into a company Jeep in Edmonton and drove to Leduc to pick up the day's instructions. Along with them rode one of Alberta's distinguished land surveyors, Oluff Inkster, and his son Roy. Oluff Inkster, already in his seventies, embraced the new era of surveying and signed all of Imperial's legal plans. By 1951 the amount of survey work had mushroomed, and Inkster agreed to take on both Turnock and Stevenson as articling students to ensure that Imperial would have a stock of qualified Alberta Land Surveyors.[17] When Lou Breton was hired as a party chief in 1951, he too articled to Inkster. Oluff Inkster finally retired in 1954. By that time, Turnock had his ALS commission and Breton was able to continue articling with him.[18] By 1960 Imperial had too much survey work for its own department to handle and began hiring survey crews on contract, including Gillmore Surveys.

*A seismic surveyor with Imperial Oil stops on a road allowance in central Alberta for a chat with a farmer [mid-1950s].*
CITY OF EDMONTON ARCHIVES, EA-122-173

surveyors, among other professions. The ensuing outcry resulted in the government dropping its proposals by 1951.

The government, nevertheless, persisted in undermining the professional standards of the ALSA questioning the necessity for ALS examinations or articling time. Three Alberta Land Surveyors, Fred Seibert, Geoffrey Hamiliton, and Robert McCutcheon, met with C. E. Gerhart, Provincial Secretary. As Jack Holloway recounted, Gerhart pounded the desk with the assertion that any man in Alberta could be taken off the street, and be trained as a surveyor in three weeks.[14] Finally, at the end of 1951, a compromise was reached. An amendment to the Alberta Land Surveyors' Act proposed exempting university graduates from articling provided they had comparable field experience.

Many university graduates during the late 1940s were ex-service men, shaped by their wartime experiences. Charlie Weir, a RCAF veteran, qualified as an ALS in 1951. Of his graduating engineering class of 1950 at the University of Alberta, seventy-three out of eighty-nine were veterans. A veterans' rehabilitation program offered free tuition and a subsistence allowance of sixty dollars a month—ninety for married men.[15] Weir had been a navigation officer with the RCAF, while classmate Ev Carefoot had been an instrument mechanic, servicing Spitfires. In April 1952, the ALSA and the University of Alberta's Extension Department ran a two-week course at the Banff School of Fine Arts on survey law and legal survey practice—primarily for the benefit of engineering students in their final year. Twelve of the twenty-four students who took the course qualified later in the year, followed by three others in 1953.[16]

The first major batch of newly qualified surveyors was ready to practice in 1950. They numbered eleven in total, followed in 1951 by eight more. Then came the big year, 1952, when twenty-four Alberta Land Surveyors received their commission. By the end of 1953, fifty-eight new surveyors had qualified in four years. They were badly needed, as each passing year brought another oil discovery. In 1950 it was at the Fenn–Big Valley area, then at Wizard Lake in 1951, Nevis, Bonnie Glen, and Westerose in 1952, and Rimbey–Homeglen in 1953. Hot on the heels of all this was the discovery of what proved to be the most significant oil field, the Pembina, around which the new town of Drayton Valley would be built.

The new generation of Alberta Land Surveyors was adaptable and ready for a world of challenges, opportunities, and technology, in an era of unprecedented prosperity. These men, who chartered the changing course of surveying in Alberta for the next thirty years or more, were poised to tackle the immediate challenges of the oil fields. The oil boom was clearly here to stay. Alberta Land Surveyors could expect a large volume of well site and pipeline survey work for the foreseeable future.[19]

## THE CHALLENGE OF SURVEYING WELL SITE LOCATIONS IN UNSURVEYED TERRITORY

Even while feverish drilling for oil field development was going on in central Alberta, the oil industry turned its eyes north. Where the oil companies went, the land surveyors went too. Surveying for the oil and gas industry was a new venture for land surveyors as well as for the oil companies, and it posed the greatest challenge for everyone in the unsurveyed territory of northern Alberta. The township system had not been fully established in this area, and some of the remote baselines had never been surveyed at all in parts of northwest Alberta, north of Grande Prairie, where geologists believed there was oil. The township system, theoretical in areas where subdivision had not yet taken place, was the basis for both well location and spacing, just as it was in subdivided areas. The calculation of the position of a well site in unsurveyed territory, where there were no established township section lines, presented problems, as did the marking of boundaries without a monument to tie them to. There was much at stake for the oil companies, as the precision of the surveys determined the drilling location and the potential success of the well. The oil companies worked to find sufficient petroleum reserves in northwest Alberta to make the building of the long pipeline to transport oil south a viable proposition, and Alberta Land Surveyors were involved at every step.

Oil companies initially had little idea of what was involved in surveying in northern Alberta. As Charlie Weir recalled, "They didn't know what they were asking for . . . they thought you could just go out and say here's the spot!" As the 1950s progressed, land surveyors in Alberta had to find ways of overcoming those northern challenges. Oil companies did not understand the problems involved in winter surveys in the bush. In the early years, they were seemingly surprised by the cost of surveying.[20]

Surveyors often began work in the north by establishing vertical and horizontal control for the geophysical teams engaged in seismic work. Oil companies hired surveyors to survey lines that would be cut out of the bush so that seismic operators could lay out cables and acquire geophysical data in preplanned patterns. The surveyors used the theoretical township grid to establish the location of seismic lines, which were then bulldozed out before the arrival of the seismic crews. In 1950 Bob McCutcheon, ALS, had a contract with Sun Oil to lay out the outline for Township 104, Range 1, West of the Sixth Meridian, about eight miles southeast of Zama Lake, which would later become a busy oil field. From Calgary, McCutcheon's survey crew drove north. As they crossed the

## Surveyors and Catskinners

The relationship between the catskinners, the guys who drove the Caterpillar tractors, and the surveyors was an interesting one. On a survey north of Manning, party chief Bill Jones, a future Alberta Land Surveyor, was less than impressed with the cats. They were doing half a mile or less a day. Jones reckoned the survey party would be there for years at that speed. On a Saturday morning, they were about seven miles from the river and Jones decided to test the men and the machines. "I bet you fellows can't make that river by tonight, bet you twenty-four beer you can't make it." They got there. From then on Jones had no problems; he knew what a cat could do when put in the right gear! [22]

Surveyors and catskinners often vied to get the best of each other—usually with practical jokes. Al Edwards, ALS, recalls the arrival of one young catskinner who had been flown in to replace someone who had taken ill. They could tell he had never been in the bush. In the morning, one of the survey crew appeared with a collapsible stovepipe: "Here kid, put this around your neck!" Surprised, the young man asked what he would want that for. "If one of those bobcats comes out of a tree," came the reply, "the first thing he is going to go for is your neck!" [23]

Chinchaga River, Armstrong MacCrimmon, the party chief, was alarmed to feel his vehicle break through the ice—fortunately, the water was only about a foot deep and they were soon free. It seemed too cold for the water to be running. They checked the thermometer—it was an unbelievable minus sixty degrees Fahrenheit! Soon they were busy running survey lines and the catskinners, contractors from Grimshaw, were following them. The survey crew lived with the catskinners in their bunk shacks and the whole train moved on periodically, leaving the approximate township outlines and several interior section lines opened behind them, for the seismic crews to follow. [21]

The seismic work itself also required the surveyor to have established both the location of each shot hole, and ground elevations for the crews acquiring seismic data. Alberta Land Surveyor Steve Cherwonick began his career on a seismic crew, as a young civil engineering student who came out from Manitoba in 1947 to work before continuing his studies. "Alberta was so good I never did go back!" In 1955 he joined the land surveying firm of Stewart, Little, Stewart and Weir as an articling student with Alex G. Stewart. He was responsible for running levels from geodetic monuments to establish elevations and also for doing compass work for directions in the location of shot holes in the north. At Rainbow Lake, he recalled, accuracy was vital because the drilling was for reef production that required precision. If the shot location was off a couple of hundred yards, the drilling rig would miss the reef. Later, when the surveyors were locating the well site, any margin of error in their position had to be accounted for, as the wells were located in the field from the seismic shot hole rather than from a theoretical position on the map. [24]

Once the oil company had the seismic information in hand, geophysicists finally decided on a location for a wildcat well to be drilled. Once again the land surveyors were called in to get accurate coordinates for the well site and survey the boundaries of the lease. This, however, was easier said than done. Without established townships, surveyors had to calculate their position from the nearest baseline, working from the known position of the baseline monument on the central meridian at the NE corner of Section 33, and then run a long open traverse line to the well location before surveying out to another monument to check their bearings for closure. In order to close northern surveys, surveyors had to resort to the age-old method of taking star shots to get their positions of latitude and longitude, because radio signals from Peace River could not be picked up that far north in the early 1950s. As Don Dawson, ALS, recalled, however, the level of accuracy was generally high, despite occasional difficulties. [25]

*Unloading supplies from an airplane belonging to California Standard at the Phillips, Hamilton and Associates camp in the Petitot Hills area, winter of 1951–52.*

JACK DEAKIN, REPRODUCED WITH THE KIND PERMISSION OF GEOFF AND CHRIS DEAKIN

These long traverses involved cutting through bush, avoiding sloughs and muskeg, as the surveyors edged their way towards the well position they had been given by the oil company. Running traverse courses was tedious back-breaking work with potential for error in calculating distances, and it required check chaining. And errors did happen. Armstrong MacCrimmon, was out two hundred feet in the survey of a well site for Home Oil in the Grizzly Hills in early 1958. It was the result of a chaining error across a frozen lake right at the beginning of the survey. The long traverse had begun from a section corner northwest of the well site, crossed the lake, and then followed a trail in a southeasterly direction. They thought everything was fine but discovered "a bust in the triangulation." While checking for closure, they discovered the angles and distances did not add up. They check chained from the baseline back to the well site. Pressed for time, MacCrimmon used a cigarette lighter to take the last bearing, and then chained out by moonlight to their camp. The rig was half up when they had to break the news by mobile telephone to the oil company at its base at nearby Edith Lake. It was a day that turned out better than expected, as he recorded in his diary: "All day waiting on word from Edith Lake—checking cal[culation]s and working up levels notes. Home decides to drill well where it is."[26]

The distances between the given well site position and surveyed legal monuments on the townships system were often simply too great to be practical to traverse in the far north, where the baseline work had been discontinued for years. In the early 1950s, some oil companies hired surveyors to cut sections of baselines, before government survey parties legally surveyed them, as a necessary preliminary job before surveys could locate well sites.

California Standard was one oil company prepared to undertake such independent surveys to

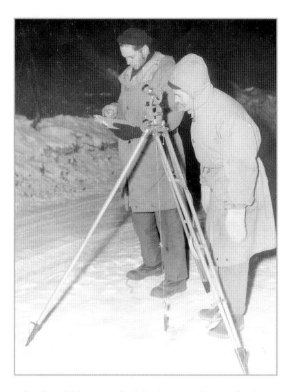

*Creighton Bildstein, ALS, (right), takes a star shot on a baseline, while a crewman takes notes and checks the time.*
JACK DEAKIN, REPRODUCED WITH THE KIND
PERMISSION OF GEOFF AND CHRIS DEAKIN

ensure accurate seismic and drilling work. In the winter of 1951–52, the company contracted survey parties totalling about thirty men from Phillips, Hamilton and Associates to run the 30th and 31st Baselines from Hay River west to the BC boundary and cut north–south on the meridians every six miles. They drove Jeeps all the way north, lived in a bunk camp with catskinners, and the oil company flew them to fly camps. The survey was a huge undertaking, and the *Edmonton Journal* even sent a leading reporter, Jack Deakin, north for a week to bring stories of adventure to its readers.

Alberta Land Surveyors Buck Olsen and Jack Webb ran a hundred miles of baseline, double chained, according to the regulations in the Dominion Land Surveyors' *Manual of Instructions*, turning off the angle every six miles at township corners for the curvature of the earth. They planted posts at every corner, each one witnessed from blazed trees. As Webb recalled, there were only six to seven hours of light, but the cats coming behind them opening up the line worked in shifts 24 hours a day, and it was hard work keeping ahead of them.

The surveyors assumed their careful notes and plans of the baselines would be sent to the director of surveys to be approved and confirmed as official plans. Geoffrey Hamilton, one of the principals

*Chaining along a survey line behind a Land Rover, season of 1951–52.*
J. H. WEBB COLLECTION

of Phillips, Hamilton and Associates, suggested that the government chip in on the cost. His request was turned down. Once the seismic was done, California Standard told them to pull the posts. "We pulled every bl—y post out all the way," recalled Webb. The subsequent running of those baselines a decade later still rankles as a waste of their efforts and the unnecessary spending of public money. As Olsen remarked, "I'm sure they aren't any more accurate."[27]

The discovery wells came in fast by the mid-1950s in northern Alberta. Surveyors themselves were caught up in the excitement of oil exploration. Armstrong MacCrimmon staked the discovery well for Home Oil Company in the Swan Hills in the mid-1950s—LSD west of the Fifth Meridian, as he recalled in an instant. It had been a three-week job, involving a thirty-mile traverse from the baseline and the running of levels along a seismic road from a geodetic benchmark on the rail line near Kinuso.[28] For the most part, surveyors never knew whether their stakes had marked the location of a dry hole or a producer, as the oil industry was bound by secrecy.[29] Charlie Weir believed that one of the wells his firm, Stewart, Little, Stewart and Weir, surveyed in 1956 was the Red Earth discovery well. After the well was a proven success, the survey company was asked to survey a number of adjacent wells in what became a major oil field over a number of seasons. It was often fifty-five below as they went in through the isolated Harmon Valley north of Nampa. The crew slept four to a tent, dependent on an airtight heater for survival. They had no power generator and what really concerned them was the absolute necessity of keeping their truck going—if it stopped for too long, it might not start again. A roster was set for three-hour intervals for someone to get up and run the truck to keep it boosted. The stakes for card games in that camp were high— whoever won passed his turn to the loser.[30]

Surveyors often had to walk three or four miles into the bush to survey a site, and during the short days of winter, it was often a race against time. As Lou Breton, ALS, recalled, his crews from Midwest Surveys often worked by flashlight to finish up. An extra half an hour could save a half-day if they had to come back. His men sometimes were less than impressed—"cold gravy with Breton" became the catch phrase while the company was working in the Swan Hills.

Others in the oil fields, catskinners and drillers, were judged to be less resilient. One survey crew was under a good deal of pressure to complete a well site survey for Union Oil west of Paddle Prairie, as the rig was coming right in behind them. All done, they noticed

## Puffing Billy

Surveyors prided themselves on their toughness and survival skills, which while perhaps not quite so exacting, were at least similar to those needed in the early days of surveying in the north. Although California Standard provided ATCO trailers for surveyors working along the 31st Baseline in 1952, at fifty below it was imperative to keep the stove, which party chief George Hedinger christened Puffing Billy, "good and toasty." If it went out, they had no water. Not that it mattered much. Washing meant dipping one's fingers in warm water and "cleaning your eye from sleep and going back to work."[31] And it was cold out there—Hedinger was thankful for the alcohol heaters that the men put in their gloves to keep their hands warm.[32]

*George Hedinger, 1952. Hedinger, who had served as a hydrographic surveyor in the Polish navy, came to Alberta in 1949. He worked on board ships in the Arctic, as well as in a bakery and an iron foundry in Edmonton, before signing on as a chainman in December 1951 with Phillips, Hamilton and Associates, a newly formed survey company in Edmonton. In 1958 he received his commission as an Alberta Land Surveyor.[33]*
J. H. WEBB COLLECTION

smoke from their tent as they trudged back. They found a Union Oil employee piling their precious supply of firewood into the heater to keep warm. When informed he could get his rig in right away, he looked aghast, and said he would have to arrange some decent accommodation for his men. Steven Cherwonick, party chief with the survey crew, recalled that the guy kept shaking his head, saying, "Mother would never believe this!" as he looked about the basic survey camp.[34]

## COMPLETION OF ALBERTA'S BOUNDARY SURVEYS

Wartime activity in Canada's northwest had broken the isolation of the North and was a catalyst for post-war exploration and the extraction of natural resources by Canadian and American companies. As neither the northern stretch of the British Columbia–Alberta boundary nor the Alberta–Northwest Territories boundary were surveyed before the war, it became imperative to do so, in order to ascertain provincial jurisdictional boundaries as oil and gas exploration moved ahead apace. The systematic aerial mapping program across Alberta, on hold since 1929, finally went ahead, making the demarcation of the boundaries urgent in order to establish control points that would allow accurate plotting of topographical points. The completion of the two boundaries was undertaken almost simultaneously.

In February 1950, a commission was again established for the British Columbia–Alberta boundary, with the Surveyor General of Canada, Bruce Waugh, serving as Chairman and Jack Holloway, ALS, representing Alberta. Robert Thistlethwaite, DLS, BCLS, ALS, led the field party, which struck out in summer 1950 along the meridian some thirty-two miles north of Fort St. John. The old-style laborious reconnaissance on foot was a thing of the past. Aerial photos taken by the RCAF were used daily to locate the best camp spot and to assess the terrain they were heading into. The first seventy miles were mostly thick spruce, requiring pack horses and axemen to forge the way. At the end of the summer season, it was decided, as the terrain north of where the Hay River crossed the boundary was swampy, to resume in winter using bulldozers. This proved tricky—it was February before the ice could support the machines' weight. The survey became a race against time before spring thaw, and was dogged by bad weather.

A third field season began in late 1951, when William N. Papove, DLS, ALS, BCLS, assumed charge. Eschewing Caterpillar tractors, he reverted to pack horses and brawn, and organized aircraft to fly in supplies; this involved locating predetermined sites. Airdrops, which included hay bales, were precarious, as it was difficult to find and pinpoint a marked spot from the air. It was wooded country, and as the survey progressed, line cutting operations frequently had to be interrupted

---

### Restoration Surveys

Many of the monuments just built by surveyors were destroyed by the bulldozers with seismic parties. Surveyors were aghast at this destruction, which in many cases included legal township monuments. In 1953, Director of Surveys Carl Lester sent out the first of many government survey parties to restore monuments in areas where damage had resulted as a result of exploration. Surveyors' complaints were finally heeded, and by late 1954 the oil companies were beginning to flag the monuments before the bulldozers arrived.[35] Destruction of legal monuments did, however, continue, and so did the necessity of sending out government restoration survey crews. In 1956 a government survey crew under George Palsen, ALS, restored 526 section monuments that had been destroyed by oil company and seismic crews.[36]

to make sleigh roads to move camp. By the end of the season thirty-seven more miles of the boundary had been surveyed and thirty-one monuments built. On March 28, two Stinson aircraft picked up the survey party, and the horses and dog teams set out for Hay River. Yet another field season was required in 1952–53. George Palsen, DLS, ALS, BCLS, was in charge. He had easier terrain and weather to deal with, and used dog teams through the more open country, setting out from an Imperial Oil airstrip in the upper Hay River area that November. In January 1953, he finally established a monument where the Alberta–Northwest Territories boundary intersected the line.[37]

The Alberta–Northwest Territories Boundary Survey began in 1950, taking up where Richard Cautley, DLS, ALS, had finished the demarcation of thirty miles of the line around Smith Settlement in 1925. The Geodetic Survey provided the precise latitude observations to control the survey, which was undertaken in the same manner as baselines completed earlier by the Topographical Surveys Branch. Cecil B. Donnelly, DLS, ALS, led the survey party across the frozen muskeg by tractor train. The use of Caterpillar D7 tractors with bulldozer blades to do the preliminary clearing of the line proved hazardous, as it was not always easy to gauge the depth of frozen crust on a muskeg, and the cats required a frost depth of at least fifteen inches. On one occasion, a TD18 tractor disappeared in the mire. Radio calls for help brought out a heavier D8 tractor all the way from Hay River. Using a block and tackle arrangement, it was able to pull the lighter machine to the surface. The men eventually managed to dry it out, warm it up, and put back it in service. The next field season, winter 1951–52, was marked by particularly savage weather—snowstorms, winds, and fog. All caused problems for surveying and resulted in the crew suffering frostbite.[38]

David Holmberg, later an Alberta Land Surveyor, was first a chainman and then first assistant to Cecil Donnelly, on the survey. The men, he recalled, would be up at 5:00 AM for breakfast. By 7:00 AM they strapped on their snowshoes and headed for the end of the line; it might be a one- to a four-mile walk. "When noon came along we just stopped and built a fire— warmed up the sandwiches." Before it became dark they headed back to camp for supper. The camp was moved when the line was about five miles away. The

⧼∞⧽

## The Oil Industry: Always in a Hurry

"Always, always, always . . . because once they make up their minds— they might take 6 months or a year to get it all organized—but once they make up their minds they are going to drill, then it's money and everything has to be coordinated– the surveyors have to be there, the landmen have to do their jobs, the cat operators are there and everybody has to do his job on time. . . . Any holdup is money—there's a lot of money involved—it's the same now as it was way back then. Hurry up and wait, but mostly jump and how high can you jump when you go." Lou Breton, ALS [39]

⧼∞⧽

*A mounder works on monument 98-1, with a standard post, trench and mound, on the Alberta–British Columbia boundary, June 19, 1950.*

DIRECTOR OF SURVEYS OFFICE, MONUMENT BOOK, POSITIONS AND DESCRIPTIONS OF MONUMENTS ESTABLISHED ON ALBERTA–BRITISH COLUMBIA BOUNDARY, 1950–51

*"Cat" train on the move, Alberta–Northwest Territories Boundary Survey, 1950–51.*
ALSA, WEIR ALBUM

technical crew rolled up their belongings, and took down their tent, and went to work on the line. At the end of the day, they walked in the direction of the new camp, always relieved to find it, as the trail cut for moving was some distance from the line.[40]

The urgency of the survey was apparent when oil company prospectors appeared near the line, ploughing out roads for seismograph-equipped trucks. As the official report on the boundary noted, "For staking purposes they were intensely interested in the location of the boundary—so much so that the surveyor felt obliged to warn them not to molest any pickets along the line."[41] The winter season of 1952–53 brought better weather, but more problems with the D7 tractor that required the services of a mechanic from Fort Smith. Cecil Donnelly led his crew on the final stretch of the 310-mile survey to complete the boundary in summer 1954.

## THE CALL FOR CONTROL SURVEYS FOR THE OIL AND GAS INDUSTRY

It was apparent by the mid-1950s that there was insufficient survey control for cost-efficient surveys of well site positions and seismic lines for oil companies by independent surveying companies. Where the township system was not in place, surveyors from competing companies found themselves working in the same localities, resulting in duplication of effort. And they knew there were errors—errors that could affect the positioning of a drilling rig and the bottom line for an oil company. They were further discouraged that the arduous and detailed surveys undertaken for the oil industry did not have any official standing, although they were required by government regulations controlling the oil and gas industry. Well site plans defined the limit of interest of the oil company's lease, rather than a property boundary that required registration at the Land Titles Office. Surveyors nonetheless worked to a level of accuracy that was set by the Surveys Act, which required all surveys to be tied to the township system. Surveyors took the initiative in pushing the director of surveys to extend the baselines, and argued that if there were insufficient numbers of government surveyors available, then the government should contract surveyors in private practice to the work, which indeed turned out to be necessary.

Government surveys for extending the township system began in 1956 with a survey party establishing twelve miles of control meridians in townships that had been subdivided in the Pembina oil field to assist surveyors locating well site locations. They also established vertical control to assist in the determination of well site elevations. The survey party carried a line of levels from the precise Canadian geodetic benchmarks, and the provincial benchmarks established during the field season were subsequently plotted on a published map.[42] During 1957 more such work was done in the Pembina Valley, as well as in the Whitecourt area.

Land surveyors worked closely with the Canadian Petroleum Association (CPA), and in summer 1957 the Alberta Land Surveyors' Association suggested setting up a working committee with representatives from the CPA, the Alberta Oil and Gas Conservation Board, and the ALSA along with the director of surveys, to advise the Surveys Branch on the planning of each season's control survey

*Winter conditions on the Alberta–Northwest Territories Boundary Survey meant taking a saw to cut a ham!*
D. Holmberg Album, reproduced with the kind permission of Dora Holmberg

work in new oil and gas fields.[43] The CPA committee was duly struck—spearheaded by Alberta Land Surveyor Jack Hill—to investigate a standard system for surveying in unsurveyed territory that would allow the oil industry to maintain a registry of wildcat well traverses.[44]

In late 1957, the ALSA also presented a brief to the Royal Commission on Northern Development, arguing for a systematic approach to the completion of baseline work in Alberta's north as the basic frame of reference governing the activities of the oil industry. It was favourably received. The report, published in March 1958, pointed to the necessity of accurate surveys to ensure that oil wells were spaced correctly in accordance with the regulations in place. The problems resulting from distant baselines, it contended, placed "a serious financial burden on resource development."[45]

In 1958 the Alberta Surveys Branch duly began a systematic program of extending the township system and establishing elevation benchmarks as they went. In the north, winter surveys worked best, and by spring 1958, government survey parties had established 24 miles of central meridian—the line running north–south from the NE corner of Section 33 on the baseline—in the Red Earth Creek area north of Nampa, while another party cut twelve lines of meridian north of the Whitecourt–Valleyview Highway in the vicinity of Iosegun Lake.[46] Land surveyors in private practice were eager to know what was being done. In January 1959, the ALSA received a map from

*A helicopter ferries and positions a survey control tower near High Level, while the survey party prepares to connect the tower to footplates placed in the permafrost.*

R. A. BASSIL COLLECTION

the Director of Surveys Office showing the proposed work for the next three years, which aimed to complete the 24th through the 28th Baselines, and continue running the central meridian in those areas.[47] The pressure for extending the baselines in the oil-producing areas of northwest Alberta, from both industry and surveyors, was mounting. By January 1961, 160 miles of new baselines and 24 miles of central meridian lines and control chords had been surveyed, along with 178 miles of section lines.[48] By year's end, northern baseline surveys had been completed up to and including the 29th Baseline. Plans for the completion of the 30th, 31st, and 32nd Baselines between the Fifth and Sixth Meridian were scheduled for 1962.[49]

Along with the call for baseline and meridian surveys, Alberta Land Surveyors consistently argued for a registry of approved plans of survey for oil and gas surveys. Surveyors left markers, either an iron spike or pipe, on all control traverses. If plans and field notes were publicly available, then subsequent surveys could tie in to their coordinates as in any other survey plan.[50] From late 1959, under new well site survey regulations, only Alberta Land Surveyors could undertake well site surveys, and all well site plans and control traverses were subsequently approved by the director of surveys and filed with the Department of Lands and Forestry.[51]

The ever-expanding oil and gas industry prompted the Alberta government to experiment with newly available technology to establish further control points to assist surveyors in more efficient location of oil and gas wells in Alberta's north. In 1969 and 1970, Alberta Land Surveyor John Deyholos, from the Director of Surveys Office, was in charge of placing a network of approximately fifteen permanent control towers that were integrated with the baseline boundary monuments of the township system on the ground at intervals of twenty-five to thirty miles. The towers were between forty-five and sixty feet high, and looked somewhat like windmills. The idea was that oil and gas wells could be located directly by observing the towers, minimizing the need for cutting a line and doing lengthy traverses from a baseline.

The distances between towers was measured using an airborne instrument called the Autotape. This network of permanent towers was tied into the Geodetic Survey of Canada framework—the North American geodetic control network NAD 27—and after a mathematical adjustment, the NAD 27 coordinates for the towers were known. The next phase was to measure from the NE corner of Section 33 on the baselines to two of the permanent towers using an untried method. Transponders were mounted on each of the permanent towers, a camera was set up on the NE corner of Section 33 pointing directly overhead, and a TV monitor was mounted in a helicopter. When the operator viewed the image of the helicopter on the monitor crosshairs, he pushed the button to measure the distances to the towers. This allowed calculation of the NAD 27 coordinates of each NE 33.

The camera/monitor system was known as the Airmark. The Autotape and Air Mark systems were supplied and supported by Canadian Engineering Surveys. The weather did not always co-operate and there were sometimes difficulties in establishing strong enough signal strength to get a reliable measurement. Dick Bassil, ALS, one of the government surveyors who worked on this project, noted it was cutting-edge methodology and technology. It proved, however, not to be as accurate as had been hoped, and surveyors subsequently working on the ground in the area of the control towers only found them useful when in close proximity.[52]

By the mid-1950s, oil companies had also turned to the foothills of Alberta. The problem of ade-quate survey control for oil exploration became acute in the rugged terrain of the foothills of the Rocky Mountains, where the Dominion Land Survey system of townships had never been fully extended. Surveyors had complained bitterly about the impossibility of running baselines on the sides of mountains more than thirty years before. Now surveyors working in exploratory areas for oil companies faced even greater challenges in the foothills than in the north. The terrain forced them to run long traverses with multiple short courses from existing section corners, and the error margins in computations for slope correction in chaining distances were a headache.

There were existing triangulation points in the foothills that had been established earlier by the federal Surveys and Mapping Branch to control aerial mapping. Alberta Land Surveyors argued that they offered a more accurate starting point than the practice of establishing theoretical baselines for such traverses. If these triangulation points, surveyors suggested, were given legal status, then any subsequent legal surveys should be carried out by reference to such points.[53] In 1959 the Canadian Petroleum Association, representing oil companies, approached Alberta's Department of Mines and Minerals with a proposal for a special type of precise trilateration survey.

It was an advance in surveying technology—electronic distance measurement (EDM)—that allowed this work to be done. The all-new microwave Tellurometer was a portable instrument that allowed surveyors to measure long distances. Ilmar Pals, an Alberta Land Surveyor with the Director of Surveys Office, who had immigrated to Canada from Estonia, brought valuable know-ledge from Europe of early EDM technology and mathematical adjustments.[54] In 1959 Pals led a control survey using helicopters to land crews on high points where they established Tellurometer stations with a line of sight. They then measured between any two given stations to produce dis-tances. The control network was tied into established geodetic coordinate points to ensure its accuracy. All Tellurometer stations were also tied to the nearest corner section, as surveyors could then work from coordinates relative to the NE corner of Section 33 on the baseline to allow them to locate well sites in terms of the township system.[55]

During a second season of work in 1960, the weather proved more cooperative, the survey party became more experienced with the new technology, and the helicopter pilot had perfected his drop-off techniques. By the end of the season, a total of eighty-nine Tellurometer stations had

*A survey crew working under Ilmar Pals, ALS, using a Tellurometer at a triangulation station in the foothills.*
R. A. Bassil Collection.

been established, and eleven existing baseline monuments had been tied to the traverse network in Townships 25 to 53, Ranges 4 through 20, West of the Fifth Meridian. A total of 716 miles of line were measured, which established control over an area of forty-six townships.[56]

In May 1961, the Department of Highways issued a second edition of the control plan with the plotted positions of all points established or used during the 1959 and 1960 field seasons, with tables showing elevations, geographic coordinates, azimuths, and distances.[57] These markers were tied into NAD 27, which Alberta also adopted for provincial control. The foothills control markers were also used to provide tighter control for the federal NTS 1:50,000 maps.[58] Surveyors were now able to go into the foothills armed with maps showing the positions of fifty to sixty markers that would give them coordinates from which they could determine their position for locating a well site.

## Surveying for Pipeline Rights-of-Way

From the early 1950s, the survey of pipeline rights-of way went hand in hand with surveying oil and gas well sites. Although oil companies shipped the first consignments of oil from Leduc by railway tank cars, and used tanker trucks for small distances, cheaper transport of oil was to be achieved through pipelines serving the local Alberta market, the rest of Canada, and ultimately export markets in the United States. All pipelines carrying either oil or gas from producing wells require legal right-of-way surveys, as they affect the title of all lands they pass through. These right-of-way surveys required a good deal of work at the Land Titles Office even before beginning fieldwork. The surveying of oil pipelines was relatively easy in the level terrain of central and southern Alberta, but required more careful calculations of elevations in hilly areas, where strategically placed pump stations were needed to ensure the flow of oil. Along with grade, location surveyors had to be aware of geological faults and the potential for ground subsidence.[59] The firms of Phillips, Hamilton and Associates, along with Stewart, Little, Stewart and Weir, and Canadian Engineering Surveys of Edmonton, became specialists in pipeline surveys, working with aerial photos and topographical maps to determine their final location and right-of-way. Although oil company landmen were supposed to discuss all angles of the project as it affected landowners, sometimes they were, as Charlie Weir recalled, a little lax. Working with landowners also became part of the land surveyor's job on pipelines.[60]

The bulk of survey work was for flow lines, gathering lines, and transmission lines within the province. A number of Alberta Land Surveyors were also involved with the construction of large-diameter main transmission pipelines, which moved Alberta's natural resources to the rest of Canada and to the US following 1949 federal legislation that governed pipelines crossing provincial boundaries. The larger survey companies that contracted to do sections of these national jobs had to expand. They took on enough men to run twenty to thirty crews, and bought the necessary extra vehicles and equipment to get the job done. On such jobs, a surveyor would run at least three crews on a section of pipeline—a line crew and two tie crews. The surveyor worked the line crew running alignments for the pipeline, planning monuments, and leaving spikes at any intersections—such as a road allowance. The tie crews then ran the ties to the section lines.[61] There was always a good deal of computing involved, which also required extra manpower with the right technical skills.

The first of these huge engineering feats undertaken was the Interprovincial Pipeline, built in 1950 to carry oil from the Redwater field, northeast of Edmonton, to Superior, Wisconsin, on the Great Lakes, from where it could be shipped to Ontario. By early 1949, production overcapacity encouraged the companies that were to form Interprovincial Pipe Line Company to begin location and survey work even before they could incorporate in accordance with federal legislation that was expected to be passed by parliament in June 1949.[62] Engineers decided on the size of the pipe and the pumping station requirements, and the preliminary route was determined from an aerial photo survey that was also used to provide detailed contour maps for land surveyors to work from. Underwood and McLellan of Saskatoon were hired by Imperial Oil in March 1949 to begin the final location surveys and the right-of-way surveys on the ground between Edmonton and Regina, via Provost. Alberta Land Surveyor Dave Ferguson, of their Edmonton branch office, led one of the company's two survey parties, which had completed almost 150 miles of right-of-way surveys—even before the Pipeline Act became law.

In spring 1950, construction began, as crews drove large ditching machines to cut a five-foot trench along the route, followed by the pipe stringers and welders. The pipe, twenty-inch diameter on the stretch from Edmonton to Regina, was then coated and wrapped and laid in the trenches that stretched a full 1,129 miles. Cleanup crews finished their work and the cameras flashed in September as Premier Manning turned a valve at the Edmonton pumping station and Alberta crude oil began its initial journey out of the province.[63]

The Trans Mountain Pipeline, built in 1951–52, was the next major pipeline that Alberta Land Surveyors played a part in. Engineers determined that a twenty-four-inch buried pipeline over seven hundred miles long could be built to carry crude oil from oil fields in the Edmonton area through the Rocky Mountains to the west coast—where oil was being imported—and that it would be an all-Canadian route. The big challenge was determining the exact route through the mountains. An initial decision, based on topographical maps and aerial reconnaissance during 1950, was made to go through the Yellowhead Pass and then south via the Nicola Valley and the Fraser Valley to Burnaby. Trans Mountain Pipelines then asked a prominent Dominion Land Surveyor to investigate the route by foot on the ground. The surveyor was none other than Guy Blanchet, who had proved his skills on the routing of the Canol pipeline from Norman Wells to Whitehorse in 1942. "It's difficult in places but feasible!" was Blanchet's general verdict, having walked the line. Trans Mountain trusted his judgment and completed an engineering study in conjunction with a field study and further aerial photography to determine and mark on the ground a final location route for the pipeline, whose construction would be managed by Canadian Bechtel.

In summer 1952 the right-of-way surveys began, with 112 men in the field at their peak. Jack Webb was one of several Alberta Land Surveyors with Phillips, Hamilton and Associates of Edmonton, the survey company contracted for the legal surveys on the Alberta section of the line and also the most difficult stretch, from Kamloops to Merritt in British Columbia. Webb wrote a comprehensive account of the pipeline survey, *The Big Inch*, published in 1991.[64] He described the long hours spent in the Land Titles Office searching out registered plans and titles, under both provincial and federal jurisdiction, that would be affected by the right-of-way, even before they went in the field. Beginning in Alberta, the fieldwork was carefully planned to meet tight deadlines, and Phillips, Hamilton and Associates put two twenty-man survey crews in the field, one led by Jack Webb and the other by Lawrence (Buck) Olsen.

The first fifty miles were through farmland and posed few problems, and the original township survey monuments were largely in place. However, the muskeg and mountainous country as they neared the Yellowhead Pass made progress slower, and so did the lousy weather. On average, the crews surveyed 2.7 miles a day in Alberta. According to Webb, "The chainages . . . had to show ties to the edge of farmland, water edges, sloughs, power and telephone lines, all roads and trails, other right-of-ways, type of trees, muskeg, coulees, buildings, fences, creeks . . . and anything else that did not move, which might have had an affect on the proposed pipeline." Webb's survey crew determined the all-important elevations using Cooke levels with split bubbles and a level rod graduated into tenths and hundredths, and tied their findings into geodetic benchmarks. Permanent benchmarks were then placed every four miles along the route, at least fifty feet from the line and marked by a five-inch galvinized spike driven into a pole or tree, or an 'X' chiselled in rock. The axemen were kept busy clearing and blazing the south boundary of the sixty-foot right-of-way, which was marked with iron posts. Orange and red paint was daubed on fence posts to mark where the pipeline crossed a fence line. In some areas it was necessary to deviate from the original planned route, and then extra pickets and bunting were left to mark the deviation. On reaching the Jasper Park boundary, a Dominion Land Surveyor was required to do the right-of-way through Crown Lands, so the indefatigable seventy-two-year-old Guy Blanchet, once more out of retirement, joined the team.[65]

Bechtel was pleased with the survey work of Phillips, Hamilton and Associates and asked them to continue the work on the difficult British Columbia section from Kamloops to Kingsvale, south of Merritt. In order to meet provincial survey requirements, Geoffrey Hamilton, one of the principals of the firm, made an arrangement with a British Columbia Land Surveyor, Clare Underhill, to oversee the BC sections. By the third week of July, all had moved to hotter climes in the valleys of BC. Olsen's crew began in Kamloops, while Webb's crew, based in Merritt, struck out northwest. By fall 1952, pipe-laying crews were hot on the heels of the land surveyors, laying the sections of pipe that were brought into the nearest rail siding and then transported by truck to the line. A year later, the first oil from Alberta arrived in Burnaby, British Columbia.

All through the 1950s, land surveyors had plenty of work surveying rights-of-way for the myriad smaller feeder pipelines, such as the 120 miles of pipeline running from the Sturgeon Lake Oil Field to the Trans Mountain Pipeline near Bickerdike.[66] Gradually a web of underground pipelines developed that crisscrossed rural areas and carried oil and gas to the province's ever-proliferating refineries and processing plants. Two main gas pipeline systems served the domestic market in Alberta. Northwestern Utilities served towns north of Red Deer and Edmonton, and Canadian Western Natural Gas Company, served Calgary and southern Alberta.[67]

By the 1950s, just how big Alberta's gas reserves were was becoming clearer, and the Alberta government's initial resistance to pressure from the federal government to supply gas to the east, gave way. In 1951 parliament granted a charter to Trans Canada Pipelines, an American subsidiary, to build a gas pipeline from Alberta to Montreal. But all was not destined to happen without a debate that became a flashpoint in national politics. It took years to sort out the finances, ownership, and routing of the pipeline. Eventually in 1954, federal cabinet minister C. D. Howe succeeded in forcing the emergence of a new company out of two rival companies, Western Pipelines and Trans Canada Pipelines. Ex-Alberta cabinet minister N. Eldon Tanner, with the backing of Alberta's Premier Manning, was at the helm of the new company, which retained the name Trans Canada Pipelines. After a debate that rocked the country, the Liberals eventually pushed a bill through parliament in 1956. It guaranteed the federal government would cover 90 percent of the construction cost in the west, while sharing the cost of the section through northern Ontario with the Ontario government.

In the meantime, Alberta had covered all bases on the home front. Fearful of any encroachment on provincial jurisdiction through the pipeline, Manning set up the Alberta Gas Trunk Line, a partially government-owned company, to gather and transmit gas within Alberta.[68] Alberta's gas pipeline system already in the ground, along with projected new lines to form a 550-mile gas

## Alberta Land Surveyors Undertake Mineral Claims outside Alberta

In the early 1950s, there was a frenzy of activity in mineral exploration in the Yukon and the NWT that set a trend for Alberta Land Surveyors to work outside the province in Canada's North. Phillips, Hamilton and Associates surveyed gold claims east of Yellowknife in the early 1950s. As Buck Olsen recalled, there were plenty of abandoned prospectors' cabins left from the last gold rush of 1930s for them to take over—no need for tents. The company also surveyed claims south of a gold mine already in operation at Yellowknife. Wardair flew the survey parties in and out. They landed in winter on a lake while the ice was still in, with sufficient supplies to carry them through the breakup period. After spring breakup, the plane could land on the water with more supplies. On one such occasion, Max Ward himself was the pilot. While he was out on the ground helping Buck Olsen and his survey crew to unload supplies, one of the other passengers on board was quietly replacing a gold brick from the mine with a fake. The thief later disembarked, his crime undetected. The story goes that the brick ended up in Australia.[69]

gathering grid, would feed into the Trans Canada Pipeline that was to run east from Empress on the Alberta–Saskatchewan boundary. Only three hundred metres of the Trans Canada Pipeline actually lies within Alberta.[70] Underwood McLellan and Associates, along with Phillips, Hamilton and Associates, surveyed various stretches of right-of-way in Saskatchewan and Manitoba. All the drafting of right-of-way plans for the Trans Canada Pipeline in the western provinces was done in the Phillips, Hamilton office in Edmonton.[71]

Debate as to whether the oil and gas industry should develop on a national or a North American continental basis, was complicated by Canadian provincial–federal relations. When Tory Prime Minster John Diefenbaker assumed power in 1958, he set up a Royal Commission on Energy, and the result was the formation of the National Energy Board in 1959. The board assumed federal regulatory responsibility for pipelines crossing Canada, interprovincial marketing of natural resources, as well as the export of oil, gas, and electricity. At the same time, the National Oil Policy was set in motion. In furthering exports of gas and oil to the United States, Ottawa chose to import oil into eastern Canada, while encouraging the export trade of oil south from Alberta. The result was a growing integration of Canadian and American energy policies during the 1960s.[72]

## SMOOTH SURVEYING IN THE SIXTIES

During the 1960s, many of the difficulties initially encountered in surveying for oil sites in the north and the foothills were smoothed out. Surveyors had forged solutions to many of the problems, survey control was improving and plans were on file, and transportation by air to isolated places made for greater convenience. Surveyors saw that oil companies were hiring people with experience who understood better what was involved in surveying in isolated areas and specific circumstances.[73] And finally, technology was advancing to allow for an overall greater efficiency in speed and accuracy. Surveying for the oil and gas industry gradually transformed into a more manageable and routine line of work.

Survey crews found access to northern well sites easier by the 1960s, as by that time the sheer number of seismic lines allowed access routes from a baseline without much axe cutting. From the late 1950s, the introduction of chainsaws made the work of axemen much easier in the bush of northern Alberta. As Bill Jones, ALS, recalled, everyone had them the minute they were available. By the early 1960s, the snowmobile was also making life easier, but survey crews still had to chain, check-chain, and plant monuments on the well site traverses.[74]

During the 1960s, each of Jones' crews had a snowmobile while doing winter well site work in northern Alberta. Survey companies were beginning to purchase snowmobiles rather than relying on oil companies to supply them as they saw fit. But Lou Breton noted the Twin Track Alpine he purchased for Midwest Surveys around 1965 was none too reliable, and he usually had to spend all night servicing it for the next day. This early machine was also underpowered. Only one person could ride it going up hills to bring in equipment—the rest of the party had to trudge through snow as before.[75] On one occasion, Breton loaded a snowmobile on a Twin Otter and set off north to check the accuracy of an isolated well site location. Breton managed to locate Peerless Lake using a map, and once overhead was able to guide the pilot to the well site. The plane landed the survey party in thirty below temperatures. They got the snowmobile going and got into camp. Breton used the snowmobile to pack a trail up and down the seismic line, in order to chain it. Having reestablished the line, he discovered the well site was indeed in the wrong location.[76]

Helicopters were increasingly used for surveys in mountainous areas during the late 1950s and into the 1960s. There was no extra half an hour when the survey party depended on a helicopter pickup, however, or the survey party might spend a cold night in the northern bush. Helicopters were not very reliable in the early days and sometimes were alarmingly under-powered for working in the mountains. Lou Breton experienced a rather nerve-wracking survey while working for Amoco, when the survey party was flown to the top of a mountain each morning from a base camp in an underpowered helicopter. The only way the pilot could get up was to fly the helicopter toward the side of the mountain—all aboard being sure they would crash, until he caught an updraft, and then he would "just spiral up like a hawk." When he got to the top, he dropped them off. Going back down was almost as bad, as the pilot "tippytoed" the helicopter to the edge of the mountain and just went straight down.[77]

The ever more demanding oil industry was the driving force behind land surveyors' adoption of new technology available in Alberta from the mid-1950s on. It provided the impetus to try for the new cost efficiencies these technologies promised and sufficient income for surveying companies to purchase them. The Odhner and the Facit were among the first of the mechanical calculators. Alberta Land Surveyors also eagerly adopted another model, the Curta, already in use in Europe since 1947, when it became available in Alberta. They all worked much the same way. "You would punch the numbers in and then crank it . . . if you were multiplying a six-digit number by a six-digit number you punched in one of the six-digit numbers then you cranked the thing . . . you hit a carriage to move it over one, you cranked again for the next number, you had to crank it six times to enter all six numbers . . . it would roll up the answer."[78] Surveyors still had to look up the natural functions, but it reduced the amount of work doing calculations quite considerably, and consequently reduced the margin of error in transposing.[79]

A couple of Alberta surveying firms working for the oil industry used Tellurometers by the early 1960s. Dave Usher, ALS, principal of the firm Usher and Associates, who purchased one in spring 1959, pioneered its use in private practice. As Usher recalled, it was a Master Remote model, MRA 100, and it cost ten thousand dollars—

## Electronic Distance Measurement

The introduction of EDM technology was a major boon to land surveyors. It allowed for the measurement of distance between two points by electronic methods that were based on sending a modulated beam of light or a microwave with a known frequency out from one electronic unit or reflector to another at the distance to be measured. The beam was returned from the second unit, and the phase difference of the returning modulation was recorded, and ultimately allowed its conversion into a distance.[80] The ability to measure distances without having to chain them out on the ground was a tremendous breakthrough in saving time and costs in running survey crews.

The first of the EDM instruments was the Geodimeter. Designed in Sweden, it measured distance by sending a light beam to a reflector unit on a tripod that would return it. Surveyors could then compute measurements based on the speed of light. The Geodimeter was used largely for establishing triangulation baselines for major first order geodetic surveying projects.

Next came the Tellurometer. It was developed by Dr. T. L. Wadley, of the South African National Institute for Telecommunications Research, in 1956. It used a microwave rather than a light beam. The master unit sent out a microwave signal. The second unit intercepted the wave and reflected it back. Based on the time it took to travel between the two points, the distance between them could be computed. Air temperature, pressure, and humidity, all affected the speed of the microwave, requiring meteorological observations to be made at each unit, even before any measurements could be made. The first Tellurometer, the MRA 1, was introduced in Canada in 1957. It arrived with a terse instruction—"If anything goes wrong, kick the power pack." The first Tellurometer power pack had a vibrator that occasionally stuck, so kicking the power pack was an effective way of loosening it.

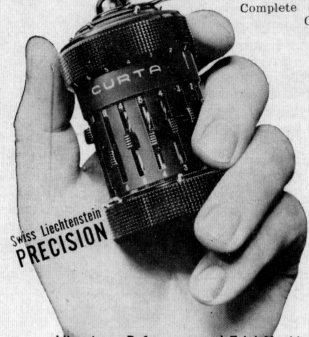
*Advertisement for the Curta in* The Canadian Surveyor, *October 1953.*

"a lot of money in those days."[81] It took him and his survey crew some time to figure out how to work it and to check its accuracy against chaining, as it had not yet been approved for legal surveys in Alberta. He ran one test at Airdrie, working from a helicopter hovering over a point between the two units. Once confident that it worked, Usher used it for surveying well site locations, such as one on Crowsnest Mountain. Doug Barnett, who worked on Usher's survey crew, found the Tellurometer had sufficient range to allow them to measure two points across the valley that were four or five miles apart.[82]

Dave Usher used the Tellurometer to mark portions of the Alberta–British Columbia boundary line for resource development. This was difficult work, as determining the watershed line between boundary monuments presented quite a challenge. They ran a series of levels and gave it their best estimate. The Tellurometer was large and heavy, as was the twelve-volt car battery that powered it, and it was hard work carrying it up mountains.

The Tellurometer certainly sped up survey work "You could measure long distances at the flick of a switch," recalled Jack Webb.[83] Doug Barnett found its operation not quite that simple. There was a lot of fiddling and adjustment to be done, as well as the meteorological corrections. He recalled that it took at least half an hour to take a measurement, depending on the distance itself and the terrain.[84] Manufacturers of the Tellurometer advertised the need for minimal training and personnel as one of its benefits, which also included cutting the cost of triangulating or chaining, and the ability to operate under the most adverse weather conditions, day and night! Whatever exaggeration may have crept in, the Tellumometer certainly made surveying easier. Its great benefit was that although the surveyor still needed a line of sight, it was no longer necessary to chain the distance through the bush.

In the early 1960s, the oil economy slowed a little in Alberta. There was less work for surveyors, and while established companies were busy, there were fewer opportunities for young men to get into surveying, either with larger firms or on their own. By the mid-1960s, new oil and gas discoveries such as Mitsue Gilwood in 1964, and Rainbow Keg in 1965, brought further optimism and more survey work. The new frontier of technical challenge for surveyors working for oil and gas companies had, however, shifted into the Arctic Circle. Dome Petroleum put in the first drilling rig on Meville Island in 1961, and drilling began in the Beaufort Sea by 1966. In 1967 Shell discovered gas on Sable Island. This marked the beginning of the arctic drilling programs that would come to fruition during the 1970s, bolstered by the federal government's aim to establish Canadian sovereignty in the Arctic. Many Alberta Land Surveyors shifted their focus to the far North to survey for oil and gas companies.

After the frenzy of the developing oil industry on the 1950s, when Alberta's land surveyors watched every twitch of its powerful tail, the 1960s were a period of consolidation. The decade was a time

## Trading Benchmarks

Establishing elevations is an essential part of carrying out well site location as well as pipeline, and seismic surveys. Oil companies need to know the surface elevations to target formations accurately. During the course of several years of work, Hamilton and Olsen (the successor firm to Phillips, Hamilton and Associates from 1956) amassed a benchmark data system. They used a standard-sized tag and a method of placing benchmarks at regular intervals, tying from one to another to ensure closed circuits. In the office in Edmonton, new benchmarks were plotted on one inch-to-a-mile topographical maps and placed in a numbered card filing system. With ten thousand benchmarks, it was the most comprehensive and retrievable system in Alberta, and it saved their clients in the oil industry a lot of money. "We traded benchmarks with other surveyors," as Buck Olsen recalled. The company charged a nominal fee to those it did little work with or who were working for oil companies that were not among its clients.[85]

of quiet, steady sailing on smooth political seas for the energy sector, and so too for surveyors working in the oil and gas industry in Alberta. The oil patch provided survey firms with most of their work, either directly or indirectly. The royalties from oil fired Alberta's economy on all fronts, and surveys were needed for the massive infrastructure program that was launched—the building of roads, rights-of-way for communication and utility services, and the laying out of new urban subdivisions that marked Alberta's transformation in the 1950s and 1960s into a prosperous modern province that became the envy of Canada.

CHAPTER 12

# Shaping Modern Alberta
*Surveying for Urbanization and Infrastructure*

ALBERTA CATAPULTS INTO A FRENZY OF MODERNIZATION

Albertans flocked to urban centres and sought jobs in the new economy fueled by the exploding oil and gas service industries from the 1950s through the 1970s. Alberta's royalties from oil grew dramatically as production rose from 7.7 million barrels in 1946 to 143.7 million in 1956, giving the Alberta government massive revenues for capital expenditure.[1] The speech from the throne in the Alberta legislature in 1950 spelled it out—there was money for roads, bridges, hospitals, recreational facilities, an extensive program of aerial survey mapping for forestry, rural electrification, and cost-sharing schemes to be undertaken with the federal government for irrigation projects in southern Alberta.

The dream of suburban life with community facilities—new schools, hospitals, and parks—became a reality for many as cities and towns expanded. Albertans' love affair with the car blossomed, and everyone became more mobile as Alberta's road system rapidly expanded and improved. In the country, electric power and telephone service made life on the farm easier as progress became the buzzword on everyone's lips. Countless surveys were required for new infrastructure and building projects of all kinds. Alberta Land Surveyors, already busy with surveying for the oil and gas industry, scrambled to lay out new suburban subdivisions, as well as right-of-way surveys for roads, railways, utilities, and irrigation ditches, for the development of a modern infrastructure. The 1960s and 1970s saw an expansion of Alberta's survey control system, and the efforts of the profession to keep abreast of the rapid pace of change and evolving technology through its educational programs.

SURVEYING FOR A NEW URBAN LANDSCAPE

At the end of the war, Alberta embraced suburban living. The acute need for housing started a construction boom calling on the services of surveyors in the major cities—Edmonton, Calgary, and Lethbridge. During World War II, zoning and bylaws had fallen by the wayside due to housing shortages, which were particularly acute in Edmonton as the city was inundated with servicemen and their families. In the post-war years, planning became the watchword in Alberta with the appointment of town planners and regional planning commissions that worked towards a long term goal of orderly urban development following modern international models. In 1937 the position of director of town planning became part of the responsibility of the director of surveys, cementing the traditional link between planning concerns and the land surveying profession.[2] When Jack Holloway was appointed director of surveys in 1947, he worked closely with municipal officials by advising on town planning and ultimately approved the resulting subdivision plans drawn by surveying companies. He became chairman of the Edmonton District Planning Commission, set up in 1950, and later was chairman of the Provincial Planning Advisory Board. Land surveyors laying out new subdivisions in Alberta's towns or major urban centres became increasingly involved with planning authorities, legislation, and regulations in the course of their work.

*Jack Holloway, ALS, exchanges a few words with Prince Philip while his wife Joyce (left) shakes hands with Queen Elizabeth, in Edmonton during the Royal visit in 1959.*
ALSA, J. W. HILL COLLECTION

Alberta adopted the neighbourhood unit, which was promoted by American Clarence Perry as early as 1929 and had been adopted in Toronto in 1945.[3] Noel Dant, Edmonton's Town Planner from 1949, was a major proponent of neighbourhood planning and brought planning experience from Britain, eastern Canada, and Chicago. The neighbourhood was a distinct residential area with a curvilinear design, cul-de-sacs and well-defined boundaries cut off from major thoroughfares. In contrast to the established square grid of avenues and streets of pre-war Alberta, the neighbourhood, it was argued, provided a safe, stable community atmosphere for children. The planners sought to foster neighbourliness and a civic sense of community by incorporating a school, park, and small local shopping areas within walking distance for residents. As the Canada Mortgage and Housing Corporation (CMHC) was happy to fund house buyers in modern neighbourhood units, land developers were encouraged to plan and build them.

Parkallen was the first new neigbourhood subdivision in Edmonton; it was designed by Noel Dant and surveyed by Alex G. Stewart, ALS. It was the very first survey job that George Walker, a young engineering graduate, worked on when he joined Stewart's firm in 1950 to article with Alex Stewart. Stewart, he recalled, drove him out to meet his party chief, Charlie Weir, who was already at work. "Charlie showed me . . . the plan of subdivision he had just started to lay out for Parkallen and then had me operate the transit while he booked notes and the chainmen drove iron posts and wooden hubs. About 5 PM we packed up, adjourned to the old Strathcona [Hotel], and after a few drinks, headed home. The next morning I was informed that as Charlie had to head south to survey a well site, I had to take over his crew and carry on with the subdivision."[4] It was sink or swim in those days and George Walker swam.

Walker recalled that things were so busy in Edmonton that his boss was often overheard on the telephone telling clients that it could be up to a year before he could free up a survey crew to do a job for them. "I made up my mind that I would start up my own practice and specialize as an *urban surveyor*."[5] George Walker soon found a niche in urban municipal work and housing development in Alberta, when he was invited by the town of Stettler to provide its municipal engineering. Walker qualified as an Alberta Land Surveyor in 1953, and the following year went into partnership with Dick Newby, ALS, who was also an engineer. Together they set up a practice that offered integrated engineering and survey services—a pattern that was to become prevalent during the next decades.

In Edmonton land surveyors laid out forty-four neighbourhood units between 1950 and 1963. Surveyors prefer to measure a straight line, and the introduction of curvilinear designs, pie-shaped lots, and crescents in new subdivisions presented many a headache. Some of the old-time surveyors were not enthusiastic about the vision of modern planners. Alex Stewart expressed his apprehension in 1958: "I can see all these curvilinear lots that are being surveyed all over the province and I think that an awful lot of people are going to find that their corners are laid wrong." Stewart feared that surveyors would take a financial loss working in new subdivisions. "I am just hoping the surveyors will get their pencils sharpened and figure out what they should charge for such lots that are every kind of shape, curves on the side, curves on the back, curves everyplace, and tangents and curves mixed up; it can be an awful chore."[6] Dave Usher, ALS, who surveyed many such suburban lots, recalled that indeed it was difficult work and took hours and hours to calculate the curves using logarithms. George Walker noted this was strictly a mathematical problem, but the real problem came in later, in servicing these lots and the right-of-way surveys required for utilities.[7]

Alex Stewart—who sat on the Edmonton Interim Development Appeal Board, 1934–1962, and the Provincial Planning Appeal Board[8]—was not a man to change his mind. Although his firm continued to lay out new subdivisions in Edmonton, he continued to criticize the new crescents. "I think we have too many in Edmonton," he argued in 1964. "Some planners seem to have them on the brain. They are costly and a devil to get around."[9] Ironically, in November 1953, Noel Dant, Edmonton's planner and chief proponent of curvilinear designs, got lost in the North Glenora subdivision that he had designed himself. The adoption of names rather than numbers for curved streets

## Devon, Alberta's First Model Town

The townsfolk in Leduc were not impressed with the transient population of roughnecks and seismic operators that inundated their town with a host of trailers in 1947. Accommodation was scarce. Imperial Oil's plans to expand the townsite got an icy reception, so the company decided to build its own townsite for its employees. Imperial chose a site on the west side of the discovery field close to the Saskatchewan River, and drew up an outline plan. Jack Holloway, Director of Surveys, in his role as provincial town planner subsequently drew up a detailed plan for the model town.[10] Alberta Land Surveyor Alex G. Stewart then laid out the townsite from this plan. Imperial constructed water, gas, and sewer lines, and its new production office was complete by May 1948. The first of Devon's prefabricated houses, heated by natural gas, was soon going up. Many of Imperial's permanent employees, most married with children, soon made Devon home. Imperial built commercial business premises on the main street. These, like the houses, were handled by Devon Estates for purchase or lease. In January 1950, Devon was incorporated as a village—a village that boasted a skating rink and a swimming pool among its burgeoning facilities. An expansion to the town was soon required, and Imperial had its own survey department do the work.

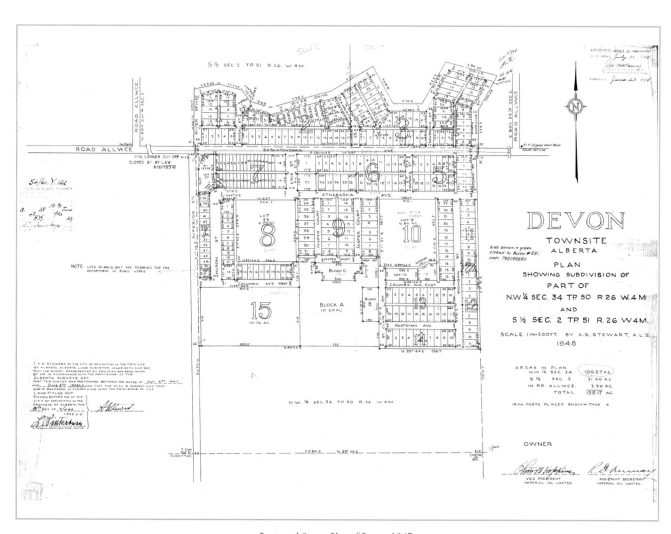

*Registered Survey Plan of Devon, 1947.*
LAND TITLES OFFICE, PLAN NUMBER 720HW

remained an issue with the public.[11] Curved streets and crescents were, however, here to stay.

In Edmonton undeveloped grid subdivisions required extensive surveys to incorporate them into new neighbourhood unit subdivisions. Subdivisions laid out in the pre-World War I boom on the grid system often took little account of the conditions on the ground. This resulted in situations where ravines ran through subdivision blocks, cutting lots, lanes, and streets in such a way as to leave useless portions, cutting off adjoining blocks from normal street access, and wasting land.[12] Many such subdivisions were never developed, and had been cancelled or reverted to city ownership for non-payment of taxes. Where the city controlled abandoned subdivisions, they were easily incorporated into complete new neighbourhoods in the 1950s, through replotting schemes, that took the natural contours of the land into account. Where individuals retained ownership of lots within old subdivisions, landowners of 60 percent of the lots had to agree to the replot.[13]

Most of the city's survey firms worked on these replotting surveys, which involved consolidating all parcels of land within the subdivision, drawing up a new subdivision plan, and then redistributing the land among the landowners to approximate their previous holdings. Surveyors found themselves dealing with the myriad of interests represented by different city departments before the replot ever went to City Council for ratification. Surveyors sometimes had to deal with city officials making changes after the plans had been prepared. In April 1953, the city's legal department noted "both the Crestwood plan and the plan of Glenora prepared by Charlie Weir, ALS, have been delayed in registration by decisions that have extended the original scope of the plans."[14] The replotting of a small part of a subdivision was also necessary for neighbourhood service stations or larger retail outlets, such as for a Safeway between 123rd and 124th Avenue, which Dave Usher, ALS, surveyed in February 1954.[15]

In Calgary the pace of development and building was even more dizzying as young families established themselves in burgeoning neighbourhood suburbs. In 1944 Calgary's population stood at 97,241; by April 1960 the city accommodated 235,428.[16] Land surveyors found that the pattern of development in Calgary was a little different than in Edmonton. The City of Calgary did not own as much land as Edmonton did, and private developers led Calgary's expansion, buying land, laying sewer and water lines, constructing roads, and building houses. As a result, unlike in Edmonton, it was not the city that provided the basic services that would later be added to the house owner's taxes, but the developer, who built the infrastructure and added it to the price of the house up front.[17] From the early 1950s, developers bought up land outside the city limits with dizzying speed. Once construction was underway, the developers applied for annexation within the city of Calgary to ensure the extension of city utilities and services to connect with the infrastructure they were putting in place. Calgary was surrounded by ranches in the early 1950s. In less than two decades it became a

*Alex G. Stewart, DLS, ALS.*
ALSA, WEIR ALBUM

*Geoffrey Hamilton, ALS. In 1961 Geoffrey Hamilton was appointed City Commissioner in charge of Planning and Development in Edmonton, a position he held until 1965. He was instrumental in passing Edmonton's new zoning bylaw of 1960 and the city's General Plan in 1967, which marked the culmination of years of interim planning for Edmonton's future growth.*
GLENBOW ARCHIVES, NA-3262-1

city transformed, as suburbs reached by new arterial roads stretched as far as the eye could see.

Calgary's land surveyors laid out the city's first post-war subdivisions on the neighbourhood model. Ley Harris, ALS, laid out the neighbourhood subdivision of Glendale in 1957 off Seventeenth Avenue, which, at that time, marked the far western edge of the city. Alberta Land Surveyor Bob McCutcheon's solid reputation brought Norman Trouth, the general manager of Kelwood Corporation, Calgary's biggest land developer, to his door in the mid-1950s. It was the beginning of a relationship that would sustain his survey firm, and later that of his partners—Wolley-Dod and MacCrimmon Surveys—for nearly two decades.

Kelwood prepared their own plans, incorporating current concepts from California that included rolled curbs. They usually had some rough grading work done on the streets and then handed the plans over to the land surveyors. A subdivision survey required a three-man crew, an instrument man and two chainmen, to establish the lot corners.[18] Armstrong MacCrimmon recalled that Haysboro was among the Kelwood subdivisions surveyed by his firm. It was on land purchased from Harry Hays, Calgary's well-known mayor, and extended south of the city for sixteen blocks as far as today's Southland Drive. Kelwood also developed Willow Park, where the lots surrounded a golf course. Willow Park was built on a farm purchased by Kelwood for a million dollars from Freddie Percival, who boasted a British earldom but made Calgary home. MacCrimmon first worked on surveying the boundary of the Willow Park golf course in 1963, and then laid out the lots for houses.

E. V. Keith Construction Company built the innovative subdivision of Willow Park. In 1967, on a tour of developments in the San Diego area, Keith saw luxury homes surrounding a man-made body of water called Lake San Marcos. Why not in Calgary? he mused. Keith determined the idea was feasible, and drew up plans for the surveyors to lay out Calgary's newest subdivision—Lake Bonavista, with full recreational facilities, an inn, and shops around a lake within the neighbourhood.[19]

By the 1960s, the planning of neighbourhood units in isolation was abandoned in favour of integrated planning that involved commercial retail catchments and arterial traffic routes. Planners moved towards the development of larger residential units through outline unit or sector plans, which envisaged the unit plan and its implementation to be a public responsibility, while the infill planning was left to the private developer.[22] These new communities would be formed by grouping neigh-bourhoods around a town centre linked with the larger city by freeways—modern Alberta had arrived. In Edmonton the largest of the six communities planned was Millwoods. It was designed to cover six thousand acres, and construction began in 1972.

Subdivision continued apace in Calgary all through the 1960s, and like Edmonton it showed a shift to the larger outline unit plan from the earlier neighbourhoods. Wolley-Dod and MacCrimmon Surveys tackled the survey of the new community of Glenmore, which covered two thousand acres. In comparison, the neighbourhood of Fairview, which they had surveyed ear-lier, comprised two hundred acres. Walker and Newby also surveyed several unit developments from the mid-1960s, including Northhaven and Bayview.[23] In the new community of Acadia on the southeast edge of the city, the area was large enough to employ both survey firms. Maple Ridge, which lay west of Deerfoot Trail, comprised six different parts. Armstrong MacCrimmon recalled that his firm surveyed parts one and five into lots in March 1967.[24]

By 1967, Canada's centennial year, Calgary's downtown skyline, which reflected in the glass of its large modern buildings, was emerging. The Husky Tower (renamed the Calgary Tower in 1971), built for Canada's centennial, defined and helped to revitalize the city core. Alberta Land Surveyors looked to the future that summer, presenting visitors to the Canadian Petroleum Exposition in Calgary with an exhibit on modern surveying. During the 1970s, many land surveying companies provided engineering survey services for the boomtown of Calgary. The city boundaries would go on extending into the 1980s, as one subdivision after another stretched south and west from the city centre.

In contrast to Calgary, Edmonton's neighbouring communities largely resisted annexation and remained under local jurisdiction as they expanded. In the 1950s, a number of satellite towns developed within easy commuting distance of Edmonton. The first of these, Campbell Town, later renamed Sherwood Park, lay within the municipality of Strathcona, whose independence came from its tax base on refinery row. Carved out of farmland belonging to Alf Hooke, Minister of Municipal Affairs,[25] the proposed subdivision was developed by J. W. Campbell with the help of an American financier. An initial plan designed by Danny Makale of the Edmonton Regional Planning Commission was dropped in favour of a plan drawn by the developer.[26] The new plan allowed extra lots, but it was not in accordance with provincial planning regulations. The curved streets were fifty to sixty-six feet wide rather than the regulation eighty to one hundred feet, and no lanes were pro-vided. Political controversy raged in the press, but the county of Strathcona and the Provincial Planning Advisory Board ultimately approved the plan.[27]

In September 1953, Jack Holloway as chairman of the Provincial Planning Advisory Board, wrote a lengthy letter to the editor of the *Edmonton Journal*, defending his decision to approve the plan against the arguments of City Planner Noel Dant. He emphasized that the plan did not envisage a satellite town, but rather it aimed to provide housing for employees in the industries in the municipalities east of the city. Alberta Land Surveyor Dave Usher laid out the first part of the new subdivision of Campbell Town in summer 1955. Al Willie, a party chief with W. D. Usher and Associates, recalled it was the first subdivision work he had been involved with where there were lots back to back with no alleys.[28]

On the northwest fringe of Edmonton, St. Albert remained separate from the city. George Walker surveyed Grandin Park, Sturgeon Heights, and Mission Park, which were among the first St. Albert subdivisions of the 1950s designed by the Edmonton Regional Planning Commission. His firm then provided an integrated engineering and survey service for planning development in St. Albert under the 1957 ammendment to the Town and Village Act.[29] Stony Plain expanded in the 1950s, and a number of its new housing blocks, originally part of the Dominion Experimental farm, were subdivided by W. D. Usher and Associates of Edmonton.[30]

By the early 1950s, Edmonton, Calgary, Red Deer, and Medicine Hat all had district planning commissions, which were responsible for planning within adjacent municipalities. Red Deer took

### Surveyors and Rural Residential Subdivisions in the 1970s

Acreage living became all the rage in the 1970s in Alberta. Surveyors were intimately involved in the planning of these subdivisions as well surveying them, and as a result became experts in planning legislation. Surveyors used maps that had five-foot contour intervals to choose the best sites for building and suitable road access lines in drawing up plans. The developers then forwarded the application to the Provincial Planning Board for approval[36] Ted Rippon, ALS, Surveyor to the Land Titles Office, along with Wally Youngs, Director of Surveys, represented the expertise of surveyors on the board.[37]

a unique approach to control development on its edges by annexing a corridor around the city, thus in effect becoming the landowner and potential developer for the future, while maintaining a green public space.[31] In 1953 the province introduced extensive subdivision regulations, under the Surveys and Expropriation Act of 1951, to ensure the suitability of the land to be subdivided, which included taking into consideration the topography, the economical provision of utilities, traffic flow, and the view from each lot.[32] Developers were often frustrated by how long it took to get their projects off the ground, and were pleased when in 1953 local planning bodies became approving authorities for proposed subdivisions.

Surveyors worked as quickly as possible in the interest of their clients to get provincial approval and the stamp of the director of surveys on their plans of survey for a new subdivision. Once the subdivision was laid out, building contractors hired surveyors to determine elevations at the lot corners and mark out the foundations of buildings. Often the surveyors returned once more to the subdivision after the houses were up to do a location survey. The surveyors produced a plan showing exactly where the building was on the lot, along with distances to the property lines.[33] This plan, called a Building Location Certificate, was required by CMHC, and by the mid-1950s it required the signature of an Alberta Land Surveyor.[34]

The firm of Walker and Newby worked closely with house builders and land developers. Walker joined HUDAC Edmonton—a local branch of the Housing and Urban Development Association of Canada, which represented house builders.[35] Walker found attending their dinners and meetings during the 1960s and early 1970s good promotion for his company. In 1976 he joined the Board of Directors of HUDAC Edmonton and in 1978 was elected president—the first non-builder to hold the office. In this position he acted as liaison between HUDAC and a number of planning committees and task forces in the city, including the Mayor's Advisory Committee on the General Plan of 1979, which was to set the course for Edmonton's next stage of development through the 1980s and 1990s. Walker sat on the Alberta Council of HUDAC and received several awards for his work in improving the residential construction industry. He was also involved with the Urban Development Institute, the organization that represented the interests

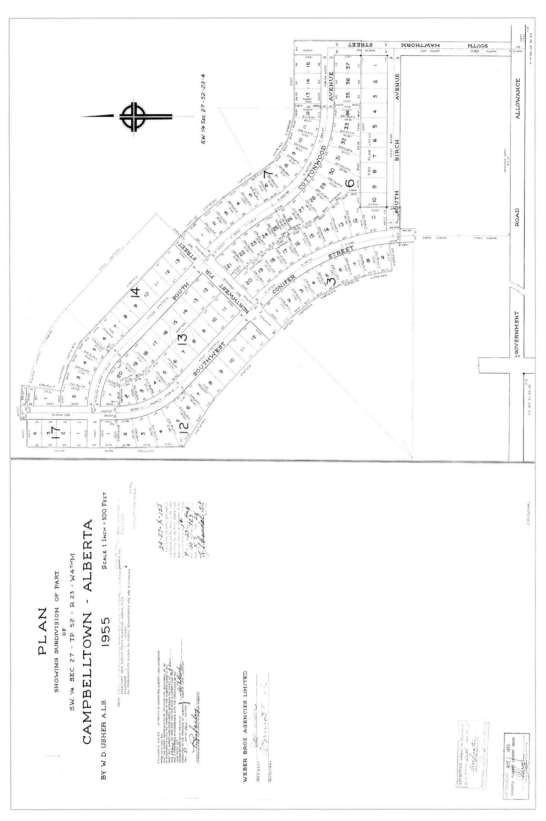

*Townsite subdivision survey plan for Campbell Town, now Sherwood Park,*
*showing the streets called after trees, Conifer, Birch, and Cottonwood.*

LAND TITLES OFFICE, PLAN NUMBER 723 KS

of land developers, and served on the committee that negotiated the first private development servicing agreement with the City of Edmonton.[38]

### CHARLIE SNELL, ALS, ASSERTS TERRITORIAL PROPRIETARY IN RED DEER

Land surveyors in the 1950s and 1960s did not have to be competitive—there was more than enough work to go around. They undertook projects at the invitation of their clients, and charged them according to tariffs set out by the Alberta Land Surveyors' Association. While many surveyors worked in the general geographic area where they were based, others worked all over the province, and no one had a stranglehold on all the business in one area. Charlie Snell, of Red Deer, however, had a long-standing unofficial relationship with the City of Red Deer, who hired him to do all its municipal work for decades. Snell regarded the survey marks in the city as his work, and along with his notes, they were not to be relinquished for the use of anyone else. By the 1950s, the demand for survey work had grown to such an extent that Snell was occasionally faced with the fact that other companies were hired to do land surveys in Red Deer.

In 1953 George Walker was hired by a lawyer to do a survey to solve an issue involving property encroachment on a Red Deer city sidewalk. Snell accosted him on the street and asked him what he thought he was doing. Walker explained that he was looking for the survey marks on the sidewalk; Snell advised him to get the hell out of town.[39] Walker was not the only surveyor that Snell tried to run out of town, and finally the council members of the Alberta Land Surveyors' Association had to address the issue when it came to a head in 1956. The firm of Stewart, Weir, Stewart and Williams of Edmonton was hired to do a subdivision survey within a larger survey plan previously surveyed by Snell. Snell refused to release his survey plan so that the certificate of title could proceed. He alleged the city had promised that he would get this work himself. Without the survey plan and the certificate of title, Donald W. Williams, the surveyor from Edmonton, could not proceed. Alex Stewart appealed to the ALSA to have Snell register his survey plan so the survey could go ahead. Snell countered that as he kept all of Red Deer's plans in his office and incidentally replaced missing posts as required, he would incorporate Williams' subdivision plan with his outline plan and submit the combined plan.

The Alberta Land Surveyors' Association Council dismissed this idea and told Snell to produce his plan. Council ruled Snell could not reasonably claim the right to embody Williams' plan within his own—not least as it violated the Alberta Surveys Act, which stated that the surveyor responsible for the work on the ground must sign the affidavit under which it is registered. The ALSA subsequently recommended to the City Commissioner in Red Deer that the city take steps to clarify its position on employment of Mr. Snell for surveys required by the city. "The situation in Red Deer is unique," the ALSA admitted, "in that [Snell] has been for many years the only local source of reliable survey information . . . ." Charlie Snell, it was suggested, might be retained by the city as a survey consultant, but on the issue of relocation of corner posts, it would be more appropriate to have a salaried land surveyor on staff.[40] Despite all this, Charlie Snell remained a respected surveyor, having the distinction of being the only Alberta Land Surveyor to serve four terms as president of the ALSA.

*The banquet held at the Macdonald Hotel in Edmonton during the annual general meeting of the Alberta Land Surveyors' Association, January 22, 1958, concluded with a dance.*

ALSA, WEIR ALBUM

The pent-up demand for cars during the war years exploded with a splurge of vehicle buying in Alberta and elsewhere across North America. Albertans faced a major obstacle in enjoying their new cars—the roads. Drivers vied to tell the worst horror stories of trips on the province's roads. Public opinion, spearheaded by the ever-growing Alberta Motor Association, was developing a short fuse behind the wheel of shiny stylish new models. The booming oil industry needed better and wider highways for transporting drilling equipment, and planners in urban areas were trying to deal with the first inkling of traffic problems. Public criticism of the highways in the late 1940s happily coincided with the Alberta government's willingness and ability to do something about it. The province, awash with oil and gas royalties, also gathered increased revenue from car registrations and gas taxes, which jumped from $7 million in 1946 to a staggering $25 million by 1956.[41]

In 1951 the Highways Branch of the Department of Public Works became a department in its own right. Carl Lester, Director of Surveys, and the Surveys Branch were transferred from Public Works to Highways—a sign of the importance of roads in the years ahead. Gordon Taylor, Minister of Highways, would make his reputation with the much-touted Alberta blacktop that motorists craved. By 1954 a new road map had been produced by the Department of Highways, indicating which routes were paved. By the end of the decade, Taylor's department had spent $280 million on modernizing Alberta's roads—building new highways, widening and straightening roads, and building bridges.[42] Alberta's main north–south artery between Edmonton and Lethbridge, Highway 2, had a hardtop, as did many of the main east–west highways that linked to it. Albertans were on a roll that was kick-started by the oil industry—they had the cars, they had the roads, and they had the money to pay for it all.

### Carl Lester, ALS

A legend among Alberta's surveyors, Carl Lester was director of surveys from 1950 to 1963, and all the surveyors who received their commissions faced him in their oral examination, conducted by the ALSA's board of examiners. Woe betide the man who got his terminology wrong or referred to a survey post as a pin. As many surveyors remember, Lester would "go up one side of you and down the other if you ever said pin."[43] One of his favourite questions to ask was, "What is the most important piece of survey equipment?" The correct answer was, "a shovel."

From its main office in Edmonton, the Department of Highways sent out location survey parties and right-of-way buyers ahead of the land survey crews marking rights-of-way. In 1951 there was so much work that five right-of-way buyers were kept busy, one based in Lethbridge, one in Calgary, and the rest working from Edmonton. They negotiated three thousand agreements for expropriating land, as well as damages for land affected by construction.[44]

Each season, location surveys continued apace in areas where the oil and gas industry desperately required adequate roads. When oil was discovered at Swan Hills in 1958, a location survey for a road between Fort Assiniboine and Swan Hills was immediately undertaken.[45] When the location surveys were complete, the land surveyors moved in to survey the right-of-way. The new road was urgently needed; the forestry trail along the route from Fort Assiniboine was so bad that truckers, headed for the new town being laid out at Swan Hills, were forced to hire bulldozers to pull them through.[46] By September 1960, 350 people lived in Swan Hills, with a further 700 at the nearby Home Oil base camp, and by the end of October the highway was open.[47]

Most of the surveys carried out during the 1950s and 1960s were for new main provincial

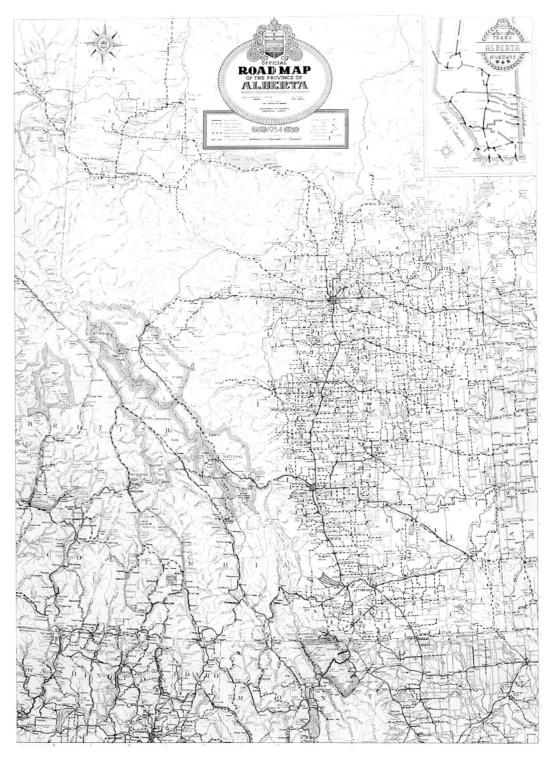

*Official road map of Alberta, 1954.*
PAA, 74.464/193

## Township Subdivision Continues in Alberta's North

By the 1950s there was demand once again for the subdivision of townships for agriculture. Since 1930 the provincial responsibility for township subdivision rested with the Surveys Branch, but from 1951, surveyors were so busy with highway work that the director of surveys had to employ surveyors in private practice for a number of seasons. Survey parties with Phillips, Hamilton and Associates of Edmonton subdivided townships in the Battle River and Valleyview areas, Hugh Pritchard, ALS, laid out township sections in an area south of High Prairie, and Knox McCusker worked in the Blueberry area as well as along the banks of the Peace and Clearwater Rivers.

McCusker reflected on the changes since 1929, the last time he did township work: "The modern labourer is hopeless on a survey job without mechanical support to do the work for him. Bought a new Chev. car [sic] so was able to be home almost every weekend during the season as the work was only one hundred miles away from home. Big contrast to the old days. I was wondering what old W. H. Selby, who ran the base I worked off, in 1904 would have said had he come back to see the goings on in camp of the subdivider—a modern truck in camp, the like never dreamed of in those days, a monster pushing out the lines and seven radios all tuned in on high, all blaring forth 'Irene Goodnight.' A table with all available produce of Canadian farms and California citrus groves in place of sow belly and beans. He doubtless would blame the dream on liquor."[48] The subdivision of townships in northern Alberta was destined to continue intermittently as the demand for homesteads and other settlement needs arose. Alberta's North, it seemed, was endless.

highways and for widening existing highways. From the early 1950s, there were about ten district surveyors working in the province at any one time. Alberta Land Surveyors Albert Tonsoo and Peter Baptie were the district engineers and surveyors in southern Alberta, based out of the Calgary Office of the Department of Highways. Ted Rippon, ALS, was based out of Edmonton, and Ilmar Pals, ALS, in the Peace River district. Others included Don Dawson and Paul Hargrove, and Tom Cuff. Cuff had the distinction of having been photographed by Canada's most distinguished photographer, Yousef Karsh, who later revealed his identity when he sent him a print. Cuff used to joke, the story goes, that it was he who had made Karsh famous. Later in the decade, Alberta Land Surveyors Jerry Iwanusiw, Roman Skierkowski, and Mike Tarczynski also held positions as district surveyors.

Each district surveyor had an assistant, who was often an articling student, and organized his own survey crews, hiring men in the district as chainmen. Many of the crew returned seasonally, May to October, year after year. Most crews had four members: an instrument man, two chainmen, and a picket man or a mounder. Over the winter months, the surveyors and their assistants did desk work, drafting plans, and arranging the cancellation of roads that had been cut off by a new highway.

Each year the number of miles surveyed increased. In 1953 survey crews began the season's work in May, and by October they had surveyed 551 miles of main highways. The following year twelve crews ran 711 miles of main highways.[49] Director of Surveys Carl Lester was hard pressed to keep a sufficient number of parties in the field, and in summer 1954, he hired three surveyors in private practice to work in improvement districts in the Nanton, Calgary, Rocky Mountain House, and Pigeon Lake areas. Bob McCutcheon, ALS, of Calgary ran fifty miles of main highway; the firm of Stewart, Weir, Little, Stewart and Williams completed twenty-eight projects despite horrendously muddy conditions on the dirt roads where they were working.[50] In 1956 work opened up to private surveyors for new roads in the Rocky Mountain House and Drayton Valley areas.[51]

Government surveyors made numerous legal right-of-way surveys for widening roads in local improvement districts to give an extra 16.5 feet on each side of the sixty-six-foot road allowance so it would be a one-hundred-foot-wide road. Clayton Bruce, assistant to Peter Baptie from 1957 until 1962, when he received his ALS commission, found that in hilly country, it was often impossible to get a direct line of sight between two points. One solution was a technique called interlining. The surveyor

*Member of a Department of Highways survey crew under Wally Youngs, ALS, near High Prairie in 1953, with instrument set up beside a Chevrolet panel truck.*
D. HOLMBERG ALBUM, REPRODUCED WITH KIND PERMISSION OF DORA HOLMBERG

used a trial and error process to get his instrument in line between the two points. When the surveyor had accomplished this task, he could see from his interlined point C to endpoint A as well as from point C to endpoint B, although it was not possible to see directly from A to B. This was less time-consuming than the alternative of running an offset line, and avoided the calculations to get the actual distance between the two points.

Clayton Bruce's whole crew worked together as circumstances dictated. John Standish, an experienced chainman, was an expert at finding iron posts, taking the topsoil off and scraping carefully. In the Medicine Hat area, windy days were a problem. Bruce kept the instrument work ahead of the chainmen, and everyone pitched in to dig pits and mounds on days that the wind made instrument work impossible.[52] During the 1950s, surveyors used pits, two feet by two feet and one foot deep, to mark the boundaries at intervals of twenty chains (1,320 feet) along roads. Farmers, however, had problems with them. Frequent complaints of broken axles on farm machinery poured into the Department of Highways. In 1964 a switch was made to steel marker posts, and these have been used to the present.[53]

Highway survey crews were in the field all summer; they lived in rented accommodation or in tent camps. Survey crews in southern Alberta generally only moved camp two or three times a season, driving each morning to the survey location. Bob Baker, ALS, and Ernie Tessari, ALS, generally set up a camp at the edge of a town, which allowed them to get electricity. At Redcliff, they had a camp in an undeveloped part of a subdivision, where they could link their own power pole to a transformer. While the surveyors still slept in tents in the early 1960s, they did have an office trailer. The cook also had a trailer and provided meals that were so good the men put on weight, even though they were chaining eight miles in a day! Finally, Tessari and Baker persuaded the director of surveys to agree to survey crews living in hotels rather than camps. They pointed out that there was little point in spending time hauling propane and water, and digging toilet holes, and that

### Keep Off the Greens!

In 1955, when the provincial highway between Stettler and Big Valley was being surveyed, the golfers on the course at Stettler were somewhat surprised to see the survey crew appear. No golf clubs in hand—but they had spades, and they were heading for the fairways. The golf course had previously been subdivided, and the surveyors were required to tie into the original township posts. The golfers were understandably somewhat hostile, but intrigued to see the original wooden posts. Fortunately, none of them was located on a green![54]

*Ted Rippon, ALS, digging for survey evidence on a survey for Highway 54 in summer 1955. Hermann Kohlschein kneels with dip needle in hand. The dip needle was a magnetic compass held in a vertical position. Instead of pointing magnetic north, the dip needle rested horizontally until it sensed iron and then began to dip in that direction. The dip needle was used to locate iron posts before the introduction of magnetic locators.*

R. F. BAKER COLLECTION

it took extra men to run the camp. From then on, the surveyors received a daily allowance, which proved to be both cheaper and time-saving.[55]

All in all, it was a pretty comfortable life for road survey crews in southern Alberta in comparison to that of their counterparts up north, who were faced with muskeg, mosquitoes, and mud. As Clayton Bruce recalled, Bob Baker, his colleague in the Calgary office, often came back from a meeting in Edmonton with their boss, Wally Youngs, then director of surveys, circulating the rumour that they would be sent north for the next season. "It never happened!" laughed Bruce, so he remained with the Department of Highways, finally severing his thirty-four-year association with the Department in the early 1990s due to government downsizing that resulted in contracting provincial highway survey work.[56] The dry south, however, had its own drawbacks, including the choking dust on gravel roads, which often meant that with each passing car, surveyors had to wait for half an hour before they could take another observation.[57]

The long-awaited Trans-Canada Highway became a reality with the optimism of the 1950s, as the federal government agreed to split the cost of the two-lane national highway from coast to coast with the provinces. The selection of its route through Alberta involved vigourous political lobbying that was reminiscent of the debate surrounding the route of the CPR seventy years previously. Once again the Yellowhead route lost out, as did a southern route through Lethbridge and the Crowsnest Pass. The chosen route closely followed the CPR line west from Walsh through Medicine Hat, past the Suffield Airbase, to Calgary, and on through the Kicking Horse Pass.

Once the engineers with the Location Branch of the Department of Highways had detailed a route, and the right-of-way buyers had negotiated the purchase or expropriated the land required, the legal survey of the boundaries could begin. Albert Tonsoo, ALS, was the surveyor in charge of the right-of-way surveys on the Alberta section of the Trans-Canada Highway from the Alberta–Saskatchewan boundary to the Banff Park gates, where Dominion Land Surveyors took over. Beginning in 1952, Tonsoo worked west from the Alberta border to Calgary.[58] The first Alberta stretch of the Trans-Canada, from Walsh to Calgary, opened in 1954. Meanwhile, the location surveys for the section west from Calgary to the Banff Park boundary caused a major holdup, as the preliminary route bisected the grazing lands on the reserve of the Stoney Nakoda at Morley. No one had consulted the band, who objected to the route. Public opinion in Calgary swung behind the Stoney Nakoda, and even the *Calgary Herald* berated the minister of highways for his high-handedness. Finally a settlement was negotiated, and the Stoney Nakoda accepted the route in exchange for twenty-thousand additional acres of land and fenced underpasses for their cattle to move freely.[59] In 1956 Albert Tonsoo's survey crew finally continued the right-of-way surveys.

The survey began within the boundaries of the city of Calgary, out along Sixteenth Avenue, through Shouldice and Bowness, before hitting open country. Tonsoo set up a camp at Bowness and the survey crew commuted daily to their survey location. They followed instructions prepared by the Department of Highways, working from the location plan, and marked stations with steel posts on the boundary line at each deflection, or in other words, each curve. The plan indicated where there was a deviation from the standard width of the road and extra width was required.[60] The survey crew, however, had a difficult problem to solve as they neared the mountains.

A thin ribbon of the township grid had been surveyed following the railway as it snaked through the Bow corridor. The Trans-Canada route was never far from the Bow River, but every section line they needed to tie the right-of-way line into was on the other side of the river. The government refused to issue a boat. The first time the crew crossed the river, it was in a shallow place where the water was only up to their waists, so they set out confidently. They had not bargained for the current. "The rocks were rolling under us, and of course we had everything on our backs, all the equipment," as Ernie Tessari, Tonsoo's second assistant, recounted. They got across and back without mishap, but decided then and there on an alternative method. The next morning they drove out all the way to the park gates and spent all day building a raft. They cut a number of good poles, and set off downstream. They started picking up section lines as they drifted down the river, running them up the mountain from the riverbank to find the old iron posts from the 1880s. They then left the line well referenced on both sides of the bank. Day after day they ran section lines until they got back to where they had crossed the river and left off the highway survey. Then they cut the raft loose and let it go.[61]

The crew then resumed the survey, picking up the lines as they progressed west. Bob Baker remembers that curious ranchers showed up on horseback to chat. At Morley, the Stoney Nakoda chief rode out to meet them and watch the work through the reserve.[62] When the survey party reached the Banff Park boundary, they tied the right-of-way into the park boundary markers and recut the demarking line. By this time it was almost

Christmas week, and in the New Year the return to a desk to draft plans was probably welcome. The Trans-Canada Highway finally opened almost six years later, in September 1962.

The surveying and construction of Alberta's new Highway 2, an American-style freeway between Calgary and Edmonton, was a major undertaking, and not without controversy. Location surveys in the late 1950s routed Highway 2 to bypass Red Deer and most of the main towns along the way by a short distance. The exception was Wetaskiwin, where the route lay some thirteen miles west, skirting the four reserves near Hobbema, despite the fact the town was more than a little put out about lost business.

Surveyors marked out a three-hundred-foot wide right-of-way to allow not just four lanes,

## Surveyors Disrupt Concert

Matt Wuhr, DLS, was one of the surveyors who worked in Alberta on Dominion Lands during the 1950s. He ran surveys in the national parks, and in 1956 was asked to determine the difference in elevation between Lake Louise and the rail line. "Why, I don't know," Wuhr recalled. "But we did it. I pounded a post in the flat wall right below the piano in the ball room of the Chateau Lake Louise put the elevation on it. [An hotel official] came out and gave me s__. He said 'What are you doing that for?' I said, 'Well, I was ordered to do this.' He said, 'Well, I'm going to change your order. You're disrupting our concert.' I said, 'I can't help it.' We got her in. Then he left us alone. It's still there too!" [64]

*Terry Skinberg, ALS, with his instrument set up on the roof of a building serving as the mortuary, which was located on the centre line of the new highway to be built through Fort McMurray, 1963.*

R. F. Baker Collection

but the six or eight lanes touted by Gordon Taylor, Minister of Highways. The first section of the new divided Highway 2, from Calgary north to Penhold, opened in October 1958. In 1960, beginning with a section between Nisku and Leduc, additional sections of the highway were constructed with four lanes. Surveyors faced new challenges in right-of-way surveys for the overpasses and cloverleaf interchanges. The approach roads required sweeping curved alignments coming off a straight level road. By March 1967, a total of forty-two interchanges had been built in Alberta. [65]

The building of roads and grading continued unabated in the 1960s. Land surveyors with the Department of Highways produced over 250 right-of-way plans each year. In 1963–64, for instance, Wally Youngs, Director of Surveys, approved a total of 340 plans. [66] At the same time, the municipal districts were also submitting road plans prepared by Alberta Land Surveyors in private practice. New roads often required right-of-way surveys for new bridges, such as the ones over the North Saskatchewan at Devon, Drayton Valley, and Genesee.

The demand for roads in Alberta stretched as far as Fort McMurray, where in the early 1960s there was only a five-mile stretch of road south to the Bitumount plant at Waterways. The Department of Highways drew up plans for a new bridge over the Athabasca to replace the winter bridge—logs across the ice similar to a corduroy road—and for a new highway through the town and north to the tar sands. Bob Baker was sent north by the director of surveys to do the necessary surveys over four summer seasons, beginning in 1961. He flew north from Edmonton, having loaded his equipment on the Northern Alberta Railway. When he got to Fort McMurray, he searched out a vehicle, but all that was available was a 1927 Ford Model T. While out on the river surveying the abutments for the new bridge, Baker heard the trappers coming downstream on the ice with their yapping dog teams. It would be a while yet before the automobile became a factor at Fort McMurray, as the road from Edmonton was not completed until 1966. [67]

By the mid-1960s, the Department of Highways had established a Planning Branch that conducted a range of traffic studies to determine the future highway upgrading and improvements needed throughout the province. In 1965, all rural municipalities were invited to participate in a rural road study that divided Alberta into nineteen study areas, to determine where the province required a secondary highway system. Engineering and planning consultants almost exclusively carried out these secondary highway studies. In the Vegreville area comprising four counties, for instance, the principal consultants, the surveying firm of Stewart, Weir, Stewart and Watson, in conjunction with Walker and

Newby, provided planning services.[68] The 1970s saw the beginning of the construction of Alberta's secondary highway system, which is still being expanded in the twenty-first century.

## RAILWAY RIGHT-OF-WAY SURVEYS

Acquisition or sales of railway land required surveys so that the land title could be altered. There were numerous circumstances in which a railway might need to acquire land, including land cave-ins along the track, or the need for additional trackside storage, and all required a survey plan. In summer 1953, Ross Tate, a Manitoba Land Surveyor with the Canadian National Railway (CNR) spent a summer under Joe Doze, ALS, resurveying the right-of-way of a CNR spur line from the east into Red Deer. In 1960 Tate transferred to Edmonton and was commissioned as an Alberta Land Surveyor in 1963. He was in charge of all legal surveys for the CNR which were handled through the real estate branch located in Edmonton.[69] During the 1970s, the CNR surveyed the rights-of-way for more recently built railway lines in northern Alberta, as resource development continued to expand. One was for the Alberta Resources Railway, from Hinton to Grande Prairie, constructed by the Alberta government in the 1950s to accelerate the development of coal, timber, and oil production. The CNR also surveyed the right-of-way for the Great Slave Lake Railway. Completed in 1964, it linked Peace River to Hay River on Great Slave Lake, with an extension to Pine Point, where there were lead and zinc deposits.

Alberta Land Surveyor Pete Muirhead, who joined the CNR in 1976, worked on the right-of-way survey of the Great Slave Lake Railway. As they were dealing with a track already in place, he and his crew worked with plans from the construction engineer to set the centre line up and take shots on the curves to show the type of curve and to calculate a legal centre for a replacement circular curve and get rid of the spirals. Knowing the degree of curve on the central curve, they calculated what the

### Public Relations

Surveyors increasingly found themselves dealing with the public on right-of-way surveys. On one highway northwest of Edmonton, a service station owner was furious because the road would now go behind his service station, and in the process of cutting the preliminary line, the location crew had cut down his prized spruce trees. When surveyor Ernie Tessari arrived to do the right-of-way survey, he went out to see the site and meet the landowner. Over a cup of coffee, he calmly explained what he had to do. When he returned to his hotel, he found an urgent message from the director of surveys telling him not to go out to the site, as the landowner was armed and dangerous![70]

Assault was rare, but occasionally things did turn ugly, such as an incident south of Calgary on the right-of-way for the power line from the Langdon sub-station to BC during the 1960s. Survey crew member Art Knudson, out to do the right-of-way survey for a power transmission line, parked his vehicle at the entrance to a farm to be crossed by the wires. He noticed a truck barrelling down the road towards him. To his alarm, a man with a balaclava over his head jumped out, clutching a roll of barbed wire with intent. Knudson, who later became an Alberta Land Surveyor, was badly scratched up, but managed to get back in his truck and get away.[71]

transitional curves should be and posted the line. The chainmen came in behind them. Then at night, Muirhead did the calculations necessary to get closure so that they could tie the line into whatever property parcels were required along the line.[72]

During the 1960s, the web of Alberta's railroad system in the rest of the province had begun to unravel, just as its highway system expanded. Blacktop highways, private cars, buses, and trucks with greater capacity for haulage, meant many branch rail lines were becoming unprofitable and the abandonment of lines began. In 1969 the federal government froze sixty-three hundred miles of prairie branch lines until 1977, and instigated a study as to their fate. Ultimately, relentless erosion of rail services continued through the 1970s and 1980s, finally culminating in the deregulation of the railways in 1996.

In 1977 a gifting agreement was struck between the federal government and both the Canadian Pacific and the Canadian National Railway. When the tracks were taken up, the federal government bought back the land. The Department of Public Works had the responsibility of transferring the land to the municipalities to dispose of—often to farmers for cattle grazing. An amendment to the agreement gave the provinces first right of option on railway right-of-way land, prior to going to the municipalities.[73] In Alberta, Ross Tate, ALS, who had joined the Department of Public Works in Edmonton in 1972, had the job of searching titles and deeds for the transfer of abandoned railway rights-of-way. The legacy of early problems with railway right-of-way titles was apparent, as in many cases descriptions were hard to follow and many CPR titles proved to be erroneous.[74]


## SURVEYORS HELP TO PROVIDE ALBERTANS WITH UTILITIES

Infrastructure for utilities and communications required right-of-way surveys. From 1946, the Director of Surveys Office issued the permits for any utility lines—power, water, sewer, and telephone—that affected public roads and road allowances, and examined all right-of-way surveys for registration at the Land Titles Office. Miles and miles of transmission and distribution power lines were put in through the 1950s and 1960s, as rural Alberta got electricity. The Director of Surveys Office issued 193 permits for new power lines in 1951–52, 265 permits in 1953–54, and in the following year, a further 272. By 1955 the number of utility lines had expanded to the point where the director of surveys asked the Location Branch of the Department of Highways to examine the permit applications in order to avoid complications that might arise in the subsequent development of highways once the lines were in place.[75]

Surveyors were kept busy working for the power companies who were putting in the lines. In 1956–57 alone, surveyors submitted 233 utility plans to the Director of Surveys Office.[76] These plans were surveyed for private corporations or municipal authorities, for the most part for Calgary Power or the City of Edmonton. By 1957 Calgary Power supplied 65 percent of the province's power, the City of Edmonton 21 percent, and Canadian Utilities, 8 percent. The cities of Medicine Hat and Lethbridge, along with Northland Utilities, provided the small percentage remaining.[77]

In southern Alberta, Wolley-Dod and MacCrimmon Surveys did most of the survey work required by Calgary Power. W. D. Usher and Associates, based in Edmonton, opened a branch office in Camrose to have a crew on the spot for right-of-way surveys for transmission lines belonging to

Canadian Utilities, who were expanding their network in the area. The power companies sometimes needed other surveys too. W. D. Usher and Associates, for instance, surveyed the boundary of the area that was to be flooded for the dam at the Battle River power plant.[78] Surveyors also worked for the rural electrification associations, cooperatives that bought power to distribute to farms from the main transmission lines. The rights-of-way under power lines were surveyed, but local residents could farm the land under them or grow gardens. Surveyors were kept busy with right-of-way surveys for power lines during the 1960s as Alberta's production of electricity soared to meet the demands of the increasing Alberta population. In 1961–62 alone, 576 permits for transmission lines were approved, and 699 more the following year.[79] More and more high-voltage transmission towers were built to carry power lines. The right-of-way for high voltage wires was generally only posted on the ground at the intersection of the right-of-way with road allowances, so farmers had no interference with their operations on the ground other than the immediate area around the towers.[80]

Albertans were also demanding more telephones for business, home, and farm use. In 1950 there were ten thousand people waiting for a telephone in the area served by Alberta Government Telephones (AGT).[81] Updating the system, including automatic exchanges and individual rather than party lines, required a good deal of survey work. Government surveyors with the Survey Branch of the Department of Highways did the right-of-way surveys for telephone lines and for the network of microwave sites for transmission. The system expanded in 1958, and required surveys for a number of radio telephone sites, and many miles of right-of-way for buried cable.[82] During the 1960s, further right-of-way surveys were required as AGT extended its rural service by underground cable, rather than overhead wires.

By the 1960s, an increasing number of rights-of-way crossed each other, particularly in urban areas. The complications of numerous rights-of-way along any given highway or urban street were apparent to surveyors. In the early 1970s, the firm of Stewart, Weir, Stewart and Watson promoted the idea of utility corridors and multi-use corridors. The concept was to set aside land to run parallel rights-of-way, thus conserving land, minimizing environmental impact to a narrow band, and simplifying issues of land ownership in relation to rights-of-way. The Alberta government took up the idea, and in 1974 hired Stewart, Weir, Stewart and Watson to undertake the Athabasca Tar Sands Corridor Study, which recommended multiple-use corridors for transport, not only of oil and gas but also for road traffic. Utility corridors would also help to solve the problems of numerous rights-of-way in urban areas, where streets contained water lines, power lines, gas lines, sewer lines, telephone lines, and sidewalks in addition to the paved roadway. In 1974 the first sections of the Edmonton Transportation/Utility Corridor were in place. The Calgary Transportation/Utility Corridor, initiated in 1979, included a right-of-way for a projected ring road, oil and gas pipelines, and power transmission lines, along with lines for municipal services. By the 1980s, Alberta Land Surveyors had clearly established the corridor concept in Alberta.

## IRRIGATION SURVEYS CONTINUE

Alberta Land Surveyors continued to play a leadership role in post-war irrigation schemes. The construction of the St. Mary River Dam in 1951 marked the beginning of the modern phase of irrigation development in southern Alberta. Alberta Land Surveyor Penrose Melvin Sauder, Director of Water Resources for Alberta and involved with irrigation schemes in southern Alberta since the 1920s, noted in 1942 that the area in southern Alberta that could potentially be irrigated was much greater than the supply of available water was capable of irrigating, and that future development would have to be based on storage of high and flood waters.[84] Sauder was the first manager of the Western Irrigation District from 1944 until 1960.

Surveyors with the federal Prairie Farm Rehabilitation Association (PFRA), established in 1938 to assist post-Depression recovery, undertook numerous surveys in connection with irrigation schemes. One was the Homestead Settlement Scheme at Hays, where land to be irrigated could be taken out at ten dollars an acre. The PFRA took over unused small canals in place, built in 1917 by the Canada Land Company enlarged them, and extended the network further in the early 1950s. Dalton Martin, ALS, who ran five survey crews at Hays, laid out the farm lots from the edge of the canals.[85] Once the surveyors had done their preliminary work, catskinners prepared the lateral ditches and then the specialized work of final levelling of dirt began. Lloyd Haverhold, who took a homestead at Hays, was one of the men who did the dirt levelling work. The surveyors left instructions as to height, depth, angle, and slope, as well as the distance to be worked. After he finished the ditch to grade within an inch, the surveyor would return with his instrument to check that all was as it should be so the water would run as planned.[86]

By the 1960s, the development of sprinkler technology, first wheelmove and then pivot sprinker systems, meant that surveyors no longer ran right-of-way surveys for open ditches. Rather, they ran rights-of-way for buried pipelines that carried water from existing ditches to the delivery point, located in the centre or close to the centre of a field to be irrigated. Takeshi Okamura, ALS, undertook many reconnaissance trips prior to undertaking such surveys in the Bow River Irrigation District in the 1960s, and this required driving for miles and miles down canal banks. Once he fell into a washout with his car—just the back wheels left up on the bank! He managed to jack the car up using fence posts as a bridge to get himself out. He drove fast in those days. The gravel roads had canal crossings "and of course they were always elevated and boy, I'd be airborne for a long ways . . . before I hit the road again!"[87]

## The Challenge of Natural Boundaries

Surveyors conducting right-of-way surveys for pipelines, roads, railways, a myriad of utility lines, and lakefront summer cottages on Gull Lake and Pigeon Lake, ran into problems with natural boundaries in the 1950s and 1960s. As surveyors worked with township survey maps, they discovered that river courses were often some distance from where they had been fifty years earlier, affecting the current ownership of any given parcel of land. How to deal with this posed a conundrum. There was a conflict between English common law, which held that the boundary of a property shifts with the natural accretions or recessions of the shoreline, and the Public Lands Act of Alberta, which held that the original shoreline marked on the township survey remains the boundary regardless of natural forces of change and erosion. In 1958 the Alberta Land Surveyors' Association referred the matter to the Attorney General's department for a solution. A verdict came in 1959. Notwithstanding the Public Lands Act, the rule of English common law was to prevail in Alberta, as it had been consistently upheld in the courts. It was now clear that government departments would have to change their approach. The Land Titles Office would have to make the necessary adjustments as surveyors resurveyed natural boundaries as they found them on the ground.[83]

## MUNICIPAL CONTROL SURVEY NETWORKS

The compilation of plans required in planning for subdivisions and associated infrastructure of roads and utilities revealed some of the weaknesses inherent in a system without geodetic control. In urban areas, the initial survey marks were posts in the ground, but gradually many had to be made in concrete sidewalks. As these marks in turn disappeared due to development, it became increasingly difficult to do retracement surveys in order to tie in new surveys.

In Calgary, many of the survey marks—which comprised a startling array of marks, from standard posts to metal plugs and bolts in concrete along with chisel marks on buildings—made by early surveyors led to a good deal of confusion. Those placed by the city's most famous surveyor, Allan Patrick, had become rare finds by the 1960s. Surveyors, unable to find the survey marks shown on old plans, had to spent a good deal of time running trial lines and interpreting what evidence they had.

Edmonton, divided by the North Saskatchewan River, had to deal with a different vertical datum on either side. From 1959 to 1962, planning for the city of Edmonton was simply divided into two sections, north and south.[88] This meant that any plan spanning the river was out of kilter.[89] This coordinate system did not tie into established benchmarks or the township system. By the early 1960s, as Edmonton began to build freeways extending across the city, the problem came to the forefront. Dave Usher was hired by engineers working on the city's new freeways to develop a temporary coordinate grid that crossed the river to allow for engineering surveys. In 1966, after more than a decade of planning, the decision went ahead to build both the Quesnell and Capilano bridges across the North Saskatchewan River. Engineers required the skills of surveyors for the very precise location work needed to locate the piers for these bridges. Hans Nederveen, ALS, with W. D. Usher and Associates, was in charge of these surveys. They required setting up temporary control points on each bank; the Capilano Bridge was especially challenging because it was curved and so required lengthy calculations.[90] These problems were found across Canada by the 1960s, and the implementation of control survey networks became the solution.

Calgary was the first city in Alberta to implement a control survey, largely due to the unflagging efforts of Alberta Land Surveyor Ken Pawson. In 1961 Pawson joined the city's Engineering Department as a land surveyor to do legal surveys on city property. The dynamic Pawson brought international experience of control surveys with him, and in 1961 he headed up a committee struck by the ALSA to look into control surveys in the province. He ultimately persuaded the City of Calgary to undertake a control survey. In an article in *The Canadian Surveyor*, Pawson explained why a control survey was so crucial. He pointed out there was in fact no way to calculate with accuracy the bearing and distance between any two points at opposite sides of the city, as it would require measuring out a route going from one plan to the next. "The only practical system yet devised to bring order to a mass of adjoining and interlocking surveys is control based on a coordinated network of reliable, indisputable monuments, located in safe positions, to which individual surveys, legal or otherwise, are tied systematically by methods aimed at obtaining and maintaining the desired accuracy."

As the project got underway Pawson pointed out that "a control system does *not* in any way upset, disturb, or call into question established legal property boundaries, rather it simply makes it easier to locate accurately all the other surveyed boundaries tied into it." The control survey also solved some of the problems associated with curvilinear subdivision design, as the bends could be tied to permanent survey control monuments. "As surveys are tied into a common grid, they will, in time, fit together like the bricks in a house, each one capable of being located relative to a sound framework. Under the present system of non-coordinated surveys we are simply throwing bricks together with no framework, and hoping that we will finish up with a house."[91] The network was filled in with practical assistance from the federal Department of Mines and Technical Surveys, and the cooperation of the provincial Surveys Branch in Edmonton, over the next couple of years.

As urbanization in Alberta continued, the associated challenges of surveying continued to mount. A City Control Survey Program was instigated through an amendment to the Surveys Act in 1966.[92] In Edmonton, a control survey similar to Calgary's was finally begun, driven by the efforts of Alberta Land Surveyor Geoffrey Hamilton, who, in his position as City Commissioner, was able to loosen the Edmonton City Council's purse strings. W. D. Usher and Associates was one of the firms that worked for the city in establishing permanent control monuments. The reconnaissance and monumentation was completed for one hundred stations during 1966.[93] They used geodimeters for distance measurement, as they were more accurate than the tellurometers for the shorter distances required for city work.[94] Control surveys were also undertaken in other cities. By March of 1967, the City of Red Deer had established 164 stations and Medicine Hat had established 68.[95] Lethbridge, Grimshaw, and Fairview joined the ongoing program, which accelerated from 1968. By 1973 Grand Cache, Grand Prairie, Camrose, Strathmore, Cochrane, Airdrie, Okotoks, and High River were also participating.[96]

In the early 1970s, government surveyors under the Director of Surveys Office, involved in developing a geodetic control network for Alberta for small-scale mapping, played a significant role in urging municipalities to tie into the larger provincial network. Dick Bassil, ALS, had the job of making presentations to town councils, explaining how a control system would allow for accurate large-scale computerized mapping required for the planning and location of bridges, water and sewer pipelines, fire hydrants, and other infrastructure. The Municipal Integrated Surveying and Mapping Program (MISAM) was launched in 1974 and many of Alberta's municipalities, from Medicine Hat to Peace River, were eager to sign up—the government paid for 85 percent and the municipalities paid for 15 percent. Municipal control surveys would ultimately tie into the provincial control survey network. They not only allowed the accurate mapping of property boundaries and infrastructure, but also provided a base for the integrated Geographic Information Systems (GIS) computer programs that would develop during the 1980s.

## New Technology and Demands for More Training for the Surveying Profession

In 1962 Jim Clark, President of the Alberta Land Surveyors' Association, urged his colleagues to keep abreast of scientific advancement in the field and to keep an open mind on the use of electronic instruments—such as the tellurometer, geodimeter, and electronic computers—as solutions to survey problems.[97] Computers were to prove the greatest breakthrough in technology. The Surveys Branch of the Department of Highways used a computer to do the calculations for the City Control

Survey Program from 1966. Ernie Tessari faced enormous difficulties in first setting up a government computer with a program that could handle the data, and then to get a program up and running to do the geodetic adjustments. In fact, it took all night to run an adjustment on a whole network. It was, as Tessari recalled, an exciting time as technology advanced.[98]

In the early 1970s, several Alberta survey firms bought their first computers, including Stewart, Weir, Stewart and Watson, who acquired an LGP 30. "It was a great big old hunk of machinery— about the size of a deep freeze," as Reg Watson recalled.[99] W. D. Usher and Associates had the same model. The magnetic drum of the computer made quite a racket when it was switched on. The computer sped up the production of survey plans, as the computations increased the level of accuracy. The potential for changing the surveyor's work process was immediately evident. In 1971 Charlie Weir forecast that, by the year 2000, the computer would lead to the involvement of the surveyor in the process of storing and retrieving environmental data. Land titles, he said, "would be stored in a computer with push button retrieval," and "along with the usual Land Titles information on each parcel of land, there would also be stored much environmental, personal and social information which would allow the automatic production of maps showing selected information which could be utilized in land use, planning, or engineering projects."[100] And indeed it came to be in 2000, with the digital submission and retrieval of survey plans.

As computers evolved from the mid-1960s, there was increasing concern that technology would outstrip the profession, and it was apparent that advanced training would be required to keep surveyors on the cutting edge of technology. The demand for surveyors was increasing, and as technology advanced, young men going into the profession without university degrees needed more training than was available at the Southern Alberta Institute of Technology (SAIT), as the Alberta Institute of Technology and Art was known from 1960.

An expansion of surveying programs at the province's two technical institutes began in the mid-1960s. In 1966 a two-year Surveying Technology Program was established at the Northern Alberta Institute of Technology (NAIT), headed by Doug Barnett, ALS. Barnett investigated a work–study program at Northeast University in Boston, and from 1975–85, NAIT students were offered a similar three-year cooperative education program with six-month work placements to get practical on-the-job experience.[101] Hugh Pritchard, ALS, joined Barnett at NAIT as an instructor from 1967 to 1970, followed by Ken Berg, ALS, from 1970 to 1996. A total of fifty graduates from the NAIT Surveying Technology Program obtained their ALS commission between 1972 and 1995. In southern Alberta, a similar program taught by Alberta Land Surveyors, including Jim Clark, Zenny Swydnycky, and Neil Coy, was offered at SAIT.

From the early 1970s, increasing numbers of women were taking training in surveying. Approximately ten percent of the students

### Survey Technicians Society

By the late 1960s, survey firms were expanding to meet the demands of industry and municipalities. The sheer volume of work meant that Alberta Land Surveyors employed skilled technicians for field and support work and drafting prior to checking and signing plans. In 1967 a meeting of about forty people, including the president and secretary of the ALSA, met in Red Deer to discuss the formation of the Alberta Society of Technicians and Technologists, which would launch its own certification process to establish criteria for membership. ALSA Secretary Jack Holloway projected that the new society would quickly have about one hundred members. It was established in 1970, and in 1980 adopted the name the Alberta Society of Survey Technicians and Technologists. By 2000, now known as the Alberta Society of Surveying and Mapping Technologies, it had a membership of 225.

## The ALSA Office

In 1967 Jack Holloway, handed over the reigns of the Alberta Land Surveyors' Association to Bob Baker. In that year the ALSA rented suite 218 in the new Bonnie Doon Shopping Centre on Edmonton's south side. Here the ALSA Council met for many years, and the records of the Association were filed, along with the beginnings of a library. Jack Holloway had a detailed plan of advice for Baker—for managing files and records, articled pupils, registration, membership list, examinations, Council transactions, annual and general meetings, ALS News—newsletter for members—and on it went. "I can't think of anything else," Holloway finally concluded. "Except a few things. . . . You will encounter problems and situations that cannot be reduced to a rule written in a guide book. All you can do is play it by ear and use your common sense. So good luck and *ne bastardi carborundum*, as Carl Lester use to say."[105] Bob Baker evidently heeded such wisdom; as secretary-treasurer and registrar, he successfully single-handedly ran an increasingly complex and expanding organization for over a decade on a part-time basis. Nevertheless, it was obvious by the late 1970s that the running of a modern professional organization required a full-time position, with support staff, to carry out its mandate.

In October 1977, Ken Allred, ALS, took over as the first full-time secretary-treasurer and registrar of the ALSA, and hired an assistant. In 1981, Allred's position broadened into the role of executive director, which still included the role of secretary-treasurer and registrar. When he left the position in 1991, the ALSA hired Brenwyn Cooley, who had a business background rather than being a land surveyor. She served as executive director from 1992 to 1997. The separate statutory position of registrar was filled by Jerry Rasmuson, ALS. In 1997 Brian Munday, MBA, became executive director, and in 2004 he and seven other full-time staff moved the office from the CN Tower to the Phipps—McKinnon Building, its sixth home, at 10020-101A Avenue.

at NAIT, as Doug Barnett recalled, were women, and a few went on to qualify as Alberta Land Surveyors. Judy Morrison (née Tarzwell), the first woman to take Neil Coy's SAIT survey courses—and who later received her ALS commission in 1977—had registered under her initial and no one was any the wiser until she showed up in class. Coy recalled that she was a crackerjack at math: "She was so good . . . she could make out matrices practically in her head!"[102]

Land surveyors in Alberta, as across Canada, stressed the need to bring qualifications up to a degree level, and there was a move to encourage universities to expand their course offerings in surveying. "Times are changing," warned Ted Rippon, president of the ALSA, in January 1967. "Today profound advances are being made in the electronic and electro-optical measuring devices, electronic computers and there are endless possibilities of automation in photogrammetry. Geodetic controls are now a reality in many of our cities. With the increasing use of photogrammetry and the increasing scale of engineering projects, a high standard of control survey is essential. If the surveyor is to take control of these complex and specialized operations, he will require a thorough basic training in science and a broad education in surveying subjects in order to cope with problems of the future."[103]

Land surveyors, many practitioners agreed, needed a university degree to ensure that these areas of emerging expertise would remain the domain of the land surveyor. Rippon warned: "At all times and at particularly at the present, our profession is being evaluated against others, and educational requirements form an obvious and easy means of evaluation." He pointed out that there were thirteen professional bodies in the province whose qualifications fell within the jurisdiction of the Coordinating Council of the University of Alberta. "The time to move for a university degree to serve to the profession in the western provinces is now," Rippon argued. "The future depends on us as members of the profession whether we are relegated to the ever-narrowing field of legal surveys or whether we grasp the potential of the future."[104]

The Special Committee on University Education led by Dave Usher prepared a submission pressing for a surveying engineering course at the University of Alberta. As a result, survey options were established in the engineering faculty. As Tom Swanby, outgoing President of the ALSA, noted with satisfaction at the annual general meeting of the ALSA in March 1968: "It is now up to us to do some public relations in Alberta high schools, technical schools and

## Blazing a New Trail

Jarmilla Marie Satra received her commission as an Alberta Land Surveyor on June 30, 1976. She was the first woman to do so. Satra came to Canada from Czechoslovakia in 1968 with a degree in surveying engineering from the Prague Technical University. Having undertaken further studies in cartography at the University of Alberta, she began articling for her ALS commission under Charlie Weir in 1973. Coming from Europe, where one-third of her graduating class had been women and where women formed a more significant part of the workforce, Satra was surprised to find there were none in the surveying profession in Alberta. She found it difficult to even buy winter boots in her size for fieldwork. "Ladies don't do that kind of work," she was told.[106] Satra was a surveyor with the firm of Stewart, Weir, Watson, Heinrichs and Dixon, and undertook field surveys for oil and gas well sites, pipeline rights-of-way, road widening, and subdivisions, until she was laid off due to the economic recession in 1982. In 1980 Satra received her CLS commission, and she was soon practicing as a Canada Lands Surveyor, running surveys on Indian reserves, and in the Northwest Territories.

Other trailblazers were Lorraine Hortness, a graduate in mathematics who qualified as an Alberta Land Surveyor in 1990, and Connie Petersen. Petersen, with a degree in surveying engineering at the University of New Brunswick in hand, headed west to Alberta in 1977. Through the 1980s, she worked for a number of surveying companies in British Columbia and Virginia, as well as in Alberta. In 1998 she received her Alberta Land Surveyor commission, and began to run Maltais Associates Surveyors' branch office in High Level, where she was soon elected as a town councilor.[107]

amongst ourselves and our employees to ensure students are found to take the courses offered."[108]

From the late 1960s, the Survey Science Program at the University of Alberta offered an amalgam of courses—geography, engineering, computer science, and law—through the Geography Department. It was not a fully fledged program and was weak in the area of technical surveying.[109] In 1974 Alex Hittel, ALS, manager of surveying at Shell, proposed a Geodetic Research Institute at the University of Calgary. This floundered, but it stirred up further discussion about university education. In 1977 a seminar, "Education for Professional Surveyors in Western Canada," was held in Alberta and sponsored by the national and western provincial surveying associations, the Canadian Petroleum Association, and the Association of Professional Engineers, Geologists and Geophysicists of Alberta. Surveyors had the backing of industry and found an ally in Dr. Mike Ward of the Civil Engineering Department at the University of Calgary. Finally the support and funding fell into place. In 1979 the Surveying Engineering Program, headed by Dr. Edward Krakiwsky, P.Eng., Ph.D., as professor and chairman, took in the first students. Sessional instructors were employees of Shell, which also presented an undergraduate scholarship. It was, as Dave Usher noted, a milestone in the history of the surveying profession in Canada.[110] Alberta would subsequently lead the way in geomatics into the twenty-first century.

CHAPTER 13

# The Future in Their Sights
*Surveyors Transform the Profession for the Twenty-First Century*

The beginning of the new millennium was a milestone for the human instinct to both look over its shoulder and to look forward into the unknown; this was apparent among surveyors as much as the rest of society. The last decades of the twentieth century were tumultuous ones for Alberta Land Surveyors. Following the economic crisis of the early 1980s, land surveyors in a rapidly modernizing world sought to ensure the highest professional standards in the public interest. The simultaneous revolution in technology—improved EDM measurement and the emergence of GPS, a dizzying level of computerization and software capability, and rapid telecommunications—changed the tools of the profession. New legislation mirrored these changes. As the twentieth century drew to a close, surveyors continued to undertake many of the kinds of surveys they had in the past, such as subdivisions, rights-of-way, and oil and gas well sites, but also were expanding into new areas where their skills and expertise were applicable.

## "THE DIRTY EIGHTIES"

After the conflict in the Middle East and the OPEC crisis of 1973, Alberta's oil industry hit dizzying new heights of production and profits as oil prices spun out of control in the new global market. By summer 1980, in the aftermath of the Iran–Iraq war, world oil prices hit forty dollars per barrel. The number of oil and gas wells drilled kept climbing: five thousand in 1976 alone, and a staggering seven thousand in 1980.[1] Surveyors could hardly keep up with the demands of oil and gas work, even as seventy-four new Alberta Land Surveyors received their commissions between 1976 and 1978. An explosion of activity was evident in Fort McMurray and the first synthetic crude pipeline came on stream in 1978. Alberta's Conservative government under Peter Lougheed championed the province's prosperous hard-nosed self-reliance as the economy boomed and buildings went up everywhere. Everyone, it seemed, was getting rich in Alberta.

On October 28, 1980, Albertans got a rude shock. The federal Liberal government in Ottawa announced the National Energy Program (NEP). It was designed to strengthen Canadian ownership, encourage energy self-sufficiency, and protect all Canadians from the surging world oil prices. It introduced federal taxes and price controls that would reduce Alberta's monopolization of the

Canadian oil industry and see Alberta selling oil at seventeen dollars per barrel. Fairness for all Canadians was the declared intention of the NEP, but Albertans did not buy it. It was condemned as an infringement on Alberta's provincial jurisdiction over her resources, and Peter Lougheed led the howl of outrage from Alberta. "The Ottawa government, without negotiation and without agreement, simply walked into our homes and occupied the living room," he declared on a TV broadcast.[2]

The oil industry slowed down overnight. "One day we were busy. The next day we had no work," recalled John Holmlund, ALS. The NEP "was the single most devastating thing that happened in our business."[3] Numerous rigs were taken down and moved south over the border in fall 1980. Alberta Land Surveyors were dismayed; they carefully watched to see how the politics of a legal battle and public opinion would play out between the provincial and federal government. Lougheed retaliated with cutbacks in oil production and shelved plans for Exxon's $8 million Cold Lake heavy oil mega-project. At the same time, he promised Albertans he would try to mitigate the effects of the NEP through cutting corporate taxes, increasing public spending, and diversifying the economy. On September 1, 1981, after rounds of provincial–federal negotiations to strike a compromise on modifying the details of the NEP, a deal was struck. Just as the third round of Alberta's cutbacks came into effect, a five-year agreement established a two-tier energy pricing system. It would, however, be some time before land surveyors would see the benefits. Simultaneously, the world demand for oil fell, and prices with it; high interest rates and recession worldwide gave Alberta's economy a beating from which it would take years to recover.

Surveyors were somewhat stunned, and survey companies were forced to lay off staff and close down branch offices. As Charlie Weir, ALS, recalled, his firm, at the time known as Stewart, Weir, Stewart, Watson, Heinrichs and Dixon, let half its staff go and consolidated survey crews. For some survey companies, it was a hard lesson learned and they began to diversify their client base. For HDS Focus Surveys, John Holmlund recalled, the goal was to no longer be subject to the cyclical pattern of the oil industry. The firm expanded into British Columbia, established an engineering branch within the company, and strengthened its presence overseas by providing assistance in the upgrading of land administration systems in developing countries.[4] Most survey companies were able to keep going, but their profit margins fell dramatically. It would take ten years for them to recover. No wonder many surveyors called the decade the dirty eighties.

In 1982 surveyors gathered at the annual general meeting of the Alberta Land Surveyors' Association, asked their council to immediately approach the Alberta government to institute programs that would generate employment in the field of land surveying during the deepening economic recession. By 1983 the building market had been plunged into the doldrums. Housing starts were slow; Genstar, one of Canada's largest construction companies, closed its office in Calgary in 1984. Surveyors' services were no longer in high demand for laying out subdivisions or surveying for large new building construction projects such as those that had characterized the 1970s skyline.

Some Alberta Land Surveyors argued in 1982 for the introduction of a mandatory minimum schedule of fees for survey services, but were not successful in getting their motion passed by the membership. By April of 1983, however, Alberta Land Surveyors were prepared to accept a minimum tariff of fees.[5] In April 1984, in his opening address at the annual general meeting of the Alberta Land Surveyors' Association, President Dick Bassil acknowledged the past year had been one of the most difficult of the last seventy-five years for Alberta's land surveyors. The profession had expanded and structured its companies to meet the demands of the boom days leaving itself open to vulnerability should the economy turn. It had happened. The issue was now what should be done in the present to avoid a compromise in services to the public. "Procurement policies, bidding practices, contract arrangements, and fee schedules are all under review, hopefully to ensure that acceptable professional and technical standards are provided now and the needs of the demands of the public are met in future," he warned. He suggested that short-term solutions needed to be found in concert with long-term objectives.[6]

## An Olympic Moment

Calgary's winning bid to host the 1988 Winter Olympic Games brought optimism and a renewed vitality to the city's economy. As the work began several years in advance, it was a boost for a city reeling from the economic downturn. Land surveyors played their part in the legacy of facilities constructed for the Games. In spring 1988, at the height of Olympic excitement, several surveyors shared their experiences with the surveying community in *Boundaries*, a magazine published by the ALSA.[7]

In 1984 Frank Halahuric, ALS, did surveys for the bobsled and luge track at Olympic Park, which required a high degree of accuracy and a dense survey control network. As Halahuric explained, "The need for precise positioning can be appreciated when you consider the speeds attained by the sleds on their descent down the course and the probable disastrous results should the proper geometry not be adhered to." They did the calculations for shape checks, for which they had to employ various "gadgets and gimmicks" in addition to more conventional survey techniques and equipment.

Out at Nakiska, a crew with McWilliam Surveys was surveying for the construction and mapping of the downhill ski slopes on the east face of Mount Allan. They struggled through a metre of snow on a 34 percent slope, working above the treeline to establish accurate elevation points at strategic locations that could be seen from the area to be developed. "I recall fighting waist-deep snow to get to our vehicle at night, only to hear the radio telling us there was no snow on Mount Allan," noted Dave McWilliam, ALS. Their job was then to establish and profile the three proposed chairlifts, called Bronze, Silver, and Gold, and the upper temporary Platter lift. This meant spotting the ground location of the top and bottom terminals of each lift and running a straight line between the two.

Unconventional methods were required due to dense bush. "We cleared a 'tear-drop' opening in the trees from the theodolite end of the line. Then we attached a weight to a cable which in turn was slung from a helicopter. The helicopter was then directed to hover over the opposite end of the line we wished to establish. The instrumentman simply sighted the rotor shaft of the helicopter and our direction was established. Then followed two or three days of bush cutting and a day of profiling and the lift line was ready for construction." The surveyors then used the lift lines as a base framework to lay out the ski runs. Once the runs were in place, McWilliam Surveys established additional control points for subsequent aerial mapping of the site.

Wolley-Dod and MacCrimmon Surveys undertook a number of Olympic projects, the most interesting and challenging of which provided surveys and plans for the International Broadcast Centre at Stampede Park. It was not as straightforward as it initially seemed due to the proliferation of utility lines that served the secondary lines to concession stands on the grounds. They all had to be located and marked before transmission cables could be installed. The problem was the utility lines had been installed over a hundred year period with no records. "Dig with caution" became the watchword! Then they located two satellite dishes on specific coordinate points, in conjunction with a huge AGT tower to receive transmissions from Canada Olympic Park some fourteen kilometres northwest. It required difficult calculations to orient the dishes to pick up the signals. All in all it was, in Alberta Land Surveyor Bill Wolley-Dod's estimation, "the most complex endeavour of its kind ever undertaken by this firm."

And then there was the survey for locating the legacy bricks at the Olympic Plaza. Twenty thousand bricks were purchased; each donor was allowed twenty-one characters engraved on his or her brick. As opening ceremonies approached, organizers realized it would be necessary to design a placement and locator system, as the bricks could neither be produced nor placed in alphabetical order. Land surveyors solved the conundrum with true Olympic spirit. They devised a grid system that used Olympic venues in Calgary to name the lines. Twenty blocks, with names such as Ski Jumping 1, were laid out separated by grid lines that were distinguishable by a caulked cutline and a lettered locator brick. How to catalogue the legacy bricks between the lines became the next hurdle. As Syd Loeppky, ALS, recalled, "Forty-three land surveyors, their wives, and friends spent approximately 200 man hours on their hands and knees writing down the inscription on each brick after they had been placed." Once the catalogue was complete, it was fed into a computer that assigned a coordinate to each brick, and it can now be retrieved through City Hall. A plaque at the Plaza commemorates the efforts of the Alberta Land Surveyors' Association in devising the mini land information system for this unique Olympic site.

## SURVEYORS MOVE TOWARD GREATER PROFESSIONALISM

The beginning of the 1980s in Alberta marked a crisis in the energy sector, but also a new climate of government philosophy towards professions and occupations. It urged a greater degree of self-regulation for professions and partnerships between the public sector and private industry in bringing services to Albertans. In May 1978 the government tabled policy that challenged professions to justify their existence and endorsed the view that professions should set their own standards and accept the responsibility of enforcement, in order to ensure the interests of the public.[8]

Alberta Land Surveyors had been self-regulating since 1910, but the ALSA quickly moved to update the Alberta Land Surveyors Act to clearly define the exclusive field of practice of Alberta Land Surveyors. It set out to establish more standards, and mechanisms by which surveyors could regulate their profession more closely. The Land Surveyors Act of 1982 for the first time recognized and authorized members of the profession to incorporate and practice as a corporation or as a surveyors' partnership. The amendments to the Act now meant that the corporation, not merely the individual land surveyor, had to take responsibility for the plans it produced. In addition, practitioners were required to carry professional liability insurance and corporate practitioners were

*Paul Methuen and James Hume of the ALSA Professional Audit Branch,*
*dig to check survey evidence, near Indus, May 1991.*
ALSA, MISCELLANEOUS PHOTO COLLECTION

required to take out a permit to practice. The first corporate permit, P001, was issued to Hunter Survey Systems. The permit number is also stamped on every iron post placed by the permit holder. These regulations also ensured that majority control of any company rested with Alberta Land Surveyors. As ALSA President Bill Hunter pointed out to the members in 1983, this was for the protection of the surveyor as well as for the protection of the public."[9]

The Act of 1982 also established a Practice Review Board to advise on areas of practice, the development of educational standards, and requirements to keep pace with technology. Then in 1987, the Director of Surveys Office, in step with government downsizing and budget reductions that ran parallel to deregulation, announced that it would cease to examine survey plans prior to registration at the Land Titles Office. Now individual practitioners had to assume full responsibility for their plans. The ALSA took steps to strengthen professional standards by instigating a post-registration monitoring of plans.[10] On March 1, 1988, the Alberta Land Surveyors' Association appointed Bill Wolley-Dod as Inspector of Surveys in charge of the Association's newly established Professional Audit Branch. The ALSA received a kick-start fund of one hundred thousand dollars from the Alberta government, and ongoing funding was ensured through a ministerial order, which ultimately made the ALSA responsible for the manufacture, sale, and distribution of survey monuments.

In 1992 the ALSA decided to broaden the scope of practice review, and in 1994 initiated the Systematic Practice Review Program, headed by a director and administered by the Practice Review Board, which takes its direction from the Council of the ALSA. The program now ensures accountability and quality control through both a full internal and external audit of all survey companies once every five years. The audits keep current director Lyall Pratt, ALS, his assistant Don George, ALS, and a technologist busy year-round. The review involves an office interview and assessment—to evaluate staff experience and expertise, systems and procedures, and equipment—as well as a random plan check for compliance with all pertinent acts, regulations, and other documents covering surveying procedures. The random plan check includes examining the field notes used to prepare the plan and a field inspection to look at the evaluation made of the survey evidence, which involves digging and scraping to find the original evidence. All these components of the Systematic Practice Review Program are designed to assist Alberta's land surveyors in providing the public with quality services.

Alberta Land Surveyors, always ready for debate, had varying opinions about these initiatives; many missed the plan-checking services of the Director of Surveys Office. Today most companies, particularly the larger firms, have in-house plan-checking departments. The commitment of Alberta Land Surveyors to maintaining high standards is reflected in the highturn out for the "Getting it Right" Seminars. These two-day seminars, held in cooperation with the Land Titles Office, deal with quality control from a survey, evidence evaluation, and plan examination perspective.[11]

## LEAPS AND BOUNDS IN MEASUREMENT TECHNOLOGY

By the late 1980s, a new instrument—the total station—became available to surveyors. This instrument did it all. Set on a tripod and battery operated, it measured vertical and horizontal angles as well as distances, and recorded this data in an electronic field notebook, either internal or mounted externally. This data collector allowed for interfacing with a computer in the office. The total station sped up surveys in remote areas, as the fieldwork could quickly be checked and plans prepared. Its greatest advantage was that it cut down on potential human error in recording angles and distances. Some surveying firms were quicker than others to adopt it in the late 1980s. It was not without its drawbacks. Although many technologists learned to use the instrument quickly and efficiently, a total station did not replace the need for notes and diagrams to assist in interpreting the data.[12] In addition, an electronic filing system can cause problems without adequate backup. As John Haggerty, ALS, has remarked, "It's easier to lose than a piece of paper."

In the early 1980s, the US Department of Defense developed a new satellite navigation system—Global Positioning System (GPS). It was soon available for geodetic positioning, and by the mid-1990s, its associated technology on the ground was widely adopted by land surveyors. Today the Global Positioning System consists of twenty-four satellites orbiting the earth twice a day at an altitude of twenty thousand kilometres, in six orbital planes at 55° degree inclination to the equator. "Each satellite receives and stores information from special controlling ground stations, carries very accurate atomic clocks, and emits signals on two carrier frequencies intended for ground receivers."[13] By measuring the travel time of the signal transmitted from each satellite, the receiver computes its distance from the satellite. With simultaneous distances from at least four satellites, the receiver can calculate its position. GPS works twenty-four hours a day in any weather, and has increasingly become an effective and efficient measuring tool for surveyors.

GPS technology has evolved very quickly, making a larger amount of data available as more satellites are in orbit and better signals are received on the ground. At the same time, the speed of the processing of the data has increased, producing positions in real time rather than with hours of delay. The earliest static GPS receivers used in the field had to be downloaded into a computer to compute the position. Today's GPS technology, the easily portable Real Time Kinematic (RTK) system, has a radio link between a base station and a rover receiver, allowing for immediate computing of the required position. The GPS systems with base station and rover used in the field by land surveyors differs considerably from the popular hand-held GPS units, both in terms of cost and accuracy. These hand-held units give accuracy to approximately ten metres, whereas the units used by land surveyors give precision to approximately ten millimetres.

Like all new technologies, GPS has its detractors and promoters. However, the adoption of GPS by the land surveying profession for surveying boundaries provides an advantage over the use of total

*A survey crew from The Cadastral Group working with a RTK system for GPS positioning in central Alberta.*
ALSA, MISCELLANEOUS PHOTO COLLECTION

stations and conventional surveying methods. It does not require a line of sight, it has an increase of speed and accuracy with which it can position points in relation to one another over large distances, and it makes it feasible to tie all land surveys into the geodetic reference frame.[14] Furthermore, it allows flexibility in the field for project completion, as not all measurements have to be made at once. GPS positions in the field must, however, be independently confirmed, by tying the GPS co-ordinates into established survey monuments on the ground to ensure accuracy and reliability. It is still just another tool used to evaluate survey evidence and define property boundaries. Not all Alberta Land Surveyors use GPS for all jobs. In urban areas, in particular, many surveyors continue to use total stations because of the interference with GPS signals from high buildings, and because it remains more cost-effective and efficient in the urban core.

## COMPLETION OF PROVINCIAL SURVEY CONTROL

The demand for better maps and a survey control infrastructure that would support the integration of all levels of land-related information continued to mount during the 1980s. The programs initiated during the 1970s within the provincial Bureau of Surveying and Mapping, and developed in partnership with federal surveying agencies, municipal governments, and the surveying profession, were accelerated to complete the establishment of survey control networks in urban centres and throughout rural Alberta. In urban areas, land surveyors in private practice made connections from the control markers into monuments in the land survey system, while in less accessible areas of northern Alberta, they were tied in by government survey crews.

Advances in measuring technology have played a major role in advancing this work. Government land surveyors using EDM Systems, Inertial Survey Systems (ISS), and, by the 1990s, Global Positioning Systems (GPS), measured these networks. The municipal survey control fabric, with control markers spaced at three hundred to eight hundred metres spacing in major urban centres, supports urban development. It allows for 1:1000 and 1:5000 large-scale mapping. The provincial survey control fabric consisting of markers at a spacing of ten kilometres by twenty kilometres supports resources development. Marker information is stored in digital form, and index maps provide a guide to the precise location of all markers.

During the late 1980s, Henry Palindat, ALS, and Harold Von Hollen, ALS, led survey crews in northern Alberta to establish Alberta Survey Control Markers (ASCM) according to coordinates previously established by federal crews. Flying in on a daily basis by helicopter from their camp, usually set up at either a fishing or a logging camp, they located these positions, which were usually in accessible areas where it was easy to install markers. They replaced the temporary federal markers—aluminum caps on a rebar—with a helix pipe eight feet long with an ASCM cap. From each ASCM, crews cut a line to find evidence on the nearest baseline and then tied into it, thus strengthening the relationship of the Alberta Township system to the ASCM network.[15] A monument commemorating this achievement was erected in the grounds of the Alberta Legislature in 1987.

In 1996 the province completed the provincial base-mapping coverage with a cash injection of $5 million provided by the major utility companies.[16] Today there are thirty thousand survey control monuments in place across Alberta that have been readjusted from NAD 27 to the new North American Datum, NAD 83. (Based on a mathematical model of the earth, NAD 83 uses earth-centred coordinates on a newly defined ellipsoid, and has no fixed initial point.) As a result, Albertans now enjoy property boundaries and a mapping infrastructure that is envied around the world.

### The Development of Satellite Positioning

The acceleration of the American space program and satellite development inadvertently impacted the practice of land surveying. By 1967 the US Navy Navigation Satellite System, called Transit, was available for civilian use. Observation consisted of recording the Doppler shift (the change in frequency of the radio signal emitted by the satellite) as it passed overhead. The rate of change was relative to the receiver's distance from the satellite. The position of the satellites was known and therefore the receiver's position could be determined from multiple Doppler shift measurements.[18] As the satellites had their own positional frame of reference, accurate positions could be established outside of surveyed territory. The most immediate civilian application of this technology was for exploration and government mapping projects in remote areas—such as the Canadian High Arctic. The offshore oil industry was quick to see its value. In the early 1970s, Alex Hittel, ALS, who worked for Shell Canada, was a pioneer researcher of applications of Doppler positioning methods in Canada.

## SURVEY PLANS GO DIGITAL

In spring 1997, the Land Titles Office began the process of putting registered survey plans on computer—the Survey Automation Project. Registration, archiving, printing, and distribution would all be done at the click of a mouse. Land surveyors were first required to submit their plans on a disk in a TIFF file. For land surveyors, this was a big change; even as they had moved from hand drafting on linen to computerized drafting onto Mylar, the end product had always been a hardcopy plan that was brought to the Land Titles Office for registration. On June 1, 1999, a six-month phase-in period began to iron out any problems in the process while not holding up the registration of plans, which required surveyors to submit both a hard copy and a digital file. Digitization has sped things up. In the words of Alberta Land Surveyor Duncan B. Gillmore, who received his commission in 1956, "it is more convenient now, definitely."[17]

## Checking of Instruments

From the 1870s, surveyors were required to check their chains for accuracy, through the Dominion Observatory and later the National Research Council. So, too, do surveyors now using EDM and GPS. The Director of Surveys Office maintains four EDM calibration baselines in the province, including one just east of Edmonton north of Highway 16. They have seven or eight markers, pipe piles driven thirty feet in the ground for stability, for which there are published coordinates and distances. Here, Alberta Land Surveyors can test their instruments by measuring between the pillars in various combinations to verify the accuracy of their instruments. Similarly, there are now GPS base nets that provide a standard to check GPS receivers and their resulting measurements. The base nets comprise five to six stable pillars with published values, similar to the EDM baselines, which form a network of triangles with distances ranging from 500 metres to 150 kilometres. Each pillar has a forced centre affixed to the top on which a surveyor's satellite receiver is placed. The results are compared with the known published values to ensure the reliability of the surveyor's GPS system and that the operator is correct. Just as they did in the early twentieth century, today's surveyors seek independent measurements to eliminate the possibility of blunders and improve accuracy.[19]

Alberta Land Titles simultaneously introduced its new Survey Plan Index System (SPIN) database system available via the internet. (It is now known as the Spatial Index System). It gave surveyors and other clients quick twenty-four-hour access to search and download survey plans—at a cost—directly from their offices. Surveyors were no longer bound by office hours or remoteness of location to get started on a survey project.

The Alberta government also decided it should no longer be in the business of managing the provincial mapping base and in 1996 set up Spatial Data Warehouse to do so. Its agent, AltaLIS, assumed the responsibility of integrating all registered survey plans into the provincial mapping base. In 1999 a cadastral mapping integration fee was introduced, to be collected by the Land Titles Office on digital registration of a survey plan.[20] The efficiency of the SPIN system and integrated mapping has given Alberta Land Surveyors an edge over their colleagues in other provinces.

SURVEYS IN THE FIELD: CHANGE AND CONTINUITY

Surveyors continue to carry out many of the types of surveys that have shaped the landscape of the province. Township subdivision is no longer ongoing, and Alberta's provincial boundaries are fixed, but other surveys—such as those needed for the oil and gas industry, massive new urban subdivisions, irrigation projects, and new Indian reserves—are always in demand. Political, social, and economic change has posed new circumstances and demands as to what is required, and at the same time, new technologies have emerged, resulting in modifications of standard practice in how the work is done.

By the mid-1990s, Alberta was back on track in resource development. The oil and gas industry had revived and was back to its pre-1980 level of activity. The fortunes of land surveyors turned also, and once again surveying in the oil and gas patch was in heavy demand. Just as happened in the 1950s, surveyors had their phones ringing and crews in the field at a moment's notice. The 1990s saw an expansion of survey firms. As new technologies came on stream in the oil and gas industry, the survey work required brought new challenges, and that solutions were facilitated by the new level of computer-assisted calculations and drafting.

In the early 1990s, for instance, Shell required a sulphur pipeline to run forty-five kilometres from the sour gas plant at Caroline to the plant at Harmattan, which produced sulphur pellets. Shell hired the survey firm of Stewart, Weir and Company to survey the right-of-way and to undertake engineering construction surveys. Reg Watson was the surveyor in charge of their branch office in Sundre. The pipeline was one of the first hot sulphur pipelines built in the world. Manufactured in Europe, it was a double pipe; the centre pipe carried hot sulphur and the outer jacket contained hot water that was circulated from each end of the pipe to maintain temperature and keep the sulphur liquid. The survey crews used total stations to set out the construction specifications. The bends in the pipe were critical to avoid stress on the metal, and the pipeline had to maintain an even depth of two metres of ground cover all the way through. Part of the surveyor's job was also to ensure that the construction was done according to the specifications for laying it in ground. Watson spent a good deal of time in the office doing the computing to make sure the curvature was maintained. All the figures had to be printed out for the construction engineer, and then the survey crews remeasured and checked the pipe in the ground to make sure it was right.[21]

During the 1990s, Alberta Energy and Utilities Board (EUB), the successor to the Oil and Gas Conservation Board, increased its requirements for surveys for oil and gas well sites. The survey

*Henry Palindat, ALS, takes notes while Kurt Edwards takes a sun shot over an Alberta Survey*
*Control Marker on a baseline north of Zama City, 1988.*

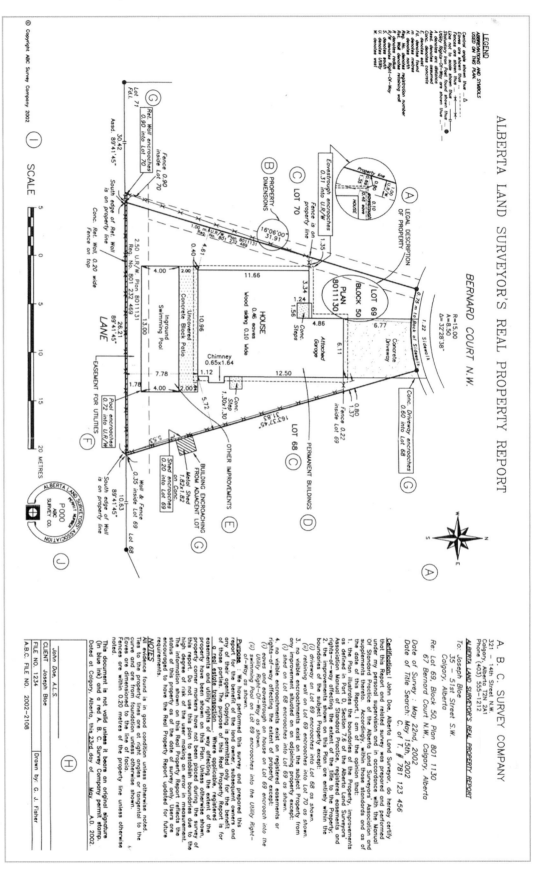

ALBERTA LAND SURVEYOR'S REAL PROPERTY REPORT

A prototype of an Alberta Land Surveyor's Real Property Report.
ALSA

work became more complex in order to provide the amount of information that had to be included on the plan. Surveyors had to show not only the proximity of natural features including water courses, historically significant areas, and tracts of native prairie, but also residences, airstrips, and the nearest town, where relevant. In 2000 Alberta Environment introduced additional requirements to note areas of alkali, flood plains, and gradient along proposed access roads. In addition, municipalities needed to know about visibility distances at the point where the well site access road meets the government road allowance. The surveyor gathered and mapped all the data in an ever-widening net of geographic and spatial information.

Urban surveying saw another development with the introduction of Real Property Reports (RPR) in 1987. This was another milestone in raising standards in providing a service to meet the needs of the public. The RPR replaced the Building Location Certificate that had been introduced in the 1950s, but by the 1980s was found to be lacking in the kind of detail and accuracy required for urban development. The certificate merely confirmed the location of the building and indicated there was no obvious encroachment but gave no other details. The RPR ensured that anyone buying a house, business, or property of any kind knows exactly where the boundaries of the property are, as well as the location of any improvements, and is made aware of any encroachments on the property.

Conversely, an RPR offers anyone selling a house today protection from future legal liabilities or complications that could occur if a property fails to meet municipal requirements after the sale is agreed. Problems relating to boundaries or encroachments that were previously unknown will come to light when an RPR is undertaken. Having a current RPR in hand means mortgage lenders and real estate agents can avoid costly delays in completing property transactions. An RPR is used to obtain a certificate of compliance with land us e bylaws and fire codes.

House buyers or vendors often come into contact with an Alberta Land Surveyor for the first time when they enter the real estate market and are advised to get an RPR for their property. The surveyor will explain that in preparing an RPR, he must search the title of the property and all pertinent encumbrances registered against it, search for all plans relating to the boundaries of the property, and do a field survey to determine the

## Back to Fred Seibert's 26th Baseline

In summer 1986, Edward Titanich was party chief on one of the three-man crews tying in Alberta Survey Control Markers to the 26th Baseline west of Fort McMurray, which had been surveyed by Fred Seibert in 1914. They kept a record of the evidence found and its condition as they worked west. At NE Section 31, Township 100, Range 21, West of the Fourth Meridian, Titanich found the iron post had been cut off and pinched at the bottom, while at NE Section 36, Township 100, Range 21, West of the Fourth Meridian, he noted that the iron post was leaning slightly north and the pits were in very poor condition. Again the iron post was shortened; it was only .86 of a metre long. Something, Titanich concluded, was definitely strange about the iron posts that Seibert had used along the western reaches of the baseline, and they did not match the township plan or the field notes Titanich had in hand. On NE Section 35, Township 100, Range 19, West of the Fourth Meridian, there was no trace of any evidence. Titanich paced back and forth a hundred metres in each direction with a metal detector—but no luck. As they continued the survey, they found one mound that had part of a threaded axle for a post, and then wooden hubs made from tree branches were used along the baseline going west. All in all, Titanich concluded, the evidence suggested that there was a metal shortage when the baseline was surveyed.

Edward Titanich was curious and later dug through Seibert's correspondence with the surveyor general.[22] It turned out that when Seibert's scow broke up in the Long Rapids in May 1914, those "lost supplies" had contained iron posts—no wonder the notation in his diary was terse. The ingenious Seibert had used boulders for benchmarks wherever possible, to save iron posts. "The iron posts not used for bench marks were used for section posts in place of those posts that had been left with the broken scow at Long Rapids and which did not get down to the line until it was completed," he reported in March 1915.[23] Clearly, he did not have enough, so he cut the ones he had to stretch them further, although he never admitted this to Surveyor General Edouard Deville. It took seventy-three years to discover his dilemma—the survey evidence will always tell the story.

## The Monumentation of Lot Corners

When the new Surveys Act came into force on June 9, 1988, one significant change was the requirement that all lot corners be monumented with iron posts. Lot corners were marked (usually with wooden posts) under regulations in place prior to 1912. But since the first provincial Surveys Act of 1912, surveyors were required to monument only the block corners, corners on a curve of constant radius, and deflection points on a block, using statutory iron posts. Between 1912 and 1988, any marker placed on a lot corner in Alberta usually did not, in fact, govern the corner of the lot; surveyors had to find the iron posts on the block corner and then mathematically calculate the location of lot corners when required. Over the years, this became confusing for both surveyors and landowners, and the question arose as to why the corner at the back of the lot could not be used! In the 1950s, the ALSA adopted a good practice resolution indicating the best practice was to place either wooden posts or iron bars at all lot corners. In 1988 the problem was resolved. Now a surveyor working on an urban property must consider the date of the original survey, and keep in mind whether the post marking the lot corner or the block corner should be used as the governing monument.

*Richard Beaumont, ALS, CLS, (left) consults with First Nations cutting crew while clearning new Indian Reserve boundaries for Treaty Land Entitlement at Pine Lake in Wood Buffalo National Park, 2002.*
Bernie Brotischi, Natural Resources Canada, Legal Surveys Division

*The Calgary Crew. Standing, Armstrong MacCrimmon, Lloyd Cridland, Lyle Ford, Alex Hittel, John Matthyssen, Terry Hudema, Ed Scovill, Kneeling, Dave Williams, Hal Falkenberg, Tony Melton, Al Jamieson, Dave Marquardt, (missing, Robin Arthurs).*

M. A. MacCrimmon Collection

## An Old-Time Survey

On a warm sunny day in April 1994, a number of Alberta Land Surveyors headed out on Calgary's streets with a transit, rods, chains, and shovels, along with other survey equipment of a hundred years earlier. They were two motley crews complete with rodmen, chainmen, and picketmen, clad in checked shirts and sporting suspenders. Their mission? To show Calgarians celebrating the city's centennial how surveys were done a hundred years earlier. Curious onlookers learned how the heart of downtown Calgary was surveyed by Archibald McVittie, DLS, in 1883, and that it lies within Township 24, Range 1, West of the Fifth Meridian, surveyed the same year by Charles La Rue, DLS. As the survey crews, one from Edmonton and one from Calgary, chained east down Ninth Avenue, they were greeted by riders from the Tsuu T'ina First Nation. The surveyors bore gifts of tobacco and blankets, and the Tsuu T'ina lit sweet grass for a symbolic peace pipe smoked in a circle at Fort Calgary. Outside old-time canvas tents, the surveyors brewed up coffee and simmered stew over a fire.

actual dimensions of the property and location of improvements—all of which will be shown in the final plan.[24]

Another area of change as the twenty-first century begins involves the surveys undertaken for First Nations. During the course of the twentieth century, there have been changes as to who is authorized to survey reserves. Although most of the land entitlements for Alberta's First Nations

*A potential land surveyor of the future.*
SCIENCE ALBERTA FOUNDATION

were surveyed as reserves in the late nineteenth and early twentieth centuries, ongoing surveys of reserves were carried out gradually by Dominion Land Surveyors. The surveyor general, following the Natural Resources Transfer Act of 1930, retained responsibility for all Dominion Lands, including Indian reserves. Alberta is obliged under the agreement of 1930 to transfer lands to the federal government in order to fulfill outstanding Treaty Land Entitlement claims from Treaties, 6, 7, and 8.

In the 1960s, things began to change as First Nations demanded more effective service. Surveys for reserves were carried out by the surveyor general's staff, who were sent to the field for periods of six months at a time. Service was improved by the establishment of a regional office of the Legal Surveys Division, Department of Energy, Mines and Resources in Edmonton in 1972, and with the work of government surveyors being supplemented by contract surveys with Alberta Land Surveyors in private practice. Work also increased as, in the 1970s, the Government of Canada made a commitment to settle those land entitlements that were outstanding.[25]

In 1995, in anticipation of the creation of a self-governing Association of Canada Lands Surveyors and the passage of the Canada Lands Surveyors Act, the surveyor general decreed that only Canada Lands Surveyors could survey on Canada Lands (formerly known as Dominion Lands).[26] While internal surveys on reserves are undertaken by a Canada Lands Surveyor, surveys in connection with reserve boundaries in Alberta must be carried out by a surveyor who holds both a CLS and an ALS commission. However, for new reserves being established under Treaty Entitlement Lands, the boundaries must in fact be surveyed by an Alberta Land Surveyor, because the lands are held by the province prior to transfer. Legal Surveys Division, Natural Resources Canada, in cooperation with the province, issues instructions for the reserve boundary surveys that are done on contract by Alberta Land Surveyors.

As First Nations strive to forge new land management practices on their lands, they deal with myriad issues, from oil and gas leases to housing and infrastructure rights-of-way. Land surveyors do more than survey boundaries; they provide services that

---

❧

### "Made to Measure"

Hundreds of kids now know what a land surveyor does because of an initiative by the Alberta Land Surveyors' Association in partnership with the Science Alberta Foundation's "Science in a Crate" program. It is geared to complement the Grade 8 mathematics curriculum that includes shape and space measurement, transformation, three-dimensional objects, and two-dimensional shapes. In 2002 Jay Abbey, ALS, a member of the ALSA Public Relations Committee, along with then articling pupil Jarl Nome, joined Science Alberta staff in a brainstorming session that resulted in the "Made to Measure" crate, filled with seven activities.[27] "That was then, this is now," for example, looks at composite area estimation—students use a stereoscope to view and work at aerial photographs to determine if a farm is the same size as a current map indicates. Such experiential work may be the key to students thinking about a career in land surveying from an early age.

❧

aim to balance traditional beliefs with current land management practices. As Aboriginal governance structures change, consideration of the fundamental structure of the land registration and survey system within Aboriginal lands has raised the issue of new models for both these components of a land tenure system.[28]

The registration of survey plans for Métis settlements, established in the 1930s, has changed following legislation passed by the Alberta government in November 1991, which conferred self-government and ownership of land in fee simple to Alberta's Métis settlements. When the late Gordon Haggerty, ALS, surveyed the boundaries of the eight settlements, he took settlement staff in the field with him to discuss the township system and its monuments, and to explain how to read a survey plan. He also gave talks to Métis schoolchildren on the significance of survey monuments.[29] The Métis Settlement Land Registry was also created in 1991 to register and record all interests within settlement lands. Therefore, land surveyors doing surveys for oil and gas well sites of pipelines must register plans of survey with the Métis Settlement Land Registry, as the Land Titles Act does not apply to Métis land, in order to ensure complete registration of an interest in the land.[30]

## Looking Ahead and Keeping Faith with the Past

Sometimes when looking into the crystal ball, it is the past that emerges. In 2001 Alberta Land Surveyors found themselves ending an old debate—called reciprocity in 1910, now called internal trade and labour mobility. In 1994 the federal and provincial governments signed the Agreement on Internal Trade. Its purpose was to reduce barriers to the movement of persons, goods, services, and investments within Canada, and by the late 1990s, both levels of government were pushing all self-governing professions, including land surveyors, to make their own side agreements to increase labour mobility. Ron Hall, a member of the Council of the ALSA, represented Alberta Land Surveyors in forging an agreement among surveyor associations across Canada that would allow land surveyors in good standing within a Canadian jurisdiction to acquire a commission in another jurisdiction more easily. It was argued that asking a land surveyor moving from one province to another to serve articles was an artificial barrier, a view that was debated vigorously. The surveyors decided that a land surveyor would not be examined in subjects that he or she had previously been examined in. Land surveyors across the country, with the exception of those in Prince Edward Island, came to a consensus, and the Interprovincial Labour Mobility Agreement was finally signed in June 2001.

⌘

### "It Runs in the Family"

When John Haggerty, ALS, went into surveying, he was following in the footsteps of his late father Gordon Haggerty, ALS. Among land surveyors, this was not unusual. In fact over the years, Alberta's land surveyors as a group have shown a marked tendency to have surveying run in the family, be it father and son, brother and brother, or father and son-in-law. Joseph Doupe and his son Jacob were both Dominion Land Surveyors who surveyed in Alberta in the 1890s, while two brothers from England, Richard W. and Reginald H. Cautley, were founding members of the ALSA. The late Alan Spence, ALS, surveyor at the Land Titles Office for thirty years, was the grandson of Allan Patrick, one of the first Dominion Land Surveyors to live in Alberta. Later examples of father and son include Richard Heacock, ALS, son of the late George Heacock, ALS, and Duncan C. Gillmore, ALS, who practices with his father, Duncan B. Gillmore, ALS. Bruce Barnett, ALS, also followed in his father Doug's footsteps, and more recently a father–daughter tradition has been established by Ashley Robertson, ALS, whose father is a Manitoba Land Surveyor.

⌘

*Ashley Robertson, speaking at the annual general meeting of the Alberta Land Surveyors' Association, April 2001, shortly before receiving her commission as an Alberta Land Surveyor.*

ALSA, AGM 2001 ALBUM

Alberta, due to its strong economy, saw more land surveyors from other Canadian jurisdictions apply to become Alberta Land Surveyors than did all other provinces. At its 2004 annual general meeting, the ALSA welcomed the first two Alberta Land Surveyors (Geoff Hobbs, a British Columbia Land Surveyor, and John Landry, a Canada Lands Surveyor) to receive their commissions under the terms of the agreement.

Many recently qualified Alberta Land Surveyors pursued a degree through the University of Calgary's Geomatics Engineering Department. Along with traditional survey courses, students take courses in GPS, GIS, hydrography, remote sensing, digital imaging, and high-precision surveys as well as attend a survey camp. Whether a graduate of Geomatics Engineering or any other program, the student then applies to the Western Canadian Board of Examiners for Land Surveyors, established in 1980, to assess his or her educational qualifications. The board, which assesses students across the prairies, issues a certificate that allows the student to apply to the relevant provincial survey association in order to article. In Alberta, students with two years minimum articling experience sit professional examinations set by the ALSA before the final oral examination to qualify as an Alberta Land Surveyor.

Attracting young people to the profession in order to ensure the next generation of land surveyors is a recurring issue for surveyors, as it is for all professions. Surveying requires strong mathematical ability, but, as Rob Radovanovic, ALS, pointed out as an articling student in 2002, "it remains a fact that few high school councillors advise an honours student who loves maths and science to become an Alberta Land Surveyor." Radovanovic suggested that more students should be encouraged to enter the Geomatics Engineering Program at the University of Calgary, with a career in land surveying in mind. By December 31, 2004, the number of active Alberta Land Surveyors hit 323, of which eight were women, and today there are more surveyors practicing in Alberta than ever before.

History works in cycles, shifting slightly in emphasis or direction as the circle turns, but "the more things change, the more they say the same," as the expression goes. Land surveyors today continue to deal with many of the same issues as their predecessors—the need for maintaining professional ethics and standards in times of economic change; keeping up with technology; seeing the need for further educational requirements; and meeting the demands of the social, political and economic climate in which they work.

As land surveying moves into the twenty-first century, the technologies that surveyors now use are supported by modern telecommunications. Surveying has quite simply sped up as survey crews can e-mail and fax field data from a truck in the field. Even in remote areas of northern Alberta, the office is never more than a satellite phone call away if problems arise that need to be discussed.

Once it arrives in the office, the field data is immediately transformed, through computer assisted drawings, into plans that can be ready and checked in relatively short order and e-mailed to a client in any location.

Surveyors find themselves in an expanding profession as geomatics has become the buzzword for the new means and applications for managing spatial information. Land surveyors now take a multi-disciplinary approach and do many types of work beyond their exclusive area of practice: cadastral surveys, the survey of legal property boundaries. The new power of computers in the application of Geographical Information Systems (GIS) allows survey compa-

Ceremonial piping of Ken Allred, newly inducted President of the Alberta Land Surveyors' Association, into the president's ball during the annual general meeting, 2001. Don Jaques, Ken Allred, Larry Pals, John Haggerty, and Bob Baker.
ALSA, AGM 2001 ALBUM

nies to produce a range of mapping services for different clients. These include, for example, maps showing all well sites and pipelines in a given area for an oil or gas company or all the buildings and information required for maps and plans for emergency response personnel at the local level. Asset mapping for municipalities is another application of GIS, and surveyors using photogrammetry can tie potholes, sewers, or light posts into previously established municipal survey networks.

However, whatever its benefits, computer technology throws up new challenges, particularly in the area of software compatibility and database interface, along with copyright issues such as those arising from the generation of digital plans for clients. The tools may have made surveying more convenient and efficient, but surveyors now do more and are asked to include more on their survey plans. As environmental regulations increase, for example, there are more stakeholders who want more out of a plan that may be produced for any one client.

The surveying life has become undeniably easier: quads cut down on sore feet and motel rooms are more comfortable than tents, but the weather and the bugs are just as bad and the urge to tell a story or two over a drink remains just as strong. One thing, however, never changes—the importance of the original surveys to today's work. Surveying always requires looking for the original survey evidence—no survey crew takes a truck out without a shovel. Surveyors are dependent on the job done by the surveyors who went before them. In a sense, they are historians as they examine old plans, and archaeologists as they scrape away layers of dirt—detectives looking for evidence, like Sherlock Holmes. They always seek the original mark laid down by their predecessors, and tie into a position established in the past to create the boundaries and property parcels of tomorrow.

## The Rust Mark

The old man said it wasn't there;
As I checked the ground with methodic care
For the iron post so badly sought
Which at the corner marked the spot.

No sign of iron the compass drew
Although a bit of junk was threw
Around the place which was the bond
For all the lands it bordered on.

A spade I took to turn the sod
While the old man thought it rather odd
For he said that in his four score and ten
No one yet had found that 'pin'.

The sod was black with grass roots strong
And these I cut and laboured on
Till down into the clay I got
And scraped the ground to find the spot.

At first the signs were not so clear
Since roots had caused the clay to shear
But soon the scraping began to show
A round rust stain of long ago.

The old man came and with his knife
Took off another slice
And by his smile I really knew
He could see the rust mark too.

Gordon Haggerty, *Rippling Rhymes* (Edmonton: Diamond Willow, 1984),
reproduced with the kind permission of Mary Ellen Haggerty.

# Endnotes

ABBREVIATIONS

ALSA – Alberta Land Surveyors' Association
LAC – Library and Archives Canada
PAA – Provincial Archives of Alberta
UAA – University of Alberta Archives


PREFACE

[1] David Thompson, *David Thompson's Narrative, 1784–1812*, ed. Richard Glover (Toronto: The Champlain Society 1962), 89.


CHAPTER 1

[1] See Dava Sobel, *Longitude: the True Story of a Lone Genius Who Solved the Greatest Scientific Problem of His Time* (New York: Penguin Books, 1996).

[2] Turnor's survey work was used for the early map of the North American interior published in Britain by Arrowsmith in 1795.

[3] Thompson, *Narrative*, 3.

[4] Thompson, *Narrative*, 55.

[5] Correspondence, Alexander MacLean to David Thompson, May, 1791, 1792, 1794, HBC Archives, A/5/3, cited by Richard Glover in introduction to Thompson, *Narrative*, xxiv.

[6] David Thompson, *Travels in Western North America, 1784*-1812, ed. Victor G. Hopwood (Toronto: Macmillan of Canada, 1971), 6–7.

[7] Thompson, *Narrative*, 89.

[8] Ronald Schorn, *Planetary Astronomy. From Ancient Times to the Third Millennium* (Texas: A&M University Press, 1998), 40. The achromatic lens combined two separate lenses ground from materials with complimentary refractory lengths to reduce the chromatic aberration found when using the object lens ground from a single piece of glass.

[9] W. S. Stewart, "David Thompson's Surveys in the North-West," *Canadian Historical Review* (September, 1936): 289–303.

[10] Thompson, *Narrative*, 121.

[11] Thompson, *Narrative*, 122.

[12] Thompson, *Travels*, 259.

[13] D'Arcy Jenish, *Epic Wanderer. David Thompson and the Mapping of the Canadian West* (Toronto: Doubleday Canada, 2003), 218–219.

[14] Thompson, *Travels*, Appendix, 327.

[15] Thompson, *Travels*, 13–15.

[16] Jenish, 285–290.

[17] See Douglas Owram, *Promise of Eden: the Canadian Expansionist Movement and the Idea of the West, 1856–1900* (Toronto: University of Toronto Press, 1980).

[18] Irene Spry, *The Palliser Expedition. An Account of John Palliser's British North American Exploring Expedition, 1857-1860* (Toronto: The Macmillan Company, 1963), 165, 277, 285–87. Spry's lively account is based on based on Palliser's extensive but rather dry reports.

[19] *Letters from the 49th Parallel, 1857–1873: Selected Correspondence of Joseph Harris and Samuel Anderson*, ed. C. Ian Jackson (Toronto: The Champlain Society, 2000), xlix.

[20] Diary of Captain Roderick Cameron, PAA, 93.134.

[21] The Angle of the Lake of the Woods, as it became known, was re-surveyed in 1925, returning the contested piece of land to Canada.

[22] Jackson, xcvff.

[23] Albany Featherstonhaugh, *Narrative of the operation of the British North American Boundary Commission, 1872-76* (Woolich: 1876), 27, 66.

[24] Featherstonhaugh, 34–35.

[25] Samuel Anderson, *The North-American Boundary from the Lake of the Woods to the Rocky Mountains.* A paper read March 27, 1876, to the Royal Geographic Society, 262.

[26] Anderson to his mother, August 1, 1874, quoted in Jackson, 439.

[27] Anderson to his mother, July 21, 1874, quoted in Jackson, 436.

[28] Anderson to his mother, August 1, 1874, quoted in Jackson, 441.

[29] Anderson, 254.

[30] George Mercer Dawson, *Report on the Geology and Resources of the Region in the Vicinity of the Forty-ninth Parallel from the Lake of the Woods to the Rocky Mountains*. (Montreal: Dawson Brothers, 1875), 298.

[31] Anderson to his mother, August 23, 1874, quoted in Jackson, 446.

[32] Dawson, 299.

[33] Anderson to his mother, August 23, 1874, quoted in Jackson, 446.

[34] Spry, 276–77.

[35] Fleming, who quit the CPR in 1880, was instrumental in having international standard time adopted, based on hourly variation to Greenwich Mean Time in 1884.

CHAPTER 2

[1] Debates of the House of Commons (1883), 874, quoted by Chester Martin, *Dominion Lands Policy* (Toronto: Macmillan Company of Canada, 1938), 232–33.

[2] See Don Thomson, *Men and Meridians: The History of Surveying and Mapping in Canada, Vol. 2, 1867–1917* (Ottawa: Department of Energy, Mines and Resources, 1967), 4–19; and George Stanley, *Louis Riel* (Toronto: Ryerson, 1963), for narrative accounts of these events.

[3] Stanley, 110–117.

[4] W. D. Stretton. *From Compass to Satellite: A Century of Canadian Surveying and Surveyors, 1882–1982* (Ottawa: 1982), 21.

[5] Canada. *Annual Report* of Department of the Interior for Year Ending June 30, 1874.

[6] For more on federal control in the North-West, see Morris Zaslow, *The Opening of the Canadian North, 1870–1914* (Toronto: McClelland and Stewart, 1971), Chapter 4. This remained so, even after the creation of the provinces of Saskatchewan and Alberta in 1905, right up to 1930.

[7] This large area was further divided in 1882 into four districts. The three districts to the south, Assiniboia, Saskatchewan, and Alberta, were represented in the Council of the North-West Territories, but Athabasca to the north was not.

[8] For a detailed and more technical account of King's work in the Edmonton area, see Douglas Barnett, "Early Surveys and Settlements in Central Alberta," unpublished manuscript, 2001, held by PAA and City of Edmonton Archives.

[9] King to Russell, April 8, 1878, LAC, RG 88, vol. 298, file 0463.

[10] Barnett, 50.

[11] Aldous to Russell, December 12, 1879, PAA, 85.34, box 1, file 1a,

[12] Aldous to Russell, December 10, 1880, PAA, 85.34, box 1, file 1a.

[13] *Ibid.*

[14] *Ibid.*

[15] Canada. *Annual Report* of the Department of the Interior for the Year Ending June 30, 1879, Report of Montague Aldous.

[16] Under the Dominion Lands Regulations of 1881, all odd-numbered sections within twenty-four miles of the railway line could be sold by the CPR main line as the company saw fit, while odd-numbered sections outside this area could be sold at a fixed amount, subject to the authority of the governor in council of the NWT to dispose of them otherwise. This "anticipated the selection of indemnity land by the CPR, and the vote of railway land subsidies in addition to the main line subsidy for the CPR." Kirk N. Lambrecht, *The Administration of Dominion Lands, 1870–1930* (Regina: Canadian Plains Research Centre, 1991), 17–18.

[17] The contract is today on display in the CPR's inner corporate sanctum in Montreal.

[18] Zaslow, 28.

[19] Association of Dominion Land Surveyors, *Annual Report*, 1912, 61, cited in Thomson, 42–43.

[20] In March 1879, in expressing his view that it was an error to disband the special survey parties, Russell had urged yearly employment. L. Russell, Surveyor General, to J. S. Dennis, Deputy Minister of the Interior, March 28, 1879, LAC, RG 88, vol. 87, file 0242.

[21] Russell to Dennis, December 2, 1880, LAC, RG 88, vol. 87, file 0242.

[22] In 1883 Charles Biggar, DLS, Assistant Inspector of Surveys, noted that the red paint on the iron posts, required by the third edition of the *Manual of Instructions for the Survey of Dominion Lands*, was often already partially washed off and that a great many posts were without tin plates. Surveyors reported that the tops of the posts broke off, making it impossible to fasten the tin plates (Biggar to Deville, August 30, 1883, PAA, 85.34, box 2, file 51).

[23] Dennis to Russell, 16 February, 1881, LAC, RG 88, vol. 87, file 0242.

[24] Canada. *Annual Report* of the Department of the Interior for Year Ending June 30, 1881, Report of the Surveyor General.

[25] Just to complicate matters further, a Second System of Survey, with some minor technical differences, had been used in southeast Saskatchewan during 1880–81.

[26] See Barnett, 61.

[27] LAC, RG 88, vol. 87, file 0092, 1880-81.

[28] Aldous to Russell, December 1, 1881, PAA, 85.34, box 1, file 2.

[29] Memorandum, Inspector of Surveys, [1880s], LAC, RG 88, vol. 303, file 0984; King to Deville, December 22, 1885, LAC vol. 298, file 0447.

[30] Aldous to Russell, June 23, 1881, PAA, 85.34, box 1, file 2.

[31] King to Russell, January 11, 1879, LAC, RG 88, vol. 298, file 0463; Aldous to Russell, November 10, 1881, PAA 85.34, box 1, file 2; C. A. Magrath, Statement of Expenses, PAA 85.34 box 4, file 137.

[32] LAC, RG 88, vol. 87, file 0287, file 0321.

[33] LAC, RG 88, vol. 88, file 0913.

[34] Canada. *Annual Report* of the Department of Interior for the Year Ending June 30, 1881, Report of Lachlan Kennedy, DLS.

[35] Canada. *Annual Report* of the Department of the Interior for the Year 1882, Report of O. J. Klotz, DLS, DTS.

[36] Canada. *Annual Report* of the Department of the Interior for the Year 1882, Report of Thomas Drummond, DLS.

[37] Canada. *Annual Report* of the Department of the Interior for the Year 1882, Report of C. A. Magrath, DLS.

[38] Canada. *Annual Report* of the Department of the Interior for the Year 1883.

[39] *Macleod Gazette*, July 14, August 4, 1883.

[40] Memorandum from Deville to the Minister of the Interior, May 13, 1884, PAA, 85.34, box 3, file 88.

[41] Roy to Deville, January 24, 1884, PAA, 85.34, box 2, file 52.

[42] Correspondence, *passim*, 1883–1886, PAA, 85.34, box 2, file 41.

[43] Deville to Russell, September 4, 1883, PAA, 85.34, box 3, file 94.

[44] Memorandum, Cost of Dominion Land Surveys, May 14, 1895, LAC, RG 88, vol.87, file 0242.

[45] Donald G. Wetherell and Irene Kmet, *Town Life Main Street and the Evolution of Small Town Alberta, 1880–1947* (Edmonton: University of Alberta Press and Alberta Community Development, 1995), 2.

[46] *Macleod Gazette*, March 6, 1883.

[47] Correspondence, *passim*, PAA, 85.34, box 2, file 31.

[48] Max Foran, "The CPR and The Urban West, 1881–1930," in *The CPR West: The Iron Road and the Making of a Nation*, ed. Hugh A. Dempsey (Vancouver: Douglas & McInytre, 1984), 94.

[49] J. Egan, General Superintendent, to Van Horne, August 1, 1883, Glenbow Archives, NA-2856-5.

[50] McVittie to Deville, January 1, 1885, PAA, 85.34, box 4, file 155.

[51] They were: Montague Aldous, John Stoughton Dennis Jr., Thomas Drummond, Thomas Fawcett, Otto Klotz, John McAree, Charles Magrath, Allan Patrick, Louis B. Stewart, William Thompson and Fred Wilkins.

[52] Hart to Deville, November 22, 1883, PAA, 85.34, box 3, file 83(A).

[53] Deville to A. Cotton, Secretary of Association of Dominion Land Surveyors, March 12, 1885, LAC, RG 88, vol 88, file 0983.

[54] Although meetings foundered by 1894, the Association was to revive from 1907 with a renewed burst of Dominion Land Survey activity, particularly in Northern Alberta. See Thomson, 60–67.

[55] J. N. Wallace, "The coming of the Dominion Land Surveyor," *The Canadian Surveyor*, April 1940, 11. A total of seventy surveyors worked on all the various subdivision surveys, along with Indian reserves, river lots, and town sites, carried out in Alberta to 1883.

## CHAPTER 3

[1] Olive Dickason, *Canada's First Nations: A History of Founding Peoples from Earliest Times* (Toronto: McClelland and Stewart, 1992), 281, 284.

[2] Canada. *Annual Report* of the Department of the Interior for the Year Ending June 30, 1879, Report of A. P. Patrick, DLS, DTS.

[3] Dickason, 300.

[4] William Ogilvie, 'Field Notes of a Surveyor,' *Alberta Historical Review* (vol.22, no.2), 2, quoted in James G. MacGregor, *Vision of an Ordered Land: The Story of the Dominion Land Survey* (Saskatoon: Western Prairie Books, 1981. Republished Edmonton: Alberta Land Surveyors' Association, 1999), 50.

[5] Canada Lands. ILR, Registration #X 10557, OCPC 400.

[6] Canada. *Annual Report* of the Department of Indian Affairs, for the Year 1883, Report of L. Vankoughnet, Deputy Superintendent General of Indian Affairs.

[7] Canada Lands. FB 6062, Nelson's Book, PC 115, 1889, *Descriptions of Plans of Certain Indian Reserves in Manitoba and NWT*, Indian Reserve (Blackfoot) No. 146.

[8] *Indian Treaties and Surrenders, Vol. 2* (Ottawa: Queen's Printer, 1891).

[9] See Treaty Seven Elders and Tribal Council with Walter Hildebrandt, Dorothy First Rider and Sarah Carter, *The True Spirit and Original Intent of Treaty Seven*, (Montreal: McGill-Queen's University Press, 1996), 263–269.

[10] Canada. *Annual Report* of Department of Indian Affairs for the Year 1883, Report of the Superintendent of Indian Affairs.

[11] Canada. *Annual Report* of the Department of the Interior for the Year Ending June 30, 1879. Appendix 8, Report of A. P. Patrick to Lindsay Russell, Surveyor General, January 12, 1880.

[12] Klotz to Deville, January 31, 1884, PAA, 84.34, box 3, file 71.

[13] Charles Magrath, "Casting Bread Upon the Waters," *The Canadian Surveyor*, 1935.

[14] Freeman to King, July 18, 1884, PAA, 72.84, 12-k.

[15] Canada. *Annual Report* of the Department of the Interior for the Year 1887, J. S. Dennis, Inspector of Surveys.

[16] UAA, William Pearce Papers, 74-169, 9/2/6/2/7. In 1937, DIA amalgamated with parts of other Departments to form the Department of Mines and Resources, and its survey section was closed down. The records and subsequent responsibility for Indian reserve surveys was transferred to the Surveyor General. Indian Reserve Survey records were incorporated within Canada Lands Surveys Records in 1960.

[17] Diary of John C. Nelson, 1885, LAC, RG10, vol. 3831, file 63465.

[18] Canada. *Annual Report* of the Department of Indian Affairs for the Year 1886, Report of John C. Nelson, in charge of Indian Reserve Surveys.

[19] *Ibid*.

[20] Nelson to Superintendent of Indian Affairs, November 12, 1883, LAC, RG10, vol. 3807, file 52935.

[21] Canada. *Annual Report* of the Department of Indian Affairs, for the Year 1887, Report of John C. Nelson, in charge of Indian Reserve Surveys.

[22] Ostlund & Company to Department of Indian Affairs, April 25, 1935, LAC, RG 10, Vol. 7765, file 27,103-2.

[23] Canada. *Annual Report* of the Department of the Interior for the Year Ending 1893, Report of Jas. Wilson, Blood Agency.

[24] Nelson to Deputy Superintendent General of the Department of Indian Affairs, April 20, 1892, LAC, RG 10, vol. 7765, file 27, 103-1.

[25] Canada Lands, FB31614, *Indian Treaties and Surrenders,* Vol. III (Ottawa: 1912)

[26] Canada. Annual Report of the Department of Indian Affairs for the Year Ending June 30, 1903, Report of A. W. Ponton in charge of surveys in Manitoba and the NWT.

[27] Canada. Annual Report of the Department of Indian Affairs for the Year Ending June 30, 1903, Report of A. W. Ponton in charge of surveys in Manitoba and the NWT.

[28] Canada Lands, FB 31614, *Indian Treaties and Surrenders*, Vol. III (Ottawa: 1912).

[28] Canada. Annual Report of the Department of Indian Affairs for the Year 1893, Report of A. W. Ponton, Assistant Surveyor.

[30] Ted Byfield ed., *Alberta in the 20th Century. The Great War and its Consequences*, Vol. 4 (Edmonton: United Western Communications Ltd.1994), 110–111.

[31] Canada. Annual Report of the Department of Indian Affairs for the Year Ending March 31, 1912, Survey Report, James McLean.

[32] Dickason, 294.

[33] Lambrecht, 9.

[34] PAA, 86.418, 426, Edmonton Settlement.

[35] See Margaret R. Stobie, "Land Jumping," *The Beaver* (Winter, 1982), 14–21.

[36] Instructions for Survey of Fort Saskatchewan and Victoria, August 25, 1884; Kains to Deville, February 10 and 12, 1884, PAA, 85.34, box 4, file 130,.

[37] Magrath to Deville, October 6, 1884, PAA, 85.34, box 4, file 137.

[38] Canada. *Annual Report* of the Department of the Interior for the Year 1885.

[39] Canada. Department of the Interior, *Annual Report* for the Year 1889, Report of P. R. A. Belanger, DLS.

[40] Undated memorandum, Deville to Minister of Interior, [1880s], LAC, RG 88, vol. 301, file 0741.

[41] Deville to A. M. Burgess, Deputy Minister of the Interior, November 21, 1887, LAC, RG 88, vol. 301, file 0741.

[42] A. M. Burgess to Dewdney, January 30, 1890, LAC, RG 88, vol., 301, file 0741. The reason cited was the tendency of the Métis not to reside permanently on their river lots.

CHAPTER 4

[1] Pearce to Flynn, 11 September, 1890, UAA, William Pearce Papers, 74-169, 9/2/7/1-1.

[2] Reprinted in *Lethbridge News*, July 31, 1895.

[3] Address to Dominion Land [Surveyors] Association January 19, 1891, UAA, William Pearce Papers, 74–169, 9/2/7/2–6.

[4] A. Burgess to William Pearce, January 21 and February 12, 1891, cited in E. A. Mitchner, "William Pearce: Father of Irrigation," Ph.D. thesis, University of Alberta, 1966, 26.

[5] The Bill followed the Australian precedent, which almost extinguished riparian rights, unlike the situation in the United States of America where their retention was causing many administrative difficulties.

[6] A. E. Cross to Pearce, April 13, 1894, UAA, William Pearce Papers, 74-169, 9/2/7/2-9.

[7] Burgess to Pearce, October 4, 1894, UAA, William Pearce Papers, 74-169, 9/2/7/1-5.

[8] Dennis to Deville, June 18, 1894, PAA, 85.34, box 26, file 834.

[9] Canada. *Annual Report* of the Department of the Interior for the Year Ending June 30, 1895, Canadian Irrigation Survey, Part II, report of J. S. Dennis Jr.

[10] *Ibid.*, 38.

[11] Canada. *Annual Report* of the Department of the Interior for the Year 1894, Report of A. O. Wheeler, DLS.

[12] *Ibid.*

[13] John Gilpin, *Quenching the Prairie Thirst* (Lethbridge: St Mary Irrigation Project, 2000), 17.

[14] Deville to Wheeler, May 22, 1895, PAA, 85.34, box 5, file 202.

[15] Canada. *Annual Report* of the Department of the Interior for the Year Ending June 30, 1895. Canadian Irrigation Survey, Part II, report of J. S. Dennis Jr., 2–44.

[16] Wheeler's report for 1899, received December 9, 1899, PAA, 85.34, box 28, file 884.

[17] Edouard Deville, *Photographic Surveying: Including the Elements of Descriptive Geometry and Perspective* (Ottawa: Government Printing Bureau, 1895), v.

[18] Diary of A. O. Wheeler, DLS, 1895, PAA, 79.27, Diary #5742.

[19] Canada. *Annual Report* of the Department of the Interior for the Year 1896, Report of J. S. Dennis Jr., Chief Inspector of Surveys, Reports of A. O. Wheeler, for seasons of 1895 and 1896.

[20] Canada. *Annual Report* of the Department of the Interior for the Year Ending 1897, Report of A. O. Wheeler, DLS.

[21] Deville to Wheeler, September 6, 1895, PAA, 85.34, box 5, file 202.

[22] Wheeler to Deville, September 21, 1895, PAA, 85.34, box 5, file 202.

[23] Canada. *Annual Report* of the Department of the Interior for the Year 1897, Report of Arthur Wheeler, DLS.

[24] *Ibid.*

[25] Canada. *Annual Report* of the Department of the Interior for the Year 1897, Preliminary topographical map of a portion of the foothills region from micrometer surveys by Division B of Canadian Irrigation Surveys, 1895–6, Sheet A.

[26] October 7, 1897, PAA, 85.23, box 6, file 223.

[27] Wheeler to Deville, March 27, 1895, LAC, RG 88, vol. 95, file 1706.

[28] Correspondence between Wheeler and Deville, November 1898 to March 1899, LAC, RG 88, vol.95, file 1706.

[29] Wheeler to Deville, December 23, 1899, PAA, 85.34, box 28, file 884.

[30] Wheeler to Deville, February 18, 1900, PAA, 85.34, box 28, file 884. The map in question was not published as a result.

[31] Memorandum of Instructions for the Guidance of Dominion Land Surveyors employed in surveying and preparing returns of Right-of-way for Irrigating Ditches and works in connection therewith [Draft 1893], UAA, William Pearce Papers, 74–169, 9/2/7/1–3.

[32] See Glenbow Library Map Collection, G3503/Ir-146J4.

[33] Pearce to Dennis, Calgary, January 28, 1898, UAA, William Pearce Papers, 74–169, 9/2/7/1–2.

[34] Dennis to John F. Faraho, December 21, 1898, UAA, William Pearce Papers, 74–169, 9/2/7/1–9.

[35] See Alex Johnston and Andy A. den Otter. *Lethbridge: A Centennial History* (Lethbridge: The City of Lethbridge and the Whoop–Up Country Chapter, Historical Society of Alberta, 1985), 40.

[36] Andy A. den Otter, *Civilizing the West: The Galts and the Development of Western Canada* (Edmonton: University of Alberta Press, 1982), 206.

[37] *The Diaries of Charles Ora Card. The Canadian Years 1886–1903*, ed. Donald G. Godfrey and Brigham Young Card (Salt Lake City: University of Utah Press, 1993), 417–18.

[38] Otter, 222.

[39] Gilpin, *Quenching*, 21.

[40] Canada. *Annual Report* of the Department of Interior for the Year 1899.

[41] North-West Territories, *Annual Report* of the Department of Public Works, Irrigation Branch, 1900.

[42] Renie Gross and Lea Nicoll Kramer, *Tapping the Bow* (Brooks: Eastern Irrigation District, 1985), 155.

[43] Gilpin, *Quenching*, 69 ; Report on the Progress of Surveys of Dominion Lands pt. 1, 4, LAC, RG 88, vol. 405, file 23/262-883-9.

[44] Gilpin, *Quenching*, 69, 17; Lawrence B. Lee, "The Canadian–American Frontier, 1884–1914," *Agricultural History* Vol. 40, No. 1 (October, 1966), 278.

[45] Pearce to Dennis, January 9, 1902, UAA, William Pearce Papers, 74–169, 9/2/7/1–9.

[46] Gilpin, *Quenching*, 60.

[47] John Gilpin, *Prairie Promises: History of the Bow River Irrigation District* (Vauxhall: Bow River Irrigation District, 1996), 3–11.

[48] Pearce to Magrath, quoted in Keith Stotyn, "The Development of the Bow River Irrigation Project, 1906–1950." MA. thesis, University of Alberta, 1982, 53.

[49] Gilpin, *Prairie*, 51.


CHAPTER 5

[1] PAA, 87.141, GS, book #7, The Statutes of Canada 1880, chapter 25, section 91, and Statutes of Canada 1886, as chapter 50 section 107 and 108.

[2] Canada. *Annual Report* of the Department of the Interior for the Year 1890.

[3] Canada. *Annual Report* of the Department of the Interior for the Year 1886, Report of George P. Roy, DLS.

[4] Canada. *Annual Report* of the Department of the Interior for the Year 1886, Report of C. A. Biggar, DLS.

[5] Canada. *Annual Report* of the Department of the Interior for the Year 1887, Report of the Surveyor General; Report of J. S. Dennis, Inspector of Surveys.

[6] Mitford was located between Cochrane and Morley on the banks of the Bow, and was abandoned when the CPR built a station at Cochrane. It is now a locality.

[7] Correspondence, *passim*, PAA, 85.34, box 28, file 867; Diary of F. W. Wilkins, 79.27, DLS Diary # 5566.

[8] Canada. *Annual Report* of the Department of the Interior for the Year 1888, Report of J. S. Dennis, Inspector of Surveys. Mr. McMillan was most likely James McMillan, DLS, an Ontario Land Surveyor. The services of a trail commissioner seems to have limited application as surveyors working in the Edmonton area had no such recourse.

[9] Diary of T. D. Green, DLS, 1888, PAA, 79.27, Diary # 4753; Canada. *Annual Report* of the Department of the Interior for the Year 1888, Report of T. D. Green, DLS.

[10] Canada. *Annual Report* of the Department of the Interior for the Year 1889, Report of R. P. Belanger, DLS.

[11] Canada. *Annual Report* of the Department of the Interior for the Year 1887, Report of the Chief Inspector of Surveys.

[12] See John S. Nicks, "Road Construction in Alberta" (Reynolds-Alberta Museum, Background Paper No. 4, 1983), 1–21.

[13] Canada. *Annual Report* of the Department of the Interior for the Year 1894, Report of E. W. Hubbell, DLS, 1894.

[14] Diary of E. W. Hubbell, DLS, 1895, PAA, 79.27, Diary # 5838.

[15] Canada. *Annual Report* of the Department of the Interior for the Year 1894, Report of F. W. Wilkins, DLS.

[16] Dennis to Wilkins, July 5, 1894, PAA, 85.34, box 5, file 198.

[17] Diary of Fred Wilkins, DLS, 1894, PAA, 79.27, Diary #556.

[18] Canada. *Annual Report* of the Department of the Interior for the Year 1898, Report of the Surveyor General.

[19] Department of Public Works, NWT, to Deville, March 7, 1900, LAC, RG 15, Department of Interior, Vol. 347, Reel T-13069.

[20] Canada. *Annual Report* of the Department of the Interior for the Year Ending June 30, 1902, Dominion Survey, 1901–02.

[21] See PAA, 83.199, Alberta Department of Transportation Records.

[22] Driscoll to Pearce, November 3, 1903, PAA, 85.34, box 13, file 427b.

[23] LAC, RG15, Department of Interior, vol. 347, reel T-13068, memorandum from the Survey Records Branch to the Department of Interior, April 10, 1905.

[24] LAC, RG15, Department of Interior, vol. 347, reel T-13068.

[25] The provincial ledgers of payment attest that the rate of compensation was often disputed. If a first ruling was protested, a second ruling followed often with a second protest. The date of payment or "no compensation" was noted after the amount ruled against the owner's name and land location. Ledgers for 1913–41 indicate that the bulk of payments were made during the 1930s. PAA, 87.141, Book #9.

[26] These tents were later shipped to Wetaskiwin and Fort Saskatchewan for the same purpose.

[27] Canada. *Annual Report* of the Department of the Interior for the Year 1892, Report of the Surveyor General, Report of J. S. Dennis, Chief Inspector of Surveys, Report of C. F. Miles, DLS, and Report of J. Gibbons.

[28] Canada. *Annual Report* of the Department of the Interior for the Year 1892, Report of J. S. Dennis, Chief Inspector of Surveys.

[29] Deville, correspondence *passim*, 1884–1907, LAC, RG 88, vol. 301, file 0719.

[30] Correspondence, *passim*, PAA, 85.34, box 6, file 245.

[31] Canada. *Annual Report* for the Department of the Interior for the Year 1892, Schedule of Surveys for 1892.

[32] Canada. *Annual Report* of the Department of the Interior for the Year 1893, Immigration Branch, Report of R. L. Alexander.

[33] Canada. *Annual Report* of the Department of the Interior for the Year 1895, Report of J. E. Woods, DLS.

[34] PAA, Township Survey Map Twp 40-1-W5; Field Notebook of J. E. Woods, DLS, PAA, 83.396, Field Notebook # 1419, Twp 40-1-W5.

[35] Diary of J. E. Woods, DLS, 1895, PAA, 79.27, Diary # 5736.

[36] Canada, *Annual Report* of the Department of the Interior, for the Year 1892, Report of J. S. Dennis, Chief Inspector of Surveys.

[37] Field Notebook of Arthur Wheeler, DLS, 1892, PAA, 83.376, 1178a.

[38] Cautley to Surveyor General, December 21, 1903, PAA, 85.34, Box 13, 422a.

[39] Canada. *Annual Report* of the Department of the Interior for the Year 1896, Report of E. W. Hubbell, DLS.

[40] North-West Territories. *Annual Report* of the Department of Public Works, 1901.

[41] The system was developed by Robert Torrens of New South Wales, Australia, in the 1850s.

[42] Field Notebook of Arthur Wheeler, DLS, 1892, PAA, 83.376, 1178a, 1177, 1175a.

[43] Canada. *Annual Report* of the Department of the Interior for the Year 1893, Report of E. W Hubbell, DLS.

[44] Canada. *Annual Report* of the Department of the Interior for the Year 1895, Report of E. W Hubbell, DLS.

[45] Diary of E. W Hubbell, 1895, PAA, 79.27, Diary # 5838.

[46] Canada. *Annual Report* of the Department of the Interior for the Year 1895, Report of J. E. Woods, DLS.

[47] Canada. *Annual Report* of the Department of the Interior for the Year 1895, Report of E. W Hubbell, DLS.

[48] *Ibid.*; Diary of E. W Hubbell, 1895, PAA, 79.27, Diary # 5838.

[49] DuBerger to the Minister of the Interior, November 16, 1898, PAA, 85.34, box 6, file 232.

[50] McLean to Deville, August 2, 1899, PAA, 85.34, box 6, file 233.

[51] O'Hara to Deville, August 8, 1900, PAA, 85.34, box 6, file 240.

[52] O'Hara to Deville, May 29, 1900, PAA, 85.34, box 6, file 240.

[53] T. G. Rothweel to Deville, August 12, 1901, PAA, 85.34, box 8, file 294.

[54] Surveyor General to Deputy Minister of the Interior, May 12, 1902, PAA, 85.34, box 8, 300.

[55] Duberger to Deville, November 7, 1902, LAC, RG 88 vol. 89, File 2032.

[56] Wallace to Deville, January 6, 1903, LAC, RG 88, vol. 89, file 2032/pt3.

[57] Deville to the Deputy Minister of the Interior, September 1, 1904, PAA, 85.34, box 16, file 482.

[58] Deville correspondence, *passim*, LAC, RG 88, vol. 89, file 2049.

[59] Pearce to Deville, January 6, 1903, LAC, RG 88, vol.89, file 2049.

[60] Canada. *Annual Report* of the Department of the Interior for the Year Ending June 30, 1904, Report of the Surveyor General, 1904.

## Chapter 6

[1] Canada. *Annual Report* of the Department of the Interior for the Year 1884, Report of William Ogilvie, DLS.

[2] William Ogilvie, *Report on the Peace River and Tributaries in 1891* (Ottawa: S. E. Dawson, Queen's Printer, 1892), cited in Daniel Francis and Michael Payne, *A Narrative History of Fort Dunvegan* (Vancouver: Watson and Dywer, 1993), 92.

[3] See Donald G. Wetherell and Irene Kmet's comprehensive study, *Alberta's North: A History, 1890–1950* (Edmonton: University of Alberta Press, Canadian Circumpolar Press, Alberta Community Development, 2000), for background and context on northern Alberta.

[4] McLean to Deville, July 17, 1897, PAA, 85.34, box 6, file 200.

[5] Frank Oliver to Clifford Sifton, April 13, 1897, PAA, 85.34, box 6, file 220.

[6] McLean to Deville, 31 August, 1897, PAA, 85.34, box 6, file 220.

[7] *Edmonton Bulletin,* July 4, 1898.

[8] *Edmonton Bulletin,* August 15, 1898.

[9] *Edmonton Bulletin*, July 18, 1898.

[10] UAA, William Pearce Papers, 74.169, 9/2/6/3/9, Cornwallis King to William Pearce, n.d., cited in David Leonard and Victoria Lemieux, *The Lure of the Peace River Country: A Fostered Dream* (Calgary: Detselig, 1992), 104.

[11] HBCA, A.12/403/1 fo.1, cited in *Athabasca Landing: An Illustrated History*, by Athabasca History Society, David Gregory and Athabasca University (Athabasca: Athabasca History Society, 1986), 32.

[12] McFee to Dennis, November 28, 1898, UAA, William Pearce Papers, 74.169, 9/2/6/3-8.

[13] *Edmonton Bulletin*, September 21, 1899.

[14] See Joan Weir, *Back Door to the Klondike* (Erin: Boston Mills Press, 1988).

[15] Canada. *Annual Report* of the Department of Indian Affairs for the Year 1902, Report of A. W. Ponton, DLS.

[16] Canada. *Annual Report* of the Department of Indian Affairs for Year Ending June 30, 1906, Report of Surveys in Treaty 8.

[17] *Ibid.*

[18] David Leonard, *Delayed Frontier: The Peace River Country to 1909* (Calgary: Detselig Enterprises, 2000), 84–85.

[19] The two commissioners were Jean Arthur Côté (not to be confused with surveyor Jean Leon Côté) and Major James A. Walker, a retired NWMP officer. Charles Mair, one of the two secretaries assisting Côté and Walker, later published a

book, *Through the MacKenzie Basin: a Narrative of the Athabasca and Peace River Treaty Expedition of 1899* (Toronto: William Briggs, 1908) detailing the events surrounding the Treaty and Half-Breed Commissions.

[20] See Leonard, *Delayed,* 85–94.

[21] Correspondence between Talbot and the Surveyor General, *passim,* PAA, 85.34, box 27, file 856; Canada. *Annual Report* of the Department of the Interior for the Year 1902, Report of A. C. Talbot, 1902.

[22] Deville Memorandum, February 15, 1905, PAA, 85.34, box 10, file 339.

[23] Canada. *Annual Report* of the Department of the Interior July1, 1906 to March 31, 1907, Report of the Surveyor General.

[24] Canada. *Annual Report* of the Department of the Interior for the Year Ending March 31, 1910.

[25] Canada. *Annual Report* of the Department of the Interior for the Year Ending March 31, 1915, Report of the Surveyor General.

[26] Deville to the Deputy Minister of the Interior, February 19, 1907, LAC, RG 88, vol. 111, file 3374.

[27] See Leonard, *Delayed,* 181–183.

[28] Canada, *Annual Report* of the Department of the Interior for the years 1905, Report on Immigration. The Peace River Block of British Columbia had few settlers. Three and half million acres had passed to the Dominion Government in north-east British Columbia as part of the negotiated arrangements to bring BC into Confederation in 1872.

[29] Deville to Holcroft, April 24, 1908, PAA, 85.34, box 29, file 908.

[30] LAC, RG 88, vol.405, file23/262-883-9, pt.1.

[31] David Leonard, "The Last Best West," unpublished manuscript, 2003.

[32] The 1916 *Bulletin* also covered the Peace River Block of BC.

[33] Deville to Holcroft, December 23, 1907, PAA, 85.34, box 29, file 908.

[34] Memorandum, stamped January 17, 1908, LAC, Vol. 89, file 1105.

[35] Deville to Oliver, June 20, 1907, PAA, 93.217, Jean Gustave Côté Papers, file 15.

[36] Resolution, November 10, 1908, UAA, William Pearce Papers, 74.169, 9/2/6/3-10.

[37] Deville to Deputy Minister of the Interior, December 13, 1912, LAC, RG 88, vol. 342, file 13081.

[38] Greisbach to Roche, December 16, 1913, PAA, 85.34, box 44, file 1456.

[39] Deville to Private Secretary to the Minister of the Interior, December 23, 1913, PAA, 85.34, box 44, file 1456.

[40] Canada. *Annual Report* of the Department of the Interior for the Year 1884, Report of William Ogilvie, DLS.

[41] *Edmonton Bulletin,* July 4, 1898.

[42] J. W. Pierce, Draft Report, February, 1916, PAA, 85.34, box 51, file 1659.

[43] Blanchet to the Surveyor General, Report on the Survey of the 23rd Baseline, between the Fourth and Fifth Meridian , PAA, 85.34, box 39, file 1238.

[44] Correspondence, *passim,* PAA, 85.34, box 47, file 1559.

[45] Report of explorer on condition of Cache No. 1, PAA, 85.34, box 43, file 1420.

[46] Minister of the Interior to his Royal Highness in Council, October 3, 1914, PAA, 85.34, box 43, file 1420.

[47] Memoranda, January 31, February 9, 1916, PAA, 85.34, box 43, file 1420.

[48] Fred Seibert, Address to Alberta Land Surveyors' Association, Annual General Meeting, 1960.

[49] Typescript, PAA, 94.157.

[50] Claude McLaughlin, oral history interview with Cheryl Ingram, 1975, PAA, 75.199.

[51] *Ibid.*

[52] Fred Seibert, Address to Alberta Land Surveyors' Association, Annual General Meeting, 1960.

[53] Claude McLaughlin, oral history interview with Cheryl Ingram, 1975, PAA, 75.199.

[54] *Ibid.*

[55] St. Cyr to Deville, January 11, 1909, PAA, 85.34, box 19, file 584.

[56] Diary of James Wallace, DLS, 1904, PAA, 79.27, Diary # 7712.

[57] Fred Seibert, Address to Alberta Land Surveyors' Association, Annual General Meeting, 1960.

[58] PAA, 85.43, box 43, file 1411.

[59] Barry Glen Ferguson, *Athabasca Oil Sands: Northern Resources Exploration, 1875–1951* (Edmonton: Alberta Culture/Canadian Plains Research Centre, 1985), 21–22. The potential petroleum pool in Turner Valley south of Calgary was also placed under reserve.

[60] Correspondence, *passim,* PAA, 85.34, box 34 & 35, file 1089a and b.

[61] Côté to Deville, October 2 and 11, 1911, PAA, 85.34, box 39, file 1238. In 1912 George Macmillan, DLS, ran part of the 20th Baseline west of the Fourth Meridian on both sides of the Athabasca River, while Blanchet ran the 19th Baseline west from the Fourth Meridian.

[62] Correspondence, *passim,* PAA, 85.34, box 51, file 1653; Diary of Fred Seibert, DLS, 1914, PAA, 79.27, Diary #14118.

[63] Seibert to Deville, October 10, 1915, PAA, 85.34, box 51, file 1653.

[64] Diary of Fred Seibert, DLS, 1915, PAA, 79.27, Diary # 14977.

[65] Seibert to Deville, October 10, 1915, PAA, 85.34, box 51, file 1653.

[66] Fred Seibert, DLS, 1915, PAA, 79.27, Diary # 14977.

[67] PAA, 85.34, box 51, file 1659, Pierce, Draft Report, February 1916.

[68] Ibid.

[69] Pierce to Deville, April 15, April 27, 1915, PAA, 85.34, box 51, file 1659.

[70] Pierce to Deville, August 10, 1915, PAA, 85.34, box 51, file 1659.

[71] William Ogilvie, Exploratory Surveys, Reprinted from the report of Proceedings of the Association of Dominion Surveyors, 1892-93, CISM Journal ACSGC (Autumn, 1992), 311.

[72] Claude McLaughlin, oral history interview with Cheryl Ingram, 1975, PAA, 75.19.

[73] Pierce to Deville, July 5, 1915, PAA, 85.34, box 51, file 1659.

[74] Pierce, Draft Report, February 1916, PAA, 85.34, box 51, file 1659.

CHAPTER 7

[1] See Leslie Bella, Parks for Profit (Montreal: Harvest House, 1987).

[2] Memorandum of instructions to Thomas Fawcett, 27, March 1884, signed by Deville, PAA, 85.34, box 4, file 118.

[3] Fawcett to King, July 28, 1884, PAA, 85.34, box 4, file 118.

[4] Memorandum, December 4, 1885, PAA, 85.34, box 4, file 118.

[5] Memorandum of Fawcett's application for a transit instrument free of charge, March 4, 1885, PAA, 85.34, box 4, file 118.

[6] Arthur Wheeler, The Selkirk Range (Ottawa: Government Printing Bureau, 1905), 32–33. In 1905 Wheeler noted the survey had limitations, as the reference marks placed every mile on the CPR telegraph poles did not stand the test of time, being replaced or rotting out.

[7] Canada. Annual Report of the Department of the Interior for the Year 1887, Report of J. J. McArthur, DLS.

[8] Canada. Annual Report of the Department of the Interior for the Year 1886, Report of J. J. McArthur, DLS.

[9] Correspondence, passim, PAA, 85.34, box 24, file 707 & 724.

[10] McArthur to Deville, November 25, 1889, PAA, 85.34, box 24, file 764; McArthur Report, January 23, 1891, PAA, 85.34, box 24, file 765.

[11] Drewry to Deville, January 30, 1892, LAC, RG 88, vol. 91, file 1226.

[12] See Sid Marty, A Grand and Fabulous Notion: The First Century of Canada's Parks (Ottawa: NC Press, 1984).

[13] Canada. Annual Report of the Department of the Interior for the Year 1887, Report of Arthur Saint Cyr, DLS.

[14] E. J. Hart, The Place of Bows. Exploring the Heritage of the Banff-Bow Valley, Part 1 to 1930 (Banff: EJH Literary Enterprises Ltd., 1999), 209.

[15] Deville to Walker, May 13, 1913; Walker to Deville June 19, 1913; Walker to Deville, June 23, 1913, PAA, 85.34, box 45, file 1475.

[16] Pearce to Deville, August 1913; Deville to Pearce, September 2, 1913, LAC, RG 88, vol. 141, file 13732.

[17] Correspondence, passim, LAC, RG 88, vol. 357, file 1606.

[18] Douglas to Deville, June 15, 1899, PAA, 85.34, box 6, file 234.

[19] Saunders to Deville, August 18, 1899, PAA, 85.34, box 6, file 234; Walker to Deville, June 23, 1913, PAA, 85.34, box 47, file 1475.

[20] Correspondence, passim, LAC, RG 84, A-2-a, vol., 2206, W46.

[21] O'Hara to Deville, February 16, 1912, LAC, RG 84, A-2-a, vol. 2206, W 46, Part I. He actually surveyed two sets of lots. The lots on the northeast corner of the lake were later cancelled at the request of the National Parks Branch, leaving the second set of lots that are now in the townsite of Waterton.

[22] O'Hara, draft report, February 21, 1911, PAA, 85.34, box 34, file 1055.

[23] Correspondence, passim, LAC, RG 84, A-2-a, vol. 2206, W46.

[24] Deville to R. H. Campbell, Department of the Interior, November 4, 1909, LAC, RG 84 -A-2-a, vol. 527, J46. In June 1911, the area of the park was altered so that newly surveyed lines running ten miles each side of the GTP defined the northerly and southerly boundaries. (L. Pereida, Department of the Interior, to H. R. Charlton, General Advertising Agent, Grand Trunk Railway System, July 24, 1911, LAC, RG 84, A-2-a, vol. 527, J-46, T-12985).

[25] University of Alberta Library, Special Collections, R. C. W. Lett Collection.

[26] C. J. Taylor, The Railway and Jasper National Park, Parks Canada, unpublished manuscript, [9].

[27] Deville to Herriot, Instructions, May 1,1911, PAA, 85.34, box 39, file 1244.

[28] Herriot Report, February 29, 1912, PAA, 85.34, box 39, file 1244.

[29] Ibid.

[30] Canada. *Annual Report* of the Department of the Interior for the Year Ending March 31, 1912, Report of the Chief Superintendent Dominion Parks, 1912.

[31] National Parks Branch File J., 19, vol. 1, Deville to Harkin, Memorandum, April 12, 1913, quoted by W. F. Lothian, *A History of Canada's National Parks*, Vol. III (Ottawa: Department of Indian Affairs, 1979), 52.

[32] Diary of Hugh Matheson, DLS, 1913, PAA, 79.27, Diary# 13439.

[33] Matheson to Deville, June 26, 1913, LAC, RG 88, vol. 345, file 13379.

[34] Matheson to Deville, September 13, October 15, 1913, LAC, RG 88, vol. 345, file 13379.

[35] Lothian, 68.

[36] Diary of Hugh Matheson, DLS, 1913, PAA, 79.27, Diary# 13439.

[37] Matheson to Deville, Feb 6, 1915, LAC, RG 88, vol.348, file 13885.

[38] White to Harkin, August 24, 1916, LAC, RG 84 A-2-a, vol. 527, J46.

[39] Matheson to Deville, March 6, 1914, LAC, RG 88, vol. 348, file 13885.

[40] I am indebted to G. Zezulka-Mailloux for allowing me to consult an early draft of "From the Ground Up: Contouring the World of M. P. Bridgland", a biographical profile of Bridgland to be published in association with the Bridgland Repeat Photography Project at the University of Alberta.

[41] M. P. Bridgland, Typescript "Photographic Surveying in Canada" 1918, 2, LAC, RG 88, vol. 208, file 16178. This account was later published as *Topographic Surveying*, Bulletin 56 (Ottawa: Department of the Interior, 1924).

[42] Deville to Director of Forestry, March 8, 1917, LAC, RG 88, vol. 361, file 16533, cited in Zezulka-Mailloux.

[43] Surveyor General to Secretary, Department of the Interior, May 29, 1900, LAC, RG 88, Vol. 112, file 4072, pt 2.

[44] Wheeler to Deville, July 1, 1914, LAC, RG 88, vol. 185, file 5429.

[45] Memorandum, February 16, 1914, LAC, RG 88, vol. 357, file 16061.

[46] Harkin to Deville, February 27, 1917, LAC, RG 88, vol. 361, file 16545.

[47] See Robert W. Sandford, *The Canadian Alps, The History of Mountaineering in Canada*, Vol. 1 ( Banff: Altitude, 1990).

[48] See Wheeler's own account of the formation of the Alpine Club of Canada in the *Canadian Alpine Journal*, vol. 26, 1938. He notes that it was Fleming who first broached the idea of an Alpine club in 1883.

[49] Esther Fraser, *Wheeler* (Banff: Summerthought, 1978), 74–75.

[50] Wheeler to Deville, April 19, 1913, LAC, RG 88, vol. 345, file 12785.

[51] Instructions to J. E. Woods, March 20, 1900, PAA, 85.34, box 27, file 251; Deville to Woods, July 12, 1900, PAA, 85.34, box 27, file 854.

[52] Woods to Deville, August 1, 1901, PAA, 85.34, box 8, file 290.

[53] Canada. *Annual Report* of the Department of the Interior for the Year Ending June 30, 1901, Report of J. E. Woods, DLS.

[54] Surveyor General to Deputy Minister of the Interior, May 12, 1902, PAA, 85.34, box 8, file 300.

[55] See *The Coal Mining Industry in the Crow's Nest Pass*, compiled by Sharon Babaian from research papers by Lorry Felske (Alberta Culture, Historic Sites Service, 1985), 1–17.

[56] J. Brian Dawson, *Crowsnest: An Illustrated History and Guide to Crowsnest Pass* (Canmore: Altitude, 1995), 27.

[57] See Anne (McMullen) Belliveau, *Small Moments In Time: The Story of Alberta's Big West Country* (Calgary: Detselig, 1999).

[58] Green to Deville, January 20, 1909, PAA, 85.34, box 31, file 960.

[59] Green to W. W. Cory, Deputy Minister of the Interior, January 31, 1910, PAA, 85.34, box 31, file 960.

[60] Green to Deville, October 19, 1908, PAA, 85.34, box 31, file 960.

[61] Deville to Oliver, December 19, 1908, PAA, 85.34, box 31, file 960.

[62] Memoranda, February 12 and 15, 1912, PAA, 85.34, box 37, file 1135; Deville to Cumming, October 25, 1913, PAA, 85.34, box 46, file 1522.

[63] Frank Smith was actually appointed mine manager at Pocahontas, but never did assume the position, presumably because he decided to buy shares in the company. (PAA, 77.237/280a)

[64] See Jasper and Yellowhead Museum and Archives, 78.01.63, typescript on the Pocahontas–Moosehorn Creek Coal Basin, by B. R. Mackay.

[65] Canada, *Annual Report* of the Department of the Interior for the Year Ending March 31, 1912; *Edson Leader*, September 26, 1912.

[66] PAA, 77.237/280b, 1914.

[67] Correspondence, *passim*, PAA, 77.237/280c.

[68] J. G. Côté, "J. L. Côté, Surveyor," *Alberta History* (Autumn 1983), 31.

[69] Special permits were also granted along railway rights-of-way or areas to be opened for settlement. These permits did not convey the property rights that leases did and were issued by order-in-council.

[70] See Kelly Buziak, *Toiling in the Woods: Aspects of the Lumber Business in Alberta to 1930* (Wetaskiwin: Friends of the Reynolds-Alberta Museum Society, 1992).

[71] Hart, 99.

[72] Wheeler to Deville, February 5, 1900, PAA, 85.34, Box 28, file 884.

[73] Canada. Department of the Interior. *Forestry Branch Forestry and Irrigation* (Ottawa: 1911), 60.

[75] Canada. *Annual Report* of the Department of the Interior for the Year Ending March 31, 1911, Report of the Superintendent of Forestry.

[74] Correspondence, *passim,* PAA, 85.34, box 42, file 1386.

[76] Correspondence, *passim,* PAA, 85.34, box 49, file 1600.

[77] Correspondence, *passim,* PAA, 85.34, box 39, file 1236.

[78] Correspondence, *passim,* PAA, 85.34, box 49, file 1600.

[79] *Report of the Commission Appointed to Delimit the Boundary Between the Provinces of Alberta and British Columbia, Part I. From 1913 to 1916* (Ottawa: Office of the Surveyor General, 1917), 89.

[80] R. W. Cautley, DLS, "'Highlights of Memory,' Incidents in the Life of a Canadian Surveyor," copy of a typescript held in the Archives of British Columbia, 106, Whyte Museum of the Canadian Rockies, 025.5, C31p.

[81] Ibid., 111.

[82] The Geodetic Survey of Canada was established in 1909 to determine, with the highest degree of accuracy possible, the position and elevation of points across Canada. These monumented positions provided survey control and have evolved into a national coordinate system, now known as the Canadian Spatial Reference System.

[83] Wheeler to Peters, July [?] 1924, LAC, RG 88, vol. 246, file 18500.

[84] Wheeler to Peters, August 11, 1924, LAC, RG 88, vol. 246, file 18500.

CHAPTER 8

[1] Wetherell and Kmet, *Town,* 6–7.

[2] Memorandum, Natural Resources Intelligence Branch, to Deputy Minister, October 1, 1918, LAC, RG 15, vol. 1098, 2613585.

[3] Ann Holtz, "Small Town Alberta: A Geographical Study of the Development of Urban Form," MA thesis, University of Alberta, 1989. Holtz's research, in conjunction with scrutiny of plans forms the basis of the discussion of the survey of Alberta's townsites above.

[4] *Manual of Instructions for the Survey of Dominion Lands* (Ottawa: Topographical Surveys Branch, 1913), 13–15.

[5] See Douglas Barnett, *Ed Barnett: Pioneer of Alberta,* 2001, ALSA library H0752.

[6] Holtz, 54.

[7] *Claresholm Review*, May 1, 1908.

[8] Holtz, 103.

[9] Glenbow Archives, NA-789-21.

[10] Howard Palmer and Tamara Palmer, *Alberta: A New History* (Edmonton: Hurtig Publishers, 1990), 13.

[11] *Henderson's Directory*, Edmonton, 1912.

[12] *Edmonton Journal,* May 13, 1912.

[13] Max Foran and Heather MacEwan Foran, *Calgary: Canada's Frontier Metropolis, An Illustrated History* (Calgary: Windsor, 1989), 123, 126.

[14] Survey notebooks, *passim,* Glenbow Archives, Herbert Harrison Moore Fonds, M866.

[15] *Calgary Herald*, November 10 and 13, 1911.

[16] Glenbow Archives, Map Collection, 92.02, Calgary, 1910, ke.

[17] Glenbow Archives, G3504, C15, 1913.

[18] City of Edmonton Archives, EAM 16, 1909.

[19] *Annual Report* of the Alberta Land Surveyors' Association, 1913, President's address.

[20] *Annual Report* of the Alberta Land Surveyors' Association, 1964, address by L. E. Harris.

[21] *Annual Report* of the Alberta Land Surveyors' Association, 1913, President's address.

[22] *Annual Report* of the Alberta Land Surveyors' Association, 1914, President's address.

[23] *Annual Report* of the Alberta Land Surveyors' Association, 1914, R. W. Cautley, "Government Control of Townsite Subdivision."

[24] This was Wolf of the later Ottawa firm of Wolf, Cotton, and Co.

[25] The analysis of survey firms below is based on information found in street directories, *Henderson's* and *Wriggley's*, from 1889.

[26] *Edmonton Journal* clipping, special number, 1913, PAA, 93.217, Jean Gustave Côté Papers, file 15.

[27] *Edmonton, 1910,* City of Edmonton Archives.

[28] *Fort Macleod Gazette*, April 19, 1887.

[29] Bond and contract documents, PAA, 85.34, box 15, file 480; box 17, file 509.

[30] Partnership agreement May 15, 1912, PAA, 93.217, Jean Gustave Côté Papers, file 15.

[31] *Calgary Herald*, September 3, 1910.

[32] *Annual Report* of the Alberta Land Surveyors' Association, 1912.

[33] City of Edmonton Archives, Planning Clipping File, Morell and Nicholls Report, 1912.

[34] PAA, NA, 9010N36, 1912. The Calgary City Council, with missionary zeal, distributed 500 copies of Mawson's report throughout Alberta.

[35] Foran and Foran, 132–133.

[36] For a full discussion of the 1913 Town Planning Act, see David G. Bettison, John K. Kenward and Larrie Taylor, *Urban Affairs in Alberta* (Edmonton: University of Alberta Press, 1975), 18–21.

[37] LAC, RG, 88, 168, file 2099, Horace Seymour, obituary.

[38] *Annual Report* of the Alberta Land Surveyors' Association, 1915.

[39] Letter dated February 21, 1906, UAA, William Pearce Papers, 74-169, 9/2/6/4–4.

[40] Correspondence 1906–09, *passim*, UAA, William Pearce Papers, 74-169, 9/2/6/4–4.

[41] In fact, the ALSA itself undermined this ruling by inviting three Dominion Land Surveyors, Belanger, Fontaine, and Lonergan, who had worked extensively in Alberta but who were not residents, to be members without sitting the exam. Belanger, however, refused on principle. (*Annual Report* of the Association of Dominion Land Surveyors, 1912).

[42] While the surveyors of the day considered the 1910 meeting as the first meeting, subsequent confusion emerged whether the 1910 or the 1911 meeting was considered the first annual general meeting. For a full discussion of the issue, see *ALS News*, June 2002, 9.

[43] ALSA, Minutes of the Annual Meeting of the ALSA, January 17, 1911.

[44] Alberta. *Alberta Land Surveyors' Act*, 1910.

[45] ALSA, Minutes of the Examining Committee of the ALSA, February 1, 1911.

[46] Cited by J. H. Holloway, *A History of the Alberta Land Surveyors' Association* (Edmonton: ALSA, 1964), 12.

[47] ALSA, Minutes of the Annual Meeting of the ALSA, January 16, 1912.

[48] ALSA, Council Minutes, February 21, 1913.

[49] *Annual Report* of the Alberta Land Surveyors' Association, 1912.

[50] Canada. *Annual Report* of the Department of the Interior for 1912, Report of the Surveyor General.

[51] Deville to Charlesworth, August 17, 1910, LAC, RG 88 vol. 337, file 11728.

[52] B. F. Mitchell to Deville, August 8, 1901, LAC, RG 88, vol. 337, file 11728.

[53] Correspondence, *passim,* LAC, RG 88, vol. 333, file 10624.

[54] *Annual Report* of the Alberta Land Surveyors' Association, 1913, 1915.

[55] PAA newspaper clipping, *Edmonton Capital*, January 23, 1912.

[56] Jean Gustave Côté, Papers, newspaper clipping, *Edmonton Capital*, January 23, 1912, PAA, 93.2217.

[57] Alberta. Chapter 13, *Alberta Surveys Act*, 1912.

[58] Alberta. *Annual Report* of the Department of Public Works, 1906, Report of the Director of Surveys.

[59] R. A. Bassil, "Outline of the History of Director of Surveys Office," ALSA Research files.

[60] Memorandum, E. Deville, October 21, 1907, LAC, RG 88, Vol. 327, File 4009.

[61] Surveyor General to Clark Sweatman & McIntyre, solicitors for the CNR, January 25, 1909, LAC, RG 88, Vol. 331, File 10204.

[62] Cartwright to Deville, April 30, 1912, LAC, RG 88, Vol. 327, File 4009.

[63] Jacob L. Doupe retired as Chief Surveyor of the CPR in 1932 and was succeeded by Wilfred Humphreys, DLS, ALS.

[64] *Annual Report* of the Alberta Land Surveyors' Association, 1914.

[65] ALSA, biographical research files.

[66] *Annual Report* of the Alberta Land Surveyors' Association, 1915,

[67] *Annual Report* of the Association of Dominion Land Surveyors, January 1919, President's address.

CHAPTER 9

[1] Byfield, *Vol. 4,* 326–31.

[2] Alberta. *Annual Report* of the Department of Public Works, 1918, Report of P. N. Johnson, District Surveyor and Engineer.

[3] Canada. *Sessional Paper* No. 25a, Report of the Topographical Surveys Branch, 1920.

[4] Correspondence, *passim,* PAA, 85.34, box 55, file 1797.

[5] Fawcett to Deville, November 13, 1918, PAA, 85.34, box 56, file 1808; correspondence, *passim*, PAA, 85.34, box 55, file 1797.

[6] LAC, RG 88, vol. 95, file 1707.

[7] Cautley, 105.

[8] Correspondence, *passim,* PAA, 85.34, box 55, file 1797.

[9] Cautley, 106.

[10] Norris to Deville, September 15, 1920, PAA, 85.34, box 58, file 1897.

[11] *Ibid.*

[12] Soars to Deville, April 29, 1920, PAA, 85.34, box 57, file 1866.

[13] Hotchkiss to Deville, May 20, 1920, PAA, 85.34, box 58, file 1895.

[14] Purser to Deville, May 22, 1920, PAA, 85.34, box 58, file 1903.

[15] ALSA, Biographical File.

[16] Obituary for H. Seymour, *Canadian Surveyor,* July 1926; LAC, RG 88, vol.168, file 2099. He finally returned to Alberta in 1929, to take up the appointment as Director of Town Planning.

[17] Address of A. G. Stewart at the Old Timers' Banquet, Alberta Land Surveyors' Meeting, 1959, printed in *The Canadian Surveyor,* supplement, 1976, 428.

[18] ALSA, Register of Members. By that time the ALSA, however, had lost members, due to the war and the death of several older members, reaching an all-time low of 37 members in 1937.

[19] Canada. *Sessional Paper* No. 25a, Report of the Topographical Surveys Branch, 1920.

[20] *Ibid.*

[21] Canada. *Annual Report* of the Department of the Interior, for the Session of 1920, Report of the Topographical Surveys Branch.

[22] Hotchkiss to Deville, May 28, 1920, PAA, 85.34, box 58, file 1895.

[23] LAC, RG 88, vol. 258, File 18776 pt. 1.

[24] Canada. *Sessional Paper* No. 25a, Report of the Topographical Surveys Branch, 1921. Hotchkiss later became an ALS in 1922.

[25] Canada. *Sessional Paper* No. 25a, Report of the Topographical Surveys Branch, 1922.

[26] Hotchkiss to Deville, May 28, 1920, PAA, 85.34, box 58, file 1895.

[27] LAC, RG 88, vol. 405, 23/262-883-9, pt.1, Summary of Surveys, Alberta.

[28] Canada. *Annual Report* of the Department of the Interior 1922, Report of the Topographical Surveys Branch.

[29] Deville to Narraway, April 17, 1919, LAC, 85.34, box 57, file 1871.

[30] PAA, 85.34, box 57, file 1886.

[31] LAC, RG 88, vol. 386, file 18583.

[32] Canada. *Annual Report* of the Department of the Interior for the Year Ending March 31, 1928.

[33] Narraway to Cumming, September 14, 1922, PAA, 85.34, box 59, file 2037.

[34] Paper read before the Alberta Land Surveyors' Association, 1921, LAC, RG 88, vol. 405, 23/462-883-9, pt. 1.

[35] Peters to Deputy Minister of the Interior, February 17, 1927, LAC, RG 88, vol. 167, file 1996.

[36] ALSA, biographical research files, memoirs of Knox. McCusker, unpublished typescript ca. 1954, 56.

[37] William Stretton, *From Compass to Satellite: A Century of Canadian Surveying and Surveyors, 1882–1982* (Ottawa: Canadian Institute of Geomatics, 1982), 114.

[38] Bridgland to Cory, December 30, 1927, LAC, RG 88, vol. 167, file 1966.

[39] Memorandum Peters to Cory, September 11, 1925, LAC, RG 88, vol.10, Geodetic Survey pt. 1.

[40] Paper read before the Alberta Land Surveyors' Association, 1921, LAC, RG 88, vol. 405, 23/462-883-9, pt. 1.

[41] *Annual Report* of the Alberta Land Surveyors' Association, 1923.

[42] LAC, RG 88, vol. 405, 23/262-883-9, pt.1. Between 1905 and 1929, the Dominion Government spent a total of $6,769,227.83 on surveys in Alberta.

[43] Peters to McCusker, September 4, 1928, PAA, 85.34, box 62, file 2131.

[44] Typescript Form, statement of surveys to be performed by W. H. Norrish, DLS, during the season of 1917, PAA, 85.34, box 54, file 1748.

[45] Canada. *Annual Report* of the Department of the Interior, for the Session of 1920, Report of the Topographical Surveys Branch.

[46] Canada. *Sessional Paper,* No. 25 a, 1921, Report of the Topographical Surveys Branch.

[47] Statements of Surveys to be performed by W. H. Norrish, DLS, during the season of 1917, PAA, 85.34, box 54, file 1748.

[48] Deville to Glover, May 22, 1917, PAA, 85.34, box 54, file 1737.

[49] Deville to Glover, June 26, 1917, PAA, 85.34, box 54, file 1737.

[50] Correspondence, *passim,* PAA, 84.34, box 57, file 1855.

[51] *Journal of the Dominion Land Surveyors' Association,* July 1923.

[52] Norrish to Deville, September 21, 1917, PAA, 85.34, box 54, file 1748

53 Deville to Norrish, April 11, 1918, PAA, 85.34, box 55, file 1797.

54 Narraway to Deville, June 22, 1918, PAA, 85.34, box 55, file 1797.

55 Norrish to Deville, August 14, 1918, PAA, 85.34, box 55, file 1797.

56 Canada. *Annual Report* of the Department Interior, for the session of 1920, Report of the Topographical Surveys Branch.

57 General Report by R. C. Purser, 1921, PAA, 85.34, box 59, file 2009.

58 *Annual Report* of the Association of Dominion Land Surveyors, 1925.

59 Alberta. *Annual Report* of the Department of Public Works, 1919.

60 Dominion of Canada. Department of Railways and Canals, Highways Branch. Bulletin No. 7, *The Canadian Highway and its Development* (Ottawa: 1925), 5.

61 Alberta. *Annual Report* of the Department of Public Works, 1924, Report of J. D. Robertson, Deputy Minister.

62 County of Lamont, Municipal District of Wostok, Council Minutes, 1928–1930, *passim.*

63 Alberta. *Annual Report* of the Department of Public Works, 1922, Report of Homer Keith, District Surveyor and Engineer.

64 *The Canadian Surveyor*, July, 1924; Alberta. *Annual Report* of the Department of Public Works, 1924, Report of C. A. Davidson, Highway Commissioner.

65 Alberta. *Annual Report* of the Department of Public Works, 1928–1929, Report of P. N. Johnson, Director of Surveys.

66 *The Canadian Surveyor*, July 1926.

67 Pinder to McLeod, June 25, 1927, Glenbow Archives, George Zouch Pinder Fonds, M973, box 4, file 186.

68 Tom Pinder to Ken Allred, March 12, 1982, ALSA, G. Z. Pinder research file.

69 Report for Field Season, 1931, Glenbow Archives, George Zouch Pinder Fonds, M973, box 13, file 338.

70 Canada. *Sessional Paper* no. 25a, Report of the Topographical Surveys Branch, 1921.

71 Canada. *Sessional Paper* no. 25a, Report of the Topographical Surveys Branch, 1922.

72 William Christie General Report April 30, 1927, PAA, 85.34, box 62, file 2128.

73 See Pat Myers, *Sky Riders: An Illustrated History of Aviation in Alberta, 1906–1945* (Saskatoon: Fifth House Publishers/Friends of Reynolds–Alberta Museum Society, 1995), 52–55.

74 Memorandum, May 23, 1923, LAC, RG 88, vol. 155, file 18236.

75 Memorandum, Director of Surveys to Deputy Minister of the Department of the Interior, December 30, 1924, LAC, RG 88, vol. 155, file 18232.

76 Memorandum, Peters to the Deputy Minister of the Department of the Interior, December 30, 1924, LAC, RG 88, vol. 155, file 18232.

77 Report on Civil Aviation, 1924, Ottawa: 1925, cited by Thomson, 12.

78 Report upon the use of Vertical Aerial Photographs on Land Classification and Topographical surveys summer of 1924 by R. H. Knight, LAC, RG 88, 18465, pt. 3.

79 Report of Photographic Operations. High River, Season, 1924, LAC, RG 88, vol.156, file 188465, pt.2.

80 Report on field operations, 1925, Richard Knight to Director of Topographical Survey of Canada, October 28, 1925, PAA, 85.34, box 62, file 2125.

81 LAC, RG 88, vol. 155, 18232.

82 Brownlee to Stewart, March 26, 1928, LAC, RG 88, vol. 266, file 19240/1.

83 Thomson, 274.

84 LAC, RG 88, vol. 392, file 19870, pt1.

85 *Annual Report* of the Association of Dominion Land Surveyors, 1925, President's Report.

86 Wallace, 8.

87 Côté, 32.

88 Memorandum from Pearce, February 17, 1927, LAC, RG 88, vol. 210, file 16275.

89 Memorandum from Frederic Peters to R. A. Gibson, Acting Deputy Minister of the Interior, May 22, 1930, LAC, RG 88, vol. 214, file 166675.

90 Tom Pinder to Ken Allred, March 12, 1982, ALSA, Biographical File, G. Z. Pinder.

91 Holloway, 40.

92 Correspondence, *passim*, LAC, RG 84, Canadian Parks Service, Series A-2-a, vol. 192, part 9.

93 T. S. Mills, *Canada's Highway–Banff to Jasper*, LAC, RG 84, Canadian Parks Service, Series A-2-a, vol. 192, part 10.

94 Correspondence, *passim*, LAC, RG 84, Canadian Parks Service, Series A-2-a, vol. 192, part 10.

95 Meridians of the Dominion Lands System," published in 1921, cited by J. H. Holloway and J. W. Hill, "Alberta–Saskatchewan Boundary Surveys, *The Canadian Surveyor* (July 1954).

96 Holloway and Hill, 236-238.

[1] ALSA, Research files, Biographical File.

[2] *Ibid.*

[3] Cited by Myers, 163.

[4] Myers, 163.

[5] Palmer and Palmer, 283.

[6] J. A. Wilson, "Aerodrome Construction for the British Commonwealth Air Training Plan, 1940." Paper presented to the Montreal Branch of the Engineering Institute of Canada, October 3, 1940, typescript, 13. DOT Library, Ottawa.

[7] See Myers, 154.

[8] Wilson, 16.

[9] The Civilian Aviation Division was transferred from the Department of National Defence in 1936. The senior official with the Department of Transport in charge of all the development of all airports for the war effort on the home front was Alexander McLean, a WWI pilot who had grown up around Innisfail.

[10] Wilson, 13.

[11] Wilson, 11, 13.

[12] Holloway, 42.

[13] Palmer and Palmer, 284.

[14] See Carl A. Christie, "The Northwest Staging Route: A Story of Canadian–American Wartime Co–operation," in *For King and Country: Alberta in the Second World War*, ed. Ken Tingley (Edmonton: Reidmore, 1995), 213–228.

[15] ALSA, Research files, Biographical File.

[16] *Ibid.*

[17] K. S. Coates and W. R. Morrison, *The Alaska Highway in World War II: The US Army of Occupation in Canada's Northwest* (Norman: Oklahoma University Press, 1992), 31, 35.

[18] K. McCusker, newspaper cuttings, ALSA, Biographical File; E. I. Carefoot, "Knox Freeman McCusker, DLS, ALS" in *ALS News*, Winter 1983; Knox McCusker, "The Alaska Highway," *The Canadian Surveyor*, July 1948.

[19] Ontario government employees R. N. Johnston and K. H. Siddall brought their expertise in aerial photo work for highway location to the project. Thomson, Vol. 3, 90.

[20] Palmer and Palmer, 284.

[21] Coates and Morrison, 53.

[22] J. Clark, interviewed by M. A. MacCrimmon and J. Haliday, January 17, 2000, ALSA, OH10:1.

[23] ALSA, Biographical File, K. McCusker.

[24] Thomson, Vol. 3, 93–94.

[25] Coates and Morrison, 31, 35, and 65.

[26] Coates and Morrison, 171–173.

[27] See Thomson, Vol. 3, 156–163.

[28] UTM coordinates are based on a traverse Mercator projection, applied to maps of the earth's surface from the Equator to 84° north latitude and 80° south latitude.

[29] W. D. Usher, unrecorded telephone interview with J. Larmour, June 1, 2004.

[30] M. A. MacCrimmon, interviewed by J. Horn, ALS, November 22, 1999 and March 25, 2000, ALSA, OH8:1 and 16.1; unrecorded interview with J. Larmour, October, August, 2003.

[31] D. Martin, interviewed by R. Baker, ALS, August 10, 2000, ALSA, OH30:1.

[32] "History of the 2nd Canadian Survey Regiment, RCA," typescript privately held.

[33] *Report* of the Annual Meeting of ALSA, January, 1942.

[34] ALSA, Research files, Biographical File.

[35] Alberta. *Annual Report* of Department of Public Works, Surveys Branch, for Year Ending March 31, 1944.

[36] See Robert Bothwell, Ian Drummond, and John English, *Canada, 1900–1945* (Toronto: University of Toronto Press, 1987), 375–387.

[37] *The Canadian Surveyor*, January 1945.

[38] *The Canadian Surveyor*, October 1943.

[39] *Report* of the Annual Meeting of Alberta Land Surveyors' Association, January 1945, President's address.

[40] Ted Byfield, ed., *Alberta in the 20th Century Vol. 9: Leduc, Manning and the Age of Prosperity, 1946–1963*, (Edmonton: United Western Communications, 2001), 102.

[41] John Webb, *Along the 55th in '55: Dawson Creek, BC, to Hopedale, Labrador: The Mid Canada Radar Defense System, 1955–1969* (Saskatoon: J. H. Webb, 2004), 5.

[42] Louis Sebert, "Military Surveys," in *Mapping a Northern Land, The Survey of Canada, 1947–1994*, ed. Gerald McGrath and Louis Sebert (Montreal: McGill-Queens University Press, 1999), 154.

[43] Major D. H. G. Thorne, "The Mid Canada Line, 1958–1965," http://www.lwilson.ca/mcl.htm.

[44] Webb, 24.

[45] C. Weir, interviewed by L. Frederick, February 22, 2000, ALSA, OH12:1.

[46] Webb, 24.

[47] Webb, 35.

[48] C. Weir, interviewed by L. Frederick, February 22, 2000, ALSA, OH12:1.

[49] *Ibid*.

[50] Webb, 30, 35.

[51] Major D. H. G. Thorne, "The Mid Canada Line, 1958–1965," http://www.lwilson.ca/mcl.htm.

[52] *Ibid*.

[53] P. Lypowy, interviewed by C. Weir, June 13, 2000, ALSA, OH23:1.

[54] Byfield, *Vol. 9*, 104.

[55] P. Lypowy, interviewed by C. Weir, June 13, 2000, ALSA, OH23:1. The legacy of the Primrose Weapons Range of 1952, now known as Cold Lake Weapons Range, was a long-standing grievance held by the First Nations affected by the loss of traditional hunting, trapping and fishing grounds. In 1975 the Canoe Lake First Nations of Saskatchewan, and in 1985, the Cold Lake First Nations, filed specific claims alleging that the original compensation had been inadequate, with severe economic and social repercussions. Canada's initial rejection of such claims led to a court case, which, in 1992 recommended a negotiated settlement. This settlement was finalized under a special cabinet mandate. In July 2002, the federal government announced an agreement whereby the Cold Lake First Nations now have access to the range, as well as new reserve lands south of its boundary, which had been an area of traditional access routes to the lands of the range.

[56] J. E. Underwood and R. A. McLellan, *A Consulting Engineer's Partnership* (Saskatoon: Mercury Printers, 1958), 48–49.

[57] E. Carefoot, interviewed by C. Weir, February 29, 2000, ALSA, OH14:1.

[58] P. Lypowy, interviewed by C. Weir, June 13, 2000, ALSA, OH23:1.

[59] Underwood and McLellan, 50.

[60] E. Carefoot, interviewed by C. Weir, February 29, 2000, ALSA, OH14:1.

CHAPTER 11

[1] ALSA, Biographical File, A. P. Patrick.

[2] North America's first oil field was developed around Petrolia in Ontario.

[3] Only a few lots were ever sold, but the townsite remained freehold property until the 1960s.

[4] Graham MacDonald, *Where the Mountains Meet the Prairies: A History of Waterton County* (Calgary: University of Calgary, 2000).

[5] J. W. Hill, "Surveying for the Oil Industry," *The Canadian Surveyor* (July 1959), 325.

[6] This was in large part due to the flaring off of approximately 1 trillion cubic feet of gas from the gas cap, thus depressurizing the reservoir.

[7] PAA, Information files, Redwater.

[8] "Synopsis of surveys by provincial and federal governments during 1950," *The Canadian Surveyor* (April 1954), 41; Geoff Hamilton, "Surveying for the Oil Industry," *The Canadian Surveyor* (July 1951), 36–7.

[9] These were B. Mitchell, R. V. Heathcott, C. C. Fairchild, and R. H. Cautley, followed by A. Patrick in 1948, and C. Magrath in 1949.

[10] *Report* of the Proceedings of the Annual Meeting of the Alberta Land Surveyors' Association, January 1946.

[11] Holloway, 49.

[12] *Report* of the Proceedings of the Annual Meeting of Alberta Land Surveyors' Association, January 1947.

[13] Holloway, 52–53.

[14] Holloway, 55.

[15] C. Weir, interviewed by L. Frederick, February 22, 2000, ALSA, OH:12.

[16] Holloway, 54–56.

[17] G. Turnock, interviewed by A. Main, March 15, 2001, ALSA, OH 41:1.

[18] L. Breton, interviewed by B. Doyle, November 7, 2000, ALSA, OH 34:1.

[19] "In the Province of Alberta," *The Canadian Surveyor* (April 1954), 116.

[20] C. Weir, unrecorded interview with J. Larmour, May 21, 2004.

[21] M. A. MacCrimmon, unrecorded telephone interview with J. Larmour, May 22, 2004.

[22] W. H. Jones, interviewed by A. Main, December 2, 2000, ALSA, OH35:1.

[23] A. Edwards, interviewed by L. Frederick, August 17, 2000, ALSA, OH27:1.

[24] S. Cherwonick, interviewed by B. Doyle, March 20, 2000, ALSA, OH15:1.

[25] D. F. K. Dawson, interviewed by D. Lipinski, November 9, 1999, ALSA, OH6:1.

[26] M. A. MacCrimmon, interviewed by J. Horn, November 22, 1999, ALSA, OH8:1; M. A. MacCrimmon Field Diary, 1958, private collection,.

[27] L. Olsen, interviewed by K. Allred, January 26, 2001, ALSA, OH17:1; J. Webb, interviewed by C. Weir, April 14, 2000, ALSA, OH18:1.

[28] M. A. MacCrimmon, interviewed by J. Horn, November 22, 1999, ALSA, OH:8:1.

[29] C. Weir, unrecorded interview with J. Larmour, May 21, 2004.

[30] S. Cherwonick, interviewed by B. Doyle, March 20, 2000, ALSA, OH15:1.

[31] G. Hedinger, interviewed by B. Doyle, November 19, 1999, ALSA, OH7:1.

[32] These were small containers filled with cotton wool that was soaked with alcohol and burned from a lit knot inside.

[33] G. Hedinger, interviewed by B. Doyle, November 19, 1999, ALSA, OH7:1.

[34] S. Cherwonick, interviewed by B. Doyle, March 20, 2000, ALSA, OH15:1.

[35] *Report* of the Proceedings of the Annual Meeting of the Alberta Land Surveyors' Association, 1955, President's report.

[36] Alberta. Department of Highways, *Annual Report,* Surveys Branch for the year ending March 1956.

[37] See *Report of the Commission Appointed to Delimit the Boundary Between the Provinces of Alberta and British Columbia* (Ottawa: Office of the Surveyor General, 1955); Doug Barnett, *The Demarcation of Alberta's Boundaries* (unpublished manuscript, 2003), 233–51.

[38] See *Report of the Commissioners Appointed to Direct the Survey and Demarcation of the Boundary Between the Province of Alberta and the Northwest Territories* (Edmonton: Alberta–Northwest Territories Boundary Commission, 1956).

[39] L. Breton, interviewed by B. Doyle, November 7, 2000, ALSA, OH34:1.

[40] D. Holmberg, interviewed by L. Frederick, November 2, 2001, ALSA, OH36:1.

[41] *Report of the Commissioners Appointed to Direct the Survey and Demarcation of the Boundary Between the Province of Alberta and the Northwest Territories* (Edmonton: Alberta–Northwest Territories Boundary Commission, 1956), 32.

[42] Alberta. Department of Highways, *Annual Report*, Surveys Branch, Report for the year ending March 31, 1957.

[43] *Report* of the Proceedings of the Annual Meeting of the Alberta Land Surveyors' Association, 1958, Minutes of a meeting of the Oil Field Surveys Committee, August 30, 1957.

[44] *Report* of the Proceedings of the Annual Meeting of the Alberta Land Surveyors' Association, 1959, Report of Oilfield and Northern Surveys Committee.

[45] *Report of the Royal Commission on the Development of Northern Alberta* (Edmonton: The Commission, 1958), 107.

[46] Alberta. Department of Highways, *Annual Report,* Surveys Branch, Report for the year ending March 31, 1958.

[47] *Report* of the Proceedings of the Annual Meeting of the Alberta Land Surveyors' Association, 1959, Report of Oilfield and Northern Surveys Committee.

[48] *Report* of the Proceedings of the Annual Meeting of the Alberta Land Surveyors' Association, 1961, Report of Oilfield and Northern Surveys Committee.

[49] Alberta. Department of Highways, *Annual Report,* Surveys Branch, Report for the year ending March 31, 1960; *Report* of the Proceedings of the Annual Meeting of the Alberta Land Surveyors' Association, 1962, Committee on Oil Field and Northern Surveys.

[50] Hill, 328.

[51] *Report* of the Proceedings of the Annual Meeting of the Alberta Land Surveyors' Association, Appendix G, Report of Oilfield and Northern Surveys Committee, 1961.

[52] C. Weir, unrecorded interview with J. Larmour, May 21, 2004.

[53] *Report* of the Proceedings of the Annual Meeting of the Alberta Land Surveyors' Association, 1958, J. W. Hill, "Notes on Oil Field Surveys Committee Report."

[54] R. A. Bassil, unrecorded interview with J. Larmour, May 14, 2004.

[55] *Ibid.*

[56] *Report* of the Proceedings of the Annual Meeting of the Alberta Land Surveyors' Association, 1961, Report of the Northern and Oil field Survey Committee; Alberta. Department of Highways, *Annual Report,* Surveys Branch, Report for the year ending March 31, 1961.

[57] *Report* of the Proceedings of the Annual Meeting of the Alberta Land Surveyors' Association 1962, Report of the Northern and Oil Field Survey Committee.

[58] Hill, 327–28.

[59] Adam Chrzanowski, "Engineering and Mining Surveys," in McGrath and Sebert, 493.

[60] C. Weir, interviewed by L. Frederick, February 22, 2000, ALSA, OH12:1.

[61] W. Jones, interviewed by A. Main, December 2, 2000, ALSA, OH 35:2.

[62] Underwood and McLellan, 43.

[63] D. G. Waldon, "The Longest Oil Pipeline in the Western World," in *Dusters and Gushers: The Canadian Oil and Gas Industry*, James Hillborn, ed. (Toronto: Pitt, 1968), 127.

[64] John H. Webb, *The Big Inch: Surveying Trans Mountain Pipe Line, 1951–52* (Saskatoon: J. H. Webb, 1991). The account below is based on Webb's account in the *Big Inch* as well as on ALSA oral history interviews with John (Jack) Webb and Lawrence (Buck) Olsen.

[65] A number of Alberta Land Surveyors worked intermittently as associates with the Phillips, Hamilton and Associates Trans Mountain survey crews. As recalled by Jack Webb, they included Oluff Insker, Leonard (Dick) Newby, Creighton Bildstein, Rae Sutherland, William Jones, as well as others who later qualified as Alberta Land Surveyors—George Hedinger, Duncan Gillmore, John Sikal, Allen Edwards, Pete Muirhead, and Roger Vossen.

[66] "Alberta, Summary of Activities for 1954," *The Canadian Surveyor* (1954), 605.

[67] *Alberta: province of opportunity; a survey of the resources and facilities offered to industry by the province of Alberta, of its present industrialization, and of future probable growth and industrial oportunities in the province* (Calgary: Calgary Power Ltd., 1958), 131.

[68] Palmer and Palmer, 302–303.

[69] L. Olsen, interviewed by K. Allred, March 29, 2000, ALSA, OH17:1.

[70] *Alberta*, 110; Alex Osborne, Chief Surveyor, Trans Canada Pipelines, telephone conversation with J. Larmour, May 31, 2004.

[71] Underwood and McLellan, 53.

[72] Glen Toner and Francois Bregha, "The Political Economy of Energy," in *Canadian Politics in the 1980s*, ed. Michael S. Whittington and Glen Williams (Toronto: Methuen, 1984), 115–116.

[73] C. Weir, unrecorded interview with J. Larmour, May 21, 2004.

[74] W. H. Jones, interviewed by A. Main, December 2, 2000, ALSA, OH35:1.

[75] L. Breton, interviewed by B. Doyle, November 7, 2000, ALSA, OH34:1.

[76] *Ibid.*

[77] *Ibid.*

[78] E. Teassari, interviewed by J. Haggerty, January 1, 2003, ALSA, OH51:1.

[79] S. Cherwonick, Interviewed by B. Doyle, March 20, 2000, ALSA, OH 5:1.

[80] For a full discussion, see George Babbage and Allen C. Roberts, "Geodesy in Canada, and International and Interprovincial Boundaries," in McGrath and Sebert, 28–29.

[81] W. D. Usher, interviewed by L. Frederick, June 7, 2000, ALSA, OH 21:1.

[82] D. Barnett, unrecorded interview with J. Larmour, May 21, 2004.

[83] J. Webb, interviewed by C. Weir, April 14, 2000, ALSA, OH18:1.

[84] D. Barnett, unrecorded interview with J. Larmour, May 21, 2004.

[85] L. Olsen, interviewed by K. Allred, January 26, 2001, ALSA, OH17:1.

CHAPTER 12

[1] Byfield, *Vol. 9*, 121.

[2] See Jack Holloway, "Development of Town and Regional Planning," in *The Alberta Municipal Councillor*, May 1962; Donald G. Wetherell and Irene Kmet, *Homes in Alberta: Building, Trends, and Design, 1870–1967* (Edmonton: University of Alberta, Alberta Culture and Multiculturalism, Alberta Municipal Affairs, 1991), 160–165.

[3] See C. A. Perry, *Housing for the Machine Age* (New York: Russell Sage Foundation, 1939); Byfield, *Vol. 9*, 210.

[4] ALSA, Biographical File, G. Walker.

[5] *Ibid*.

[6] *Report* of the Proceedings of the Annual General Meeting of the Alberta Land Surveyors' Association, 1958, Address by A. G. Stewart, at the Old Timers' Banquet.

[7] G. Walker, unrecorded interview with J. Larmour, June 17, 2004.

[8] A. G. Stewart, Obituary, *The Canadian Surveyor*, supplement (December 1976).

[9] A. G. Stewart, *The Edmontonian*, 1964.

[10] "Provincial Town Planner Directs Orderly Development," in *Within our Borders*, March 15, 1950.

[11] *Edmonton Journal*, November 10, 1953.

[12] *Replotting Scheme Procedure*, Publication #2, Provincial Planning Advisory Board, Government of Alberta, 1951.

[13] Robert Gray Graden, "The Planning of New Residential Areas in Edmonton, 1950–1976." MA Thesis, University of Alberta, 1979, 12.

[14] Assistant City Solicitor to Commissioner D. B. Menzies, April 16, 1953, City of Edmonton Archives, RG 11, class 16, file 118.

[15] Replotting surveys, City of Edmonton Archives, RG 11, class 16, file 21 and 22.

[16] *City of Calgary Municipal Handbook*, 2004.

[17] Byfield, *Vol. 9*, 216.

[18] M. A. McCrimmon, unrecorded interview with J. Larmour, June 4, 2004.

[19] Glenbow Archives, Clipping Files, Lake Bonavista.

[20] Alberta. *Annual Report* of the Department of Highways, Surveys Branch, Report for the years 1951–59.

[21] Alberta. *Annual Report* of the Department of Highways, Surveys Branch, 1969, 73.

[22] Graden, 48–49.

[23] R. Fulton, unrecorded interview with J. Larmour, June 16, 2004.

[24] Field Diaries, 1967, M. A. MacCrimmon, private collection.

[25] Hooke was cleared of later allegations that he approved the development for personal gain.

[26] G. Walker, unrecorded interview with J. Larmour, June 17, 2004.

[27] PAA, Information Files, Sherwood Park.

[28] A. Willie, interviewed by J. Larmour, April 2, 2003, ALSA, OH52:1.

[29] G. Walker, unrecorded interview with J. Larmour, June 17, 2004.

[30] A. Willie, interviewed by J. Larmour, April 2, 2003, ALSA, OH52:1.

[31] K. Allred, unrecorded interview with J. Larmour, September, 2004.

[32] Graden, 17.

[33] M. A. MacCrimmon, unrecorded interview with J. Larmour, June 4, 2004.

[34] George Walker, unrecorded interview with J. Larmour, June 17, 2004.

[35] HUDAC became the Edmonton Home Builders Association in 1984.

[36] The Provincial Planning Board was established in 1963.

[37] S. Cherwonick, interviewed by B. Doyle, March 20, 2000, ALSA, OH15:1. Steve Cherwonick did about 75 percent of the rural residence subdivisions in the County of Parkland in those years.

[38] ALSA, Biographical File, G. Walker, Nomination of George C. Walker for the Alberta Land Surveyors' Association Outstanding Service Award; G. Walker, interviewed by C. Weir, September17, 2000, ALSA, OH28:1.

[39] G. Walker, interviewed by C. Weir, September 17, 2000, ALSA, OH28:1.

[40] J. Holloway to J. A. Beveridge, June 26, 1956, Red Deer and District Archives, Charles Snell Fonds, MG 116, box V, 3.

[41] Byfield, *Vol. 9*, 121.

[42] *Ibid.*, 122.

[43] G. Walker, interviewed by C. Weir, September 17, 2000, ALSA, OH:28:1.

[44] Alberta. *Annual Report* of the Department of Highways, Surveys Branch, for the year ending March 31, 1952.

[45] Alberta. *Annual Report* of the Department of Highways, Surveys Branch, for the year ending March 31, 1958.

[46] *Edmonton Journal,* January 21, 1960.

[47] *Edmonton Journal*, September 16 and October 31, 1960.

[48] ALSA, Biographical File, K. McCusker, McKusker to Max [?], April 19, 1951.

[49] Alberta. *Annual Report* of the Department of Highways, Surveys Branch, for the year ending March 31, 1954.

[50] Alberta. *Annual Report* of the Department of Highways, Surveys Branch, for the year ending March 31, 1955.

[51] Alberta. *Annual Report* of the Department of Highways, Surveys Branch, for the year ending March 31, 1957.

[52] C. Bruce, interviewed by A. Main, March 30, 2001, ALSA, OH42:1.

[53] R. Baker, unrecorded telephone interview with J. Larmour, May 15, 2004.

[54] E. Tessari, interviewed by J. Haggerty, January 1, 2003, ALSA, OH51:1.

[55] *Ibid.*

[56] C. Bruce, interviewed by A. Main, March 30, 2001, ALSA, OH42:1.

[57] E. Tessari, interviewed by J. Haggerty, January 1, 2003, ALSA, OH51:1.

[58] *Ibid.*

[59] See Byfield, *Vol. 9*, 129–130.

[60] R. Baker, unrecorded telephone interview with J. Larmour, May 15, 2004.

[61] E. Tessari, interviewed by J. Haggerty, January 1, 2003, ALSA, OH51:1.

[62] R. Baker, unrecorded telephone interview with J. Larmour May 15, 2004.

[63] C. Bruce, interviewed by A. Main, March 30, 2001, ALSA, OH42:1.

[64] M. Wuhr, interviewed by L. Frederick, July 8, 1999, ALSA, OH1:1.

[65] Alberta. *Annual Report* of the Department of Highways, Surveys and Compensation for Land Branch, for the year ending March 31, 1967.

[66] Alberta. *Annual Report* of the Department of Highways, Surveys Branch, for the year ending March 31, 1964.

[67] R. Baker, unrecorded telephone interview with J. Larmour, May 15, 2004.

[68] See *Rural Road Inventory and Future Road Needs, Vegreville Study Area No.11,* 1966.

[69] R. A. F. Tate, interviewed by C. Weir, March 2, 2000, ALSA, OH29:1.

[70] E. Tessari, interviewed by J. Haggerty, January 1, 2003, ALSA, OH51:1.

[71] M. A. MacCrimmon, unrecorded interview with J. Larmour, June 4, 2004.

[72] P. Muirhead, interviewed by L. Frederick, May 25, 2001, ALSA, OH46:1.

[73] *Tempo*, Summer 1982.

[74] R. A. F. Tate, interviewed by C. Weir, March 2, 2000, ALSA, OH:29:1.

[75] Alberta. *Annual Report* of the Department of Highways, Surveys Branch, for the year ending March 31, 1955.

[76] Alberta. *Annual Report* of the Department of Highways, Surveys Branch, for the year ending March 31, 1958.

[77] *Alberta, province of opportunity; a survey of the resources and facilities offered to industry by the province of Alberta, of its present industrialization, and of future probable growth and industrial oportunities in the province* (Calgary: Calgary Power Ltd., 1958), 131.

[78] W. D. Usher, interviewed by J. Larmour, June 8, 2004, ALSA, OH54:1.

[79] Alberta. *Annual Report* of the Department of Highways, Surveys and Compensation for Land Branch, for the year ending March 31, 1962, 1963.

[80] W. D. Usher, interviewed by J. Larmour, June 8, 2004, ALSA, OH54:1.

[81] "AGT provides New Services," *Within our Borders,* March 15, 1950.

[82] "Annual Report, Alberta," *The Canadian Surveyor* (1958) 155.

[83] C. Weir, unrecorded interview with J. Larmour, May 21, 2004; Holloway, 66, 68.

[84] P. M. Sauder, "Irrigation in Alberta," *The Canadian Surveyor* (April, 1943), 8.

[85] D. Martin, interviewed by R. Baker, April 10, 2000, ALSA, OH30:1.

[86] Lloyd Haverhold, unrecorded interview with J. Larmour, October, 2003.

[87] T. Okamura, interviewed by B. Baker, February, 29, 2001, ALSA, OH38:1.

[88] Graden, 59.

[89] E. Tessari, interviewed by J. Haggerty, January 1, 2003, ALSA OH51:1.

[90] W. D. Usher, interviewed by J. Larmour, June 8, 2004, ALSA, OH54:1.

[91] Ken Pawson, "Establishing a Control Survey Network in Calgary," *The Canadian Surveyor* (September 1964), 293–294.

[92] Alberta. *Annual Report* of the Department of Highways, Surveys and Compensation for Land Branch, for the year ending March 31, 1966.

[93] Alberta. *Annual Report* of the Department of Highways, Surveys and compensation for Land Branch, for the year ending March 31, 1967.

[94] W. D. Usher, interviewed by J. Larmour, June 8, 2004, ALSA, OH54:1.

[95] Alberta. *Annual Report,* of the Department of Highways, Surveys and compensation for Land Branch, for the year ending March 31, 1966 and 1967.

[96] Alberta. *Annual Report,* of the Department of Highways, Surveys and Property Branch, 1972–73.

[97] *Report* of the Proceedings of the Annual General Meeting of the Alberta Land Surveyors' Association, President's report, 1962.

[98] E. Tessari, interviewed by J. Haggerty, January 1, 2003, ALSA, OH51:1.

[99] R. Watson, interviewed by J. Larmour, November 10, 2001, ALSA, OH33:1.

[100] *Report* of the Proceedings of the Annual General Meeting of the Alberta Land Surveyors' Association, 1971, Appendix C.

[101] Although successful the program ended in 1985 when NAIT introduced a semester system throughout the institute.

[102] N. Coy, interviewed by T. Ripon July, 5, 2000, ALSA, OH26:1.

[103] *Report* of the Proceedings of the Annual General Meeting of the Alberta Land Surveyors' Association, President's address, 1967.

[104] *Ibid*.

[105] "Jack Holloway Scholarship Foundation Celebrates Twenty-five years," *ALS News* (March 2000), 24.

[106] J. M. Satra, unrecorded interview with J. Larmour, September 2004.

[107] C. Petersen, interviewed by R. Baker, January 2002, ALSA, OH49:1.

[108] *Report* of the Proceedings of the Annual General Meeting of the Alberta Land Surveyors' Association, President's address, 1968.

[109] K. Allred, unrecorded interview with J. Larmour, September 2004.

[110] W. D. Usher, "History of the Establishment of a Degree Course in Surveying Engineering," *ALS News* (Fall 1979).

¹ Paul Bunner, ed. *Lougheed and the War with Ottawa, 1971–1984: Alberta in the 20th Century, Vol. 11* (Edmonton: History Book Publications, 2003), 23.

² Transcript of Premier Lougheed's Address to the Province of Alberta in Reaction to he Federal Buudget, October 30, 1980, quoted by Howard Palmer with Tamara Palmer, *Alberta A New History* (Edmonton: Hurtig Publishers, 1990), 351.

³ J. Holmlund, interviewed by J. Haggerty, April 17, 2001, ALSA, OH44:1.

⁴ *Ibid.*

⁵ *Report* of Proceedings of the Annual Meeting of the Alberta Land Surveyors' Association, 1982, 1983.

⁶ *Report* of Proceedings of the Annual Meeting of the Alberta Land Surveyors' Association, 1984, President's Message.

⁷ *Boundaries* was an occasional magazine published by the ALSA for the public, whereas *ALS News* is for its members.

⁸ "Policy Governing Future Legislation for the Professions and Occupations," tabled in the legislature by Dr. A. E. Holol.

⁹ *Report* of Proceedings of the Annual General Meeting of the Alberta Land Surveyors' Association, 1983, President's Message.

¹⁰ *Report* of the Proceedings of the Annual General Meeting of the Alberta Land Surveyors' Association, 1987.

¹¹ L. Pratt, unrecorded interview with J. Larmour, August 2004.

¹² S. Yanish, interviewed by J. Haggerty, May 24, 2001, ALSA, OH45:1.

¹³ George Babbage and Allen C. Roberts, " Geodesy in Canada, International and International Boundaries," in McGrath and Sebert, 37.

¹⁴ M. C. Pinch, "Commentary on GPS in Land Surveying," *Geomatica*, Vol. 54 (2000), 189.

¹⁵ E. Titanich, unrecorded interview with J. Larmour, August, 2004.

¹⁶ R. A. Bassil, "Digital Plan Submission – the Alberta experience," www.alsa.ab.ca.papers.

¹⁷ D. Gillmore, interviewed by C. Weir, June 12, 2000, ALSA, OH22:1.

¹⁸ Babbage and Roberts, 36.

¹⁹ R. A. Bassil, "Outline of the History of Director of Surveys Office," ALSA Research files.

²⁰ Some land surveyors thought the fast-track approach to digital submission cost their business time and money to get adequate internet connection and plotting capabilities up to speed. Others questioned paying the mapping fee, as it is the surveyor's registered plan of survey that is the mechanism for updating the provincial base-mapping system.

²¹ R. Watson, interviewed by J. Larmour, November 10, 2000, ALSA, OH33:1.

²² E. Titanich, unrecorded interview with J. Larmour, May 2003; Director of Surveys Office, Township corner inspection reports, 1989.

²³ Seibert to Deville, March 22, 1915, PAA, 85.34, box 63, file 1654.

²⁴ The Alberta Land Surveyors' Association created the RPR index (www.rprindex.ab.ca) as a searchable database accessible via the internet. Anyone, vendor or purchaser, can search a property by municipal or legal address to find out whether an RPR exists for the property. If so, an update for verification may be all that is required, reducing the cost from a new survey quite considerably.

²⁵ G. Olsson, unrecorded interview with J. Larmour, September 2004.

²⁶ The Canada Lands Surveyors Act finally came into effect in 1999. It created the Association of Canada Lands Surveyors, 117 years after it was first suggested in 1882 that Dominion Land Surveyors should be self-governing.

²⁷ See Jay Abbey, "Made to Measure, Alberta Land Surveyors make a big impact thinking inside the box," *ALS News* (December 2003), 31.

²⁸ See Brian Ballantyne and James Dobbin, "Options for Land Registration and Surveys Systems on Aboriginal Lands in Canada," A Report Prepared for the Legal Surveys Division of Geomatics Canada, January 2000.

²⁹ G. Olsson, unrecorded telephone conversation with J. Larmour, September 2004.

³⁰ See Terry Wywal, "Protecting your client's interests in Métis Settlements Land," *ALS News*, March (2002).

# Appendix

## Director of Surveys, Alberta

1905–1915 L. C. Charlesworth

1915–1922 A. P. C. Belyea

1922–1937 P. N. Johnson

1937–1946 A. P. C. Belyea

1946–1950 J. H. Holloway

1950–1963 C. W. Lester

1963–1982 C. W. Youngs

1982–1987 E. A. Kennedy

1987–1990 R. F. Baker

1990–1996 R. A. Bassil

1996–present P. M. Michaud

## Past Presidents of the Alberta Land Surveyors' Association

| | |
|---|---|
| 1911 W. Pearce | 1932 E. D. Robertson |
| 1912 L. C. Charlesworth | 1933 D. T. Townsend |
| 1913 L. C. Charlesworth | 1934 C. H. Snell |
| 1914 R. W. Cautley | 1935 P. N. Johnson |
| 1915 A. C. Talbot | 1936 T. W. Brown |
| 1916 J. L. Cote | 1937 D. T. Townsend |
| 1917 H. H. Moore | 1938 N. H. Bradley |
| 1918 A. S. Weekes | 1939 C. B. Atkins |
| 1919 P. N. Johnson | 1940 H. S. Day |
| 1920 G. W. MacLeod | 1941 A. Cormack |
| 1921 R. H. Knight | 1942 W. E. Zinkan |
| 1922 A. P. C. Belyea | 1943 C. H. Snell |
| 1923 C. M. Hoar | 1944 W. Humphreys |
| 1924 J. L. Doupe | 1945 J. W. Doze |
| 1925 P. N. Johnson | 1946 R. M. Hardy |
| 1926 B. J. Saunders | 1947 G. Z. Pinder |
| 1927 O. Inkster | 1948 C. H. Snell |
| 1928 D. T. Townsend | 1949 J. H. Holloway |
| 1929 C. H. Snell | 1950 R. McCutcheon |
| 1930 C. M. Hoar | 1951 G. C. Hamilton |
| 1931 R. H. Cautley | 1952 G. C. Hamilton |

1953  R. McCutcheon
1954  C. W. Lester
1955  W. D. Usher
1956  D. K. F. Dawson
1957  C. H. Weir
1958  W. A. Wolley-Dod
1959  L. O. Olsen
1960  C. W. Youngs
1961  E. J. Clark
1962  G. C. Walker
1963  A. J. Edwards
1964  G. Oslund
1965  W. E. Bright
1966  T. E. Rippon
1967  T. C. Swanby
1968  D. C. Holmberg
1969  D. B. Gillmore
1970  M. A. MacCrimmon
1971  R. A. F. Tate
1972  T. Okamura
1973  M. L. Sexauer
1974  R. J. Watson
1975  J. W. Hill
1976  J. Deyholos
1977  A. Hittel
1978  E. J. Tessari
1979  N. R. Mattson
1980  J. E. Rasmuson
1981  B. R. Bishop

1982  W. R. Hunter
1983  R. A. Bassil
1984  R. J. Fulton
1985  A. D. Hosford
1986  R. E. D. McCuaig
1987  L. W. Breton
1988  G. E. Olsson
1989  I. C. Maltais
1990  S. M. Loeppky
1991  G. L. Haggerty
1992  R. F. Baker
1993  H. E. Impey
1994  L. H. Pratt
1995  J. H. Holmlund
1996  W. R. Dabbs
1997  S. J. Longson
1998  A. Hittel
1999  D. R. Jaques
2000  L. M. Pals
2001  G. K. Allred
2002  D. R. McWilliam
2003  J. G. Halliday
2004  A. W. Nelson

www.landsurveyinghistory.ab.ca: A website devoted to the history of the Alberta Land Surveyors' Association—containing biographical profiles, places named by/for land surveyors, and descriptions of select survey instruments.

www.alsa.ab.ca: The official website of the Alberta Land Surveyors' Association

# A Note on Sources

There is a wealth of sources for the history of land surveying in Alberta. Interested readers should begin with published sources such as Don Thompson's three volumes *Men and Meridians, The History of Surveying and Mapping in Canada*. The series of essays in *Mapping a Northern Land, The Survey of Canada, 1947–1994*, edited by Gerald McGrath and Louis Sebert is also important for the national context.

Extensive primary sources, both archival documents and published contemporary reports and articles, chronicle the development of the profession in Alberta. The *Annual Reports* of the federal Department of the Interior contain the reports of the Topographical Surveys Branch. The extensive correspondence, official diaries and field notes held by the Provincial Archives of Alberta, and records at Library and Archives Canada in Ottawa, provide a basic profile of the work of the Dominion Land Survey in Alberta to 1930. The *Annual Reports* of the Department of Indian Affairs outline the work of its survey branch. The *Annual Reports* of the departments of Public Works of the North-West Territories, of the Government of Alberta from 1905, and of Alberta's Department of Highways from 1951, outline the work of district surveyors on surveying roads. Also useful are the official reports of the Alberta-British Columbia boundary commission and the Alberta-North West Territories boundary commission, published by the Surveyor General's Office.

The Alberta Land Surveyors' Association holds copies of its *Annual Reports* from 1911 to the present, as well as council minutes. These highlight the issues and technical concerns of land surveyors in Alberta and the development of a provincial self-regulating profession. The ALSA collection also includes miscellaneous research files, biographical research files on individual surveyors, Jack Holloway's *A History of the Alberta Land Surveyors' Association* (1964), and over 50 oral history interviews. The ALSA library has a complete run of *The Canadian Surveyor*, from 1924, along with its successors, *CISM Journal* (1988–92) and *Geomatica* (1993–). The journal published a wide range of articles from the historical to the technical, as well as annual happenings in each province.

Surviving personal papers of individual land surveyors reveal significant information on their professional lives. Most useful are the William Pearce Papers at the University of Alberta Archives, the personal papers of Jean Leon Côté at the Provincial Archives of Alberta, the Snell Papers at the Red Deer and District Archives, and the Herbert Harrison Moore Fonds and the George Zouch Pinder Fonds at the Glenbow Archives. Additionally, reminiscences and memoirs in both typescript form and as taped histories, offer first-hand accounts of life in survey camps among other topics. These are identified in the endnotes.

To trace the evolution of Alberta's earliest professional survey firms and partnerships, *Henderson's Directory*, for Edmonton and Calgary, along with corporate profiles and histories held by the ALSA, are indispensable. Newspapers, notably the *Edmonton Bulletin* and the *Lethbridge News* provide a perspective on specific issues. The Glenbow Archives and the City of Edmonton Archives hold clipping files on surveying and surveyors.

Visual sources are invaluable. In Alberta, the Glenbow Archives and the Provincial Archives of Alberta have extensive historic map collections, as does the University of Alberta. Township survey plans can be found at the Provincial Archives of Alberta, and at the Glenbow Archives. Survey plans registered at the Alberta Land Titles Office can be researched through www.spin.gov.ab.ca. Survey plans on federal lands can be found through the Canada Lands database www.lsd.nrcan.gc.ca. There are substantial photograph collections at the Provincial Archives, the Glenbow Archives, and Library Archives Canada, as well as at the ALSA.

# INDEX OF SURVEYORS' NAMES *

*The names of early surveyors and explorers, members of the North American Boundary Commission who did not later become Dominion Land Surveyors, and surveyors working prior to 1872, are listed in the general index below.

Garner, A. C., 172
Gemmell, H. W. R., 172
George, Don, 272
Gibbons, James, 86, 292
Gilmore, Duncan B., 275, 283
Gilmore, Duncan C., 283, 304n65
Gore, William S., 20, 48
Grassie, Charles, 143, 163
Green, Thomas, 60–61, 79–80, 142, 144
Grover, Arthur E., 144, 183
Grover, Len, 215

Haggerty, Gordon, 282–83, 286
Haggerty, John, 273, 283, 285
Halahuric, Frank, 270
Hall, Ron, 283
Hamilton, Geoffrey, 218, 220, 224, 235, 246, 264
Hamilton, L. A., 66
Hamilton, James F. (Fred), 162–63
Harden, J. F., 34
Hardy, R. M., 219
Hargrove, Paul, 210, 254
Harris, Ley, 139, 181, 196, 246
Harrison, A. G., 161
Harrison, Edward, 163
Hart, Milner, 18, 35
Heacock, George, 283
Heacock, Richard, 283
Heathcott, R. V., 172, 302n9
Hedinger, George, 225, 304n65
Herriot, George, 133
Heuperman, Frederick, 160–61
Heuperman, Lambertus, 160–61, 172
Hewson, T. R., 34
Hill, Jack, 229
Hittel, Alex, 267, 275, 281
Hoar, Charles M., 182
Hobbs, Geoff, 283,
Holcroft, Herbert, 106–107, 109
Holloway, Jack, 202, 220, 242, 244, 247, 265
Holmlund, John, 269
Hortness, Lorraine, 267
Hotchkiss, Cyprus, 176, 178–79
Hubbell, Ernest, 82, 86, 88–89, 93–94, 175
Hudema, Terry, 281
Hume, James, 272
Humphreys, Wilfred, 210
Hunter, Bill, 272
Hutton, J. D., 161

Inkster, Oluff, 147, 172, 197, 199, 203, 220, 304n65
Iwanusiw, Jerry, 254

Jaques, Don, 285

Jamieson, Al, 281
Jephson, Richard J., 46, 57, 153, 160
Johnson, Percy, 174, 188
Jones, Bill, 222, 236, 304n65

Kains, Tom, 29, 34, 49, 54
Keith, Homer, 186–87
Kennedy, Lachlan, 27, 29
Kimpe, Maurice, 167
King, Cornwallis, 101
King, James, 183
King, William F., 9, 21–22, 27–30, 35, 48–49, 72
Kippen, Alexander, 51
Klotz, Otto, 29–30, 35, 40, 125–26, 288n51
Knight, Richard, 147, 157, 161, 167–68, 178, 191–92
Knight, Sidney, 172
Knudson, Art, 259

Landry, John, 283
La Rue, Charles, 281
Latornell, A. Joseph, 165, 167, 172
Leitch, John S., 160
Lendrum, Robert, 95
Lester, Carl, 188, 226, 246, 252, 254
Little, Earl, 211–13
Loeppky, Syd, 270
Logan, Robert, 114
Longeran, Gerald, 95, 141, 185, 294n19
Lumb, William E., 174
Lypowy, Peter, 213–15

MacCrimmon, Armstrong, 208–9, 222, 224, 246–47,
    281
MacDonald, R. W., 159
MacFarlane, John, 196
MacLeod, G. W., 172
Magrath, Charles, 22, 30, 34–35, 40, 49–50, 67–69,
    72–74, 82, 87, 96, 155, 162, 288n51,
    302n9
Marquardt, Dave, 281
Martin, Dalton, 207, 209, 262
Martyn, Oscar W., 197
Matheson, Hugh, 134–35, 137
Mathyssen, John, 281
McAree, John, 54, 288n51
McArthur, James J., 62, 125, 127–28, 138–39, 193
McArthur, John W., 160
McCusker, Knox, 179, 181–82, 195, 202, 204–6, 254
McCutcheon, Robert, 199, 220–21, 246, 254
McDonald, H. F., 172
McElhanney, A., 175
McFarlane, Walter, 107–8
McFee, Angus, 84, 95–96, 101, 103, 162
McGrandle, Hugh, 96

Vaughan, T. R., 160,
Von Holland, Harold, 275
Vossen, Roger, 304n65

Waddell, William, 108, 172
Walker, Claude M., 129–31, 196
Walker, George, 207, 243, 250
Wallace, James N., x, 84, 95–96, 105, 107, 116, 118,
    148, 150, 194, 196
Watson, Reginald, 265
Waugh, Bruce, 197, 226
Webb, John (Jack), 224–25, 234–35, 239, 304n65
Weekes, Abel Seneca, 154–55, 157
Weekes, M. B., 197
Weir, Charlie, 211–14, 220–21, 225, 233, 243, 245,
    265, 267, 269

Wheeler, Arthur, x, 51, 60–67, 74, 88, 93, 127, 131,
    137–41, 145, 148–50, 160
Williams, Dave, 281
Williams, Donald W., 250
Wilkin, F. A., 172
Wilkins, Fred W., 43, 80, 82–83, 288n51
Wolf, Charles, E., 34
Wolley-Dod, Bill, 271–72
Woods, Joseph, 54, 82, 86, 88, 94, 141–42
Wuhr, Matt, 258

Young, William, 162, 186
Youngs, Wally, 248, 255–56

# GENERAL INDEX

Canadian Petroleum Association (CPA), 229, 231, 267

Canadian Petroleum Exposition 1967, 247

*Canadian Surveyor,* 51–52, 193–94, 238, 263

Canadian Utilities, 261

Canol Pipeline Project, 206–7, 234

Card, Charles Ora, 67–69

Carlton Trail, 28, 76

Cartwright, A. D., 170

Cascade Rapids, 118

catskinners, 222, 224–25, 227, 262

Cave and Basin, Banff, 128

Cecil Hotel, 111, 121

Central Canada Railway, 107

Chalmers Trail, 101, 103

Church of Latter Day Saints, 67–68

Chiniki, 39

*CISM Journal,* 194

City Beautiful Movement, 166

Civil Aviation Board, 202

Clearwater Forest Reserve, 138

Clitheroe, Arthur, 9

Coal leases, survey of, ix, 141–44

Cochrane, Thomas and Adela, 80

Cochrane Ranch Company, 80

Cohn, Martin, 142–43

Cold Lake Airport, 215

Cold War, x

Coleman, A. P., 140

Computers, 264–66, 268, 277, 284–85

Continental Divide, 125, 127, 130, 141, 147

Connor, John, 129

control surveys, 241, 270; for oil and gas, 228–32; municipal, 262–64, 266; Calgary, 263; Edmonton, 263–64; other cities, 264; for National Topographic System Maps, 232; provincial, 264, 274–75, 277

Cook, James, 2

Cooley, Brenwyn, 266

Cornwall, Jim, 117

Coster, George C., 9

Cottingham, W. H., 96

Cree, 37–38

Crowfoot, 38

Crowsnest Pass Forest Reserve, 140

Crozier, L. N. F., 33

Currie barracks, 215

Dant, Noel, 242–43, 247

Davies Company, 162

Davy, Mr., 60

Dawson, George M., 9–10, 14–15

Dawson, Simon J., 6

Dawson's Road, 10

Deakin, Jack, 224

defacement and removal of survey marks, 85–86; destruction of, 226,

Department of Energy, Mines and Resources, Legal Surveys Division, 282

Department of Forestry and Lands, Alberta, 213

Department of Highways, Alberta, 200, 232, 252, 254–56, 258; Location Branch, 256, 260; Planning Branch, 258

Department of Indian Affairs, 38–41, 43–44, 48, 103, 290n16; Surveys Branch, 40

Department of the Interior, 29, 31, 37, 40–41, 43, 48, 50, 53–54, 57, 67, 69, 71–73, 76–77, 84, 101, 106, 108, 110, 134, 139, 141–43, 151, 170; Canadian Irrigation Survey, 58–69, 71–73, 139, 189; Dominion Lands Branch, 20; Dominion Observatory, 276; Dominion Water Power Branch, 183; Forest Branch, 145; Geodetic Survey of Canada, 150, 180, 190, 198, 211, 227, 230, 297n82; Geological Survey of Canada, 99, 117, 142, 143, 216; Hydrographic Survey Branch, 72; International Boundary Commission, 180; Irrigation Branch, 72–73; Parks Branch, 135, 139, 182, 196, 295n21; Surveys Bureau, formation of (1922), 180–81; Timber and Mineral Grazing Lands Office, 145; Topographical Surveys Branch, 20, 25, 30, 76, 40, 84–85, 87, 91, 97, 107–8, 117, 119, 132, 137, 139–40, 180–81, 184–86, 188, 190–91, 193–95, 227

Department of Lands and Forestry, Alberta, 230; Department of Mines and Minerals, 231

Department of Mines and Technical Surveys, Surveys and Mapping Branch, 211, 231, 263

Department of National Defense, 190, 200, 213, 273, 301n9

Department of Public Works, NWT, 67, 73, 84

Department of Public Works, Alberta, 169, 192, 195, 260, Highways Branch, 129, 176, 187, 252; Surveys Branch, 169, 187, 210, 229, 252, 254, 261, 264

Department of Transport, 200–4, 211, 213–15, 301n9

Devon Estates, 244

Dewdney, Edgar, 39

digital submission and retrieval of survey plans, 265, 275–76

Diefenbaker, John, 236

Director of Surveys Office, 169, 230–31, 246, 260, 263, 272

Dolland, John, 4–5

Dolland and Company, 60

Dominion Board of Examiners, 33, 107, 219

Dominion Forest Service, 190

Dominion Lands Act (1872), 18, 33, 48, 76

Harlech Mine, 184

Harrison, John, 1

Harrison and Ponton's Map of the City of Calgary
        (1911–12), 164

Haultain, Frederick, 82

Haverhold, Lloyd, 262

Hays, Harry, 246

Hector, James, 7

Henday, Anthony, 2

Herchmer, Lawrence, 9

Herdman, Rev. J. C., 140

Heron, Frank, 175

highways, right-of way surveys for: provincial high-
        ways, 187–88; Icefields Parkway, 126, 196;
        post-World War II, 252–59; Trans-Canada
        Highway, 256–57; Highway 2, 252, 257–58

Hill, James Jerome, 23

Hind, Henry Y., 6

Hodge, William, 204

Holloway, Joyce, 242

Hooke, Alf, 211, 247

Horetzky, Charles, 16

Howe, C. D., 235

Howse Pass, 148

Housing and Urban Development Association of
        Canada (HUDAC), 248

Hudson's Bay Company, 2–4, 6–8, 18, 20, 46, 49, 52,
        89, 96–98, 100, 106–7, 110, 112, 118, 158

Hyatt, A. E., 137

Hydrographic surveys. See surveys, types of

Hydrographic Survey Branch, 72

Indian Act (1876), 36, 40

Indian Reserve Surveys: Beaver Lake, 42; Blackfoot,
        37–39, 46; Blood, 38, 40, 44–46: road
        right-of-way, 186; Driftpile, 103; Enoch, 44;
        Ermineskin, 44; Heart Lake, 42; Montana,
        41–42, 78; Papaschase, 41, 44; Peace River
        Crossing, 104; Peigan, 39, 46; Saddle Lake,
        42–43; Samson, 44, 46; Sarcee, 38: topo-
        graphical survey on, 189; Sharphead, 44;
        Stoney (Morley), 39, 43, 80, 256; Stony
        Plain, 44; Sturgeon Lake, 104; Sucker
        Creek, 103; Sturgeon Lake, 104; surrender
        of reserves, 44, 46, 189; Wabamun, 43;
        Washatanow, 43; Whitefish Lake, 42–43

Inkster, Roy, 220

internal trade and labour mobility, 283; agreement on
        internal trade (1994), 283

international boundary. See forty-ninth parallel

International Boundary Waterways Treaty (1909), 72

International Broadcast Centre, Stampede Park, 271.
        See also Olympic games

International Irrigation Congress, 57–58

International Joint Commission, 72

Interprovincial Labour-Mobility Agreement (2001),
        283. See also reciprocity

Interprovincial Pipeline, 233

Irrigation Branch. See Department of the Interior

Irrigation, post-World War II surveys for, 261–62

Jacob, 39

Jasper Park (Jasper Forest Park Reserve, Jasper Forest
        Park), 133, 135, 234

Jasper Park Collieries, 144

Jasper Park Lodge, 139

Joint United States–Canada Permanent Board of
        Defense, 202

Kananaskis Valley, 7

Karsh, Yousef, 254

Kelwood Corporation, 246

Kohlschein, 256

Kootenay and Alberta Railway, 142

Koney Island, Cooking Lake, 94

Kicking Horse Pass, 7, 16, 148–50, 256

Kimball, 61, 69

Klondike: gold rush, 98, 103–4, 160; surveys in con-
        nection with, 100–4

Krakiwsky, Edward, 267

Laboucan, Daniel, 93

Laird, David, 104

Lake of the Woods, 5–6, 8–11

Land Classification surveys, 177–78, 180–81, 186,
        191–92

Land Titles Act (1906), 168–71, 283

Land Titles Office, 93, 163, 166–67, 169–71, 177,
        189, 217, 228, 232, 234, 248, 260, 262,
        272–73, 275–76

Laussedat, Aime, 62

Latitude and longitude, scientific problem of, 1–2,
        4–5, 21–23

Leduc, Father Emile, 49

Leduc: oil discovery, x, 216; demand for surveys in
        connection with, 218; effect on surveying
        companies, 219; oil field, 217–18: oil com-
        panies in, 218

Lend-lease Program, 203

Lett, R. C., 133

Lieutenant-Governor, NWT, 21, 75, 78–79, 81

Lineham, John, 29, 216–17

Lines Motor Company, 186

Little, C. A., 142

Little Cascade Rapids, 119

Little Hunter, 42–43

Longitude. See latitude and longitude

Long Rapids, 98, 119, 279

218; California Standard, 218, 223, 225,
    baseline surveys for, 223–25; Dome
    Petroleum, 239; Exxon, 269; Frontenac,
    218; Home Oil, 223, 225, 252; Imperial
    Oil, 206, 217, 227, 233, 244: surveyors
    with, 220; McColl, 218; Shell, 218, 239,
    275, 277; Union Oil, 226: surveys for, 225
oil and gas leases, 117
Oliver, Frank, 52, 54, 82, 100, 106, 118, 140, 143,
    145
Olympic Games Winter 1988, surveys for, 270–71
Olympic Plaza, 271. *See also* Olympic games
Oregon Treaty (1846), 6
outfitting and supplies, 28–29, 94, 98, 109–13, 162,
    184, 194, 198, 223, 226

Pakan, 40, 42–43
Palliser, John, 7, 8, 15–17, 21, 138–139
Palliser Hotel, 169
Parker, Elizabeth and Jean, 140
Parker, Mr., 163
Pascoe, John, 57
Patricia Lake, 135
Paul, Joseph, 93
Peace River Colonization and Land Development
    Company, 106
Peace River Pass, 16
Peigan, 37
Pelican Rapids, 101
Percival, Freddie, 246
Perry, Clarence, 242
perspectograph, 65
photogrammetery. *See* survey methods, aerial photog-
    raphy
photo-topographic surveying. *See* survey methods
Pine River Pass, 16
Pinder, Tom, 188, 195
Pipelines: right-of-way surveys for, 232–36;
    Interprovincial Pipeline, 233; Trans
    Mountain, 234–35; Trans Canada, 235–36;
    Alberta Gas Trunk Line, 235; Northwestern
    Utilities, 235; Canadian Western Natural Gas
    Company, 235. *See also* Canol Pipeline
    Project
Polaris, 1
Pond, Peter, 2
Ponton, Gerald, 163
Prairie Farm Rehabilitation Association (PRFRA), 262
Primrose Lake (Cold Lake) Air Weapons Range,
    213–15, 302n55
Principal (First) Meridian, 19–20
Provincial Planning Advisory Board, 242, 247–48
Provincial Planning Appeal Board, 243
Public Lands Act, 262

Public Roads Administration, 203–5, 207
Pyramid Lake, survey of lots at, 135

Radio, 179, 198, 210, 212, 222, 227, 254, 270
Railway Act (1907), 168
railways: surveys of, 153, 155–56; rights-of-way issues,
    170–71; post-World War II, 259–60
Rates of pay: for surveyors, 95–96; for labourers, 141;
    timber berth contracts, 146–47; for
    returned men, 175–76; schedule of fees for
    surveyors, 269
Rattenbury, Francis, 133
Real Property Reports, 278–79
Rebellion of 1885, 50, 52, 77
Reciprocity, 168, 283. *See also* internal trade and
    labour mobility
Red Crow, 38, 44
Red River Settlement, 18–19, 46
Reed, Hayter, 39
replotting schemes. *See* town planning
Revillion Frères, 111
Riel, Louis, 19, 50
Right-of-way surveys. *See* railways; trails and roads;
    highways; pipelines; utilities
river lot system, 18–20, 52–54; demands for survey
    of, 46, 48–50, 52–54, 104
roads. *See* trails and roads. *See also* highways
Robbins Irrigation Company, 72
Robson Pass, 150
Rocky Mountains Development Company, 217
Rocky Mountains Forest Reserve, 143
Rocky Mountains Park Act (1887), 128,
Royal Canadian Air Force (RCAF), 190, 193, 199,
    201–3, 211–12; airbases, 200, 213–15
Royal Canadian Artillery, 215; surveying techniques
    used by, 207–9
Royal Commission on Energy, 236
Royal Commission on Northern Development, 229
Royal Geographical Society, 7, 12, 15
Royal Observatory, Greenwich, 1–2
Rowe, Lieut., 13
Rupert's Land, 6–8, 18–19, 46
Rural residential subdivision, 248
Rutherford, Alexander, 106

Samson, 44
Sarcee. *See* Tsuu T'ina
Sectional Maps: topographical surveys for, 188–89;
    aerial surveys for, 192. *See also* mapping,
    topographical
seismic, exploration, 216–18; survey of lines for, 221.
    *See also* well site locations, surveys for
Selkirk Mountains, 63, 126–27
Selwyn, Alfred, 216

Real Property Reports; right-of way surveys; well site locations

Surveys and Expropriation Act (1951), 248

Tanner, Eldon, 235
Taylor, John, 68
Taylor, Gordon, 252, 258
telegraph, 2, 16, 20–23, 122
Tellurometer. *See* electronic distance measurement
Thompson, David, ix–x, 2–6, 9–10, 16–17, 23, 139, 148, 150
timber berths, ix, 144–47
Titanich, Edward, 279
Topographical Surveys Branch. *See* Department of the Interior
Toronto Litho Company, 66
Torrens System, 93
Tory, Henry Marshall, 167
Town and Village Act (1957), 248
Town planning, 134–35, 165–66; annexation, 247–48; district planning commissions, 248, post–World War II, 241; neighbourhood unit, 242–43: in Edmonton, 243, 245; in Calgary, 245; outline units/sector plans, 246; replotting schemes, 245
township subdivision: ix, 276; township grid, 20; procedures for, 91–93; central Alberta, 87–88; east of Edmonton, 88–89; Peace River Country, 106–9; north of 25$^{th}$ Baseline, 121–23; northern Alberta 1950s, 254. *See also* Dominion Land Survey
Townsites: designs for, 151–57, 159–60; survey instructions for, 153, 169; survey of: Acme, 155; Aidrie, 153, 159; Athabasca Landing, 110; Banff, 128; Beaver Mines, 142; Bellevue, 142; Bindloss, 155; Blackfalds, 153; Blairmore (extension), 142; Bowden, 153; Burmis, 142; Calgary, 33; Camrose, 159; Cayley, 153; Claresholm, 153; Champion, 155; Chin, 155; Coleman (extension), 142; Consort, 155; Couts, 155; Czar, 153; Delburne, 157; Delia, 157; Devon, 244; Didsbury, 153; Empress, 155; Enchant, 155; Fleet, 155; Frank, 142; Fort McLeod, 32–33; Granum, 153; Hanna, 157; Hillcrest, 142; Hobbema, 46; Hughenden, 153; Jasper, 134–36; Lacombe, 156; Lethbridge, 67; Lundbreck, 142; Midnapore, 159; Millet, 153; Morningside, 153; Mundare, 154, 157; Oil City, 217; Olds, 153; Oyen, 157; Penhold, 153; Provost, 153; Raymond, 155; Red Deer, 157; Sherwood Park (Campbell Town), 247, 249; Sibbald, 157; Stavely, 153; Veteran,

155; Vegreville, 157; Wabamun, 157; Wainright, 157

Trails: evolution of, 76; administrative responsibility for, 75–76, 84; Calgary–Edmonton Trail, 77–78; colonization trails/roads for settlement, 81–84; Banff, 129–30; Fiddle River valley, 133. *See also* Trail Commissioner
Trail Commissioner, 79–81, 292n8
Transfer of Natural Resources to Alberta, 181–82, 195–96, 281
Transportation: system of, 28–29; challenges of in north, 97–98, 101, 109–13; airplanes, 197–98, 212, 223, 226–27, 236, 258; automobiles, 184–86, 192, 210, 218, 258; boats, 29, 61, 122, 125; canoes, x, 3–4, 98, 119, 122–23, 178, 197; carts and wagons, 13, 22, 28, 94, 176, 186; democrats, 184, 186; dog trains, 16, 97, 204, 206, 227; helicopters, 212–13, 230, 237–38, 270, 275 ; horses, 4, 15, 28–29, 94, 119, 120–22, 132, 137, 146–47, 226–27; Jeeps, 224; Land Rovers, 224; quads, 285; rafts, 29, 115, 123; river steamers, 28, 101, 178; scows, 101, 104, 108–9, 113, 118–19, 122–23, 179; sleighs, 28–29, 108, 113, 120, 197; snowshoes, 28; snowmobiles, 236–37; trains, 28, 46, 56, 121, 123, 133, 135, 137, 174, 176, 186, 214; tractor train, 227–28; trucks, x, 187–88, 192, 218, 254–55, 270, 284–85
Treaty Commission, 103, 294n19
Treaty Eight, 36, 54, 98, 103–5
Treaty Entitlement Lands, 280, 282
Treaty Land Entitlement claims, 281
Treaty Seven, 36–39
Treaty Six, 36, 38, 41
Trecotte, Mr., 40
Triangulation. *See* survey methods
Tsuu T'ina (Sarcee), 37–38, 280
Trouth, Norman, 246
Tumpline, 122
Turnor, Philip, 2–4, 17, 287n2
Turner Valley, 294n59; geology of, 216; discovery of gas, 217
Turner Valley Royalties, 217
Tyrell, Joseph B., 6

United States Air Force, 211
Universal Transverse Mercator coordinates (UTM), 208, 301n28
University of Alberta, 49, 138, 167, 176, 219–20, 266; Coordinating Council, 266; Survey Science program, 267
University of Calgary, 267; Geomatics Engineering Department, 283; Geomatics Engineering

# Acknowledgements

I would like to thank the Alberta Land Surveyors' Association for entrusting me with the task of writing a history of their profession in Alberta, as a centennial project for 2005. The idea was conceived by Stan Longson, who as president of the ALSA in 1997, reestablished a Historical and Biographical Committee, under the initial chairmanship of Douglas Barnett. In 1999, the committee initiated an ambitious oral history project to record personal experiences of older members and retired members of the association from the post-World War II years. Thank you to all who gave so willingly of their time. As research historian and author, I have had the privilege of working with a committed group of people serving on a succession of committees under the chairmanship of Bob Baker. Thank you all. I would also like to thank Brian Munday, Executive Director of the ALSA, who patiently shepherded the book along, drew my attention to sources at the ALSA, pinpointed significant details and provided a watchful editorial eye. Thanks also to Sharon Stecyk and Lyall Pratt at the ALSA for their assistance.

A number of Alberta Land Surveyors helped to research specific issues, and provided materials, expertise or technical explanations. Ken Allred, Bob Baker, Douglas Barnett, Dick Bassil, Les Frederick, John Haggerty, Gordon Olsson, Armstrong MacCrimmon, Allan Main, Dave Usher, George Walker, Jack Webb, and Charlie Weir all provided information and clarification. Thank you.

Special thanks to Edward Titanich and Marty Yanishewski with the Director of Surveys Office in Edmonton for their invaluable assistance in tracking materials and plans for me. In Ottawa, Alistair MacLeod, Legislative Advisor to the Surveyor General of Canada Lands, provided prompt and cheerful responses to a range of queries including biographical details on early Dominion Land Surveyors who worked in Alberta. I am grateful to Sharon Allentuck at Transport Canada's Technical Reference Centre in Winnipeg who doggedly searched out materials. Thank you, too, to staff at Natural Resources Canada in Edmonton.

As always, staff at the Glenbow Archives and Library—Doug Cass, Jim Bowman, Lindsay Muir and Harry Sanders— went out of their way to be helpful. Special thanks is owed to the Provincial Archives of Alberta, especially Marlena Wyman and Dennis Hyucak. Connie Yaroshuk made endless trips into the PAA's storage vaults, and cheerfully wheeled hundreds of boxes of papers to my desk. Thanks also to Judith Benson at the Legislative Library of Alberta, and staff at Library and Archives Canada in Ottawa, the City of Edmonton Archives, the Red Deer and District Archives, and the Whtye Museum of Canadian Rockies in Banff.

I would also like to thank a number of my historian colleagues—Doris Bergen, John Gilpin, David Leonard, and Donald Wetherell—who commented on sections of earlier drafts of the manuscript. I am especially grateful to Pat Myers for her unflagging support and encouragement, critical review of the first draft of the entire manuscript, and her advice throughout. Thanks also to Merrily Aubrey and Jim Taylor.

I am grateful to Ruth Linka and Lee Shedden at Brindle & Glass for their care and thoroughness in bringing the book to publication. And to Christine Savage for her editorial work.

And finally, I would like to thank my husband Les Bergen, for his thoughtful input and suggestions on early drafts, as well as his good-humoured fortitude throughout this project.

JUDY LARMOUR is a research historian, heritage consultant, and writer. She has a BA in History and a Higher Diploma in Education from Trinity College, Dublin, and an MA in Canadian History from the University of Alberta. For the last twenty-one years she has been involved with research and interpretive planning for many heritage and museum projects in Alberta, including the Provincial Historic Site at Dunvegan, the Reynolds-Alberta Museum, the restored NWMP Detachment Building in Canmore, and the Heritage Prairie Grain Elevator Project at the Provincial Museum of Alberta. Judy's publications include *Making Hay While the Sun Shone: Haying in Alberta before 1955* and *How to do Oral History*, and she is co-author of *Stop the Car! Discovering Central Alberta*, featured on CBC's Daybreak Alberta. She is a regular contributor to *Legacy* magazine. Judy lives on a farm near the Medicine Lodge Hills, south of Rimbey, Alberta.